GROUP TRAVEL

SECOND EDITION

Martha Sarbey de Souto, CTC

Delmar
Publishers Inc.

NOTICE TO THE READER

Cover photo by Mary M. Langenfeld with luggage and assistance by P.A. Bergner & Co./ Boston Stone, Madison, WI. Group travel luggage tags by Burkhalter Travel, Madison, WI.

Delmar Staff
  Senior Acquisitions Editor: Mary McGarry
  Developmental Editor: Sheila Furjanic
  Project Editor: Carol Micheli
  Senior Production Supervisor: Larry Main
  Art and Design Manager: Russell Schneck
  Art Supervisor: Judi Orozco
  Design Coordinator: Karen Kemp

For information, address Delmar Publishers Inc.
3 Columbia Circle, Box 15-015
Albany, New York 12212

Copyright © 1993 by Delmar Publishers Inc.

1 2 3 4 5 6 7 8 9 10 XXX 99 98 97 96 95 94 93

Library of Congress Cataloging-in-Publication Data

de Souto, Martha Sarbey.
    Group travel / Martha Sarbey.—2nd ed.
        p.   cm.
    Rev. ed. of: Group travel operations manual. 1985.
    Includes index.
    ISBN 0-8273-3514-8
    1. Travel agents—Handbooks, manuals, etc. I. de Souto, Martha
Sarbey. Group travel operations manual. II. Title.
G154.D4 1993
338.4′791—dc20   92-32756
                                                           CIP

TABLE OF CONTENTS

For the wonderful, professional members of the
travel industry with whom I have been affiliated through the
Institute of Certified Travel Agents (ICTA), The Pacific Asia Travel
Association (Norcal PATA), and San Francisco Women in Travel...
who gave me their support through this project.

ABOUT THE AUTHOR

Martha "Marty" Sarbey de Souto, CTC, brings to her book over thirty-five years of experience in the group travel field. Her background includes handling group operations, group travel sales (both wholesale and retail), frequent tour escorting, itinerary planning and costing, writing tour brochures, editing travel newsletters, and preparing marketing and advertising campaigns.

With a B.A. in journalism from the University of Arizona, the author began her career in the area of student travel in New York City. Subsequently, she worked with professional medical and dental overseas convention programs, then in the area of academic study tours and overseas campus programs, and then with special-interest agricultural study tours and trade missions. She also spent three years as vice president of marketing for a large cruise operator and another three years as vice president of a Latin American specialty wholesaler.

She teaches a variety of group tour packaging and wholesaling classes at the community college level for Cañada College in Redwood City, California, for the University of California Extension, and for Echols Travel Training in San Francisco. In 1978, she developed the travel industry certificate program and curriculum for Vista College in Berkeley, California, and is still active there as instructor, curriculum developer, and as chairman of the travel industry advisory committee for the college.

The author is past president of San Francisco Women in Travel, and has served on the Board of Directors of the Northern California chapter of the Pacific Asia Travel Association (NORCAL PATA). She is a frequent contributor to *TravelAge West*, and *ASTA Agency Management*, the magazine of the American Society of Travel Agents. The first edition of this book won her the prestigious Crest Award by the American Society of Travel Agents (ASTA). She was selected as outstanding travel agent in the country by *Travel Weekly* in January 1983.

The author lives with her husband José, in Berkeley, California, where she owns her own travel writing and consulting firm, Sarbey Associates.

ACKNOWLEDGEMENTS

I wish to express appreciation to my many business colleagues who graciously offered their professional input: Ralph Davis of Travel Insurance Services for his insurance expertise, Jeffrey R. Miller for his legal guidance, and Frances Friedman for sharing tour escorting information. Also Dorothy Purdie for her common-sense budget guidance, Henry Eaton of Dix and Eaton Public Relations for his marketing and public relations advice, and both Carol and Greg Bauer of Harvest Travel for their travel agency management insights.

To past employers, Jack Dengler who gave me my start at SITA Tours in New York, Joe Howard of Howard Tours, Inc., who taught me tour operations, and John Bell at Golden Bear Travel. A special post-humous remembrance goes to Ken Goy of Cal-Farm Travel who gave me my freedom in marketing tours for 10 years of my professional life.

To my students at Canada College, Vista College, and Echols Travel Training, all here in Northern California, on whom I practiced my theories over the years. A special word to all those instructors who have used the first edition of this book as text during the past seven years and offered their suggestions for this new edition.

I owe a particular word of gratitude to my triumvirate of editors at Delmar: Mary McGarry, Sheila Furjanic, and Susan Merrill, without whom I might still be in never never land.

I also wish to thank the following reviewers for their thorough evaluation of the manuscript and valuable suggestions.

Pat Antonellis, Dean Junior College, Franklin, MA
Sue Urie, Nationwide Travel Training College, Richmond, BC
Jeffrey Miller, Ward, Klein & Miller, Gaithersburg, MD
Jim Tjaden, Maple Woods Community College, Kansas City, MO
Mary Beth Walsh, Moraine Valley CC, Palos Hills, IN

I am particularly grateful to the American Society of Travel Agents (ASTA) for granting a Crest Award for the first edition of this book; I hope they will feel this revision lives up to, and perhaps surpasses, the first edition.

And on a strictly personal note, a big kiss to my dear husband, José, who put up with papers all over the house, calls at all hours, and many a weekend when I was unavailable as a playmate while I completed this work.

 **PREFACE**

As a student living in Europe in 1954, I grew to abhor those busloads of "Ugly Americans" touring the continent and swore that I would never condescend to be one of *them*—those people who raced through 2,000 years of history on a three-week tour consisting mostly of one-night hotel stands and a view of the natives through a tinted motorcoach window.

Strange then that I should ultimately have found group travel to be one of the primary educational forces in the world today and at the same time one of the most exciting business careers possible. Group travel in the '90s is no longer simply hordes of uninitiated travelers being pushed and pulled from country to country. On the contrary, it has become a highly specialized and diversified field encompassing not only the traditional tours, but also a wide variety of group projects for very sophisticated travelers. It ranges from conventions, sales incentives and all kinds of international meetings to trade missions, treks, white river rafting adventures and overseas campus in-residence programs. It might include Christmas shopping junkets to Hong Kong, theatre or opera tours, wine-tasting seminars, or study programs at sea. In short, the arena of group travel is today an extremely imaginative and stimulating field, offering a unique opportunity to those entrepreneurs and employees willing to make their way in a group travel career.

Yet, very little exists in the way of formal education or training for this challenging field. Most travel agency preparatory courses devote no more than perhaps a lecture or two to the entire field of group travel, as instructors scurry through weeks of airline ticketing and quick skill preparation in an effort to give students entry level training for typical retail agency employment. At the other end of the spectrum, most university programs, while perhaps looking at tourism as it affects the ecology or economy of a country, seem not to train the theorist how to put his or her idealism to work in a practical career in which one can bring together interdisciplinary studies and "do good" in the world and still make a living.

And, if academic institutions (be they at university level or vocational school level) have failed in teaching group travel, it may be partially because there have not been the necessary textbook source materials. Teaching group tour packaging myself the first year to a small class, I was able to photocopy sufficient materials from my office to use as samples and was able to call on my own experience and that of friends and colleagues in the group travel field. However, as classroom size grew, this became unwieldly and as inquiries for my classroom materials started coming in from other instructors across the country and from travel agents, tour operators, and outside salespeople I began to realize the need for a text.

This second edition reflects many of the changes wrought by airline deregulation and by the age of computerization. It also addresses new developments in this fast-changing industry as more and more specialties and sub-specialties of tours have developed.

I hope this new edition may also meet the needs of a new kind of reader—ranging from the community college or proprietary college student to the university level student. I hope it will also prove helpful to the adult who is retraining for a new career or for the individual who may already be active in the travel industry but now seeking specialization in the group field.

This book, then, is designed to be used by both the student of tourism and by members of the travel industry who hope to increase their skills. It is highly personal, being a synthesis of more than thirty-five years experience in the group travel field and of seventeen years of teaching group travel in the college classroom. Many of the opinions expressed herein are merely that—personal opinions reflecting experiences, both positive and negative, throughout my group travel career. Your experiences may prove different, and as times and techniques change we can all certainly adapt to new ways of thinking and new methods of approaching things. It is hoped you can bear with me through some of the "how-to" practicalities and through some of the necessary pedantics—never losing sight of the contagious excitement and personal fulfillment which is the essence of the group travel field today.

Marty Sarbey de Souto, CTC
Berkeley, California

▷ 1

GROUP TRAVEL: THE POSSIBILITIES

LEARNING OBJECTIVES

After completing this chapter, you should:

- ❑ Understand the breadth and extent of the group travel business
- ❑ See that group travel is more than just tours
- ❑ Know why individual travelers are motivated to travel on group programs rather than independently
- ❑ Know who travels in groups
- ❑ Recognize the components that make up a group travel program
- ❑ See why group travel is a good product for some travelers but not for others

KEY CONCEPTS AND TERMS

Academic Market
Adventure Market
Eco-Tourism
Group Travel Program
Motivations for Group Travel
Niche Marketing
Senior Citizen Market
Special Interest Tours
Tour Components

The arena of group travel is today one of the largest and most popular areas of the entire travel spectrum. Almost anyone seeking a career in any sector of the travel industry must be prepared to deal with group travel in one way or another.

Although a highly specialized field requiring a great deal of expertise, group travel can no longer be relegated strictly to the domain of the tour operator. Those employed in the travel industry (whether with a tour operator, airline, retail travel agency, hotel, motorcoach company, or cruise line) need to deal with group travel—often on a day-to-day basis. In addition, those outside the travel industry or loosely and periodically affiliated with travel (i.e., occasional tour escorts, local guides, travel marketing and media personnel) likewise find it necessary to understand and deal with the group travel product.

Even experienced travel agents who have worked in the industry for years are finding group travel to be the most attractive segment of the industry due to the potential for profit.

GROUP TRAVEL PROGRAMS: THE DEFINITION

Webster's Dictionary defines a **tour** as "A journey for business, pleasure, or education in which one returns to the starting point."

That may be well and good for Webster's Dictionary, but for our purposes it might be modified to "Any prearranged (usually prepaid) journey to one or more destinations and returning to the point of departure. Usually includes transportation, accommodations, meals, sightseeing, and other components and is sold as a unit without price breakdown by component."

Note that these qualities of being prepackaged, prepaid and purchased as a total unit distinguish it from a fairly involved trip for a group of people who may pay as they go along and who see the cost of each item on their trip as they pay for it enroute.

But tours are not the only product when we refer to the broad spectrum of group travel—at least not tours in the traditional sense. **Group travel** today is no longer simply hordes of uninitiated travelers being pushed and pulled from country to country. On the contrary, it has become a diversified field encompassing not only the traditional tours, but also a wide variety of group projects for very sophisticated travelers.

It ranges from conventions, sales incentive trips, and all kinds of international meetings to trade missions, treks, white water rafting adventures, and overseas campus in-residence programs. It might include Christmas shopping junkets in Hong Kong, theatre or opera tours, wine-tasting seminars, or study programs on board a cruise ship.

It might include the Women's Garden Club visiting Japan to view spring cherry blossoms or an in-depth summer study/residence program for Spanish teachers in Mexico. It could mean a group of football fans wanting to attend the Rose Bowl to cheer on their team, trekkers hiking the Inca Trail in the Peruvian Andes, or a diving instructor taking his or her students to Cozumel for on-site instruction.

SAFARI ADVENTURE

14 DAYS TO KENYA
$3,995 INCLUDING AIR FARE

A safari to Kenya isn't your ordinary trip. It's extraordinary. You'll explore the plains of Amboseli and Samburu and then fly on to the game-rich Masai Mara. See Mt. Kilimanjaro tower 19,340 feet overhead as animals of every kind roam in its awesome shadow. Experience the luxuries of the Safari Park Hotel in Nairobi and the Mt. Kenya Safari Club.

FRIDAY • NEW YORK
You arrive at the Alitalia terminal at Kennedy Airport. Your Park East Tours representative introduces you to the other members of your group. Soon, you're aboard your Alitalia Jumbo Jet, flying across the Atlantic.

SATURDAY • ROME/NAIROBI
This morning, your jet lands in Rome, where you connect with your flight to East Africa.

You arrive this evening at Kenyatta International Airport in Nairobi, the Safari Capital of the world. Your Park East Tours representative welcomes you with a friendly "Jambo" (hello) and escorts you to the luxurious Safari Park Hotel, situated in exotic gardens. Overnight at the SAFARI PARK HOTEL.

SUNDAY • NAIROBI
The day is yours to relax on the magnificent grounds of the Safari Park Hotel or walk along fashionable Kenyatta Avenue. You can get your first look at wildlife on an optional tour of Nairobi National Park, just 20 minutes from the city, yet rich with lion, giraffe and zebra. You'll also find the Animal Orphanage — famed for treating orphaned, wounded and semi-tame animals. Other optional tours include Karen Blixen's home, Giraffe Manor, the National Museum or Riuki Village.

Tonight, you will have an orientation briefing at a Welcome Cocktail Party and Dinner. Overnight at the SAFARI PARK HOTEL.

MONDAY/TUESDAY • AMBOSELI/MT. KILIMANJARO
Get your field glasses and camera ready. You're off to Amboseli National Park to discover the heart of East Africa, its people and big game country. Snow-capped Mt. Kilimanjaro rises 19,340 feet to dominate every scene — whether you're gazing out the window of your lodge or the open roof-top of your minibus. Here in Amboseli, the "big five"— elephant, lion, leopard, buffalo and rhino–roam the open plains alongside the fearless Masai warriors. You may also encounter zebra, cheetah, gazelle and impala. Overnights at the AMBOSELI LODGES.

8

Figure 1.1   Park East Tours specializes in group tours to Africa. They design tours to appeal to a range of travelers from those who want an introduction to Africa to distinctive safaris for sophisticated travelers who know Africa well enough to design their own safari. (Courtesy of Park East Tours—an African Tradition.)

As you can see, the group travel product is not one product, but a vast array of products. Travel may be by plane, train, ship, or motorcoach. It may be active or inactive, be for fun or for business, or be for educational purposes. But regardless, all of these possibilities constitute the burgeoning and creative group travel industry, often simply called the "tour industry." Today, it is an extremely imaginative and stimulating field, offering a unique opportunity to those entrepreneurs and employees willing to make their way in a group travel career. (For more on career possibilities, see Chapter 2).

WHO TRAVELS IN GROUPS?

This "new" group travel field also means that today more and more travelers are attracted to group travel projects. These travelers in the past might never have considered traveling as part of a group. In fact, some of these travelers might never have considered traveling at all if it were not for some new and exciting products that stimulated them to expand their horizons.

Research firms are busily analyzing demographics, the phenomenon of the yuppies, and the effects of the first and now the second baby boom. They are alerting the travel industry to the "graying of America" and the resulting strength of the **senior citizen market**. We've all been told of **niche marketing** and advised not to market to the whole world, but rather to "find our niche" and direct our products and marketing efforts to a very specific segment of the market.

All of this may be true. However, the fact remains that the market is extremely fluid and changes daily. The industry has seen the rise and fall of many tour companies and fad tour programs. It has seen specialty markets spin off into sub-specialties, one after another at a speed so dizzying that we could hardly keep up.

We all saw the development of Club Med and the concept of all-inclusive vacation resorts. The hastle-free nature of this type of vacation was particularly attractive to singles in the 1970's and 80's. These singles have now grown up, married, and had children, and Club Med has had to grow up with them to keep its clientele. They now offer family vacations with special facilities for children—Baby, Petit, Mini, and Kids Clubs.

Over the last 20 years, we have seen the **adventure market** develop. At first, a few key companies began to attract the young and hardy climber, backpacker, and trekker who—rather than staying in cities or paying for fancy hotels—prefered to spend the bulk of their time in the great outdoors. After 20 years, many of these same adventure travelers still want their adventure, but they would prefer a nice, comfortable bed at night rather than a sleeping bag. In addition, they're willing to pay handsomely for what we now have come to call Soft Adventure trips.

Similarly, group travel on cruise ships has become more and more selective, as ships and cruise lines each developed their own personalities and specialty reputations. Not only is the market segmented into catagories of big ships versus little ships, one week cruises versus longer cruises, Old World elegance ships versus

Figure 1.2 This ad shows that club Med has changed its vacation packages to meet the changing needs of its market. Instead of offering vacations exclusively to singles, Club Med now offers family vacations. (Courtesy of Club Med Phototheque.)

chrome and plastic ships, and upscale versus not-so-upscale, but these catagories are now further segmented. For example, some of the upscale ships concentrate on the luxuries of shipboard life. Others do everything possible to attract the upscale intelligentsia with advertising that boasts about onboard enrichment lectures, unhurried dining, and good conversation with other interesting passengers (no floorshows or bingo).

Ten years ago, who would have predicted that the next big wave of travel marketing—whether for individual travelers or for groups—would be ecology-oriented? Today, so called **eco-tourism** is one of the fastest growing market segments, and ecology-oriented organizations are the hot targets of group marketers promoting programs to the Amazon or the Costa Rican cloud forest.

In summary, the question "Who travels in groups?" is answered: "almost everyone." If people are properly motivated with the right travel product, and have adequate disposable income, and view travel as a priority for spending that disposable income, then they will travel.

Yet, the opposite is also true. Many individuals may never travel in groups, even if they travel extensively. So, *why* do individuals look to group travel.

INDIVIDUAL MOTIVATIONS FOR JOINING GROUP TRAVEL PROGRAMS

The individual may join a group travel program for one of many reasons. A decisive motivation is the *money saved* by traveling in a group. Special group airfares or other group rates may offer large savings. In fact, many individuals will buy a package and throw away the land portion just to take advantage of the group airfares.

Another motivation might be *companionship*, or the desire to travel with others, hoping to meet people of similar interests with whom to share the joy of travel experiences. In fact, organizations such as social and civic clubs often like to sponsor trips because members like to travel together. Also important is a negative motivation, *fear*. The novice traveler's fear of being alone, of something going wrong, of not knowing "the ropes," of showing his or her ignorance, or of being taken advantage of in a foreign culture or milieu is a motivator. Many people also join group travel programs because they appreciate the *convenience*. Their luggage is taken care of for them and their sightseeing is planned and prearranged. In short, they are free from daily decisions or problems.

These motivations pertain to both the novice and the somewhat experienced traveler. However, many extremely well-traveled, sophisticated, and experienced travelers also join group travel programs.

One reason that an experienced traveler might join a group travel program is *destination*. Although experienced travelers may feel comfortable traveling independently year after year in Europe or Mexico, they may not feel as comfortable in places like India or Asia—in areas where cultural values and language differ radically from their own. They probably also know that in some countries, newly open to tourism, group travel is often the *only* possibility.

Still another reason experienced travelers join groups might be that they perceive participation in a specific group tour as the "in thing" to do. If the tour is a private tour, giving them access to meetings with certain key individuals or entrée to private homes or businesses, they will join for these subliminal reasons. There is also the factor of traveling with the "right" people. I have been involved in many professional travel projects, even some totally paid and hosted invitational tours. Often the first thing that the individual will ask when invited, even before asking about the tour content itself, is "Who else is going?" Many experienced travelers want to feel that they are traveling with their peers.

Many people join non-tour tours; that is, tours that are not called tours. Everyone has seen the phenomenon in recent years of companies that specialize in the trek, expedition, study program, overseas cultural experience, and so forth. These are not tours in the true sense of the word. To many people, the term "tour" is a negative word implying a different city and a different hotel every night. It implies the "If it's Tuesday, this must be Belgium" syndrome. The physician who says that he never takes tours may excitedly say that he is going to participate in an overseas on-site inspection of medical facilities in Timbuktu next summer on a program sponsored by his medical association.

WHEN DO GROUPS TRAVEL?

Now that you know who travels in groups and why, you may ask—when? Is there a particular season? Here again, "it depends."

Generally, peak season for North American vacation travelers is summer and the Christmas/New Year holidays. There is also a good-sized segment of the market that gets away from northern climes and heads for warm-weather vacations from January through March. Within these generalizations, there are many specifics and many exceptions.

The **academic market** (i.e., students, teachers, professors, administrators) is by the nature of the academic calendar, usually limited to travel during academic holidays; that is, during the summer months, spring break, and the Christmas/New Year period. It doesn't matter that airfares and other rates may be lower at other times of year.

Senior citizens usually can travel year-round, and they are a particularly attractive market for mid-week and off-season travel, since their time schedule is often flexible. Their constraint is more often money rather than time. Therefore, many year-round programs exist on the market that prove particularly popular with the senior market or with the not-so-senior, but the active, recently retired market.

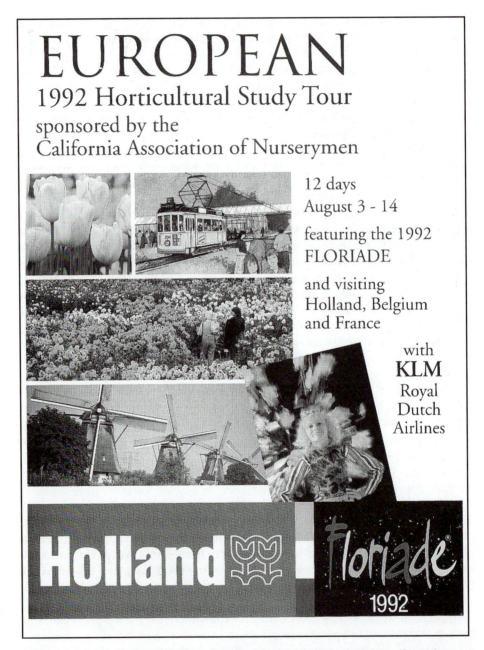

Figure 1.3 Some tours are private, sponsored by clubs, churches, or professional organizations for their members. These tours usually include events of special interest to the group like this horticultural study tour sponsored by the California Association of Nurserymen. (Courtesy of Netherlands Board of Tourism/Harvest Travel International.)

Business and professional people frequently take several short vacations to break up the year and to break up the intense pace of their day-to-day lives. They make good candidates for a one-week cruise at one time of year and then a second or third trip at another time during the year. This travel could include a golf, tennis, or ski trip—or perhaps an extension to a convention or business meeting. Family tours are usually planned around the academic calendar. Although the parents might be able to go at any time, if young people are involved, school dates dictate the travel possibilities.

In addition if **special interest tours** are being planned to meet the unique needs of specific groups, it's important to know the availability of potential markets. A trip hoping to draw accountants should certainly never be scheduled for spring prior to the U.S. April 15 income tax filing deadline. People in agriculture and agribusiness make great travelers during the winter months when the ground lies frozen over and fallow. Yet, in the spring when the first crocus peeks through, they will become restless and want to get home in time for the planting season. These people are not available for travel again until after the harvest.

Some destinations, festivities, or special events require marketing for specific times of year. Therefore, you may have to rethink your strategy. For example, skiing can only be done when there's snow, so U.S. ski tour operators' programs are probably going to be limited to the winter period of November through March in the northern hemisphere. However, such operators might offer some type of non-ski program during the mild weather months or perhaps stretch their ski season by offering ski tours to Chile and Argentina, where the winter ski season is June, July, and August.

Suppliers, such as airlines, hotels, and cruise lines, are busily dreaming up special low fares or other "deals" to entice group operators to place business with them during the supplier's weak revenue periods. But if the group operator cannot locate the market segment of the population willing to travel to Moscow in January or to the Caribbean in the hurricane season, the best price breaks in the world may prove for naught.

In summary, outbound tourism for North American travelers tends heavily toward summer and holiday periods. However, there is a substantial year-round market for specific types of tours and travelers. Peak holiday periods, such as Christmas/New Years, often are characterized by many travelers, but not necessarily group travelers, since many suppliers do not need group business at that normally busy time of the year.

THE COMPONENTS OF
A GROUP TRAVEL PROGRAM

Although group travel programs may vary tremendously in style and in the market to which they are directed, they nevertheless have a great deal in common in terms of the components that make up such programs. A typical trip will include some, but not necessarily all, of the following tour components:

1. Transportation—by air, ship, rail, motorcoach, or train.
2. Accommodations—hotels, motels, inns, dormitories, condos, lodges, etc.
3. Sightseeing—including guides and entrance fees to museums and attractions.
4. Leaderhip—a tour manager, local guides.
5. Meals—either fixed menu or *à la carte*.
6. Social events—theatre tickets, receptions, cocktail parties, nightclubs, folklore performances, and the like.
7. Transfers—meet and greet services, transportation, and baggage handling between airports, rail stations, hotels, and the like.
8. Attractions—Disneyland, Marine World, etc.
9. Special events—A music festival, Carnival in Rio parade, Olympics, Wimbledon tennis matches, etc.
10. Special interest activities—business meetings, lectures, classes, home visits, and farm stays.

The selection of components is wide, and the skillful operator learns which mix of components to use in each travel product.

PROS AND CONS OF GROUP TRAVEL

The group travel operator can provide a needed travel product to many travelers who will find traveling as a member of a group a very positive experience. Traveling as a group member will meet many of their needs and expectations (as previously discussed in "Individual Motivations for Joining Group Travel Programs."). For these travelers, joining a group program is definitely a plus.

These people appreciate the positive features of group travel. Some of the positive features include the accommodations ready and waiting for them when they arrive in each city, pre-scheduled dining reservations and theatre tickets, and compatible traveling companions. They also appreciate having the privacy of their own exclusive motorcoach, good group prices negotiated on their behalf, and entrée to certain places and events not always available to the public. Other big plusses are the expertise of a well-informed and professional enroute tour manager to handle the day-to-day details of their trip, as well as the feeling of confidence that the bulk of their travel expenses have already been paid in advance. Thus, they have no financial worries enroute.

However, there are a number of individuals for whom group travel is not a positive experience and who should not travel in groups. They will be unhappy and will wreak their unhappiness on others in the group. This might be the individual who is highly independent and unable to conform to a schedule or follow someone else's plan. It might be the person who does not wish to mix and contribute to the

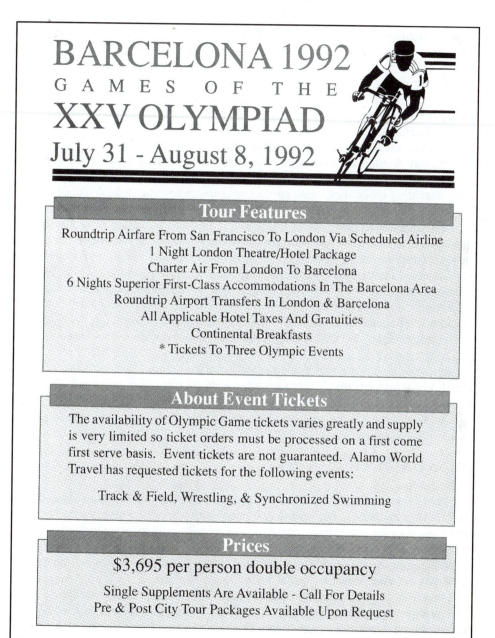

Figure 1.4 This tour to London and Barcelona was "built" around the 25th Olympiad and tickets to Olympic events are an important part of the tour package. (Courtesy of Alamo World Travel & Tours.)

overall camaraderie of the group. Some individuals want to be by themselves, rather than with others in the group. Sometimes it is not their wish to be alone, but their wish to get away from other Americans and to socialize only with the locals. Since the success (or failure) of a group travel program can often depend not only on the itinerary and events themselves, but also on the social interaction among the participants, these loners can detract from the success of the trip.

There are also individuals who do not want to follow a pre-set itinerary or travel plan. If they are enjoying one city, they resent having to leave with the group for the next city. In fact, there are a number of people who do not want to know today what they are going to be doing tomorrow. They simply like to take each day as it comes deciding when they wake up each morning what they would like to do that day. This kind of person does not do well on a group tour.

Individuals who prefer to visit one single destination in-depth, rather than to visit several destinations less thoroughly, often do not make good tour candidates. Travelers who are fussy, who complain, and who generally are not good sports and who are unwilling to "roll with the punches" can often prove a nightmare on a group tour. These people should be discouraged by a skilled travel counselor from joining a tour, since their participation will prove unsatisfactory to themselves and to the other participants. People with a history of strong leadership also find it difficult to let someone else hold the reins and they may even try to challenge the tour leader for control.

Individuals who are not in good health may find group travel a negative experience, particularly if they cannot keep up with the pace of the trip or if they find that they cannot reconcile the trip with their individual needs (e.g., special diets, a mid-day rest, or particular medical requirements).

❑ SUMMARY

The group travel arena is large and varied. It offers not only "standard" tours, but also a wide spectrum of special-interest trips. These trips encompass trips for pleasure, business, and education, and they are usually sold as prepaid package programs rather than by components.

A number of potential markets exist for the group travel product, and many programs are developed specifically for these markets. Individuals have many subliminal motivations for joining group travel programs, and recognizing these motivations helps you to design and market group trips properly. There are a number of pros and cons to group travel. Despite the many pros for most people, a certain segment of the population should not be encouraged to try group travel.

❑ *REVIEW QUESTIONS*

1. **What would be an appropriate definition of a tour?**

2. **Name four or more of the components found in a tour.**

3. **What distinguishes a "special-interest tour" from a standard tour?**

4. **Name three sample special-interest types of tours that you might like to develop.**

5. **Name four motivations for individuals to travel in a group travel program instead of independently.**

6. **Name three types of persons you would discourage from traveling in groups.**

7. **What is the academic market and when can they travel?**

8. **Name three positive features (pros) of group travel.**

9. **Name several special events: (e.g., music, sports, etc.) that might be featured as a focal point around which a tour could be designed.**

❏ *ACTIVITIES*

1. Interview a friend or classmate to determine if this individual would make a good member of a tour group.

2. Locate one special-interest tour that you may have seen in a brochure or advertisement. Make a list of organizations, clubs, schools, or other similar groups to whom you might try to sell such a trip.

3. Plan a short "sales pitch" speech that you might make to a club consisting primarily of older widows. What particular points would you include that might touch their motivations for traveling with you?

4. Put together a list of names and addresses of some major adventure tour companies in the United States. Write and tell them that you are studying group travel. Ask to see samples of some past programs.

HOW THE GROUP TRAVEL BUSINESS WORKS

LEARNING OBJECTIVES

After completing this chapter, you should:

❑ Understand the distribution process within the group travel sector of the travel industry
❑ Learn of the various employment possibilities for one wanting to work in groups
❑ Know what skills may be required of you when seeking group travel employment
❑ Understand how typical tour companies are structured

KEY CONCEPTS AND TERMS

Affinity Group
American Society of Travel Agents (ASTA)
Consumer Protection Plans
Corporate Meeting Planner
Ground Operator
Horizontal Structure
Inbound Operator
Organizer
Pied Piper
Pre-formed Group
Receptive Services Operator (RSO)
Retail Travel Agent
Retail Tour Operator
United States Tour Operators' Association (USTOA)
Vertical Structure
Wholesale Tour Operator

Many people are puzzled by the group travel business. There seem to be so many players and so many middlemen. Who does what to whom? First, let's look at the players; namely, the client organization, the retail travel agent, the retail tour operator, the wholesale tour operator, the receptive services operator, and the suppliers.

SCENARIO 1

An individual passenger wishing to enroll in an escorted tour or an independent tour package would most likely consult a **retail travel agent**. This agent, as the name implies, represents the client and suppliers. However, an agent not only represents suppliers (e.g., airlines, hotels, cruise lines) but also major tour operators. The agent acts as a broker, who searches for a tour company that has a tour appropriate for this client. The tour operator pays a commission to the travel agency for making the sale. In this case, the tour operator is a **wholesale tour operator**, because the company is selling through the retail travel agent to the public, not directly to the public.

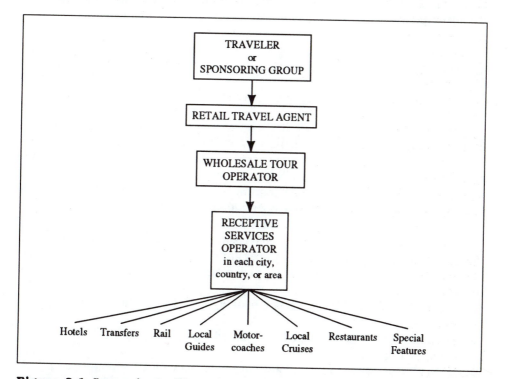

Figure 2.1 Scenario 1 The tour develops from client to retail travel agent to U.S. based wholesaler to various overseas receptive services operators, who book each supplier.

A similar situation would hold true if the individual belonged to a club, church, or employee organization and wanted to go on the trip, as well as to arrange it for the entire group. This is what is referred to as a **pre-formed group**. Sometimes it is called an **affinity group**. This is usually a group that already exists and was formed for purposes other than travel. In this instance, the group **organizer** or **Pied Piper** (i.e., the person within the organization interested in getting the group together to travel) approaches a travel agency. Or, an aggressive agency with an effective sales staff looking for group business may have taken the initiative and approached the organization. Then, the travel agency might in turn, handle the tour for the organization and choose to custom-design it and to book all reservations with suppliers (i.e., hotels, sightseeing, etc.) through a U.S.-based wholesale tour operator, rather than booking it directly themselves.

In this case, the travel agency might be remunerated by commission from the wholesaler, as when booking individual clients. However, it would be more likely quoted as a net per-client price by the wholesale tour operator. The travel agency would then be free to mark up the price to cover its time, expertise, coordination efforts, and promotional expenses. The agency's markup would also be sufficient to include a fair profit to the agency and, in some cases, an additional profit for the agency employee or sales person who generated the group business.

SCENARIO 2

Another scenario might be a retail travel agency that has its own in-house group department and staff very conversant with certain destinations. In this case, the retail travel agency might elect to bypass the U.S.-based wholesale tour operator and book directly through a **receptive services operator (RSO)** overseas in each country, city, or area. As the term receptive services operator implies, such a company receives groups; it books and coordinates services for a group coming into that particular area. Such receptive operators are also sometimes called **inbound operators**, or simply **ground operators**. In fact, if the retail travel agency (with its own group department) were very conversant with the destination, it might even elect to bypass the receptive services operator (RSO) and book directly with each hotel, each local sightseeing company, each motorcoach company, each restaurant or attraction, and so forth.

In summary, a retail travel agency booking a group tour to London, might:

❑ Book all reservations through a U.S.-based wholesaler—particularly one specializing in the British Isles.
❑ Book all reservations by fax, letter, or telephone with a London-based receptive services operator, who, in turn, handles all London services.
❑ Book all reservations by fax, letter, or telephone directly and separately with a London hotel, a London motorcoach company, a London guide service, each London restaurant, and so forth.

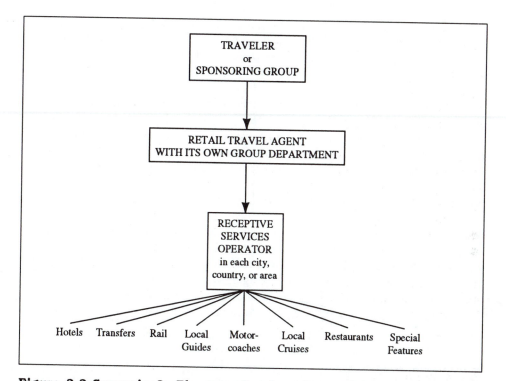

Figure 2.2 Scenario 2 The tour develops from client to retail travel agent with its own group department directly to various overseas receptive services operators, who book each supplier.

There are advantages and disadvantages to each method (see Chapter 3 for more details). Regardless of which scenario is involved, note that a retail travel agency *is* involved and is, in effect, acting as its own tour operator (i.e., a **retail tour operator**, selling directly to the client organization, not *through* any other travel company).

SCENARIO 3

In still another scenario the retail travel agency is bypassed from the outset. The club, church, or other affinity organization goes directly to a tour operator, or a tour operator solicits the client organization directly.

In this case, the client organization is booking directly with the tour operator. This may be a viable method *if* the tour operator selected by the client organization is appointed by the airlines (and thus bonded to some extent, at least up to the requirements of the Airline Reporting Corporation—ARC), and if the tour operator has joined some sort of a **consumer's protection plan** to which tour operators may subscribe.

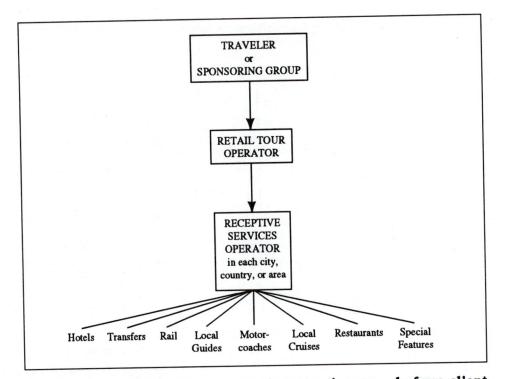

Figure 2.3 Scenario 3 The tour in the scenario proceeds from client to retail tour operator to various overseas receptive services operators, who book each supplier.

For example, tour operators may elect to join the consumer protection plan of the **American Society of Travel Agents (ASTA)** or the **United States Tour Operators' Association (USTOA)**. If the tour operator selected by the client organization does not belong to such a plan, it may prove risky to the client organization. Many small (and not-so-small) tour operators have had to close their doors and have at times taken clients' monies down with them.

This is not to imply that any tour operator not belonging to a consumer protection plan is unreliable. On the contrary, there are many excellent small tour operators that choose not to belong to such a plan because of the heavy requirements placed on them, such as large bonds tying up their cash-flow monies. But, if a client organization elects to bypass the retail travel agency and go directly to a tour operator, thinking it will save money this way, the level of expertise and protection that a good retail agency affords is missing.

As you can see, the tour operator is really the key to producing the group travel product. Whether the tour operator is wholesale or retail, large or small, nationwide or local, or a department of another travel company or a company unto itself, the concept is still the same. This is the segment of the travel industry responsible for designing and creating exciting travel products. If you wish to be

Don't Just Compare Vacation Packages. Compare What Stands Behind Them.

In these tough times, travelers are demanding more than a good value. They want assurance that their vacation dollars will be protected.

Booking packages offered by USTOA's Active Members provides that assurance. Because they are backed by USTOA's *$5 Million Consumer Protection Plan.* A proven plan that safeguards your clients from financial loss in the event of a member's bankruptcy or insolvency.

So, when comparing packages, look for the USTOA symbol. It stands for financial protection. And much more. Please contact our president, Robert Whitley, for details on our Consumer Protection Plan and USTOA.

UNITED STATES TOUR OPERATORS ASSOCIATION
211 East 51st Street, New York, NY 10022. (212) 944-5727.

20 YEARS
INTEGRITY IN TOURISM

For a list, via FAX, of USTOA members and their programs, call 800-845-6560, code #2031.

Figure 2.4   Travel agencies increasingly want to work with tour operators who subscribe to a consumer protection plan to reduce their liability. (Courtesy of USTOA.)

involved in this process, direct your efforts to this area of the industry, perhaps as an employee, perhaps as an entrepreneur.

CAREERS IN GROUP TRAVEL

If you are intrigued with working in the group travel arena, you might do so in a variety of situations:

1. As an employee of an existing wholesale tour company. You will most likely begin in the operations division to learn how groups truly operate. Perhaps you will eventually become group operations manager or perhaps move into sales and marketing. Since major tour companies are scattered around the United States, this may require you to relocate.
2. As an inside employee of a retail travel agency that is large enough to have its own group department already in place. This agency may be willing to use your talents in the operational phase, or use your sales capabilities to recruit new group business.
3. As an employee or independent contractor with a retail travel agency that does not have a group department but would like to develop one. This agency would expect you to set up such a department and to recruit the group business to support such a department.
4. As an employee of an inbound tour company, dealing in the operational phase, acting as a receptive services operator. You would learn the business by dealing in group handling from this perspective (see Chapter 15 regarding Inbound Travel).
5. As a freelance tour manager, traveling with groups as their leader. After learning in-the-field phases of tour operations, you could "come in from the cold" to work inside with a tour operator.
6. As an employee of a peripheral travel industry company, such as a hotel chain or a cruise line, dealing in group operations and sales.
7. As a **corporate meeting planner**, convention handler, or employee in an incentive house, working with large corporations on their annual employee incentive travel programs.
8. Ultimately, perhaps as an entrepreneur, setting up your own group company.

Many people who are successful in the group travel field have had experience in several of these areas. This makes them more valuable to employers because of the eclectic nature of their background and expertise.

QUALIFICATIONS FOR WORKING IN GROUPS

Working with groups requires the same basic knowledge as working with individual travel clients. In fact, perhaps it requires more. You want to begin with the usual retail travel agent skills (e.g., airline computer expertise, ability to sell and counsel, knowledge of industry products and resources, and an understanding of travel industry business practices). It also requires general business management skills, such as marketing (including advertising and preparing tour brochures); financial handling (including tour costing, pricing, accounting); personnel handling, and good inter-personal skills.

Certainly, the ability to do cold-calling and recruit group business would be a much desired quality. Of course, it is assumed that you would also have basic office skills, such as typing and a gracious telephone demeanor. Not all positions may require all of these requirements. If you are employed in a small firm, or if you are starting up a group department, you may not have the services of a secretary, a computer whiz, a receptionist, a marketing specialist, or an accounting expert.

In addition, working in groups has some specialty requirements all its own. For many people who are already accustomed to working as travel agents—whether as inside retail travel counselors or as commissioned sales persons—the change to group travel handling is often a much bigger change than anticipated. Here are some of the aspects of working in group business that make it very different from working as a retail travel consultant dealing with individual clients.

1. A retail travel counselor deals on a day-to-day basis with the potential traveler when planning an individual client's trip. With groups, the counselor may never meet the individual traveler and may miss this personal contact. This is not to say that the counselor will never meet the public. But the public you do meet will more than likely be people in the travel trade or key individuals in clubs and organizations for whom tours are being handled. If the program is being wholesaled, you will also deal with travel agents.

2. A retail travel counselor deals with individuals. A group counselor deals with volume, and everything must be geared to handling large numbers of people efficiently at one time. You must forego personal tastes (i.e., that charming country inn with only ten rooms or that elegant restaurant that will not accept a tour group).

3. A retail travel counselor deals with clients planning to travel in the relatively near future. Group handling involves planning for clients who will travel far in the future—at least a year from the first planning stages, often longer. You

Figure 2.5 Successful group tour agents have retail travel agent skills such as a pleasing telephone manner and ability to sell and counsel. But they also need a deeper knowledge of industry resources and practices, tour designing, marketing and costing. (Courtesy of Fordham University.)

don't experience the immediate satisfaction of happy clients returning and reporting on their trip. By the time a tour finally leaves, many experienced tour operators find that their interest in it has been exhausted.

4. A retail travel counselor does much of the business verbally—either in person or by phone. In dealing with groups it is vitally important to put all transactions and confirmations in writing. Therefore, written communication skills become more important. Good composition, good business letters, accurate grammar and spelling, the ability to engender enthusiasm and sell by mail are essential.

5. A retail travel counselor is subject to the flow of the day's pressures (e.g., the telephone, incoming mail, drop-in clients, and visitors). To deal successfully with groups, you must get out from under the daily pressures imposed from outside sources and follow a schedule; namely, a planned calendar. Organizational skills are very important.

6. A retail travel counselor sells a product produced by someone else. In dealing with groups, you both produce the product and sell it. This means that you are much more knowledgeable about the product, because you designed the

product and understand how it is put together. However, it also means that you must answer the difficult questions and take responsibility for your mistakes. *You* are ultimately responsible for your own product.

7. A retail travel counselor demonstrates creativity by selling well and by knowing the product line of existing tours, cruises, and other products well enough to match the right travel product to the right client. However, the constraints of time and potential profit on any one client do not afford the luxury of lengthy conversations or extended research when planning a day-by-day itinerary for just one individual. On the other hand, the time frame and profit potential of a group allows one these luxuries. It probably even requires them. You are much more likely to need a broad experience of the world, since much of the material needed to construct an interesting trip, write an exciting itinerary, or publish brochures that sell cannot always be found in traditional travel industry source books and must therefore be researched elsewhere.

HOW TOUR COMPANIES OR GROUP DIVISIONS ARE STRUCTURED

Basically, tour companies or group divisions of a travel agency are structured in one of two ways: vertically or horizontally.

Vertical Structure

A **vertical structure** is one in which one person handles an entire tour. This person plans it, books it, costs and prices it, writes the tour brochure and promotional materials, handles the bookings, prepares final documents, and dispatches it. This person may even accompany the tour and act as tour manager in the field. In other words, one individual grows with the project from the bottom up.

A vertically structured group division is most likely to occur in smaller companies or tour departments. Most notably, they're likely to occur in a one-person tour department where the group person must do virtually everything, with a little secretarial or clerical help from time to time. (See Table 2.1.)

This kind of structure has several advantages. First, the group individual knows the product thoroughly and probably can sell it well. The individual can answer almost any question about the tour, since he or she put it together in the first place. Second, the individual has total control of the project. There is no danger of too many cooks spoiling the broth, or of an important deadline date slipping through a crack and being totally missed because someone else was "taking care of it." Only one person is responsible for keeping track of deadlines and everything else! Third, a vertical structure allows for area specialization. If an individual group staff member is an expert on Asia, this person can probably best deal with clients' questions on this area. This makes the individual sound more convincing than someone who has never been there. In a company structured vertically, there might be a number

TABLE 2.1 Vertical structure of a group tour company or department. In a small company, one person must perform all functions for many different tours. As the company grows, additional employees handle additional tours in the same vertical method.

Meet with sponsoring organization to review and discuss next year.

Upon tour return, close files. Do profit/loss statement.

Travel with group as tour escort (or brief outside tour manager).

Prepare final documents/instructions for tour manager.

Prepare passengers' final documents.

Finalize with all tour suppliers.

Deal with all suppliers on an ongoing basis.

Handle individual travelers as they book onto tour.

Market the tour.

Develop tour brochure and marketing plan.

Cost and price tour.

Book all tour services with suppliers.

Design the tour.

Locate and sell the organization who will sponsor the tour.

of tour consultants. Each tour consultant would be responsible for a particular series of tours. Perhaps one consultant would take Asian tours, another would take European, and so forth.

There are, however, certain drawbacks to a vertical structure. The person handling the tour may be an outstanding sales and promotion person. However, this same individual may be a terrible operations manager who is totally inept at detail. Conversely, an excellent operations manager may be capable within the operational realm, but timid or ineffective when it comes to speaking in public or going out and calling on a prospective group account. There is also the frightening prospect of this individual's becoming ill, being out of town, or leaving the company. This leaves virtually no one else in the office who knows how to answer calls or how to handle the program.

Horizontal Structure

A **horizontal structure** is one in which a tour company (or tour department within a travel agency) is set up laterally by function rather than by tour program. This kind of arrangement occurs most often in the larger tour companies. That is, one division or individual may design and plan all tours for the company. A second division would book all space, dealing with hotels, airlines, cruise companies, and other suppliers. In fact, in extremely large companies, this booking division may be broken down into separate air, hotel, and cruise departments. Another level would be the sales division. The marketing and public relations division would be above the sales level, and perhaps other levels as well.

With this type of structure, a salesperson would have to become adept at selling all of the company's tour products—not just the area or country with which he or she is most familiar. Those who work in operations booking group hotel and air reservations, for example, would do so for all of the company's tours. (See Table 2.2.)

Here again, there are advantages and disadvantages. This kind of structure allows a top-notch salesperson to do nothing but sell and allows an operations person to devote full time to operational control and dealing with suppliers. However, a tour passes through various strata, so no one person is handling the total tour. Therefore, it requires careful supervision and checkpoints to be sure that nothing falls through the cracks.

Mixed Structure

Still other companies, perhaps inadvertently, may arrive at a mix of the vertical and horizontal structures. One person or department may initiate a tour; namely, booking the reservations, costing, and publishing it. Then, once the product is ready to promote, it may be turned over to someone else in the office who totally manages the tour to completion by handling sales, client bookings, finalization with suppliers, and dispatch.

TABLE 2.2 Horizontal structure of a group tour company or department. Different levels would perform different functions on all tours within the company.

MANAGEMENT. Supervises all departments below. Makes annual plan, budget, and goals for the company. Works on advance programming for the future. May also become involved in tour designing.

MARKETING DEPARTMENT. Develops marketing plans (and perhaps marketing budgets) for all company's tours. Handles company's advertising, promotional events, sales campaigns, brochures, and other collateral materials.

SALES DEPARTMENT. Deals with clients (or if a wholesaler, with clients' travel agents). May be broken into inside sales (handling client inquiries and bookings) and outside sales with account representatives who call on potential groups or travel agents to recruit business.

OPERATIONS DIVISION. Books all tour services with suppliers. Deals with all suppliers on an ongoing basis. Finalizes each tour with suppliers. May also cost tours (with final pricing decision made by management). May select tour managers to travel with groups in the field.

DOCUMENTATION DIVISION. Prepares final documents, air tickets, departure packets for travelers.

ACCOUNTING/FINANCE. Handles all day-to-day accounting functions, payments to suppliers, clients' payments, employee payroll and fringe benefits, end-of-tour profit and loss statements, bank statement reconciliations, and projection of cash flow needs. Works with management on company budgets, tax matters, and state and federal compliance requirements. May perhaps do weekly ARC reports also if company is ARC-appointed.

SUPPORT STAFF. May include switchboard/receptionist function, file clerk, secretarial, and clerical functions, depending on size of company.

This method's prime advantage is that it removes one staff person or one department from the day-to-day pressures and allows them time to be concerned with future tours. They constantly work ahead a couple of years. Frequently, a tour consultant may be so busy working on this year's tour that it is impossible to stop the momentum and find time to set up next year's trip. Then, by the time this year's tour is dispatched, it is too late to get reservations for next year.

❑ SUMMARY

There are three primary scenarios for handling group tours: (1) from the client to a retail travel agency to a U.S.-based wholesaler; (2) from the client to a retail travel agency to the receptive services operator overseas or directly to individual overseas suppliers, thus bypassing the wholesaler; and (3) from the client to a tour operator, bypassing the retail travel agent.

Careers in group travel are varied. Many careers are within group tour operators or departments; other careers are with peripheral travel companies involved with groups. The qualifications for working in group travel not only include basic retail travel agent skills, but also many other additional skills. Tour companies and group divisions are usually structured in one of two ways: vertically or horizontally. The structure of the company will determine the type of employment opportunities and job descriptions.

❑ REVIEW QUESTIONS

1. What is the difference between a retail tour operator and a wholesale tour operator?

2. Why do we often think of a retail travel agent's role as that of a broker?

3. What is a Pied Piper and what is his/her role in the group travel field?

4. If a retail travel agency is quoted a net per client price for a group tour, how does the retail agency make its profit?

5. What are two other commonly used terms for a receptive services operator (RSO)?

6. What is the role and what are the actual duties of a receptive services operator?

7. **Why are writing skills a much more important qualification for working in the group business than for working as a retail travel counselor?**

8. **In which company structure would you learn the most about all phases of the group business—vertical or horizontal?**

❑ *ACTIVITIES*

1. Contact a local tour company and ask for an informational interview with the manager or owner. In the interview, determine how the company is structured, what types of job descriptions exist within the company, and what specific skills the owner looks for when hiring personnel.

2. Locate several organizations in town that have already done group travel programs. Ascertain the kind of program, the success or failure, the problems that the organization may have had, and how the program was handled—through a retail travel agent? a wholesaler? a receptive services operator?

3. Analyze your own skills for future employment in the group travel field. Make one list of your qualifications that you feel are a "plus" for working in groups. Make a second list of "minuses" of personal qualifications or skills that you feel you lack. Develop a written plan about how to enhance your chances for employment in groups by developing these missing qualifications and skills.

4. Write to the United States Tour Operators' Association (USTOA) and request information on what a tour operator must do to qualify for USTOA membership in terms of bonding, references, and so forth.

▷ 3

ENTREPRENEURSHIP IN GROUP BUSINESS

LEARNING OBJECTIVES

After reading this chapter you should:

- ❑ Understand why group business is so attractive as a business endeavor
- ❑ Know the preventive legal planning required when beginning a group business
- ❑ Know what types of business insurance should be considered for a new tour company/division
- ❑ Understand the various banking, budget, and financial considerations you should investigate
- ❑ Be more knowledgeable about special requirements in personnel staffing
- ❑ Have an idea of office location, layout, and equipment needs

KEY CONCEPTS AND TERMS

Booking Direct
Defaults
Errors and Omissions (E and O) Insurance
Escrow Account
Group Operations Manager
Liability Insurance
Net Plus Markup
Preventive Legal Planning
Principal
Responsibility Clause
Travel Promoters' Law
Trust Account

You have decided that you want to "get into groups," as we say in the industry. But perhaps you do not want to be an employee working for an existing operator or in the group department of a travel agency, although this experience would certainly be a wonderful background for an entrepreneurship.

ENTREPRENEURSHIP IN GROUP TRAVEL

Perhaps what you really want is to open your own tour company. Or, perhaps you are a travel agency owner or manager who would like to open a group department within the agency. Where do you start?

You should probably begin by assessing your own motivations to see if they are sensible, businesslike, and realistic. Many tour companies have come and gone in past years for a myriad of reasons including the following:

- ❏ Under-capitalization
- ❏ Inability to locate and sell sufficient group business
- ❏ Personnel without group specialty experience
- ❏ Unwillingness or inability to take financial risk and operate without income from groups during the start-up year
- ❏ Unwise spending habits, and
- ❏ Bad business decisions

Also, bad timing affected many companies that opened in a year of world crisis and that did not have the cash flow to see them through to better times.

Unfortunately, many people simply jump into group handling because of its excitement and income possibilities. In fact, sometimes people don't even make a conscious decision to handle groups; a group simply arrives on their doorstep, and before they know it, they're "into groups."

WHY HANDLE GROUPS?

You may decide to handle group business for many reasons. These reasons might include building a list of clients, expanding the base of potential future travelers, developing repeat tour projects, and filling in weak business periods in the office. Other reasons are less directly connected with business. They might include helping a friend or client who is involved with a group or assisting new and inexperienced travelers to attempt that first trip. (This is a trip that they might never be able to take without help.) But the primary fact remains that group business is attractive because, if handled properly, it offers the greatest profit potential.

Many will refute this statement. They say that if they devoted the same amount of time and involvement to 30 independent passengers as to a group of 30, then

TravelAge
WEST
January 28, 1991

Gulf War Rocks U.S. Travel Industry

Agencies Face Cutbacks

By MICHELLE SULLIVAN
and ANN WILLIAMS

LOS ANGELES — There are strong signs that the U.S. recession and the Persian Gulf war are taking a toll on travel agencies, one of which is the dramatic increase in agency closures reported by the Airlines Reporting Corp.

The number of travel agencies that closed voluntarily jumped 768% in December, to 165 agencies, compared with the same month in 1989, the ARC said. For the year, voluntary deletions were up 31%, to 1415.

The number of agencies declared in default dropped slightly in 1990, from 872 to 868, but increased 9% during the month of December, according to the ARC. The number

Continued on page 56

Figure 3.1 World crises, such as war or economic recession, discourage travel. This can put travel agencies and tour operators out of business if they do not have adequate cash flow and long-term financing to see them through. (TravelAge West Magazine.)

they would be ahead financially. If this is the case, it is probably because the tours are not being priced properly. The reason that you can make more money on a group of 30 than on 30 individuals is not because of volume handling or because the commission is earned 30 times over. It is because group tour business allows a company to establish its own markup on its tours, and thus frees the company from working under the commission system.

No matter how many individual bookings you handle, the earnings on those bookings are still limited to those that can be obtained from suppliers. These earnings are usually 10 or 11 percent on an air ticket sold in conjunction with a land tour and an airline's approved itinerary (IT) number. They are usually a basic 10 percent on tours and cruises, plus whatever overrides accrue because of volume bookings or through tenacious negotiating with suppliers. But even when selling tours and cruises, and even when dealing with volume, the earnings are still restricted to a commission rate that someone else has established. While this commission can be attractive when compared to the commission usually received on individual bookings (particularly if overrides are involved), these earnings are still not as attractive as they could be if the tour were built from scratch. When designing a tour, using a **net plus markup** pricing system, you're free to work with *net* rates, and then cost in your operating expenses. Then you can determine your profit needs and mark up the net rates accordingly to result in the earnings needed. When you build a tour this way, you step over the line from selling transportation to selling travel; that is, travel as a total concept.

For obvious reasons, existing packages—such as cruises or published tours—cannot be marked up. Why should a client buy a cruise from one travel company if its price is $100 higher than the same cruise being sold by another company down the street! If a company is just beginning in group business, it might want to sell a group into an existing product such as a cruise or tour, learning how to handle group business in this way and being content with the commission the supplier will grant.

However, as you and your personnel become more knowledgeable about group handling, and somewhat braver and more adept at the whole group process, you will want to package your own tours. Packaging a tour involves custom designing a trip to the particular needs of a specific group or projected clientele. In this way, you control the entire tour. Namely, you control its components, its quality, its pricing, and so forth. Control of the tour's components means control of potential earnings. Since you determine the amount of profit built into the trip, you control the expenses and make the operational decisions that affect the pricing and the profit. This freedom from working under the commission system gives you a wide latitude to be creative in including non-commissionable features in an itinerary and to design tours that standard tour operators are not offering, or tours that may appear unfeasible or unprofitable to others.

The higher profit potential also gives you the freedom to hire personnel (e.g., a good group operations manager), at a higher salary level than a usual retail travel consultant. In short, your higher earnings will support higher salaries. It also may allow you to be more generous with commissioned salespeople who are involved in bringing in group business to your company. Many commissioned salespeople will want part of the profit of group business and will not be content with their usual commission split arrangement with a travel agency. They will want a split of the total earnings on the project (including markup, overrides, volume savings, and so forth), not merely a split of commissions.

Once it has been decided that you do want to handle group business, it is important to make sure that you really are ready to handle it. Do you have access to sound legal advice? Is your insurance adequate for group risks? Is your accounting system prepared to track group profit or loss? What about financing? Has a structural format been designed? What about special layouts, personnel, and supplies? Many decisions must be made. Let's take a look at a few of these.

LEGAL PREPARATION

In the interest of **preventive legal planning**, your attorney should be consulted *prior* to embarking on a new group endeavor. You will want legal advice whether you're opening a group department in an existing travel agency, opening your own tour company from scratch, or simply handling a large group project within your already formed company.

If you are opening a group department of an existing travel agency, there are not as many considerations as in a startup operation. The existing travel agency probably already holds all of the necessary local business licenses, minimum insurance, and appointments with cruise lines and airlines (through the Airline Reporting Corporation ARC). The ARC appointment carries with it certain minimum bonding requirements that the travel agency has presumably already fulfilled, based on its present volume of air business. The ARC could, however, require an increase in bonding amount if the new group business brings substantially higher volume of air sales.

If yours is a start-up tour company, not operating within the confines of a travel agency already appointed by the ARC, then more legal preparation will be required. In this case, you will need to address such issues as local business license(s), insurance (see pg. 38), and any specific requirements in your state.

In your new company, if you do plan to issue air tickets in-house, you, in effect, become a travel agency, even if you only plan to sell tours and not individual travel. This means that you will have to obtain ARC appointments in order to receive airline ticket stock. In addition, you will have to structure your new company to comply with all ARC rules and regulations. These rules and regulations include, among other things, the ARC required bonding, the proper storage of ticket stock on-site and in a safety deposit box in a bank, and the submitting of a weekly ticket sales report to the ARC area bank, whether or not you issue air tickets every week. There are also ARC requirements regarding the specific qualifications of the individual you hire as your "qualifier." A suggested source for further information is *Guide To Starting and Operating a Successful Travel Agency* by Laurence Stevens. Also you will want to review the ARC's own publication *ARC's Industry Agent's Handbook*.

Note that a travel agency owner's decision to become involved with group business can change the agency's status from an agent for an existing principal (as when selling a group into an existing tour or cruise) to a **principal** (as when packaging one's own tours). In the past, it was customary for most travel agencies to book overseas land tours through their favorite U.S.-based tour wholesaler. Thus, they remained an agent and not a principal. They also had someone else within the reach of the U.S. court system to share a defense with them in the event that they were sued by our increasingly litigious consumer public.

However, with the advent of the fax machine, which made direct booking overseas possible with relative ease and speed, many travel agencies have become principals without ever realizing it. It should be noted that the law requires that the name of the principal be disclosed in all literature published. The U.S. judicial system does not look favorably on travel programs where the consumer cannot easily ascertain who's in charge and easily determine to whom to forward a complaint (or perhaps a lawsuit).

California has a **Travel Promoters' Law**, which, among other things, requires that anyone involved in the offer or sale of air or sea transportation register with the California Attorney General's Office and pay the required registration fee. Hawaii and some other states have enacted similar laws. The California law requires that a travel promoter maintain a trust account and requires that you deposit 90 percent of all sums received therein or, in lieu of that trust account, maintain an adequate bond. (See Figure 3.2 and further information on trust accounts on pg. 42.) Currently in California, ARC-appointed travel agencies are exempt from the Travel Promoters' Law. However, you and your attorney should carefully check all similar requirements that may exist in your particular state.

Whether you are starting a company from scratch or opening a group department in an existing travel agency, it will be necessary to prepare a standard **responsibility clause** to use in any of your tour brochures. (See the responsibility clause in the sample itinerary in Chapter 5).

If you, as an individual, are selling or putting together group travel projects under an independent contractor non-employee arrangement for a tour operator or travel agency, it is important to consult with your attorney as to your own possible personal liability. The travel industry is changing rapidly with many, many more individuals working under loose arrangements such as outside commissioned sales persons, independent contractors, and so forth.

It is important that these individuals are properly protected and that the individuals in this category know their legal status and their personal insurance protection, as well as that of the company with which they are affiliated. Many newcomers to the group field simply grab at an affiliation with a travel agency, delighted to find an agency through which they can book their first groups. Yet, they fail to query the agency's management about their own legal or insurance relationship, which may or may not protect them.

INSURANCE COVERAGE

After your attorney, the second professional you should consult is your insurance agent. Your company's insurance coverage should be reviewed in light of the decision to handle group business. This includes liability protection, errors and omissions coverage, and ways to lessen risk against such things as supplier defaults, employee illness or accident on tour, and suppliers who do not honor their contracts and commitments.

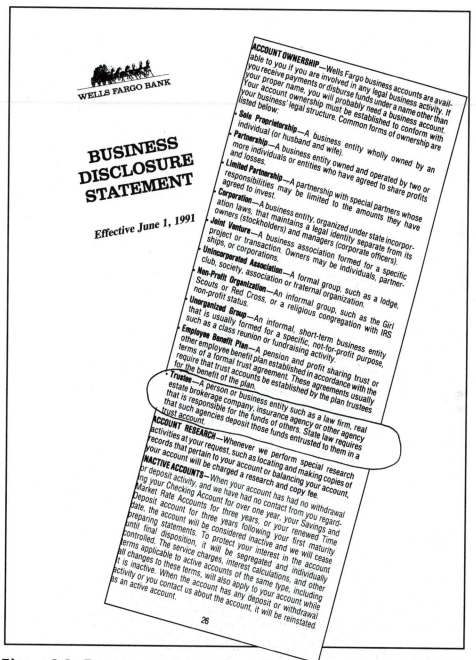

Figure 3.2 Trust accounts may be utilized to secure clients' funds. (Wells Fargo Bank.)

Liability Insurance

As a company expands into group travel and other more extensive operations, it becomes vulnerable to more kinds of liability situations. For this reason, it is essential that enough **liability insurance** be carried to anticipate and cover these problems. For example, liability insurance protects the company from a tour member slipping and breaking a leg on tour and claiming negligence and from a motorcoach going over a cliff. While most retail travel agencies probably carry a minimum of one million dollars in liability insurance, many companies involved in groups have increased their coverage to five million dollars or more, if they can find a company that will write this much coverage. Remember, if a motorcoach carrying 40 passengers goes over a cliff, and if the responsible company held only one million dollars of insurance coverage, this would amount to only $25,000 per passenger, which is not very much.

It should be noted that if you are planning to handle international tours, your liability should be worldwide liability. Also, it is possible to make arrangements with your insurance company to name a client organization (e.g., a club, church, corporation, etc.) as a rider to your company insurance policy for the duration of a specific trip.

Errors and Omissions Insurance

Errors and omissions insurance (E and O insurance) is the travel industry's equivalent to malpractice insurance. It protects the company in the event that a member of the staff (an employee or even a short-term outside contractor, such as a tour manager) makes an error causing a client hardship and expense (e.g., ticketing someone on a non-existent flight or overlooking the need for a special visa or inoculation). It is possible that if a product does not live up to the client's expectations that the client might bring suit against your company for having been negligent in the selection of a hotel or a receptive services operator, for being uninformed, or for using bad judgment. Even if your company is legally right, just the cost of bad publicity and the cost of legal defense can be extremely high. Having an errors and omissions insurance company attorney to settle such problems can prove invaluable, and the policy pays for the attorney in excess of the deductible.

Insuring Against Other Risks

If you are involved in a start-up operation, you will, of course, need the usual package of business insurance pertinent to any business. This insurance coverage includes fire, theft, on-site liability and so forth. Other possible risks must also be considered. **Defaults**, or failure to perform, on the part of wholesalers, airlines, and overseas receptive operators are a fact of life in today's economic climate. Yet, at the present time a blanket type of coverage, which one may purchase against this type of risk, does not seem to exist. Risks of this sort are often considered part of the cost of doing business. As Jeffrey R. Miller, a noted Maryland travel industry attorney, noted in his book, *Legal Aspects of Travel Agency Operation,* "In most instances, the cost of the insurance will outweigh the protection it will afford. The best protection...is to know the reputation of the tour operator or supplier you are dealing with . . . . A prudent business man or woman can be the best insurance against many of the risks faced in the travel industry."[1]

It should be noted that a client can purchase individual insurance coverage on an optional basis, and it is important that you offer this coverage. This insurance covers everything from medical/accident coverage and baggage loss/damage to cancellation penalty protection, trip interruption, and medical evacuation. Some insurance policies may also cover the default of a tour operator, airline, or cruise line. This type of optional insurance should be offered to the individual client. In fact, it should be urged. (See Chapter 10 on client handling for more details on individual client-purchased insurance.) Some travel agencies and tour operators have experimented with purchasing such coverage on behalf of their clients and packaging it into the cost of the trip, but this method has been denied validity by many states' departments of insurance. As Ralph Davis, president of Travel Insurance Services in Walnut Creek, California, recently explained, "In the state of California the client must know he is purchasing this insurance and must be advised of the premium involved and be given the opportunity to refuse the coverage if he so wishes. It cannot simply be forced upon him or her as part of the package price of the tour."[2]

Certainly, if a company is sending employees or freelance tour managers to escort tours, such risks as their lost luggage, and their illness or injury while on tour, and so forth must be considered. It is fairly easy to purchase pre-trip individual coverage for a tour manager from the same company that is providing client travel insurance. The tour manager may already have medical coverage through the company employee group plan, through a personal medical plan, or simply through Medicare. Do be aware that Medicare is not valid overseas, so if a tour manager is totally dependent on Medicare, a supplemental plan should be in force on any tour leaving the country. It is also wise to consider bonding a tour manager who will be carrying substantial funds.

FINANCIAL SAFEGUARDS OFFERED BY BANKS

Two additional financial safeguards offered by banks are escrow accounts and trust accounts.

Escrow Accounts

Another financial safeguard companies sometimes consider when paying out large sums to suppliers is a special bank **escrow account**. When money is placed in escrow, two parties agree to a certain payment and compliance arrangement. Then, they place the monies in question in the hands of a third, neutral party. This third party holds the funds until it is satisfied that the terms of the agreement are fulfilled. This arrangement is very common in the field of real estate where the monies changing hands between the buyer and the seller of a home remain in escrow until each party is satisfied that the other has lived up to his or her part of their mutual agreement.

A similar arrangement can be devised between a travel company and a supplier by naming a bank as the third party holding the funds in escrow. For example, if you were chartering a plane from an air carrier, you might want to arrange with the airline to make part of the payment for the plane before departure and the balance of the payment after the carrier has provided the return flight sector. This would assure you that your clients are not stranded abroad without homeward passage in the event that the air carrier defaults. (At least it assures that clients are not left without financial recompense). Of course, this sort of three-way escrow arrangement is only possible if all parties agree. If the chartering airline refuses to agree to the escrow arrangement, then you might want to select another air carrier.

The same type of arrangement might be set up if you were using a tour operator or cruise line to provide services. This assumes, of course, that the tour operator or cruise line agreed to the arrangement at the outset. As you can see, this would necessitate a separate escrow account and agreement between your company and each of the major suppliers used on a given tour.

A number of suppliers may not agree to an escrow agreement, because they might need the cash flow monies earlier. Furthermore, they might be afraid that the agency might try to quibble over small items at the end. Or, a supplier simply might not need the business enough to want to bother with escrow. Thus, if small amounts of money are involved, it may not be worth the trouble. However, if you have large amounts of money—as well as faith, trust, and reputation—riding on the performance of this supplier, escrow arrangements are certainly worth considering.

Many travel agencies have returned passengers' monies when a supplier defaulted to save face with the clients or to avoid a lawsuit. This has happened, even though the agency has never recovered any money from the supplier, or even though it has only received ten cents on the dollar later in a bankruptcy court. You may be able to stand a loss of this kind when only small amounts of money are at stake, or when independent clients and diversified suppliers are involved. However, with a group, when large amounts of money are at risk in the hands of one major supplier, it may not be the kind of financial risk that you want to take.

Trust Accounts

Another banking arrangement is called a **trust account**. With a trust account you open a special account with the bank for each major client organization or tour project. Ostensibly, all monies that go into this account are held "in trust," and only used for this particular travel project.

Many tour companies find that advertising that their clients' monies are "in trust" gives their company more validity. The company asks that clients make their checks payable directly to the trust account, which gives them a feeling of security. They know that their funds are not intermingled with the company's general funds. Of course, if the signatories to the trust account are the same travel company officers who are signatories to the company's general funds, nothing prevents them from moving funds from the trust account into the general fund if they need cash flow. In addition, if the company officers are bad money managers, they may just as easily manage customers' monies badly in a trust account as if the customers' monies were intermingled in the general fund. The difference is, however, that moving monies out of a trust account for purposes other than to handle the project stipulated is not just considered bad money management, but it also constitutes a criminal action. Therefore, the perpetrator is subject to criminal investigation and not merely business mismanagement.

ACCOUNTING AND FINANCING CONSIDERATIONS

Before getting into group operations, survey the accounting system that will be handling your group business and calculate some rough estimates of start-up monies needed and probable cash flow.

Accounting

The accounting system that will be handling your group business should be sufficiently sophisticated to separate all incoming and outgoing payments on a given tour project from the rest of the company's figures. Then, at the end of each trip the accountant can accurately analyze each tour project for a true profit picture. If a tour does not make the projected profit, then the figures for the actual tour can be compared to initial projections to show where things went wrong. This can be invaluable, especially in helping to cost the next tour project properly. Working in advance, the accountant can demonstrate how to assign a special code number to each tour so that all financial transactions related to that tour carry this number throughout the life of the tour project. This system works well in the simplest manual system or in the most sophisticated computerized company.

Financing

Before embarking on any large group project or before deciding to open a group department or tour company, you need to write some rough estimates of necessary start-up monies and cash flow. In all likelihood, an initial deposit from clients will be required as they join the tours. They will be billed for final payment, which probably will be due 60 days prior to tour departure, although in some cases it may even be earlier. Final payment should never be later than 60 days.

In any event, clients' money will not be available initially, and you will need funds to handle such things as advance deposits to hotels or wholesalers (wherever required) and printing brochures, direct mail, advertising, and other promotional expenses. Monies might also be needed for entertaining potential group accounts, for staff travel for on-site inspection, or for promotion. Since most tours need a one-year lead time from inception to departure date, the bulk of the clients' money (final payments) will not be available until approximately 10 months after tour start-up.

It is good business to make up a realistic budget of those monies that will have to be advanced by your company. This budget should clearly identify those monies that can not be recouped, if the tour does not materialize. Also you may need to borrow to finance the start-up cost for the tour. If so, the cost of borrowing money (interest) should be included in the tour costing. If this amount becomes a sizable amount, it is possible to look into whether the hotels, wholesalers, or cruise lines involved in a large tour project might be willing to accept an irrevocable letter of credit from your bank instead of cash. This will not eliminate the need to pay eventually (and the bank will charge interest on such a letter of credit, just as it would for a loan), but it may help the immediate cash flow situation. It also may be a good idea to meet with your company banker and establish a line of credit that might be necessary in certain unforeseen circumstances. (See Figure 3.3 on pages 46 and 47 for an example of a realistic budget.)

Always keep in mind that offering to handle a tour or opening a tour division constitutes a financial risk. If a tour fails to operate, the company must return all passengers' deposits to them. However, you have still paid for the brochure, advertising, promotion, salaries, and time involved. Hence, group handling is indeed a speculative business.

OFFICE LOCATION, LAYOUT, AND EQUIPMENT

If you are setting up a tour company from "scratch," don't pay for fancy street-front locales in high-rent downtown areas. Many successful small tour companies have started in someone's back room. Remember, you do not want walk-in clientele, who are usually shopping for nothing more than the least expensive airfare.

Therefore, high visibility is not desirable. However, if you are planning to obtain ARC appointments and thus issue your own air tickets in-house, you will need to review the *ARC Handbook* and its requirements for location and visibility of ARC-appointed travel companies.

Some tour companies that act as true wholesalers and never sell to the public directly, but only through retail travel agents, find that they do not need to have ARC appointments and issue air tickets, since they simply provide the land/sea arrangements. They let the retail travel agencies that sell their tours isssue the air tickets. Or, they simply buy the air tickets directly from the air carrier, or make a long-range arrangement with an existing ARC-appointed travel agency for them to issue the air tickets and split the commission in some sort of equitable manner. In this situation, the new tour company does not need to adhere to ARC requirements for location/visibility. (In some states, it would then have to register under the travel promoters law.)

Office Layout

If you are opening a group department in an existing travel agency, it may be necessary to rearrange the agency to allow group personnel their own private office. If this is not possible, they need at least a hidden corner where they can work without interruptions by walk-in clientele, and where they will not have to answer the general agency phones. People handling groups must adhere to their own strict schedule; they cannot permit an important option date to slip by because they were too busy that day selling a local sector air ticket to a walk-in client.

In addition, group business personnel will need extra file space, cabinets for storage of brochures and bulletins, work space in which to spread out materials, and wall space for visual calendar reminders. As the departure time draws near, agency clients or other personnel should not be tripping over boxes of baggage tags, flight bags, or departure materials being prepared for mailing.

When planning volume group business and setting up a true group department, you will also need to consider such expenses as a separate phone line (or number on a rotary line), a photocopy machine for heavy-duty, in-house printing of bulletins, a FAX, and a word processor. This electrical equipment may require an electrician's advice before it is decided where to locate the group work area.

Stationery and Supplies

Expanding into group business will mean special forms and supplies—such things as baggage tags, permanent-style name badges, passport wallets, itinerary covers, mailing labels, and perhaps flight bags. When just starting out with a couple of group tours or cruises a year, it is possible to get by with using such items sent to you by wholesalers or cruise lines that you are using.

However, eventually you will want to build your company image by giving out a nice packet of final documents with your company's name on them. Some travel agencies give their line of tours a special name, logo, and file for a registered trademark (e.g., Holiday Tours, a Division of LSI Travel Agency, Inc.). They have a special letterhead, matching envelopes, business cards, and office forms designed and color coordinated with the new name and logo.

Because many of these items (e.g., flight bags) are made in Asia , it can take several months to get them, so they should be ordered in advance. Also, adequate storage should be available for such supplies, as well as adequate facilities for handling, packing, and shipping to clients.

GROUP DEPARTMENT FIRST YEAR BUDGET

INCOME	Income	Expenses	Earnings
Premised on operating 8 projects the first year			
Winter Caribbean Cruise, 30 passengers at average sale of $2,000 per passenger @ 10% commission + 5% override commission	$11,250		
Fall Foliage Tour of New England, 25 passengers at average sale of $2,800 per person @ 10% commission + 2% override commission	8,400		
Additional income, promotional assistance funds from tour operator supplier	500		
Local Four-Day Tour for Senior Citizens, 82 passengers (2 bus loads) at $295 per passenger, average earnings $1,500 per bus	3,000		
European Garden Tour, 23 passengers at $3,700 per passenger @ average earnings $650 per passenger	14,950		
Summer Alaska Cruise, 24 passengers at average sale $2,900 @ 10% commission + 3% override commission	9,048		
High School Senior Civics Class Budget Tour to Washington D.C. by bus, 80 students @ $450 per student @ average earnings $60 per student	4,800		
Mini-Convention, 3-day/2-night land package only. 50 attendees @ $295 per person. Earnings $50 per person	2,500		
Two-week Music Tour to Edinburgh Festival, 32 passengers @ $2,950 per passenger @ $400 eanings per person	12,800		
Australia/New Zealand 18-day Tour, 22 passengers @ $5,200 @ average $750 earnings per person	16,500		
Subtotal	$83,748		
Estimate one failure. Loss of upfront expenditures for brochure printing and distribution, advertising and promotion	−2,500		
Total First Year Income from Group Department	$81,248		

Continued to next page . . . .

Figure 3.3 First year budget of group department.

EXPENSES	Income	Expenses	Earnings
Group Manager's Salary @ $2,200/month × 12 mo		$26,400	
Half-time Assistant (clerical and airline computer handling) @ $850/month × 12 mo		10,200	
Employee Fringe Benefits. Insurance, payroll deductions, vacation, familiarization trips, etc.		9,500	
Telephone @ $200/month × 12 mo		2,400	
Proportion of Rent/Utilities @ $300/month × 12 mo ..		3,600	
Furniture, 2 ea. desks, chairs, file cabinets, one word processor and other misc. items		3,500	
Stationery and Supplies		1,500	
Monthly Accounting Fees @ $150/month × 12 mo		1,800	
Start-up Accountant/Attorney Fees		700	
Postage		3,000	
Entertainment of potential group accounts		1,200	
Travel Expenses for group department staff.................		1,700	
Insurance, additional premium for increasing agency's coverage		500	
Printing Generic Brochure on new group department..		1,200	
Interest, assuming $10,000 start-up loan and another mid-year $10,000 loan, both at 14% interest		2,100	
Miscellaneous		1,000	
Subtotal		$70,300	
Contingency, 5%		3,515	
Total First Year Expenses from Group Department		$73,815	

EARNINGS

	Income	Expenses	Earnings
First Year Earnings from Group Department (of which a portion may be shared with the Group Manager)			$7,433

Figure 3.3 First year budget of group department. (Continued.)

Computers

While it is still feasible to operate tours manually in today's high-tech world, some type of computerization will be necessary. If your tour division will be attached to an existing travel agency, in all likelihood you will simply obtain an additional CRT for your new tour office and will utilize the airline computer reservations system (CRS) that the agency already has in place (e.g., Apollo, Sabre, System One, or Worldspan).

While airline reservations systems do not yet allow you to book group air space through the computer as you would book individual air reservations, you can still book the group air travel by telephone or letter. Once it is confirmed, you can input the block air into the airline CRS for further handling. Then, as individual passengers join the tour, you can add their names to the group flights and can ultimately issue each individual's air ticket in-house from the master air block. Any clients whose air travel deviates from the block air travel will have to be pulled out and individual passenger name records (PNRs) built for them before they can be ticketed.

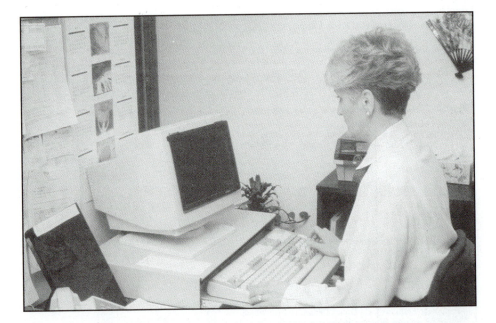

Figure 3.4 Most modern travel agencies and tour operators invest heavily in a leased computerized airline reservation system so they have access to a live system of world-wide flight schedules and current air-fares. This computer system allows them to issue air tickets by computer more quickly and efficiently. (Photo by Paul E. Meyers)

However, the airline reservations system in place in the agency does not have a facility for controlling blocks of hotel or cruise space. In addition, it does not have a facility for building individual client records with lots of custom-tailored information on each client, on their billing, on their payment records, and so forth. Remember, the airline reservations system that travel agents currently use in their offices was developed for the airlines' purpose, which was to facilitate travel agents' sales of individual air reservations—hopefully on their airline as first choice. Then these systems were augmented with the potential for sales of supplemental products such as car rentals, hotels, and so forth. In short, these airline reservations systems were never designed as a tour operator's tool.

Most tour operators find it necessary to have word processing capabilities. They build software programs designed to control hotel, cruise, or other space inventories; to track clients' charges and payments; and to control information for a number of purposes. They store master sample letters to clients and suppliers, which they can then modify for each tour. They can also store a myriad of information bulletins on various destinations, information on how to obtain a passport, information on how to pack for a specific trip, and so forth. Many operators also use desktop publishing and graphics programs to do their own tour brochures and flyers in-house quickly.

It may, therefore, be necessary for you to spend some time investigating various airline computer reservations systems, especially if one is not already in place, and if you really need one. Once again, remember that if you do not plan to issue air tickets in-house that you may not need to invest in an airline reservations system. You might simply buy your own hardware and obtain a good word-processor, spread-sheet, accounting, and desktop publishing/graphics software program. Therefore, you could operate in your own stand-alone computer hardware, which has absolutely no relationship to the airline reservations systems.

If, however, you do decide to invest in an airline computer reservations system, be sure to investigate each system and its contract thoroughly before making your decision. It's a big investment and a long-term contract, and there's a lot of "wheeling and dealing" in terms of offers, contract provisions, and so forth. If you are not thoroughly conversant with airline computer reservations systems and their contracts, it would probably be best to have your newly hired operations manager in on the decision-making process. It certainly will be necessary for your attorney to review the airline's ultimate contract offer before you sign it, since it represents such a large investment and long-term commitment on your part.

PERSONNEL

Selection of the right personnel for group handling is crucial to the success of the program. Sometimes a travel agency manager will simply assign a group to its lead agent or to the staff member perceived to have the most experience in the industry or the most free time available in their daily schedule. At other times, the travel agency manager will attempt to handle the group alone, with some operational and secretarial assistance from staff. Start-up tour companies often look to airline or travel agency personnel as potential hiring pools.

Group Operations Managers

None of these arrangements usually work successfully, because the staff person selected—even a retail travel agency manager—may not have the group operational expertise required. The primary requirement for a good group department or tour company is a strong **group operations manager**. Unless someone on the staff has had this strong group operational experience (not group sales experience), it is best to hire someone from outside the company. Table 3.1 lists some of the responsibilities of the group operations manager.

Because of the responsibility resting on this individual's shoulders, because of the previous experience required, and because of the specialized expertise needed, it is necessary to search thoroughly and to interview and screen carefully. It is best to advertise for a group operations manager openly, perhaps getting applicants from tour companies or cruise lines that operate large air/sea package programs. The usual retail travel counselor, either from the retail side of a travel agency or from the outside, is often not the best choice.

TABLE 3.1 Responsibilities of the Group Operations Manager

❏ Plan all itineraries.

❏ Negotiate with suppliers.

❏ Book all arrangements—air, hotels, ships, ground services.

❏ Meticulously control a tour project, keeping in touch with all suppliers, cutting space where necessary, finalizing all rooming lists, flight manifests, and so forth.

❏ Handle all client bookings, dealing with each client graciously by phone or in writing (or if wholesaling, dealing with each client's travel agent).

❏ Cost and price group travel projects.

❏ Prepare all written materials that the company distributes for tour clients: billings, pre-trip information bulletins, departure instructions, and final documents.

❏ Select and brief/debrief tour managers.

❏ Write promotional material to sell the tour—brochure, ads, flyers (or work closely with someone else on the staff more adept at this specialty).

It will be necessary to pay this individual a salary considerably higher than might be paid in individual retail sales. Good group people know that group business is priced on **net plus markup**. Therefore, they know that it can be marked up enough to cover a good salary. A group department's earnings are not restricted to commission sales, as in the retail side of the company. Many operations managers may also be interested in getting a percentage of the profit (not a percentage of the commissions) attributed to the group division at the end of the season. They will expect to have access to all financial figures related to their groups. In addition, they will want to have a certain amount of input into management decision making over expenses and risks related to their division, since their income may depend on these expenses and risks. This approach is also usually desirable from management's perspective, since this gives incentive to make the bottom line as profitable as possible.

Who Solicits Group Accounts?

You are now faced with deciding who will solicit the groups. Although some groups simply fall into the company's "lap," others require a planned program of attack. The usual inside travel counselors or outside salespeople may not know how to generate group sales effectively. Calling on groups requires a certain amount of assertiveness, self-confidence, elegance, business training, and group product knowledge. The inside group operations manager may be out of his or her element in making sales presentations, and the dynamic salesperson may not have enough operational knowledge to do a good job. Of course, some lucky company may find that rare combination; namely, the individual who makes a good operations manager as well as a good salesperson. For most companies, however, an alternative arrangement might be to have the operations manager accompany the salesperson on key sales calls to lend an air of credibility.

Some companies will hire special secretarial and clerical help for the group department. Some travel agencies opening group departments will ask the new group operations manager to use front-office clerical help. If this is the case, the front office personnel should be so advised by management in advance, to avoid possible resentment when the new group operations manager asks them for help.

Present staff in an existing agency should also understand that group personnel will have their own hours, their own professional lives, and their own schedules to follow. They will not be available for lunch hour fill-in or vacation backup, nor can they answer telephones when front office sales counselors are busy.

Since a new group division represents a promise of volume business to a travel agency, suppliers may suddenly start wooing the group people with luncheon invitations, familiarization trips, and site inspections. Perhaps these invitations were previously directed to others, either in the front office or the owner or manager. Jealousies and resentments could arise among those staff members suddenly left out, and this resentment should be anticipated. It should not be handled defensively and after the fact. Perhaps staff members need to be reassured by management that they will still receive their accustomed quota of perks.

OPERATING PROCEDURES

Several major decisions must be made about the way a tour company or new group division or department will be operated. These decisions determine setup arrangements.

Book Direct or Through Wholesalers?

One of these major decisions is whether to act as a primary operator and book the ground services of the tours directly (i.e., writing or faxing hotels and receptive services operators) or whether to book ground services as a total unit through a major wholesaler in the United States.

Buying from a wholesaler can save time, provide the advantage of the wholesaler's bulk buying and reputation overseas, and provide your company with the wholesaler's expertise. This can be particularly helpful when your staff is unfamiliar with the countries on the itinerary. Also, think defensively. In case of a lawsuit against your company, it means that one more company in the United States would share the defense. Buying through a wholesaler cuts down on the work that must be done in your office; that is, the amount of typing, correspondence, and mailing. So, if most of your trips are booked through wholesalers, fewer group personnel will have to be hired and the group staff will be less burdened with the operational work load, which means they can handle a higher client load.

However, working through a wholesaler has several disadvantages. Among these disadvantages are loss of identity and recognition of your company name; a total dependence on one source; and a lack of that feeling of being in control. This confidence stems from knowing that hotel reservations are confirmed because you hold a letter of confirmation on the hotel's letterhead signed by the hotel manager. Otherwise, you have to take the word of a third party. Also, with more and more bankruptcies, it is wise to pick wholesalers with extra caution. You should probably stick with the tried and true—those with good reputations and financing. Feel free to ask airlines about a wholesaler or to check with hotels about whether a wholesaler pays its bills.

In the long run, it is not only possible, but also probable that you will use a mix of booking methods. Perhaps a wholesaler will be used on some tours, particularly tours to areas with which you are unfamiliar. Other tours, particularly to areas well known to you and your staff, will be booked direct.

Wholesaling to Retail Agents

Still another decision needs to be reached as to whether your tour programs will be wholesaled once they are put together. Many retail travel agencies that have packaged a tour have discovered they own inadequate marketing power, and they have gone to other travel agencies to solicit their cooperation in selling it. Unfortunately, a commission for that other selling agent had not been costed in! It is important to anticipate every possibile cost from the outset. Think it through. Are you a retail group operator selling directly to the public (even if through a club or organization), or are you a wholesaler selling through other agents?

Sometimes semantics get in the way. Many large group operators refer to themselves as wholesalers. To them, this means that they are large, bulk group operators dealing in volume or that they have an "I can get if for you wholesale" mentality. In the true sense of the word, however, wholesaling implies selling through a retailer, not selling direct to the public.

If a tour company is setting up as a true wholesaler, this affects all of its later actions. Tour brochures will be prepared for retail agents' use as a sales tool with an appropriate empty space on the back, where retail agents can put their agency name, address, phone, and FAX numbers. Advertisements will be designed for travel industry publications, with the sales pitch directed to agents—not to the public. Even the public advertisements will direct readers to their local travel agent, rather than to the wholesaler. Furthermore, a company that is truly wholesaling will not be competing with retail agents; instead, it will be backing them, helping them, and cooperating with them. It will show films or provide door prizes at promotional evenings for their clients, share promotional expenses for their mailings, and promise not to use their clients' names and addresses for future trips, thus circumventing the travel agency.

One way or another, a company must decide if it is ultimately going to be a wholesaler or a retailer. Or, it may decide to become a wholesaler, but offer the trip through its own retail outlet as it does to other agencies. This means offering it at the same retail price and at the same commission.

❑ SUMMARY

Looking at the group travel field from the perspective of an entrepreneur is exciting; it offers one of the highest profit possibilities in the travel industry. However, it also carries a number of risks. For this reason, someone considering this arena should give it careful thought.

There are a lot of considerations in a start-up group division or company; namely, legalities, insurance, financing, accounting, locale, office setup, computerization, and personnel. Also, decisions must be made about whether you will operate as a wholesaler or a retailer, about whether you will become a principal by booking most tours on a direct basis overseas or will retain agent status, thus selling clients into the services of an existing tour operator.

The decisions are many. The delay in seeing profit may deter many. But for the individual who understands the risks, who has the cash flow, who has the enthusiasm, and who has the sense of excitement that this specialty field requires and generates, the group travel business is like no other.

❑ *REVIEW QUESTIONS*

1. Why does a group tour company or division usually not show a profit quickly—at least for the first year?

2. If there is so much risk involved in the group business, why do so many people want to try it?

3. What is the Travel Promoters' Law in the state of California and who administers it?

4. What is the travel industry's equivalent of malpractice insurance?

5. How can an escrow account protect you against a supplier's non-performance or default?

6. What kind of office equipment does a group office need? Make up a check-list.

7. Who is the key person you would have to hire to operate a group travel department?

8. As the owner of a tour company or travel agency opening a group department, how would you motivate your key employee to produce a profitable department for you?

❑ ACTIVITIES

1. Take a look at a variety of responsibility clauses in different tour brochures (sometimes called "consumer disclosure notices"). Then write one you would like for your company, if you were setting up a company. If you have an attorney (friend), have your friend look at your proposal.

2. Find out if your state has something similar to the California "Travel Promoters' Law."

3. Meet with a banking officer to obtain more information on trust accounts and escrow accounts.

4. Contact a source for your business insurance. Ascertain what protection its Errors and Omissions coverage would give you and approximate premium cost per year.

Endnotes

1. Jeffrey R. Miller, *Legal Aspects of Travel Agency Operation* (Albany, N.Y.: Delmar Publishers Inc., 1987, p. 58.)
2. Personal interview with Ralph Davis, president of Travel Insurance Services in Walnut Creek, CA.

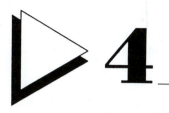

LOCATING AND SELLING GROUP BUSINESS

LEARNING OBJECTIVES

After reading this chapter, you should:

- ❏ Understand types of group travel
- ❏ Understand some criteria by which to judge whether or not a group travel project is viable for you to undertake
- ❏ Understand where to look for group business
- ❏ Understand how to present your group travel product using sales hints presented herein

KEY CONCEPTS AND TERMS

Criteria for Selecting a Group
Designing Tours for Clientele and Community
Designing a Tour for a Specific Group
Group Travel for Business
Group Travel for Pleasure
Group Travel with a Purpose
Large Operator's Approach
Motivations for Organizations to Sponsor Group Travel

The field of group travel is two-sided; namely, it's operations and sales. If sales and marketing people didn't do their job, the operations people would have no tours to operate. Conversely, if the operations people did not do a good job of operating the tours to provide the product that the sales people have promised, then the company would be hard-pressed to remain in business.

It is, therefore, important that each faction understand and respect the role that the other plays. In fact, in many cases, it may be necessary for one individual to somehow miraculously juggle both roles of operations and sales. This is true particularly in small start-up tour companies or departments.

In this chapter, therefore, we will take a look at the sales aspect.

DESIGNING TOURS FOR CLIENTELE AND COMMUNITY

Many newcomers to the group travel field ask, "Which do you do—plan the trip and then try to sell it to an organization? Or get an organization interested in working with you first and then custom-design a trip to its needs?" The answer is "Both—depending on the circumstances."

Every travel company should have a mailing list. A mailing list might consist solely of clients who have traveled with the company in the past, or it might consist of clients and prospective clients. Prospective clients are people who have requested literature or who have requested that their names be added to the list. Large companies that have been in business many years may have a list that numbers into the thousands. With such a list, you can use the first of several methods for designing tours for clientele and community. You can put together a program of tours for the year. This program may include a few of your own tours, a few cruises on which you block group space, and several short weekend trips to appeal to younger and newer travelers. (You should always try to keep a mailing list fresh by adding newcomers each year.)

The company then presents these trips as its annual program to this list of past and potential travelers. It also advertises the trips to the local community. These trips are not customized and developed for a special-interest group or professional organization or church; they are open to the public. They are preplanned, prebooked, and then offered for sale. Under this arrangement, the company first decides what products it believes its clientele will want, and then takes the risk in expending time, energy, and promotional monies to develop these products. Organizing the annual program might go something like this:

1. Create the tour concept.
2. Plan the itinerary (working within a projected price to fit the anticipated audience).
3. Book all arrangements—air, hotel, sightseeing, and so forth.
4. Cost and price the tour.
5. Publish the brochure.
6. Market the tour to the company's own mailing list, run advertisements in local publications, and so forth.
7. Handle clients from the time they first inquire about the trip to the time they depart on tour.
8. Deal with suppliers on periodic review dates and with finalization.

Figure 4.1 An enterprising agent might create tours of several counties within a state for local groups. A county tour in Indiana could feature events like the Tipton County Pork Festival. (Courtesy of the Indiana Department of Commerce Tourism Development Division and the Tipton County Pork Festival, Tipton, IN.)

9. Brief the tour manager.
10. Manage the tour enroute.
11. Handle the post-tour wrap-up.

DESIGNING A TOUR FOR A SPECIFIC GROUP

The best approach for **designing a tour for a specific group** requires contacting organizations—clubs, schools, businesses, and so forth—to encourage them to sponsor a group travel program through your company. In this case you usually custom-design the itinerary to fit the needs of the particular group. On the first sales call you often do not make a presentation for any specific trip, but simply make the contact, sell yourself and your company, and then follow up with a specific itinerary. This second method of custom-designing tours might involve the following procedure:

1. Locate the organization to which you want to sell the idea; research the organization and its previous travel history, if any.
2. Obtain the name of the key decision maker on tour matters and try to get an appointment.
3. Visit the organization and discuss trip generalities.
4. Get back to the organization, presenting several ideas with itinerary plans and rough cost estimates.
5. Ask the organization to commit to a specific itinerary and date.
6. Book all arrangements—air, hotels, sightseeing, and so forth.
7. Cost and price the tour, advising the organization of the final price.
8. Publish the brochure.
9. Market the tour to the organization's members.
10. Handle clients from the time they first inquire about the tour to the time they depart on tour.
11. Deal with suppliers on periodic review dates and with finalization.
12. Brief the tour manager.
13. Manage the tour enroute.
14. Handle the post-tour wrap-up.
15. Continue rapport with the organization's officers toward future tours.

When visiting an organization for the first time, it is helpful to have several itinerary suggestions and approximate cost figures so that you can sound knowledgeable about some areas—even if these are not the areas on which the group decides.

A LARGE OPERATOR'S APPROACH

A large operator's approach is a third method often used by some extremely large tour companies and by some cruise lines. Under this arrangement, a seasonal series of tours (e.g., a spring series of back-to-back, one-week Rhine River tours) is set up, the space is booked, and the brochure is produced.

Then the company sales representatives call on clubs, university alumni associations, professional groups, and so forth on a nationwide basis. The sales representative suggests that the group block space on a specific departure date and offers to market the tour to group members via direct mail at the company's expense. Such an approach is usually beyond the scope and financial capabilities of the average retail travel agency or small tour operator. This approach might be as follows:

1. Create the tour concept.
2. Plan the itinerary.
3. Book all arrangements—air, hotels, sightseeing, and so forth.
4. Cost and price the tour.
5. Publish a standard brochure.
6. Take the product on the road, locating organizations that wish to block departure dates and selling their group into the existing product.
7. Overprint the standard brochure in quantity, custom-tailored to show the name of the organization and the date that they have selected as their group departure date.
8. Market the tour (usually by direct mail) to the membership of the client organization.
9. Handle the clients from the time they first inquire about the trip to the time they depart on tour.
10. Deal with suppliers on periodic review dates and with finalization.
11. Brief the tour manager.
12. Manage the tour enroute.
13. Handle the post-tour wrap-up.
14. Continue rapport with the organization, with a goal of possible future tours.

Under all three methods, reservations are booked with all suppliers *before* the product is released for sale to the customer. You should never publish a sales piece, promote the tour, collect passengers' deposits (to ascertain if there is enough interest), and then try to book the tour space. This is a dangerous practice. More often than not, the flights and other reservations listed in the sales piece are not available. Then substitutions must be made, the dates changed, or the resulting prices set higher than those originally envisioned. Reputable tour companies avoid this type of operation.

DO YOU REALLY WANT THIS GROUP?

I once became involved in working with a Girl Scout troop that over a three-year period carefully and meticulously planned a summer trip to Europe by raising the funds from bake sales. Each girl eventually managed to accumulate $650 to make the trip. This is a ridiculously low price by travel industry standards, but an astronomical figure for a 15-year-old high school student.

No money was going to be made on the project by the travel agency involved, since the trip consisted of a charter flight (which in those day paid only five percent commission), a stay at a Girl Scout lodge (i.e., noncommissionable), and a do-it-yourself approach to sightseeing, with bread-and-cheese picnics along the side of the road. However, there was no way to avoid becoming involved; the Scout leader was a long-time family friend.

Figure 4.2 Intrav is a large tour operator that designs tours and sells them outside the travel agent community to organizations like the University of Rochester Alumni Association and Texas Medical Association. The company's generic brochure is overprinted with the group name and the trip is promoted via direct mail to each member. (Courtesy of Intrav, Inc. St. Louis, MO.)

Sooner or later, many of us become involved in such projects and undertake them willingly because of a genuine desire to help, because a friend or relative ensnares us, or because we cannot bear the misinformation or bad treatment that the clients are receiving elsewhere. Before you know it, you are involved.

However, good business dictates that companies cannot afford many of these goodwill projects. You should use some common sense **criteria for selecting a group**. Groups must be examined dispassionately before making a decision to become involved. Groups come in all sizes, shapes and formats. Since some are more desirable than others, before determining whether you should attempt a specific group project, you might be wise to ask the following questions.

❏ What is the profit potential? Does it warrant the involvement, time, energy, and financial risk?

❏ Is there the probability of an ongoing annual tour or is this just a one-time deal?

❑ Is there any competition? For example, is this a splinter group of an existing large-scale official tour program?

❑ Is there a certain prestige affiliated with the program? Will it lead to future tours for other similar organizations?

❑ Is there enough lead time—usually at least a year?

❑ Does the trip fit into the company's schedule? Does it fill an otherwise low period in sales, or a period when staff is not busy?

❑ Does the clientele for whom this trip is intended have the financial ability to afford it, or are they being unrealistic?

❑ Will this group lead to other similar groups, where you can use the same itinerary and the experience gained on this first trip?

❑ Will the project require extending credit, or will it be strictly pay-as-you-go business?

❑ Is there a large enough base of clientele (usually a good mailing list) to warrant any risk?

❑ Does the proposed trip and its destination meet the interest of the majority of the group membership, or just that of the group president or decision maker?

A *no* answer to any of the above questions does not necessarily mean that the project should be turned down. However, in the complete analysis, it is best to meet as many of these criteria as possible.

WHERE TO FIND GROUP BUSINESS

Some groups simply arrive a *fait accompli*. These might be a university professor convinced that he or she has a group following, a travel agency's commercial account that the agent knows is holding an overseas meeting, or an employee's daughter's senior class civics trip to the nation's capitol. But mostly, group business is located by diligent research and by going out and asking for the business.

Close to Home

Many groups are located by the company staff or by personal contact (i.e., friends, organizations to which employees belong, special interests of employees, and so forth). If company employees are members of the local Rotary Club, the golf club, or the Toastmasters Association, then, of course, they should be alert to group tour possibilities within these organizations. It is possible that your company staff members are active in a variety of community organizations. Enrolling staff members in organizations and paying their dues and monthly meeting fees may initially cost money, but ultimately the investment may pay off. (Note: this assumes that belonging to an organization is of interest to employees for reasons other than just to lure potential group business.)

IDEAS FOR GROUP BUSINESS

Agricultural and agri-business
  groups
Bridge-playing groups
Churches (for religious
  pilgrimage tours)
Conventions
Country clubs
Dive groups
Golf groups
High schools
Incentive groups
Jazz fans clubs
Literary groups
Museum associations
Music devotee organizations
Opera guilds

Professional organizations
  (e.g., teachers, nurses,
  and so forth)
Radio disk jockey listeners
  (Pied Piper)
Sailing clubs
Sales meetings
Scientific meetings
Senior citizens
Service clubs (Rotary,
  Kiwanis, and so forth)
Ski clubs
Stockholder meetings
Tennis clubs
Trade missions
Universities/colleges

Figure 4.3 Suggested sources for group business.

Staff members' interests in a specific sport or the arts offer possibilities for business. A staff member who loves classical music and has a knowledge of overseas music festivals may make a better recruiter for cultural tours than the staff member whose idea of a cultural activity revolves around the World Series. Also, your company's clients may belong to organizations that are potential group travel accounts. Clients often prove to be excellent leads into group business.

In the Larger Community

In addition to looking to your company's contacts, consider the potential from the community, the state, and even the nation. It might be a good idea to spend time at the library or county seat researching various organizations for potential group business.

One excellent source for corporate group travel accounts is Standard & Poor's *Register of Corporation Directors and Executives.* Not only does it list major firms, but it also lists the names of the companies' officers. This list allows the counselor to address a first letter or phone call to an individual, instead of to the anonymous "Dear Sir."

County offices may be helpful, particularly if they have a recreation department used by various community groups, such as YMCAs and YWCAs. Also, country clubs, police officers' associations, educational foundations, life insurance underwriters, Christmas tree growers, medical associations, and athletic organizations can be found here. Some of these may prove to be viable contacts; others may prove to be useless. Yellow Page listings under churches, schools, universities, fraternal organizations, and professional organizations can also be useful.

The diligent sales professional will not stop with the telephone book of one city or community, but will also try the state capital's telephone book. Many organizations maintain lobbyists in the capital; listings in that city's directory may be more complete.

It may be helpful to contact potential groups by categories, rather than by going out and randomly calling on individual groups. For example, if the company has just completed a successful tour for a university, it might be appropriate to use that product as a sample and call on other universities in the immediate area or out of state. The university for which you have just developed a tour may be prepared to give you the name of the contact person at other academic institutions.

SALES CALL HINTS

When making sales calls, it is important to present yourself to the client organization as a group specialist by indicating that your company is not looking for independent business but group business. Many, if not most, of these organizations will have a travel agent and will say so. The reply to this should be along the lines of "But, of course, you do. I would assume that any organization with the stature of yours would have an agency, and I assume that they are doing a good job for you. But we, as group specialists, can do much more than most travel agencies can." With this approach, I once sold a tour to an organization that owned its own travel agency! The agency was a commercial agency that was not geared to group tours or to financial risk-taking to secure volume bookings through a direct-mail promotion.

It is also a good idea to learn to think and to talk about complete packages; that is, sell a total idea, not just component parts. Travel counselors are accustomed to selling individual air reservations and hotel bookings, and they are used to quoting the airfare and the hotel per-night cost. In short, they are used to quoting breakdown charges. In selling groups, it is best to stop thinking about components and to start thinking about the total package. For example, you might explain cost to a client by saying, "I estimate that we could package a 10-day trip at slightly under $1,500, depending of course, on which hotel we are able to secure for you, time of year you select, and several other factors. There are some attractive airfares in this market, and we'd pick the one most advantageous to your organization—once I know more about your specific needs. Now, tell me such and such..." deflecting the conversation back to the direction desired.

The motivation of a group must also be considered in designing the sales approach. The motivations behind travel are varied and complex. The skilled salesperson will quickly perceive which motivations are on target in a particular sales call situation and point them out to the potential buyer as a part of the sales presentation.

WHY ORGANIZATIONS SPONSOR GROUP TOURS

If individuals have certain motivations for participating in group tours, then so do organizations. Even if you or your company do all the work on the group travel program for an organization, the officers or individuals within the organization are still investing time, energy, risk, and other factors. They could easily say that they do not want to be involved in group travel projects. Some do say that. Yet, many more do not. Many are eager to be involved in all aspects of group travel programs for their organizations. What are the **motivations for organizations to sponsor group travel**?

Probably one of the primary motivators is a *personal desire to travel*. Another reason might be *glamour*; most people outside of the travel industry still see it as a glamourous industry. It is *fun* for them to be involved. Travel is a happy subject. Deciding about travel certainly is more exciting than the day-to-day decisions many executives face concerning budget, sales quotas, and personnel problems.

Many people see a travel program as being *prestigious*. This might be true of a university that develops an overseas study program or of a professional organization that participates in a foreign meeting. It may also be perceived as *helpful*. It makes possible a group trip for employees or members at a lesser cost through group buying. It can also be a way for an organization to *raise funds*. A museum might assess (or build into the tour cost) a donation fee to each tour participant. A group tour can offer the sponsoring organization exposure or *publicity*, thus reaping recognition and perhaps eventually additional sales or business for that organization. In this way, a tour can be a form of institutional advertising.

Many businesses see travel as an excellent *motivational tool*. It is an incentive for employees to produce or sell. Many salespersons, for example, will exert themselves to make that last sale necessary to qualify for a place on the company's annual incentive trip. Such a trip cannot be measured in monetary terms. It is measured more in terms of personal satisfaction or recognition from peers and employer.

TYPES OF GROUPS

Loosely categorized, group travel probably falls into one of three major categories:

1. Group travel for pleasure (vacation).
2. Group travel for business.
3. Group travel with a purpose (other than business, often called special-interest travel).

Group Travel for Pleasure

Group travel for pleasure covers basic vacation travel in a group. Although pleasure travel can be associated with a business trip or convention, or can be associated with a pre- or post-convention pleasure trip, it is conceived as strictly for enjoyment. It can be open to the public or not, as in a private tour or cruise limited to members of a specific club, church, or organization.

Group Travel for Business

Group travel for business encompasses a variety of different kinds of travel projects. Some of these projects are more profitable than others, some are feasible for the beginner, and others are only for the experienced group specialist. In this category you find incentives, conventions, meetings (e.g., directors, stockholders, and so forth), seminars, trade missions, scientific meetings, and site inspection tours.

Group Travel with a Purpose

Group travel with a purpose might be considered an offshoot of either of the former categories, but it is really a category unto itself. It is not just transportation to get somewhere for a business purpose, nor is it travel for travel's sake or for pleasure. Rather, group travel with a purpose revolves around a specific purpose or interest. This could be sports (e.g., ski tours, diving expeditions, trekking in the Himalayas, a golf package or tennis clinic). The trip could be for education—a tour for academic credit or one offering continuing education units (CEUs), thus granting teachers a salary increase. It might be for philosophic or religious fulfillment. For instance, it could be a pilgrimage to the Holy Land or the search for a guru in India. It could be a tour with a certain lifestyle, such as living with the local villagers rather than staying in hotels. It would cover what is loosely called "special-interest tours."

Figure 4.4   This group pleasure tour has a theme of exploring Nepal and staying in the inns. (Courtesy of Mountain Travel Sobek, The Adventure Company.   Painting by John Finger.)

CHOOSING THE RIGHT GROUP BUSINESS

After deciding to go into group travel, one of the first things that you need to consider is the type of group or groups in which to specialize. With which type do you feel most capable and comfortable?

Large Versus Small Groups

A large convention may be a possibility, but can your company handle convention business? Convention and meeting business requires individual air itineraries and individual billings, as opposed to incentive and corporate business for which you bill one central source. If it is an offshore meeting (e.g., one held in Hawaii, or the Bahamas), there may be enough profit in the long haul airfare, pre- and post-convention tours, and a markup on the basic convention package to make the venture worth while. On the other hand, if the convention is closer to home, if delegates can drive or book their own air trip locally, and if the basic package is little more than a couple of nights' hotel accommodations and a registration fee, is it worthwhile to become involved?

Large conventions that involve the use of many hotels and many block flights require efficient computer handling with inventory control capacity to keep track of all those hotel beds and airplane seats. Often a special computer program must be written especially for the project. Upfront money is often required, and many large conventions are booked up to eight years in advance. Therefore, convention business is not appropriate if your company or group department are expected to show a profit within a year or two. Nor is it appropriate if cash flow is limited, if trained backup staff is lacking, and if computer capacity and toll-free telephone lines to handle client calls from all over the nation are absent.

However, smaller meetings of 40 to 50 people, although not particularly lucrative (unless overseas, and involving long haul air and a ground package), can be a starting point for anyone wishing to become involved with group business travel.

Pleasure-vacation travel—whether for a country club, church, museum, or garden club—is the easiest type of group business for the beginner in the group travel field. These tours are often planned for small, manageable groups (one busload of 40 passengers or less) and such tours are often centered around one key individual—the "Pied Piper." The Pied Piper could be the pastor who takes his congregation to the Holy Land, the museum curator, the golf pro, or the club president. Sometimes this person actively recruits a group; other times he or she may simply be a celebrity who is a "name draw" for the tour, but who does not do much active sales recruiting. Groups of this manageable size and nature give you and your company the experience necessary to go on to other more sophisticated projects.

In addition to gaining experience, you can sometimes count on a substantial profit from group pleasure travel. A group of 40 people on a comprehensive three-week tour overseas can generate the same income as a group three or four times that size attending a local convention. Profit must never be judged solely on numbers of passengers, nor on commission percentages. It should be measured in terms of bottom line earnings per total project.

❑ SUMMARY

This chapter has provided an overview of how you might locate and sell group travel opportunities, both in a local community and farther afield. Since most group business is secured by actively recruiting it, understanding an organization's motivations for sponsoring group trips and knowing how to find and approach these organizations are vital. It is also important to be able to evaluate an organization in order to determine if its group business is viable and if you and your company wish to become involved. It should never be assumed that all group business is good group business.

❑ REVIEW QUESTIONS

1. **Why might handling a local meeting not prove a particularly lucrative endeavor for you?**

2. **Why is it important for a company to add "new blood" to its mailing list continually?**

3. Name several factors you would ask yourself about a group travel project before determining if it's a viable endeavor with which you want to become involved.

4. Where might you start looking for group business in the yellow pages of the telephone directory?

5. Name at least three motivations that organizations may have for sponsoring a group travel program.

☐ *ACTIVITIES*

1. Make a list of names, addresses, and telephone numbers of 10 organizations or businesses in your community that you would approach if looking for group business. State what kind of trip you think might appeal to them and why.

2. Plan a "sales pitch" that you might make on the telephone to a secretary of a busy executive in a company or organization. Convince the secretary to set up an appointment for you with her employer.

3. Listen to the radio for a disk jockey "pitch" to the public to accompany him/ her on a trip. Jot down the pertinent facts of the offer.

4. Develop a role-play arrangement with a colleague or classmate, with one of you presenting a group travel idea, and with the other being the decision maker at the client organization.

▷ 5

RESEARCHING AND DESIGNING THE TOUR

LEARNING OBJECTIVES

After reading this chapter, you should:

❑ Understand the differences between working as a retail travel counselor and a tour designer
❑ Know the necessary lead time to ensure a successful tour project
❑ Know where to turn for research aids
❑ Know how to plan an itinerary around airfares and airline regulations
❑ Be aware of some important considerations in charting an itinerary

KEY CONCEPTS AND TERMS

Balance
Blackout Periods
Commissionable
Conditions Sheet
Foreign Independent Tour (F.I.T.)
Government Tourist Office
Incentive Tour
Itinerary Planning
Markup
Online
Pacing
Tour Designer

No part of the tour process is as exciting as the designing phase. This phase allows the planner the freedom to create imaginative travel programs. Sometimes these programs have great appeal, yet they are not available in the marketplace.

THE TOUR DESIGNER

The professional who has been working as a travel counselor before going into group tour planning has experience in booking clients on an existing travel package, such as a tour or cruise, and then individualizing it with pre-trip and post-trip independent arrangements. Such an individual probably has not been heavily involved in true itinerary design, unless he or she is one of those rare people left in the travel industry who still knows how to create a complete, independent, custom-designed trip from scratch; namely, a **foreign independent tour** (FIT).

In some ways, working as a travel counselor is like selling dresses in a department store. Salespeople in a dress department might help a customer select dresses from the rack that fit the customer in size, style, and personality. Creative salespeople might even go as far as to help their customers choose accessories that are right and that promote a total effect or image. Nevertheless, no matter how much creativity and energy salespeople bring to the job, they are limited by the merchandise in the store; that is, they are restricted in their sales efforts by the available stock.

Similarly, today's average travel counselor (who is not usually a travel designer) is selling the travel industry's version of available stock (i.e., pre-designed tours, cruises, packages, and similar products) rather than planning elaborate, individually designed itineraries, which can be very costly and time consuming.

Designing, however, as opposed to creative selling, expands the realm of possibility. Imagine the difference between a salesperson at the local department store and Christian Dior, Yves St. Laurent, or Pierre Cardin. These people are designers all, whether it's one custom-designed dress for a special client and a special occasion or an entire new fall line.

This difference between the person who sells dresses and the person who designs them is similar to the difference between the usual retail travel counselor and a **tour designer**. The dress designer brings to the drawing table a combination of business know-how, practical craftsmanship, understanding of clientele, and an inspiration from many sources. Similarly, the true tour designer brings to the task a rich background of knowledge, including travel industry skills, good business sense, marketing, and costing. Just as important, this person usually has a strong cultural base involving an eclectic background of history, anthropology, and so forth. Genuine tour designers are true Renaissance persons—artists and creators. They are much more than someone who merely throws an itinerary together by combining flights, hotel over-nights, transfers, and standard city sightseeing tours.

In the tour designer's hands, itineraries become potential travel experiences with interesting themes that answer the psychological needs of a certain type of client. The first-time traveler on a seven-day Caribbean cruise does not have the same expectations as the experienced traveler visiting Mongolia. Similarly, the motivations behind an **incentive tour** for insurance salespeople (who have earned a free trip because of their insurance sales production) would dictate an entirely different type of itinerary than those behind an educational tour for a group of teachers, although both trips might be to exactly the same destination. By understanding the clientele for whom the tour is designed, the tour designer is able to combine the proper elements into a rich, vibrant, and exciting trip, with the whole greater than the sum of its parts.

The competent designer also understands that features included in the itinerary do not have to originate within the travel industry and be commissionable. A retail travel counselor handling individual clients usually sells only **commissionable** travel products that provide a fee, or commission, for arranging travel, to ensure an income. But the tour designer knows that custom-designed group tours are priced on net and then marked up. Therefore, it does not matter if a particular tour feature is commissionable. The profit comes from **markup**, or a percentage added to the net cost to form the selling price, not commission. Hence, the designer is free to include in the itinerary fashion shows, cooking demonstrations, wine-tasting events, lectures, tours of private industries, or visits to private homes. In short, he or she is able to include experiences often unavailable to the average traveler, experiences which greatly enhance any itinerary.

A tour designer must be knowledgeable about sources. He or she must know who to contact for enroute enrichment lectures on a given subject, know which receptive services operator overseas specializes in a certain type of program, or know who moves volume groups well, as opposed to who is best at handling small, deluxe, intimate groups.

RESEARCH AIDS

Many who work year after year in tour planning and design become shortsighted and rely totally on travel industry source materials. It is, of course, necessary to be practical and to know the hotels, air schedules, and sightseeing attractions.

However, good tour planning is more than just referring to the airline computer, the *Hotel and Travel Index*, or other dependable travel industry sources. It is important to remember that many other resources exist, especially outside the travel industry. Here are a few ideas about where to find additional information:

1. Your own knowledge—from personal travel, familiarization trips, seminars, and so forth.
2. Operations Manuals/Tariffs—of receptive services operators for the countries and cities the tour will visit.
3. Brochures from other companies—read what others are doing. If the majority of tour companies are including a certain tour feature in their itineraries, it may be because it has merit.
4. Airlines—specifically those serving the countries on the itinerary.
5. An encyclopedia—unfortunately, few travel companies have one in their office. Background information from this source can be invaluable in writing interesting brochure copy.

MEMPHIS TOUR

Egypt with
Cairo, Aswan, and Luxor.

7 Days
Land only

from **$640**

BRENDAN'S TRAVEL VALUE INCLUDES

- Round-trip airport transfers
- Guided sightseeing as per itinerary
- Accommodation based on twin-bedded rooms with private bath
- Meals as indicated in the itinerary
- Complete sightseeing program as indicated in the itinerary including:
  - Giza Pyramids and Sphinx
  - Deluxe, air-conditioned overnight sleeper train to Aswan
  - Sailing on the Nile
  - Flights Aswan-Luxor-Cairo
  - Nile crossing by ferry to visit Valley of the Kings
  - Two Sound and Light Shows
- All local taxes

■ Brendan Tours flight bag and portfolio of travel documents

ITINERARY

Day 1, Sun. CAIRO, EGYPT. Upon arrival at Cairo International Airport, you will be met and assisted through formalities and transferred to your hotel.

Day 2, Mon. CAIRO. Full day visit to Giza Pyramids, the Sphinx, Cheops Solar Boat, the Valley Temple, Memphis and Sakkara Necropolis. This evening attend the Sound and Light Show. (CB,L,D)

Day 3, Tue. CAIRO-ASWAN. A full day of sightseeing in this modern city of 10 million people including the Cairo Museum, the opulent Manial Royal Palace, Cairo walls and gates — Bab Al Futuh and Bab An Nasr — Saladin's Citadel, the Alabaster and Sultan Hassan Mosques. This evening you will depart by the deluxe overnight sleeper train for Aswan. (CB,L,D)

Day 4, Wed. ASWAN. Breakfast on board your train. You will arrive in Aswan about 10:00 a.m. where you will visit Aswan Dams and Philae Temple. Afternoon sailing on the Nile to visit the Agha Khan Mausoleum. Tonight the Philae Sound and Light Show. (CB,L,D)

Day 5, Thu. ASWAN-LUXOR. Your morning will be at leisure. This afternoon a short flight to Luxor where you will visit Karnak and Luxor Temples. (CB,L,D)

Day 6, Fri. LUXOR-CAIRO. This morning you will cross the Nile by ferry to Thebes Necropolis to visit the Valley of the Kings, Valley of the Queens, Temple of Queen Hatshepsut and the Colossi of Memnon. You will also visit the Ancient Egyptian workers village at Deir el Mehinah before flying to Cairo and transferring to your hotel. (CB,L,D)

Day 7, Sat. DEPART CAIRO. After breakfast you will be transferred to the airport for your return flight. (CB)

Egypt by itself provides a fascinating vacation. Or Egypt can be taken in combination with our one week Kenya or one week Tanzania to provide a vacation of wonderful contrast.

HOTELS

Accommodation in twin-bedded rooms with private bath or shower at the following hotels or similar.

	Deluxe	First Class
CAIRO	Ramses Hilton, Sheraton, Inter-continental, Meridien, Movenpick	Nabila, Sheppards
ASWAN	Oberoi, Cataract	Kakabsha, Cataract
LUXOR	New Winter, Etap, Hilton, Isis, Sheraton	Isis

DEPARTURES & PRICES

IT1MS1BT22

Tour MEM
Departs every Sunday from September 03, 1991

Per Person Land Only	First Class	Deluxe
Twin	$640	$875
Single	745	980
Triple	590	815

Itinerary and prices are subject to change.

For any change in the itinerary, there will be a $50 per person service charge.

8

Figure 5.1 The designer of this seven-day Egypt tour properly balances time in Cairo with time in Upper Egypt (Aswan, Luxor, Karnak, Thebes). The tour also includes travel by train, boat and air for variety and pacing. (Courtesy of Brendan Tours.)

6. **Government tourist offices**—government-sponsored tourist offices for the countries on the itinerary or the consulate, if there is no government tourist office.
7. Travel Guide Books—you'll find a plethora of these at your local bookstore (e.g., Birnbaum, the Blue Guides, Fielding, Fodor, Frommer, the Insight series, Michelin). Be careful, however, for they can be out of date as fast as they're published. And they are written for the independent traveler, so many hints are not suitable for groups.
8. United States government—for example, the United States Department of State publishes a series of pamphlets entitled "Background Notes" on each country. These inexpensive pamphlets may be purchased from the Superintendent of Documents, United States Government Printing Office, Washington, D.C. 20402.
9. Organizations—such as the Organization of American States, the United Nations, Pan American Union, World Health Organization, Pacific Asia Travel Association (PATA), and others.
10. A world almanac—a vast store of knowledge on different countries, such as size, population, ethnic makeup, economy, education, agriculture, and arts.
11. The library—learn to use the *Periodical Index* to look for articles in magazines such as *National Geographic, Travel and Leisure, Gourmet, Condé Nast Traveler*, and others.
12. Bookstores—browse through sections under travel, history, geography, and political science. Some bookstores also classify by area: Latin America, Eastern Europe, the Middle East, and so forth.
13. Local Ethnic Resources—provide suggestions that travel industry resources don't know.
14. Chambers of Commerce—or local visitor's centers, which may have more details on local areas than the various National Tourist Offices.
15. An academic course—at a local college. Cultural background, history, or geography courses can be particularly helpful. Although offering long range rather than immediate help, academic courses can be useful to the tour designer who has an eye to the future.

Of course, few travel agents or tour operators have the time or budget to research fully all of these sources for just one tour. However, the creative tour designer can begin to assemble an office source library and learn from one year to the next, thus building on information gleaned previously.

LEAD TIME

Because a tour designer invests time, energy, and often personal promotional monies in a tour, it is important to have a realistic time frame in which to organize a successful tour. A minimum of one year's lead time is usually required for most group tours. A year's lead time allows three months to research, plan, negotiate,

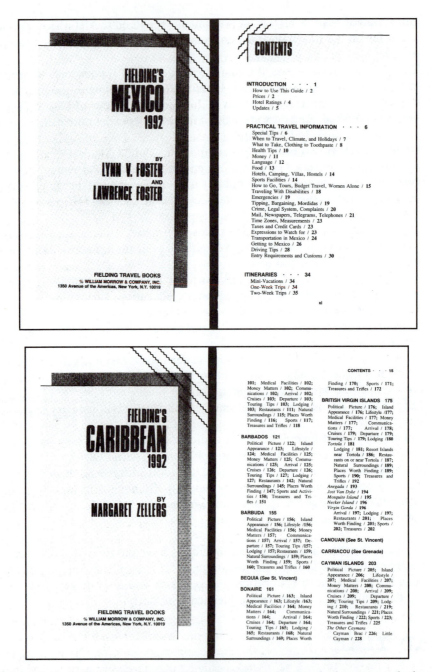

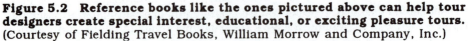

Figure 5.2 **Reference books like the ones pictured above can help tour designers create special interest, educational, or exciting pleasure tours.** (Courtesy of Fielding Travel Books, William Morrow and Company, Inc.)

book, and price the tour, as well as to produce the tour brochure and promotional materials. It allows the next six months for a promotional and sales campaign, and then leaves the final 90 days for billing, dispatch, and wrap-up. However, conventions or tours that revolve around a major event, such as the Rose Bowl or the Olympics, may require as much as a five-year lead time. Short weekend trips—such as those that might be marketed to a club, church, or a similar pre-formed target group—can be organized in less than one year.

Nevertheless, always keep in mind the one-year lead time as a rule of thumb. This rule should help a tour planner reject those tours that have little or no chance for success because of insufficient time to plan, book, promote, and finalize. It should also help keep in perspective the pressures generated by deadlines, financial need, or anxious agency owners who tend to demand a shorter time frame.

Unfortunately, many new agencies and outside salespeople hired to generate group business are placed under pressure to produce tours and generate income within six months of startup. Travel agency owners should be aware that it may be possible to secure a group commitment for a tour within six months and have it on the books for the future, but usually it is not possible to have passengers' money coming in and the group departing within six months.

ITINERARY PLANNING

Itinerary planning is the exciting yet frustrating part of tour packaging. It's the converting of the idea into a practical itinerary that works. It involves laying out the day-by-day program with all flights, sightseeing, social activities, special meals, and other components. How do you begin such an awesome task?

Start with the Airfare

Rather than arbitrarily starting out with an itinerary and then checking with the airline as to the fare, the wise tour planner researches the various airfares first and then selects the fare to be used *before* plotting the itinerary. The fare will define the conditions and restrictions of the itinerary. In other words, the itinerary is planned around the airfare, not the other way around.

For example, after researching several airfares, it might appear that the Group Inclusive Tour (GIT) airfare is the most suitable for a particular itinerary. But the GIT might restrict passengers to a total of five stops (two outbound, one at turnaround, and two inbound). Therefore, the itinerary must be planned around that restriction. Furthermore, the airfare might require that the group travel **online**, that is, on the same carrier throughout the entire itinerary. This requirement would eliminate any plan to include a city not served by that particular carrier. The tour planner should check all types of airfares, both group and individual, to ascertain which is the most suitable for the tour. However, the actual airfare itself is not the only thing to consider. Other factors may be equally important, such as flexibility, complimentaries for tour escorts, scheduling, interline arrangements with other carriers, possible upfront deposits to certain airlines (some of which may be non-refundable), and so forth.

Other restrictions dictated by airfares might be **blackout periods** when a certain airfare is not in effect or limitations in the number of days that excursion fares require. A certain airfare may not be in effect, for example, during the Christmas holiday season. Or a fare may be limited, for example, to 14/35 days. Such a fare would not be workable for a group wanting a one week tour, nor would it be suitable for those who wish to spend more than 35 days abroad. It is essential that the tour planner be aware of the ramifications and restrictions of all of the promotional fares.

Imaginative airline sales representatives accustomed to working with group tour planners recognize the importance of special promotional airfares as a sales tool. When calling on these group operators, they bring such fares to the attention of the tour planner. Other airline sales representatives, however, seem oblivious to the importance of fares and the manner in which the designer may plan an entire itinerary around a particular fare.

Of course, in certain itineraries cost may be no object, and the desired itinerary cannot be planned within the confines of the special promotional airfares. In these cases, the travel planner may decide to use a higher airfare to allow the needed latitude and flexibility.

Problem Areas First

Once the type of airfare has been established, it is time to plot a rough itinerary, working around existing flight schedules. These rough itineraries sometimes look wonderful on paper, but when flights are actually selected for the group, some of the realities of the tour business emerge, namely, infrequent flights in certain areas, undesirable departure or arrival times, and so forth. If the type of airfare planned restricts you to using a certain air carrier throughout (i.e., traveling online rather than being permitted to interline on other airlines), it will be necessary to plan the entire itinerary around that carrier's schedules. This may mean that clients may have to stay in one city longer than desired, and shorten their stay in another city.

If the plan includes a short cruise within the itinerary, it is necessary to make sure that space is available on the desired sailing date *before* plotting out the entire air schedule.

It may take some juggling to include a visit to a local market that only operates on Sundays, to avoid Tuesdays in Paris when the museums are closed, or to schedule a certain flight that operates only twice a week. If you are booking the tour directly, it will take some time to research these restrictions. On the other hand, if you are booking through a wholesaler, you will be advised in this regard, and an itinerary will be planned for you that works around these local schedules.

If the plan includes a chartered motorcoach service, it is important to know coach-originating points. For example, an excellent airfare to Amsterdam may be available, but if you plan to charter a motorcoach for the land tour in Europe that is from a bus company based in Switzerland, the airfare savings into Amsterdam may very well be cancelled by motorcoach deadhead charges. Knowledgeable tour operators start with the difficult spots first and work around them.

Charting the Itinerary

One of the easiest ways to plot an itinerary is to use a daily chart with areas for morning, afternoon, and evening activities. Of course, a simple lined pad can also be used, with one line representing each day. Whatever method is used, it is important that the itinerary indicate days of the week as well as dates. This serves as a double-check that no days have been skipped and that any free days allowed for shopping, for example, are not on Sundays or holidays when all the shops are closed.

Pacing.   This is an important factor in itinerary planning. **Pacing** is how quickly or slowly the itinerary moves, how full or empty each day is, and how the sequence of events is scheduled. If a group arrives at the hotel at 1:00 A.M., it is best not to get them up for an early sightseeing tour the next morning. If a morning of sightseeing and an evening function are planned for the same day, then perhaps the group needs the afternoon for leisure.

Often, because of a tour planner's desire to show the group everything, too much is packed into the trip. Everyone needs time to sit in a cafe, write postcards, shop, take an occasional nap, or visit the barber or beautician. If tour members are not given this time, they may either become ill, or begin to avoid tour activities. It is best to plan for free time at the outset. Remember, sick or overtired tour members do not make happy tour members. A planner should mentally walk through the tour plans day by day and ask, "Would I be overtired?"

Balance.   Another important aspect of itinerary planning is **balance**, which is introducing a variety of activities into the trip: some serious, some frivolous, some lighthearted, and some intellectual. Even though a group may be on a professional study tour, no one wants to study all the time. After an intense morning of sightseeing, almost any group enjoys a relaxing lunch with music. Similarly, it is best to plan some daytime events and some evening functions. A little music and dancing in the evening might best complement a daytime historical tour. An evening of theater, folklore, or frivolity might be needed to lighten the tone after a day's touring in an extremely poor country or drab area. Variety is the key to balance.

Evening activities.   Remember that many people join tours because they want to travel with others, make new friends, and have companionship, particularly for evening activities. An itinerary should never offer group sightseeing all day and then solitary evenings. If evening activities are not planned as an integral part of

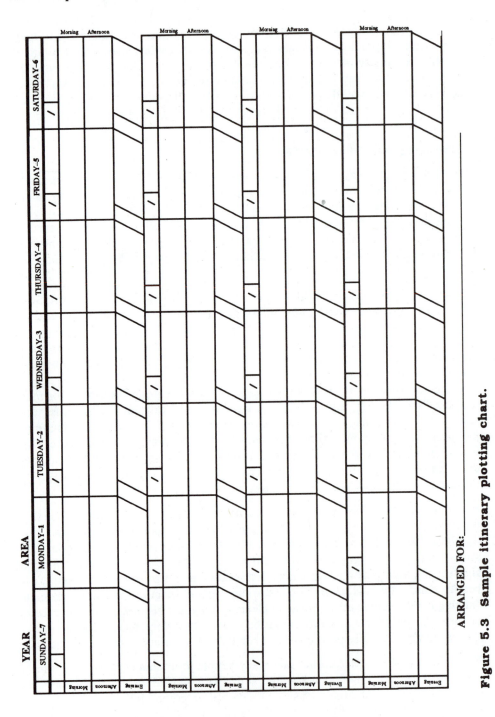

ARRANGED FOR:

Figure 5.3   Sample itinerary plotting chart.

the tour, at least some evenings on the itinerary chart should be set aside for Dutch-treat events that the tour manager can organize, so that no one in the group ever feels left out or lonely.

One-night stays.   One-night stays can be tiring. The itinerary may not look tiring on paper, but the act of moving in and out of hotels, buses, and airports and of packing and unpacking takes up a great deal of time and energy. After a couple of days on the road and a different hotel each night, tour members begin to look forward to a three-night stay in the same hotel. This gives them the opportunity to organize their suitcases, to do some hand wash, and to sleep late one morning.

First and Last Days

The two most important times on any tour are the first two days and the last day. Even if you are told that the group does not want meals included in the tour (perhaps to keep the price down), plan welcome and farewell parties, and explain to the sponsoring organization the psychological reasons why such events are important to the success of the tour.

The first 48 hours are important because first impressions are made, friendships are initiated among passengers, and a relationship of trust and respect is reinforced between the tour manager and the passengers. For these reasons, the wise tour planner pays particular attention to the first two days of the tour to be sure that the itinerary will operate smoothly. Time should be allowed for a briefing on the first day (or if arriving late after a full day's travel, the next day). An opening social event, such as a welcome dinner party or cocktail reception, is a good ice-breaker.

Memories of the tour are cemented on the last day of the tour. A wrap-up social event, such as a farewell gala dinner party, is a festive way to end a vacation. It leaves everyone with memories of happy times, a sense of camaraderie, and the desire to travel with the same company again.

SAMPLE ITINERARY

Let us suppose that a tour designer has been asked to put together a short European itinerary for a local country club. A sample day-by-day itinerary plan and accompanying terms and **conditions sheet** might look something like the European Highlights Tour in Figure 5.4.

PROPOSAL
TO THE
ROSEMONT COUNTRY CLUB
FOR A
EUROPEAN HIGHLIGHTS TOUR

Day 1, Friday, Sept. 4   DEPART CHICAGO/NEW YORK
Depart from O'Hare International Airport via TWA mid-day flight to New
York's Kennedy Airport. Transfer to TWA's international check-in
counter, where other tour participants join the Chicago group. We all
depart together via TWA early evening flight. Dinner and overnight in-
flight.

Day 2, Saturday, Sept. 5   AMSTERDAM
Early morning arrival at Amsterdam's Schiphol Airport. Here we will be
met by our local hosts and transferred to the world-famous Krasnapolsky
Hotel. Balance of the day at leisure to rest and adjust to jet lag. This
evening we'll meet for welcome cocktails and our first dinner party
together.

Day 3, Sunday, Sept. 6   AMSTERDAM
Dutch buffet breakfast at the hotel, followed by a tour briefing in which
we'll learn more about what we can expect in the days to come. Then we
head out on an introductory tour of the city. The afternoon is at leisure to
visit the Rijksmuseum or for optional independent sightseeing. In the
evening we enjoy a cruise along the illuminated canals of Amsterdam.

Day 4, Monday, Sept. 7   AMSTERDAM/HAGUE/DELFT
Dutch buffet breakfast at the hotel and full-day excursion to Aalsmeer
with the largest flower auction in the world, the Hague (seat of the World
Court), and Delft for a visit to the famed Blue Delft pottery works. We'll
stop enroute for a typical Dutch lunch. Late afternoon return to
Amsterdam. Independent dinner and evening at leisure.

Day 5, Tuesday, Sept. 8   AMSTERDAM/PARIS
Early breakfast at the hotel and then transfer to the rail station for train to
Paris. First–class compartments reserved. We can purchase lunch aboard
prior to arriving at the Paris Gare du Nord railroad station. Our French
hosts will be awaiting us and we depart directly from the rail station on an
afternoon introductory city tour of the "City of Light" visiting the Champs

**Figure 5.4 Travel agent's proposal to Rosemont Country Club for a
European tour.**

continued

Elysees, Notre Dame Cathedral, the Eiffel Tower, and all the spots we've dreamed of seeing. Late afternoon check-in at our hotel, the Meurice, conveniently located on the Right Bank near the fashion houses, the Tuileries, and the Louvre. Evening at leisure.

Day 6, Wednesday, Sept. 9   *PARIS/VERSAILLES*
Continental breakfast at our hotel and morning excursion to the Palace of Versailles. The afternoon is at leisure for shopping and independent interests. Tonight we enjoy a Night on the Town at the famed Lido nightclub, noted for its beautiful showgirls and spectacular show. Champagne and fun for all!

Day 7, Thursday, Sept. 10   *PARIS*
Continental breakfast at our hotel and then a walking tour through the Louvre to see this great museum with its vast collections. Afternoon at leisure to spend more time on our own at the Louvre or for other interests such as shopping, further sightseeing, or just cafe sitting and watching the world go by. Tonight's a free evening to sample one of the city's many gourmet restaurants.

Day 8, Friday, Sept. 11   *PARIS/ROME*
Continental breakfast at our hotel and early transfer to the airport for morning flight to Rome. We stay at the Hotel Ambasciatore on Via Veneto. Afternoon tour of the city including the Roman Forum, the Colosseum, the Pantheon, Trevi Fountain, the Spanish Steps, and other landmarks. Evening at leisure.

Day 9, Saturday, Sept. 12   *ROME*
Continental breakfast at our hotel. This morning is purposely at leisure while the city's major stores and boutiques are open. Afternoon visit to the Vatican Museum with the magnificent Sistine Chapel and Michelangelo's "Ascent of Man."

Day 10, Sunday, Sept. 13   *ROME/TIVOLI*
Continental breakfast. Today we see something of the Italian countryside as we make an excursion to Hadrian's Villa and the lovely Villa d'Este with its terraced gardens and dancing fountains. Country lunch enroute. Return to the city in time to pack and get ready for tonight's festive dinner party. We head across the Tiber River to the old section of Trastevere for an Italian farewell dinner complete with wine, folklore, and Italian songs well into the night.

Figure 5.4 Travel agent's proposal to Rosemont Country Club for a European tour. (Continued)

continued

Day 11, Monday, Sept. 14   *ROME/NEW YORK/CHICAGO*

All good things must come to an end and we head for the airport for our homeward TWA flight to New York. We say goodbye to our East Coast tour participants who leave us here. Chicago-bound members continue on via TWA to O'Hare International Airport. Welcome home.

TERMS AND CONDITIONS

Included in the tour price:

1. Round-trip economy class airfare from Chicago, via APEX (Advance Purchase Excursion) Airfare, basic season.
2. Nine (9) nights' hotel accommodation at hotels listed in the itinerary, or similar, based on two persons sharing a twin-bedded room with private bath throughout. A few single rooms are available at a surcharge of $000. Single rooms offer privacy, but do not necessarily mean better accommodations. Requests for single rooms must be made at the time of booking; however, single rooms are not guaranteed.
3. First-class rail fare, with reserved seating, between Amsterdam and Paris, as indicated in the itinerary.
4. A total of ten (10) meals, including six breakfasts (two Dutch breakfasts and four Continental breakfasts), two enroute luncheons, welcome and farewell dinner parties; (all meals are table d'hote basis in accordance with local custom; in addition are such in-flight meals as may be served by the airlines when flying at appropriate mealtime).
5. Sightseeing by private motorcoach, as shown in the itinerary, including all entrance fees, with English-speaking guides.
6. Transfer between airports, rail stations, and hotels for tour participants arriving and departing with the group.
7. Baggage handling for maximum two suitcases per person at airports, rail stations, and hotels for all group arrivals and departures.
8. All local taxes on hotels, meals, and other tour services as well as the United States departure taxes.
9. Tips to chambermaids, local guides, waiters and *maitre d'* at included tour meals, motorcoach drivers, porters at airports and rail stations, and hotel bellmen.
10. Services of a tour manager representing LSI Travel Agency, Inc.
11. Social events and special activities as listed in the itinerary, specifically the welcome party, Amsterdam evening cruise, Lido nightclub evening in Paris, and farewell party in Rome.
12. One complimentary trip, shared-room basis, to be granted to Rosemont Country Club with a minimum of 25 full-paying adult participants. This complimentary may be assigned by the club at its discretion to one club

Figure 5.4 Travel agent's proposal to Rosemont Country Club for a European tour. (Continued)

continued

member to travel with the tour group as club representative (all tour services granted to other tour members will be granted to the complimentary member; items and services not provided to other tour members are not included in the complimentary trip).

13. Three thousand (3,000) copies of a detailed tour brochure to be prepared and printed by LSI Travel Agency, Inc. at no expense to Rosemont Country Club.

14. Direct mail charges to include bulk-rate postage, envelopes, cover letter, brochure, and labor charges for circulating the Rosemont Country Club membership of approximately 3,000 members with one mailing.

15. Three quarter-page advertisement/announcements in the Rosemont Country Club Quarterly Newsletter not to exceed $275 per advertisement, plus advertisement production charges.

16. One promotional evening to include room rental, refreshments, invitations, program of speaker and/or films.

17. All necessary planning and operational charges, including liaison with overseas contacts, Rosemont Country Club, and tour passengers.

18. Packet of departure materials including all necessary documentation, canvas flight bags, and our special "Welcome to Europe" information booklet.

Not included in the tour price:

1. Personal expenses such as laundry, liquors, wines, mineral waters, phone, valet, coffee at lunch or dinner.

2. Expenses due to flight delays, strikes, bad weather or other irregularities.

3. Travel insurance.

4. Excess baggage charges, such as overweight charges or handling for more than two suitcases.

5. Individual services apart from the group.

6. Increase in tariffs or dollar exchange rate after publication date.

7. Refunds for hotel accommodations, meals, or any other tour services not used.

8. Any expense for *à la carte meal* items not included in preplanned menus under local custom, or for eating in other dining rooms or at other hours not authorized.

9. Any increase in airfares after publication date.

10. Cost of obtaining a passport.

11. Transportation between home city and Chicago.

12. Luggage handling in the United States at beginning and end of tour.

13. Those meals not specifically listed as included.

14. Customary gratuity to the tour manager at the end of the tour.

Figure 5.4 Travel agent's proposal to Rosemont Country Club for a European tour. (Continued)

continued

Conditions

Registration and deposits: An initial deposit of $200 per person is required to secure definite reservations. We regret that no space may be reserved without a deposit.

Final payment: Balance of payment is due 60 days prior to departure.

Cancellations and refunds: Full refund is guaranteed for all cancellations received up to 61 days prior to departure. Cancellations must be made in writing via letter or fax; verbal cancellations, whether in person or by telephone, are not valid. For cancellations received 60 days or less prior to departure, cancellation charge will reflect any cancellation penalties incurred by airlines, hotels, ground operators, and other suppliers involved. A special optional trip insurance policy will be available to protect against such cancellations.

Tour price: Price of the tour is premised on a minimum of 25 adult, paying participants. Should the final membership fall below this number, LSI Travel Agency, Inc. reserves the right to increase the tour price. All rates for land arrangements are based on the value of the U.S. Dollar in relation to foreign currencies and on tariffs in effect on (date), and are subject to adjustment prior to departure. Airfares are also subject to change.

Special note regarding airfare: In an effort to keep the tour price as reasonable as possible, a special APEX (Advance Purchase Excursion) airfare is being utilized and the tour price is calculated accordingly. This special fare can save one a great deal; however, it does not permit the flexibility of a full-fare air ticket and changes or cancellations in flight plans after the ticket is issued can cost an airfare cancellation fee.

Responsibility: This tour is operated by LSI Travel Agency, Inc. by contracting for services from other suppliers. LSI Travel Agency, Inc. and/ or its agents, acting as agents for the tour members, shall be responsible to tour members for supplying services and accommodations as set forth in the brochure, except to the extent such services and accommodations cannot be supplied due to force of nature, delays, or other causes beyond the control of LSI Travel Agency, Inc. If the service and accommodations set forth in the tour brochure cannot be supplied due to delays or other causes beyond the control of LSI Travel Agency, Inc., best efforts will be

Figure 5.4 Travel agent's proposal to Rosemont Country Club for a European tour. (Continued)

continued

made to supply comparable services and accommodations. If such services and accommodations cannot be provided due to the above reasons, or if the services are not used due to voluntary omission by the tour member, refunds will not be granted.

By becoming a member of the tour, a participant waives any claim against LSI Travel Agency, Inc. for any damages to or loss of property, or any injury to or death of persons due to any act of negligence of any hotels or any other persons rendering any of the services and accommodations included in the ground portion of the itinerary. LSI Travel Agency, Inc. shall not be responsible for any delays, substitution of equipment, or any act or omission whatsoever by any air or surface carrier, its agents, servants, and employees; and a participant, by becoming a member of the tour, waives any claim arising therefrom.

No refund will be made for any unused portion of the tour unless agreed to in writing prior to departure of the tour. The right is reserved to decline to accept or retain any person as a member of the tour at any time. While no deviations from the printed itinerary are anticipated, the right is reserved to make changes in the itinerary with or without notice where deemed necessary, with the mutual understanding that any additional expense will be paid by the individual passenger. LSI Travel Agency, Inc. reserves the right to cancel the tour prior to departure if circumstances permit it, in which case full refund will constitute full settlement to the passenger. The price of the tour is based on tariffs and exchange rates in effect at the time of printing the brochure and is subject to change in the event of any change in tariffs and exchange rates.

The issuance and acceptance of tickets and vouchers shall be deemed to be consent to the above conditions. The air carriers and their agents and affiliates shall not be held responsible for any act, omission, or event during the time passengers are not on board aircraft or air carrier conveyances. The passenger contract ticket in use by the airlines, steamship lines, and/or other common carriers concerned, when issued, shall constitute the sole contract between the carrier and the purchaser of this tour and/or the passenger. Air transportation on this tour is restricted to TWA.

Printed 9/1/XX

Figure 5.4   Travel agent's proposal to Rosemont Country Club for a European tour.   (Continued)

❏ *SUMMARY*

Being a tour designer is a fulfilling and creative career that requires many different qualities from being a retail travel counselor. The best designers combine an eclectic humanities background with practical travel industry know-how. It is necessary to allow a one-year lead time for most tours and to research the airfare and airline restrictions first, plotting the itinerary around these. It is also necessary to know a variety of reference sources for referral in designing an itinerary appropriate to the clientele.

❏ *REVIEW QUESTIONS*

1. Why is it not important to include commissionable features in group tours?

2. In designing a tour itinerary, what is the first thing you would research before plotting the itinerary?

3. Compare the terms *balance* and *pacing* and give samples of how each would be reflected in an itinerary.

4. What is a realistic lead time for organizing a successful tour?

5. Name four components usually included in the tour price.

6. What are four items often not included in a tour price?

❑ *ACTIVITIES*

1. Research several different possible airfares for a tour to an international destination. Compare them not only in terms of price, but also in terms of allowable stopovers, availability of tour escort complimentary, seasonality, blackout dates, and other factors. Select the fare on which you have decided and be able to justify your rationale.

2. Select one country on a proposed tour and research cities/areas that you would include on a tour to this country. Give your rationale for including the specific cities/areas in the itinerary.

▷ 6

NEGOTIATING AND BOOKING THE TOUR

LEARNING OBJECTIVES

After reading this chapter, you should:

- ❑ Know which to book first—air, hotels, or receptive services operators
- ❑ Know the advantages and disadvantages of booking cruises for groups
- ❑ Know the items for which you can negotiate with a cruise line and an airline for groups
- ❑ Know what to look for in selecting an air carrier for your group
- ❑ Know the advantages and disadvantages of booking your hotel space directly with the hotel versus through a hotel representative, sales office, or wholesaler
- ❑ Know what makes a hotel suitable for groups
- ❑ Understand certain hotel terminology so you can speak "their language"
- ❑ Understand various types of hotel rates and which are best for your tour
- ❑ Understand the role of the receptive services operator and what group services to book with this type of company
- ❑ Understand the various meal plans: American Plan, Modified American Plan, European Plan, Demi-Pension, and so forth

KEY CONCEPTS AND TERMS

Account Executive or Sales Representative
Across-the-Board
Airport Codes Versus City Codes
Amenity Package
American Plan (AP)
CLIA
Complimentaries (Comps)
Coordinating Carrier

Cruise Contract
Deregulation
European Plan (EP)
Full Pension
Gross
Gross Rates
Group Air-Booking Form
Group Desk
Half-Pension (Demi-Pension)
In/Out Dates
Interline
Modified American Plan (MAP)
Negotiate
Net
Net Net
Net Rates
On Option
Originating Carrier
Override Commission
Over-tonnage
Promotional Assistance
Rack Rate
Run-of-House Rate
Service Charge
Soft Sailings
Tour Desk
Upfront Monies
Value Added Tax (VAT)

The airfare has been selected, the itinerary has been designed around it, and a rough day-by-day plan of the tour has been sketched out. The next step is to actually book the reservations to see if the desired itinerary will really work. Very often schedules look wonderful on paper, but when they are put into operation the itinerary may not work as planned.

So, where do you start? Which comes first, the air reservation or the hotel? What if the tour planner books everything at once and then discovers that the air reservations are available but the hotel space cannot be confirmed? What if the hotel rooms are available but there is no space on the flights desired? In short, what if all the pieces of the puzzle do not fall into place easily—as they most likely will not?

START ONE YEAR IN ADVANCE

As mentioned earlier, one rule of thumb, which should avert some problems later, is to begin no later than one year in advance. Of course, there may be times when an exception is required. There may be occasions when the passengers are all pre-sold and, therefore, the lead time for sales is not necessary. But 99 percent of the time a minimum of one year's lead time will be necessary to get all reservations and prices confirmed, to have the costing and pricing done properly, and to have adequate time for promotion and sales.

BOOKING ORDER

The usual booking order is:

1. air
2. accommodations
3. receptive services operators and finishing touches.

Of course, with all rules there are exceptions. One exception occurs when a cruise is included in the itinerary. If this is the case, then the cruise should be booked first to be certain that the desired cruise date is available. Once the cruise space is confirmed, the balance of the itinerary can be built around it.

A similar situation exists if you're working around a convention date and the convention hotel is crucial to the tour. In this case, the hotel should be reserved first and then the air reservations and other arrangements made. If working around a major sporting event or show, it is necessary to confirm that the tickets are available, and then plan the itinerary around the dates or other requirements. For example, to obtain Carnival in Rio parade seats, it might be necessary to agree to buy a one-week package tour from a wholesaler or Brazilian receptive services operator. If your group is already scheduled to be in Rio for only three days, then it would be necessary either to throw away the other four days or totally rework the itinerary to accommodate the one-week Rio stay.

Another exception occurs when the hotel reservations are booked through a receptive service operator overseas. In this case, steps two and three are combined: you would book the hotels and a receptive services operator in one step. (Note: The local receptive services operator (RSO) handles the day-to-day operation of the tour in the field. (This is discussed in depth later in this chapter.)

If you design a tour that includes a cruise, and if you decide to book the hotel accommodations directly, the booking order would look like this:

1. cruise
2. air
3. hotel accommodations
4. receptive services operator and finishing touches

HANDLING A GROUP CRUISE

If this is your first group, one of the easiest ways to begin is to book the group on a cruise. A cruise is nothing more than a pre-existing, floating tour package on which you may place a group. Many cruise lines are anxious for group business. Also, a cruise can be included as an integral part of a tour. Perhaps it could be a Greek island cruise as part of a European tour or a cruise to the Galápagos Islands in a South American itinerary. A short cruise gives variety and pacing to an itinerary composed of nothing but flights, airport transfers, and motorcoach trips. Of course, cruises also have some disadvantages. A list of the pros and cons of choosing to book a group on a cruise follows.

Advantages of Cruises

❑ You may block varying amounts of space, sell what you are capable of selling, and return any unsold space to the cruise line with no further obligation to fill the space, as most contracts are non-risk contracts.

❑ You can operate the trip even if you produce only a small volume of bookings. It is not necessary to cancel the entire trip because of only a few bookings.

❑ There is one easy booking source. It's simple to operate if you are unfamiliar with the intricacies of booking overseas hotels, sightseeing tours, guides, and transfers.

❑ You probably can make as much money on a small group booked on a cruise as you can make handling an entire charter flight or other large-volume (but small-markup) project.

❑ Cruises are a popular product and the public has been pre-sold on cruising by past TV shows like "The Love Boat," through friends who have experienced cruising, by current TV advertising from some of the larger cruise lines, and so forth.

❑ You receive your commission quickly. When you pay the cruise line, you simply deduct the commission from the remittance, paying the cruise line the net cost of the cruise.

❑ It is possible to negotiate with cruise lines for **complimentaries** (i.e., a free trip for the group's organizer or conductor) and for an **override commission** (i.e., an extra commission paid by suppliers such as airlines and cruise lines to group tour operators as an incentive for group and volume business).

❑ It is also possible to negotiate with cruise lines for special extras: a welcome-aboard cocktail party; a tour of the ship's bridge, engine room, or galley; wine served at dinner and other festive touches. This type of treatment sets your group apart from other passengers and gives your group participants an incentive to travel with you again.

❑ There is excellent potential for success and for happy passengers. If you select the right ship for the right clientele, you are almost certain to bring home a group of repeat clients. And, clients like the concept of a cruise because they may visit many destinations without wasting time while transferring and packing and unpacking at each destination.

❑ A cruise is seen as an all-inclusive vacation package that incorporates transportation, accommodations, all meals, social activities, sports facilities, and entertainment features. Clients perceive a cruise as a product that permits them to have a pre-set vacation budget without a great deal of unexpected expenses along the way.

However, despite the many advantages and the popularity of cruises, there are also a number of disadvantages. It is important to be aware of some of these disadvantages before undertaking a group cruise venture.

Figure 6.1 This cruise line ad, directed to travel agents, offers them a free cabin if they reserve space for a group in at least five cabins. (Courtesy Majesty Cruise Lines.)

Disadvantages of Cruises

❑ No autonomy. The group is getting the same trip and the same itinerary as all of the other passengers. The only way to have the group feel special is to arrange for extra features on their behalf (as previously mentioned), to provide an escort or "name" leader, or to arrange for a special onboard enrichment program of lectures, seminars, meetings at sea, and other activities.

❑ No flexibility. It is necessary to take the cruise as is. The dates, the ports, and the rates are scheduled by the cruise line. It is impossible to custom design the cruise to the needs of the group (unless you are chartering the entire ship).

❑ Not all groups are right for cruises. Although cruising is an excellent vacation product for many people, for the non-touristy individual—the person who wants to see one country in depth, the intellectual who wants to get off the beaten track, or the person who hates groups—a cruise is probably not the right product.

❑ You cannot mark up the cruise price as you would when packaging your own tour. It would be imprudent to do so, since participants could buy the cruise at its tariff price elsewhere. However, it is possible to package pre- and post-cruise arrangements with some markup. These additional arrangements, when added to the cruise, make for a total package sold at a total package price.

❑ You are limited in the amount of promotional funds or complimentary trips to those that can be negotiated from the cruise line, since the tariff price cannot be marked up to cover these items. Sometimes a demanding tour organizer recruiting a group will insist on a salary or an honorarium or on taking the family along free. There is no way to provide for these demands unless the cruise line will go along with them, or unless you can absorb these additional expenses out of earnings.

❑ Early closeout. Many cruises fill quite early. Therefore, the cruise line will pressure you to sell the group space early and to return all unsold space early. This precludes late promotion and late sales. The best that can be expected is to hold the space for up to 90 days before cruise departure. In the case of lightly booked cruises (referred to as **soft sailings**) or off-season cruises, a cruise line might tend to be more accommodating. It might permit you to hold the space for up to 60 days before departure, and in some cases even up to 30 days.

❑ Cruise lines will not allot all the space in the same category or at a single price level. You will be assigned a variety of cabins in a range of prices. When a cruise is sold by itself, this range is not a problem. Clients may be offered a variety of cabin categories at various price levels, letting the client choose. However, when packaging a short cruise as an integral part of a longer tour, the variety of cabins and prices can make it difficult to standardize the total tour price.

❏ Most cruise lines keep passengers' names and addresses, and they will solicit them directly after the cruise as part of a "club" made up of their past passengers. Some cruise lines will automatically commission the originating travel company if the passengers book another cruise directly with the cruise line, provided the booking does not come from another company. Other cruise lines will simply advise you that they are soliciting your clients and will leave it up to you to get the booking. They will not commission the originating company if the client books direct with the line or with a competing travel company. Be sure to ask the cruise line its policy before booking a group. Business is hard enough to come by without having it intercepted by aggressive cruise lines. Of course, some cruise lines do not accept direct bookings.

Negotiating with the Cruise Line

The key word in dealing in cruises for groups is **negotiate**. Your primary role will be that of a go-between, trying to obtain the most favorable arrangements for the group. The clue to successful negotiation is to go into any negotiating sessions well informed about the cruise line, its ships, and its competitors. However, at the same time you must be open-minded in regards to any pre-set ideas of demanding a specific sailing date.

The best starting strategy is to investigate several cruise lines and several itineraries. First, it is necessary to determine the appropriate length of cruise and the price range suitable for the particular group. It is also important to know the "personality" of the ship being considered. Does it cater to honeymooners? Singles? The over-sixty crowd? The best way to find out the answers to such questions is to ask. An excellent source of information is Cruise Lines International Association (**CLIA**).

CLIA will be happy to provide information on its member carriers and provide information to help you to calculate such important factors as cabin size, ratio of crew to passengers, and other important information to help sell and promote cruises. (It may also be possible for you to attend one of CLIA's excellent seminars held periodically in key U.S. cities. Also, various cruise lines hold their own educational seminars and promotional evenings for the travel trade, which you should try to attend throughout the year.)

CLIA's information is thorough, even down to the history of a particular ship. For example, how many travel consultants know that the *Ocean Pearl* formerly was the *Peal of Scandinavia* and prior to that was called the *Finnstar*, that Royal Cruise Line is of Greek registry, or that Sun Line markets its cruises both in the United States and Europe and so carries an international passenger list (as compared to some lines that market strictly within the United States and carry an all-American passenger list).

Once several cruise lines have been selected, the next step is to contact them and request written information about their policy for group bookings. It is essen-

SIGN UP NOW AND EARN CREDITS RIGHT AWAY

GET STARTED ON YOUR CRUISE COUNSELLOR CERTIFICATION

CLIA's training programs get results. You and your sales staff will be able to apply proven methods of selling cruises through CLIA's new and enhanced workshops, including the innovative course, "Power Selling Techniques." So get started on earning credits toward your Accredited Cruise Counsellor and Master Cruise Counsellor awards. Improved selling skills are just a workshop away! Here's how your agency will benefit:

★ More new clients.
★ Increased revenue from existing clients.
★ Improved conversion rates of potential to real business.

And remember – you can start earning credits for the new CLIA certification programs now. Points will be awarded toward Accredited Cruise Counsellor and Master Cruise Counsellor upon successful completion of our training courses.

CLIA continues its free sales training offer: return the coupon found in your 1992 renewal kit with the completed registration form. The coupon, valued at $25, allows a second person to attend a seminar at no additional cost.

To enroll in a classroom session, mail or fax the form on the back of this page or contact CLIA, 500 Fifth Ave., Suite 1407, New York, N.Y. 10110, (212) 921-0066 or fax (212) 921-0549.

1 CRUISE VACATIONS: AN INTRODUCTION

is the entry-level course in CLIA's three-tiered curriculum for the less experienced counsellor. Upon completion, participants will be able to:
• Evaluate market data.
• Identify client needs.
• Effectively use the brochure as a sales tool.
• Make a cruise reservation efficiently.
• Demonstrate that a cruise is the better vacation value.

2 PRINCIPLES OF PROFESSIONAL SELLING

is geared toward the front line counsellor who has experience but wants to sharpen sales skills. The seminar will enable participants to:
• Qualify a client and identify buying motives.
• Recommend cruises with confidence.
• Effectively dispell any concerns that prospective passengers may have.
• Apply these techniques toward closing more cruise sales.

3 POWER SELLING TECHNIQUES (NEW)

is our newest program, recommended for all levels of expertise. A required attendance course for enrollees in CLIA's certification program, it focuses on methods to boost cruise sales. Attendees will be able to:
• Identify and address change in consumers' buying habits.
• Control the communication process.
• Evaluate and improve listening skills.
• Assess typical mistakes made in telephone selling and apply methods to improve them.

For Booking through
SABRE - ⊠ORG or **APOLLO - TD*TF/LINK**
❶ Select: Leisure Travel Directory ❷ Type Exact Name: CLIA ❸ Press: <Enter>

Figure 6.2 Cruise Lines International Association (CLIA), the trade association for the cruise industry, is an excellent source of information about cruise lines from the history of each ship to the type of clientele a particular ship entertains. The organization also sponsors many training sessions and workshops for travel agents. (Courtesy CLIA.)

tial to read the policy and to understand it before starting negotiations. Once you have read the standard group policy, call the applicable cruise line sales manager (sometimes called an **account executive** or **sales representative** and arrange an appointment to discuss the project in person. Always negotiate face-to-face whenever possible. And always deal with the sales office first, not the reservations office.

The best strategy is to enter negotiations by asking the cruise line representative to indicate which sailings they need help in promoting, thereby getting a selection of soft sailings from which to choose. Do not accept an unpopular sailing date or an inferior ship just to strike a deal. Often, however, your flexibility to move dates by several weeks can accommodate both the cruise line and benefit your company, as well as gain some tempting amenities for the group members.

Some Benefits of Cruises for Your Company and Clients

Cruises offer a variety of benefits for your company and clients. These may include higher commissions, group discounts, more generous tour leader complimentaries, brochures or shells, other promotional assistance, an offer to waive early berth deposits, an amenity package for group members, and free meeting room space on board.

Higher Commissions.   Although the standard commission on a cruise is 10 percent, a cruise line might be willing to offer up to an additional 5 percent, or even more. This could be straight commission, expressed as 15 percent **across the board** (i.e., 15 percent on all bookings from the first to last). Or, it could be 10 percent commission plus a 5 percent extra commission called an override, which is retroactive to the first booking, but payable only after the group has reached a specific number of bookings (i.e., 25 bookings). This means that if the group finalized at 20 participants, your company would receive only the basic 10 percent commission. An override is not something to be counted on, but it is an incentive.

Some cruise lines may offer a percentage override; others may offer a flat dollar amount per person. Which is more advantageous; a $25 per-head flat fee or a 1 percent override? This depends on the fare. For example, if the average cruise fare is $4,000, a 1 percent override of $40 is better than a $25 per person flat fee. Conversely, if the cruise fare is $1,500 then you would be better off with a flat $25 per person. Do not be misled by percentages. Remember that old saying: 100 percent of zero is still zero.

Another approach that some cruise lines use is to offer your company a percentage reduction for the group. Although cruise lines frown on the word "discount", it really is a reduced rate for members of a group. This is an offer that can be used effectively as a sales tool in the sales presentation to the group. Any group likes to feel special and know that it is getting a lower rate than non-group passengers.

More Generous Tour Leader Complimentaries. On a popular sailing, the cruise line might offer one complimentary berth for every 40 bookings. But on a less popular cruise, the line might be willing to grant one complimentary berth for every ten bookings. This could be a decided advantage, particularly if you are faced with selling the cruise to an organization whose board of directors is looking for as many complimentaries as possible. Complimentaries can also be helpful in generating additional income since, in many cases, you have the option to sell them.

Brochures or Shells. Many cruise lines have shells (i.e., partially prepared brochures) available from which you can develop your own brochure. (See page 162 for more information on shells.) Some lines also have standard brochures on which can be overprinted the name of the sponsoring organization, your company name, and other basic information. With the high cost of producing original brochures, this **Promotional Assistance** can mean a sizable savings, especially so if you plan to circulate a large mailing list. Often, the cruise line has photographs, graphics, deck plans, and other materials than can be used to help produce a professional-looking brochure or mailing piece. Sometimes, if you prefer to develop an original brochure rather than use the standard shell, you can convince the line to pay a share of the production costs such as typesetting, artwork, and printing.

Other Promotional Assistance. This might take the form of cooperative advertising, sponsoring a cruise night, sharing direct mail expenses, or providing videos.

An Offer to Waive Early Berth Deposits. This offer can be helpful to you in holding large blocks of space without the need to advance large deposits. Large deposits, of course, inhibit cash flow. Never hesitate to ask the cruise line to waive a deposit. Ask them to at least do so until clients' deposits start to come in. Whenever possible, try to work with clients' money, not your own.

An Amenity Package for Group Members. An **Amenity Package** could consist of such items as champagne in the group members' cabins, a gift certificate for drinks at the bar or a gift in the ship's boutique, a special welcome aboard cocktail party, or an offer to pay the expected tips to shipboard personnel on behalf of the group.

Free Meeting Room Space on Board. Meeting rooms make it possible to arrange seminars, classes, or enrichment lectures exclusively for the group. Most ships have a theatre; and since this is often unused in the mornings, many times it can be reserved for the group.

Even after all of the negotiating, it might appear that these extra benefits do not justify moving the group to an inconvenient sailing or a departure date that is not best for the group. Some groups, such as teachers' groups, are confined to the academic year; teachers have to travel during the summer months, the Christmas break, or spring break. In the case of a post-convention cruise, it is necessary to search for a cruise that immediately follows the convention dates; the convention cannot usually be scheduled around the cruise date. But even then, when limited in the choice of dates, it is still possible to query several cruise lines and compare their respective offers to see which one will work best.

It is possible that the cruise line will want to know something about your company's track record. The line may want to know what group cruise projects the company has done before; namely, destination, ship, price level, and degree of success. If your company is a newcomer to group cruises, then the line may want information on other types of groups the company has handled, such as air/land tours. Remember that the cruise line is taking a risk in setting aside a block of cabins for a company with which it has never worked. It will want to know something about the company in whose hands it is placing its product. Similarly, the cruise line will also want to know the travel history of the group: where they have traveled before, price level, and success or failure of their efforts.

Also remember that the economics of the times play a role in the negotiations. If times are good (i.e., if many people are traveling and spending, or if there are few ships in a given geographical area), then the cruise line will have the advantage. Therefore,the best you can do is negotiate the cruise line's standard written group policy. However, if people are not traveling frequently or spending heavily, or if there are too many ships cruising a given area (i.e., over-tonnage), the chances of negotiating a better deal are improved.

Seasonality can also affect your ability to negotiate. You'll certainly get a much better "deal" on a Caribbean cruise in September than at Christmas! And the very short Alaska summer season will offer better deals in May or September than July and August.

The Cruise Contract

When the cruise line has been selected and the sailing date negotiated, it is time to put everything in writing. Most cruise lines have a standard **cruise contract**; but if for some reason the line selected does not have such a contract, then it is essential to have a letter of agreement, signed by both parties that spells out in detail all the contracted for services. This cruise contract should specify the following:

- Date of departure and date of return
- Name of ship
- Name of itinerary and/or ports
- Basic commission
- Override commission, whether percentage or flat dollar amount, and number of paying passengers necessary to qualify for the override
- Number of cabins in each price category
- Complimentary policy-—how many free for how many booked, whether complimentaries are shared cabins or single-cabin basis, and whether cruise only or air/sea
- Amenity package offered to the group participants

❑ Cancellation penalties if group policies are different from those published in the cruise line's brochure

❑ Rate chart for all cabin categories, showing any special discounts for your group, rates for single, triple, and quad occupancy as well as double occupancy

❑ Any special rate for your company personnel if accompanying the group

❑ Minimum number of cabins or participants required in order for the cruise line to honor any special group rates (try to get this waived if possible)

❑ Number of shells or overprinted brochures promised

❑ Promotional expenditures promised to cover advertising, cruise nights, and so forth

❑ Option/review dates by which time a specified percentage of unsold space must be turned back to the cruise line

❑ Deposit requirements—amounts and due dates

❑ Final payment dates

❑ Whether or not shore excursion package, if pre-sold is commissionable.

Be sure to review the cruise contract carefully, to correct any errors, and to write in anything missing. It is quite possible that something promised by the sales department was not communicated to the reservation department issuing the contract. Therefore, it is important to call any omissions to the cruise line's attention. When all is agreed and in written form, a copy of the cruise contract should be signed and returned to the cruise line; another copy should be retained in the file. But before filing it away, be sure to note all review and payment dates on the master calendar so that no important date will be overlooked. See Figure 6.3 for an example of a cruise contract.

HANDLING GROUP AIR RESERVATIONS

As described in chapter 5, it is important to check airfares with several carriers before starting to plan the itinerary. Once the airfare has been checked, the itinerary planned, and the flights selected (allowing more than adequate flight connecting times), it is time to begin booking the actual space.

The first step is to confer with the airline account executive or sales "rep" at several air carriers and to determine which carrier you wish to use as the principal carrier on this tour. Similarly to negotiating with an account executive for a cruise line, it is best to meet face-to-face with your airline account executive, if possible. This airline will be designated as the **coordinating carrier** (also called the **originating carrier**). The coordinating carrier books all the group air space, whether it is online space on its own airline or **interline space,** that is using flights on other carriers. It is the coordinating carrier that will quote the airfare, advise of any flight changes, and Inclusive Tour number (IT number) if needed. (The IT Number is a code number sometimes assigned to an international tour or package by the spon-

GROUP BOOKING ACKNOWLEDGEMENT

Royal Cruise Line

One Maritime Plaza
San Francisco, CA 94111
Reservations: (800) 792-2992 (California) Administration: (800) 622-0538 (California)
(800) 227-4534 (National and Canada)   (800) 227-5628 (National and Canada)

Direct Sales: (800) 227-0925 (California and National)

AGENCY	LSI Travel Agency, Inc.
CONTACT	MARTY SARBEY DE SOUTO
ADDRESS	987 Park Drive #2A
CITY/ST	Berkeley, CA 94704

Ship: CROWN ODYSSEY
Departure Date: July 11, 19XX
Itinerary: MEDITERRANEAN HIGHLIGHTS LIS/VEN
Product/Promo: MEDH GP

Group Number: 00309

Number of Days: 12

Sales Manager:
Agency Phone #: 123-456-7890
Agency IATA #: 0043096

STATEROOM ALLOCATION

Category	Type	Deck	Allo-cation	Tariff Fare	Group Fare	Early Bird
AA	SUPR DELUX APT	PENTHOUSE		10498	8924	7874
AB	SUPR DELUX APT	PENTHOUSE		9898	8414	7424
AC	SUPR DLX SUITE	RIVIERA		9168	7793	6876
BA	SUPR DLX JR STE.	RIVIERA		8318	7071	6239
BB	SUPR DLX OUTSIDE	RIVIERA		7658	6510	5744
BC	DELUXE JR SUITE	RIVIERA, LIDO		7328	6229	5496
CA	DELUXE OUTSIDE	LIDO		6878	5847	5159
CB	DELUXE OUTSIDE	MARINA	1	6678	5677	5009
CC	DELUXE OUTSIDE	LAGUNA	1	6358	5405	4769
DA	DELUXE OUTSIDE	LAGUNA	3	6158	5235	4619
DB	DELUXE OUTSIDE	CORAL	1	5728	4869	4296
DC	DELUXE OUTSIDE	CORAL	2	5398	4589	4049
EA	DELUXE OUTSIDE	PLAYA	1	5098	4334	3824
EB	DELUXE INSIDE	RIVIERA, LIDO		4778	4062	3584
EC	DELUXE OUTSIDE	LAG,CORAL,PLAYA	1	4498	3824	3374
FA	DELUXE INSIDE	MARINA, LAGUNA		4298	3654	3224
FB	DELUXE INSIDE	CORAL		4138	3518	3104
FC	DELUXE INSIDE	CORAL, PLAYA		3978	3382	2984
	Total Staterooms		10	Port Charges	138	

Organization	LOVERS OF ARCHAEOLOGY

Promotion Arrangements

Estimated Date of Mailing/Promotion
Review Date   5/01/92
Option Date   5/15/92
Unsold block space may be recalled on review or option date indicated

Reimbursements for co-op agreements will be expedited only upon receipt of sufficient back-up.

Brochures Quantity/Type: 100 RACKS
Postage....: RCL PAYS 50%   Max $14___
        Total Commitment:..: Max $14

Early Bird Fares apply to bookings made until: 6/01/92

Group Escort Policy: 1 Per 20 AIR/SEA OR 1 Per 15 CRUISE ONLY

Amenities:

10% GROUP EARLY BIRD DISCOUNT $25 PER PERSON BAR BOUTIQUE
GRP COCKTAIL PARTY (45 MINS)   ONE BOTTLE OF WINE PER CABIN
FREE AIR FR RCL SELECT GATEWAY

Remarks:

010% commission on net amount.
ODYSSEY CLUB MEMBERS RECEIVE $100 PER PERSON SHIPBOARD CREDIT.

AGREED UPON THIS   23   DAY OF   APRIL   1992

BY

BY   TITLE
        Travel Agent

Figure 6.3 A typical cruise line contract. It does not necessarily reflect Royal Cruise Line's policy. (Courtesy Royal Cruise Line.)

soring/originating air carrier. Many carriers no longer require it.) It is the coordinating carrier that provides shells for the brochure, assists in a promotional evening, and determines on whose plate the group's air tickets must be validated.

The coordinating carrier does more than book the air. It becomes, in effect, a co-sponsor, a working partner in the tour venture. It is important to have a good working relationship with this carrier and its personnel so that the parties have a sense of mutual respect and an understanding of each other's role.

When selecting an air carrier, there are some important questions to consider.

❑   Does the carrier have good inflight service, scheduling, and equipment; or are you compelling the group to accept inferior passenger service in order to earn a higher commission or strike a better deal? If the service of two carriers is comparable, it is to your advantage to accept the best deal possible. But expect the clients to be angry about enduring a five-hour wait at Heathrow Airport in London enroute to Geneva, especially if they discover there was a direct flight to Geneva five hours earlier on another airline. Obviously, such a situation, no matter what financial savings it offers, is to be avoided.

❑   Does the airline have a group desk with which to work directly, or will it be necessary to work through a go-between or deal with a one-person local sales office? (Note: it is important to distinguish between **group desk** and **tour desk**. The group desk is the department that will process the group air reservations; the tour desk is the department that sells that particular airline's own in-house tour packages.)

❑   Does the airline have fast and accurate airfare quote capacity, or is its rate desk piled high with a three-week backlog?

❑   Will the airline willingly provide group flight confirmations and fare quotes in writing? (It is essential to have a written fare quotation in the file before publishing a brochure.)

❑   Does your staff work well with the personnel at the airline selected? Key personnel on whom you will depend will be the account executive from the sales office, as well as the people on the group and rate desks.

❑   Does the airline have suitable and attractive shells available in the quantities that you will need? Travel agencies and tour operators have been known to select a certain carrier solely because of its attractive shells or other promotional pieces.

❑   Does the airline want the business on this particular routing and at this particular time of the year? Or, does the airline give the impression that, since this is the peak season, group business is not needed for a route that is already heavily booked? Does it appear that the airline is not interested in booking low-cost, low-yield passengers such as Advance Purchase Excursion (APEX) fares or short-sector flights?

❑ Can you negotiate an override commission or other form of supplemental income and promotional monies with the carrier?

❑ What additional services might the airline offer the group enroute? For example, use of its VIP lounge? A passenger service representative to meet and assist in moving from international to domestic gates? In-flight complimentary headsets or drinks?

❑ And very importantly, must you make up-front deposits (sometimes non-refundable) to hold the space? If you do agree to pay the deposits, are you penalized by the air carrier if you do not ultimately utilize a certain percentage of the seats?

BOOKING AIR RESERVATIONS

The golden rule of group tour operations is *put it in writing*. It is also essential to *get it in writing*. Start by requesting all of the group space in writing from the coordinating carrier. At present, it is not possible to book group space (i.e., for 10 or more no-name passengers) through an automated reservation system, but this policy may change in the future. Although many airlines are willing to take group bookings on the telephone, this is not a good idea unless the phone call is followed up with a letter or fax.

Since each airline has its own system for handling group reservations, it is best to check with the airline account executive first to ascertain if the booking letter should be sent to the sales department or directly to the group desk. In some cases, sending a letter to the account executive may delay it, since he or she may be out on sales calls and may not forward it to the group desk promptly. In other cases, the airline may require that the booking letter go through the sales department before it can be processed by the group desk. If contacting the group desk directly, be sure to send a copy of the letter to the account executive as a courtesy.

Before writing to the airline, however, it is important to prepare either a reservation card or a group air-booking form. See Figure 6.4 for an example of a booking form. A **group air-booking form** is used in-house to record replies from the "controlling airline" as they are called in to the agency. It is quite likely that the airline will call today with confirmations on one or two flights, tomorrow with another, and so forth. These can be easily recorded manually on the master group air-booking form as they are called in, since the written recap of space confirmation probably will not arrive until considerably later when the bulk of the flights are confirmed. Note that this form should contain spaces to record flight dates, flight numbers, and total number of seats desired on each flight sector. It should also have a space to record the date each flight is confirmed, the name of the airline employee confirming the space, and the exact status of each flight; namely confirmed, wait-list, unable, and so forth.

GROUP AIR BOOKING FORM

Rosemont Country Club

NAME OF TOUR European Highlights Tour   YEAR 1992   DEPARTURE DATE SEPT. 4   NO. PAX 32

                  312-391-8780 SALES

CONTROLLING AIRLINE TW   PHONE 800-327-1337 GROUP DESK   PERSON Jane Johnson   RECORD LOCATOR NO. 2612

FARE BASIS (GIT, ITX ETC.) Apex

DAY OF WEEK	DATE	AIRLINE FLIGHT, CLASS	FROM/TO	ETD/ETA	CONFIRMATION STATUS, DATE, AND BY WHOM
Fri	04SEP	TW746Y	ORD/JFK	12:50/15:57	RQ 9/30/91 Jane. HK 10/06 Martin
Fri	04SEP	TW814B	JFK/AMS	18:45/07:05 +1	RQ 9/30/91 Jane. HK 10/06 Martin
			AMS/CDG	Surface	
Fri	11SEP	AF630Y	CDG/FCO	08:35/10:35	RQ 9/30/91 Jane. No reply-reserviced 10/08 Jim
Mon	14SEP	TW845B	FCO/JFK	11:00/14:10	RQ 9/30/91 Jane. HK 10/08 Jim
Mon	14SEP	TW757Y	JFK/ORD	16:30/17:56	RQ 9/30/91 Jane. HK 10/08 Jim

Figure 6.4 Group Air Booking Form.

As a checklist, it is important to include all of the following information in the booking letter to the airline:

❑ Name of tour or group organization, departure date, and year—at the top of the letter for easy identification

❑ Number of seats and class of travel for each sector

❑ Type of airfare or fare basis (Advance Purchase Excursion—APEX? Group Inclusive Tour—GIT? and so forth). Many flights are capacity controlled; there may be space on the plane but not in the fare category requested.

❑ Flight by flight, a list of each flight desired, using the proper two letter airline codes and three-letter airport codes. For example, BA 001Y SA 02 APR JFK/ LHR 19:15/08:05 + 1. (Translation: British Airways Flight No. 1, economy class, on Saturday, April 2nd, from New York, Kennedy Airport, to London, Heathrow airport, departing at 7:15 p.m., arriving at 8:05 a.m. the following date, April 3rd.)
Note: Flight numbers usually are expressed in three digits, even if two of them are zeros (some are now even four digits). **Airport codes** are used, not **city codes**. This becomes extremely important in cities that may have more than one airport, such as London with Heathrow and Gatwick; New York with Kennedy, La Guardia, and nearby Newark. Even worse is the case of Iguassú Falls; the code IGU means Iguassú, Brazil, whereas IGR means Iguazú, Argentina, located on the opposite side of the falls.

It is important to use the 24-hour time system. Although many airlines and computers in the United States are now on 12-hour times, the professional travel counselor knows that only the 24-hour time system can truly guard against what could turn out to be a mammoth error. And, as we proceed through the 1990s to the turn of the century, it is anticipated that our airline computers will ultimately interface with international reservation systems in Europe and elsewhere, so the 24-hour clock may appear on your computer screen in the future. If you are unfamiliar with this system, it is essential to take the time to learn it. Figure 6.5 illustrates the 24-hour clock.

If several legs of the itinerary are via surface (e.g., train, ship, or motorcoach), it is necessary to indicate this in the booking letter so that there are no open sectors in the continuity of the flight itinerary.

At the end of the letter, be sure to indicate what the airline should do next. It should never be assumed that the airline will automatically send a written confirmation and fare quotation; ask for it. The airline should also be asked to put in writing such things as the basic commission, overrides, shells, promotional assistance, policy on tour conductor complimentaries, and whatever else is pertinent. See Figure 6.6 for a sample airline booking letter.

It is important to have all of the details confirmed in writing in the file before starting to promote the tour so that there are no misunderstandings later. It also develops good work habits to have neat, clean, and orderly files so that anyone on

TIME	24-HOUR TIME	PRONUNCIATION
1:00 A.M.	01:00	oh one hundred
2:00 A.M.	02:00	oh two hundred
3:00 A.M.	03:00	oh three hundred
4:00 A.M.	04:00	oh four hundred
5:00 A.M.	05:00	oh five hundred
6:00 A.M.	06:00	oh six hundred
7:00 A.M.	07:00	oh seven hundred
8:00 A.M.	08:00	oh eight hundred
9:00 A.M.	09:00	oh nine hundred
10:00 A.M.	10:00	ten hundred
11:00 A.M.	11:00	eleven hundred
12:00 NOON	12:00	twelve hundred
1:00 P.M.	13:00	thirteen hundred
2:00 P.M.	14:00	fourteen hundred
3:00 P.M.	15:00	fifteen hundred
4:00 P.M.	16:00	sixteen hundred
5:00 P.M.	17:00	seventeen hundred
6:00 P.M.	18:00	eighteen hundred
7:00 P.M.	19:00	nineteen hundred
8:00 P.M.	20:00	twenty hundred
9:00 P.M.	21:00	twenty-one hundred
10:00 P.M.	22:00	twenty-two hundred
11:00 P.M.	23:00	twenty-three hundred
12:00 MIDNIGHT	24:00	twenty-four hundred

Examples:

    (1) 8:05 P.M. would be "twenty oh five"
    (2) 2:15 P.M. would be "fourteen fifteen"
    (3) 11:59 P.M. would be "twenty-three fifty-nine" (Note that many midnight flights are listed this way to be sure of date)
    (4) 9:10 A.M. would be "oh nine ten"

Notes Regarding Crossing Dateline or Time Zones

    (1) Plus one (+1) means one date later. For example, if one says "The flight leaves Tuesday at 14:00 (fourteen hundred) and arrives at 17:00+1, this means it arrives at 5:00 P.M. on Wednesday.

    (2) Minus one (−1) means one date earlier. For example, if one says "The flight leaves Tuesday at 14:00 (fourteen hundred) and arrives at 17:00−1, this means it arrives at 5:00 P.M. on Monday.

All flight times listed in airline schedules always are the local times observed in the cities specified.

Figure 6.5 The twenty-four hour clock.

LSI Travel Agency
987 Park Drive #2A
Berkeley, CA 94704
Telephone Number: 510-555-2000
Fax Number: 510-555-7210

October 17, 19XX

Mr. Jeffrey Whelan
Trans World Airlines
5678 20th Street
San Francisco, CA 94901

RE: Rosemont Country Club
European Highlights Tour
Departing Sept. 04, 19XX

Dear Jeffrey:

This will reconfirm our telephone request today for the following group space, 32 seats, economy class, APEX fare basis, throughout:

Fri.	04SEP	TW	746	SFO/JFK	12:50/15:57
Fri.	04SEP	TW	814	JFK/AMS	18:45/07:05+1
Surface				AMS/CDG	
Fri.	11SEP	AF	630	CDG/FCO	08:35/10:35
Mon.	14SEP	TW	845	FCO/JFK	11:00/14:10
Mon.	14SEP	TW	757	JFK/SFO	16:30/17:56

Now, here's what we'll ultimately need from your office to "wrap up" this project:

(1) Space confirmation, in writing.
(2) Current fare quote, in writing-both for SFO and JFK originating passengers.
(3) IT number.
(4) Your policy on override commissions.
(5) Sample shells (after seeing what you have available we'll either decide to use your shell or do our own original brochure. We'll need 3,000 shells, if we do decide to use them, and would need to know the cost, if any).
(6) Policy on tour conductor.

We look forward to working with TWA on this group and hope the tour will sell well.

Cordially,

Marty Sarbey de Souto

Marty Sarbey de Souto, CTC
Group Manager

MFS/s

Figure 6.6 Airline booking letter.

the staff can pick up the file and work from it without having to ask a lot of questions. It is conceivable that one person might negotiate and book the tour but then turn it over to someone else to operate, or that the person who booked the tour might be ill or out of the office. Hand-scribbled notes and word-of-mouth promises from the airline should be avoided.

Negotiating with the Airlines

Before deregulation, airfares were standardized on all carriers, and negotiating was nonexistent, at least as it related to commissions and overrides. Airlines did help tour operators and travel companies by "buying" large quantities of nonexistent brochures, supposedly for airline promotional use. Many other under-the-table schemes were elaborately conceived to circumvent the rules and regulations.

Today, this situation no longer exists. Today, negotiations are all open and up front. You can negotiate almost anything. But remember that you will probably be going up against experienced airline personnel who are much more sophisticated at negotiating than many travel counselors. Therefore, before going into negotiations with an airline, it is important to be familiar with some of the airline remuneration concepts associated with group travel.

Upfront Monies.   **Upfront monies** refers to money that an airline may be willing to pay your company up front (before the fact) to assist in promotional expenses; that is, monies paid before any sales result. Obviously, this is more useful than after-the-fact monies, such as override commissions. If an airline is giving you up-front help, it is sharing the risk; if the tour sells well, you both benefit; if it fails, the airline loses, too, as it already has expended the money, just as you have on a lost cause. If the airline is putting money up-front, then it can be more demanding. For example, it can insist that the promotional piece be mailed by a certain date or that it have sole occupancy of the envelope.

Higher Commission.   Prior to airline deregulation, all airlines were obligated to pay the same commissions. In the United States, it was 8 percent for an international air ticket plus an extra 3 percent for a total 11 percent if the air ticket were sold in conjunction with a prepaid land tour package with an IT number. The travel company had to put this IT code number on the air ticket to ensure receiving the 11 percent.

Today, since airline deregulation very few air carriers still follow that format. Most international airlines simply expect you to negotiate with them for the amount of commission to be granted on air tickets issued for your tour. The amount may vary depending on season, route, type of airfare, and other factors.

The airline may offer different types of commission plans. The first might be a straight commission percentage on the entire value of the air ticket (except on the tax). A second plan might be an increasing volume commission, so that on a large group you would get more commission than on a small group. A third plan might pay volume commission based on total annual sales of the travel company issuing the air tickets, whether or not the sales volume pertains to a specific tour or not. Many travel companies have such "preferred supplier" contracts already in place with certain airlines.

A fourth plan might be to pay a basic commission on the total value of the tickets and then an override commission. Such overrides are usually paid after the tour has returned and are not deducted from the weekly ARC ticket report that the company files when reporting the original ticket sale. It's important to realize that such override commissions are usually paid on the net online revenue only (i.e., after the basic air commission is deducted).

They are not paid on the total gross price of the ticket and not on the sectors flown by other airlines (interline sectors). Under this arrangement, let us assume that a company is working with an Around South America itinerary at a per person airfare of $1,000, using Varig Brazilian Airlines as the originating carrier. Varig has offered to pay you a 5 percent override on the net online Varig flight segments. Out of the $1,000 total gross fare, $600 is on Varig; the other $400 is on interline carriers such as Avianca, Argentine Airlines, and so forth. The override would be calculated as follows:

Value of air ticket, without tax	$1,000
Flights of other carriers	-400
Value of Varig's flights (gross online revenue)	600
Less basic 11% commission on $600	-66
Net value of Varig's flights, (net on-line revenue)	$ 534

You are paid 5 percent on the $534 figure, or $26.70 per passenger. That is quite different from 5 percent on the $1,000 gross ticket value, which would have been $50 per person. Note that commissions are never paid on tax.

Checking the Confirmations

Once the confirmation of space and the rate quote are received, they must be examined carefully. Information must be double-checked to make sure the flights confirmed are those requested and that the times of departure and arrival are as requested. You should also check option dates, any special sales cutoff date, special deposit date, and ticketing date pertinent to the specific airfare. Before filing the airline correspondence away, all important dates must be recorded on the master calendar for action on the appropriate date. Even if the airline doesn't require that certain dates be adhered to, it is wise to write on your calendar 90/60/30 day review dates (i.e., 90/60/30 days before departure) so that you can take the initiative and contact the airline group desk with a progress report rather than waiting for them to follow up. Such efficiency sets a professional tone. (See Chapter 11 for more details on handling 90/60/30 day reviews.)

HANDLING GROUP HOTEL SPACE

Once the flights are confirmed (or at least most of them), the next step in the booking order is to obtain hotel reservations. There are five methods of booking group hotel space:

1. Booking all hotels and other ground services through a U.S.-based wholesaler
2. Booking each hotel directly, by letter, fax, or telephone
3. Booking through a hotel chain's sales office, such as Hilton, Sheraton, Intercontinental, and so forth—if the hotel desired belongs to such a chain
4. Booking through a hotel representative (i.e., a hotel "rep"), such as John A. Tetley, Utell International, and so forth
5. Booking with the overseas receptive services operators who will be handling the tour in each country and having them include the hotels as part of their package in that geographical area.

If the itinerary is complicated, with 15 to 20 different hotels, booking methods might be combined within the same tour; certain hotels might be booked directly and others not. The following are some of the advantages and disadvantages of the different methods.

Advantages and Disadvantages of Booking Hotels Through a Wholesaler

Some advantages of booking hotels through a U.S.-based wholesaler are:

❑ Usually the wholesaler has a toll-free telephone line, and you can consult locally and quickly about hotel selection, confirmation status, final name lists, and so forth. Time and money are not expended in contacting the hotels.
❑ The wholesaler probably has better annual contract rates than you can ever hope to negotiate on an ad-hoc tour basis (unless you are booking very large volume or a series of tours).
❑ The wholesaler probably knows his hotels better than you do (e.g., their reputation, key personnel, problems, quirks, and so forth).
❑ If a problem should occur, you have local recourse in U.S. courts.

Some disadvantages of booking hotels through a wholesaler are:

❑ You do not have rapport with the hotel in your company's name.
❑ If you insist on using certain hotels that the wholesaler may not use regularly, his or her rates may not be any better than those you can secure directly.

TABLE 6.1   Booking Hotels Through a Wholesaler

Advantages	Disadvantages
Saves time and money	Cannot develop company rapport with hotels
Better annual contract rates	Low rates only on hotels used often by wholesaler
Better information about hotels	Financial risk if wholesaler is not dependable
Local recourse in U.S. courts	

❏   You must have faith in the reputation of your selected wholesaler to be sure that this company holds the space claimed. What happens if your wholesaler goes bankrupt? (See Table 6.1.)

Advantages and Disadvantages of Contacting the Hotel Directly

The following are some of the advantages of direct contact with the hotel:

❏   Information comes directly from the source. There is a confirmation on hotel letterhead signed by an hotel official. There can be no dispute later as to whether the hotel space was confirmed or not; the letter proves it.

❏   Rapport and your company's reputation are established with the hotel. The hotel people will grow to know your company. Your group will not be just tour number 6704 of a given wholesaler.

❏   There is no middleman to interpret details (or perhaps misinterpret them). You will not have to depend on someone else for information on whether rates are net or gross, if breakfast is continental style or American style, when deposit is due, or what the hotel's complimentary policy is.

Disadvantages of contacting the hotel directly include the following:

❏   Time is taken up in corresponding with each hotel property, not only at time of booking, but later when submitting booking reports, final rooming lists, payment, and other items.

TABLE 6.2   Contacting the Hotel Directly

Advantages	Disadvantages
Get first-hand information	Time consuming
Develop a personal rapport	Expense of calls/faxes
	May have to pay more

❑ There can be waiting time for answers, particularly if done by mail. If space is requested by fax, waiting time is not such a problem.

❑ The hotel may not know your company and may not give priority on space or its best rates.

❑ It's expensive to call or fax a number of hotels overseas.

❑ If the hotel people do not know your company's track record, they may demand more in terms of early deposits, final payments, and option cutoff dates than they would ask of an established group operator. (See Table 6.2.)

Advantages and Disadvantages of Using a Chain Sales Office

When a hotel chain's sales office is used, you can gain the following advantages:

❑ You build credibility with a particular chain. Even though your company may be totally unknown to the management of the Sydney Hilton, if it contacted that property directly, you might have booked the Hong Kong Hilton heavily in the past. Your company record would be known at the Hilton International sales office.

❑ As a solid client of Hilton, the international entity, your company would have more influence.

❑ Speed. One phone call does it all. The hotel chain's sales office contacts its individual property and gets back with a quick answer. (Most hotel chain offices do not have a sell-and-report policy for immediate confirmation of group space. Even they have to go to the specific property in question to request group space.)

❑ Answers are available to questions about the property. The chain office should know its own properties well enough to answer questions on such things as location, meeting room facilities, and current rates. They may, however, have to contact the property for advance rates or for answers to more detailed questions.

TABLE 6.3   Using a Chain Sales Office

Advantages	Disadvantages
Can build credibility	Use more expensive hotels
Faster	Finalization often not handled by
Qustions can be answered	the chain office—just the initial
	booking

The disadvantages of using a hotel chain's sales office include the following:

❑ The decision to use a hotel chain's sales office often means that you are limiting yourself to the larger, more expensive hotels—hotels that can support an elaborate marketing and reservation system. Perhaps the property that might be best for the group will not be selected in the interests of speed and efficiency.

❑ Even if rooms are booked initially with the hotel chain office locally, later correspondence will nevertheless be with the hotel personnel at the property itself, probably with the sales manager or the front office manager. Once the group space is confirmed, booking status reports, deposits, or final rooming assignments would not be made through the chain office. (See Table 6.3.)

Advantages and Disadvantages of Booking Through a Hotel Rep

The following are some advantages of using a hotel rep:

❑ Speed is an advantage if the rep, in turn, books the space by phone or fax. (If all the rep does is write a letter, then your company might as well book directly.)

❑ The rep can answer questions about the property if he or she really knows the property well.

There are also some disadvantages of booking through a hotel rep, such as the following:

❑ Many reps act on behalf of so many different hotels that they are not truly knowledgeable about the details of any one of their properties. Similarly, many are so busy handling independent bookings that they are not geared to han-

```
┌──────────────────────────────────────────────────────────┐
│          TABLE 6.4   Booking Through a Hotel Rep          │
│                                                          │
│  Advantages                Disadvantages                 │
│                                                          │
│  Faster service            May not know details          │
│  Questions answered        May not be geared to handling │
│                               group bookings             │
└──────────────────────────────────────────────────────────┘
```

dling group bookings, and they do little more than act as a go-between for your company. (See Table 6.4.)

Advantages and Disadvantages of Booking with a Receptive Services Operator

Many companies find it best to let their overseas receptive services operator simply include the hotels as part of their overall package of sightseeing, transfers, and so forth in their country. This is particularly convenient in rural areas. You may not know the pros and cons of a hotel in, for example, interior Brazil, whereas you may know the hotels in Rio. If it is a crucial time of the year (e.g., New Year's Eve in Acapulco, Carnival in Rio, the Olympics), the only chance of getting hotel space may be through a receptive services operator who already has large blocks of space reserved for his own packages.

Booking hotel space through a receptive services operator has the following advantages:

❑   It may be the *only* chance of getting space at certain key times of the year.
❑   These local operators know the local properties better; they have probably developed a rapport with the right personnel at each hotel and know which hotels are appropriate for which clientele.
❑   These operators can monitor the reservations locally on the spot. If it appears that the hotel is heavily oversold, they may put in a deposit for you and keep the tour group's name in front of the hotel staff.
❑   Your receptive services operator may give such a large volume of business to certain hotels that you can ride on their reputation and get better rates at those hotels.

There are, of course, disadvantages of booking through a receptive services operator. These include:

❑   The time lag is the same as if booking the hotel directly.
❑   The receptive services operator will keep a portion of the commission, or if getting a net group rate, will mark it up before quoting a price.

TABLE 6.5 Booking Hotels Through a Receptive Services Operator	
Advantages	**Disadvantages**
Can get space at key times of year	Normal time lag
Can match hotels with clientele	May charge mark-up
Can monitor reservations locally on spot	RSO could be financial risk
Can get better rates at some hotels	Pressure to use RSO's favorite hotels

❑   You must have absolute trust in the receptive services operator and must be sure that you are working with a reputable and financially sound operator. If the operator goes out of business, you will be in trouble. If you are considering working with a receptive services operator, check with your sponsoring air carrier and with some other tour companies or travel agencies that have used this RSO to determine the RSO's strengths and weaknesses.

❑   The operator may try to push you into using a hotel that you do not like. This might occur if the operator has a good relationship with that particular hotel, occur because the company gets a good override from the hotel, or occur because the company owns the property itself. (See Table 6.5.)

Choosing the Right Group Hotel

Regardless of what method is used to book the hotel space, it is important to select the right type of hotels for each specific group. Sometimes tour members are unpredictable. When they first buy the tour, they may say that a hotel room is not really that important, that they are not going to do anything other than sleep in the room, and that all they really want is a clean and comfortable bed and a hot bath at the end of a weary day. Yet, these same clients sometimes complain bitterly if the hotels do not live up to some subliminal expectations. Although clients might say that it is the "travel experience" that is most important, the two things that can quickly ruin a trip are bad hotels and a bad motorcoach. Therefore, it is important to give serious consideration to the hotels that are selected before they are booked and to evaluate them objectively and professionally. Here are some factors to consider when deciding on a hotel for a group.

❑   Location. Is the hotel centrally located in town so that the tour members can get out to shops and cafes? A central location is not so important for a quick overnight stop. However, no one wants to be stuck in a motel alongside the highway for a three-day stay. If a hotel is out of town, take into account the coach availability and costs for transfers in and out of town.

❏ Type of clientele. Do families, singles, honeymooners, or conventioneers frequent the hotel? Group members should feel comfortable and in step with the other hotel guests.

❏ Does the hotel cater to groups? Some hotels may surprise you. They may not want your group! Many groups are noisy. Groups mean suitcases lined up all over the lobby and massive check-ins and check-outs all at once.

❏ Image. Some hotels are just a place to sleep. Others are cozy country inns. Some are resorts and can be sold on the basis of their beach, golf course, or tennis courts. Some hotels are slick and modern; others pride themselves on an old-world atmosphere with afternoon tea served in the lobby.

❏ Standard level of hotels throughout the tour. You do not want a wild swing from a luxury hotel one night to a rundown one the next. An ultra-modern hotel and an old-world one might be included in the same itinerary, but they should be comparable in class. If all hotels are not the same level, then up-grade as you go along, saving the best hotel for last, not the other way around.

❏ Lobby. Check that the hotel has a lobby; a lobby is a great place for a group to meet for sightseeing in the morning or to gather over a drink in the evening. Some less expensive hotels forego lobby space in the interests of economy and are a good bet for student tours looking for budget rates.

❏ Dining room/coffee shop. Some quite lovely hotels, particularly smaller ones, may not have dining facilities, which requires that the tour members go out-side the property even for a cup of coffee. Similarly, many hotels may have a formal dining room that requires a coat and tie, but no quick informal cof-fee shop. Twenty-four hour room service is also a great amenity.

❏ Dining plan. Many hotels want to support their dining room and thus require that guests take meals at the hotel. Acapulco during the winter season is an example. And many of the better European hotels will not accept groups during peak summer months without a meal plan. When planning a tour without meals, it is important to research the policy of mandatory meals first.

❏ Ease of baggage handling. Can the hotel move baggage quickly and easily? Some charming colonial hotels in Yucatán, for example, can handle a maxi-mum of one busload of passengers at one time. If two busloads arrive at the same time, with only two small elevators and one bellman on duty, the group may not get its luggage until the wee hours.

❏ Motorcoach loading space. Is there a place for a tour bus to park to load and unload passengers and baggage? Trying to unload 40 passengers with a traf-fic police officer threatening to ticket your driver can be unpleasant.

❏ Special considerations for senior citizens. For example, consider elevators, stairs, amount of walking to/from rooms, security, and so forth.

❏ Wheelchair facilities or other needs for the physically challenged traveler.

❑ Other amenities. Find out if the hotel has a laundry, gift shop, beauty salon, money exchange, concierge, multilingual staff, spa, swimming pool, and sports facilities such as golf or tennis.

❑ Meeting facilities. If you plan to have a welcome cocktail party, briefing, or farewell dinner, does the hotel have private dining rooms available? What about meeting rooms? If meetings or a convention are involved in the trip, are there necessary facilities (i.e., audiovisual, microphone, translators, photocopy, fax, and secretarial services)?

Requesting the Hotel Space

Once the first choice of properties has been selected and the decision has been made on how to book them, it is time to request the reservations. What information does the hotel need when the booking is made? And what information must be received from the hotel in its reply to allow the tour to be priced properly?

The booking letter or fax should include the tour name, the arrival date, the departure date, and how much space is needed. It is important to specify not just the number of rooms or people, but also a breakdown on how many twin-bedded rooms and how many singles are required. In some cases, when families are involved, triples may be needed. The term *twin* and not *double* should be used. Double implies one double bed, which might be acceptable to some of the couples on tour, but not to two ladies who are strangers to each other. (The abbreviations TWB for twin with bath, DWB for double with bath, and SWB for single with bath are almost universally understood in the trade.)

The letter must specify the dates of arrival and departure, termed the **in date** and the **out date**. It should say "in January 5, out January 7," not "January 5 to 7." Meal arrangements desired should be specified. It is also helpful to the hotel to advise them of the arrival flight number and the name of the receptive services operator who will be transferring the group to the hotel. That way, if the group is late, someone will be able to find out what happened to them.

It cannot be assumed that the hotel will automatically give all the needed answers in its reply. It is best to ask direct questions and delineate what answers you expect in the reply letter. See Figure 6.7 for an example of a hotel booking letter.

Answers Needed from the Hotel

❑ Written confirmation of space, indicating specifically how many twins, singles, triples, or quads the hotel is confirming.

❑ Written confirmation of rates—rate per twin, single, triple, or quad per night. (If the hotel does not have rates available for the following year, the current rates should be requested and a percentage added to cover anticipated increase.)

LSI Travel Agency
987 Park Drive #2A
Berkeley, CA 94704
Telephone Number: 510-555-2000
Fax Number: 510-555-7210

FAXMEMO

October 17, 19XX

Mr. Hans Van der Hooten
Sales Manager
Hotel Krasnapolsky
Dam 9, 1012 JS
Amsterdam
The Netherlands

RE: Rosemont Country Club
European Highlights Tour
Arriving Sept. 05, 19XX

Dear Hans:

We would like to book another tour with you. Kindly confirm 14 twins, 4 singles for a maximum total of 32 passengers, for a three-night stay, in Sept. 05, 19XX and out Sept. 08, 19XX.

The group will arrive Amsterdam at 07:05 via TW 814 from New York and will be transferred to your property by our ground operator in Amsterdam, Transbus.

With your confirmation, please advise rates per twin and per single, and specify if net or gross and if in U.S. dollars or Dutch guilders. Also indicate any taxes or service charges applicable, as well as your policy regarding complimentary for the tour manager.

Rooms are to be reserved European Plan. Any meals taken at the hotel will be at passengers' own expense and should be charged to their personal accounts, not to the master account.

Should you have next year's room rates available now, we would appreciate them. If not, please just confirm the space and give us current rates for now.

Thank you, and awaiting word . . . .

Sincerely,

Marty Sarbey de Souto

Marty Sarbey de Souto, CTC
Group Manager

MS/s

Figure 6.7   Sample hotel booking letter that may be mailed or sent by fax to expedite.

❑ Clarification as to whether rates quoted are gross (commissionable) or net (noncommissionable) group rates. This is important, since all tour costings are done in net figures. (Note: Stay away from run-of-house rates for groups. These are fixed rates but with the hotel giving you better rooms if they are available when you check in. If a hotel can upgrade *everyone* in the group, run-of-house rates work. But if only a few are upgraded and, thus, receive better rooms than others in the group, this can cause terrible dissention in the group.)

❑ Percentage of tax.

❑ Percentage of service charge, if any, to cover gratuities to hotel staff.

❑ Policy on complimentaries for tour manager(s). Remember that there is no standard worldwide policy; each hotel will have its own. Complimentaries can range from one free bed with each 15 booked up to one free bed for each 40 booked. Sometimes complimentaries are based on a free room for so many rooms booked, sometimes on one bed for so many beds booked. Sometimes the complimentary includes group meals; sometimes it does not. The exact nature of complimentaries should always be clarified.

❑ Any special services such as meeting rooms, welcoming drink, and so forth.

When sending their confirmations, many hotels may specify review dates and payments. It is important when the confirmation comes in to record all those dates on the master calendar so that important review dates do not slip by. There may be option offerings; that is, a hotel may offer the space **on option** but expect you to reply by a certain option date, sign a contract, or submit a payment to pick up the option. If these expectations are not met, the hotel may cancel the offer automatically.

Most larger hotels today will make clear what they expect; that is, when they want payment, when they need a rooming list, and so forth. But it is wise to anticipate this at the time of requesting the space. For example, your letter might say: "Our company policy is to send you booking status reports at 90, 60, and 30 days prior to the group's arrival, with final rooming list and one night's deposit 30 days prior. Balance of payment will be paid by our office post-tour, upon receipt of your itemized bill. If this arrangement is not satisfactory, please advise." This gives your company credibility with the hotel as a serious operator. Nine times out of ten, the hotel will agree with the policy. However, there will always be times when the hotel will want one night's deposit at once to prove that you are serious; or, in some cases, such as the Olympics, it might even ask for a sizable upfront payment. These times, fortunately, will be rare. There will also be hotels that will insist on total prepayment before the group arrives. Many hotels, particularly the large chain hotels, may reply with a formal contract. See Figure 6.8 for a sample hotel confirmation.

In communicating with hotels, you will encounter jargon peculiar to the hotel industry. Any unfamiliar terms should be looked up to avoid misunderstanding. The standard glossary is *The Dictionary of Tourism*, edited by Charles J. Metelka, published by Delmar Publishers Inc.

MARTY'S INTERNATIONAL HOTEL
15 Rue Camoni
Paris, France

October 15, 19XX

LSI Travel Agency
891 Park Drive #2A
Berkeley, CA 94704

RE: Rosemont Country Club
Arriving Sept. 08, 19XX

Dear Ms. de Souto:

Thank you for your request of reservations for your Rosemont Country Club group, 42 maximum for three night in September 8, out September 11, 19XX. We are pleased to confirm 18 twins, 6 singles.

Our rates are 1000 francs net per night per twin and 760 francs net per night per single. In addition there is an 8% tax and 20% service. Rates include continental breakfast.

We will be happy to provide one complimentary single room for your escort with a minimum of 40 paying passengers in the group.

An initial one night's deposit is due now. Final payment and rooming list are due 30 days before arrival.

With all best wishes for success in your sales endeavor.

Sincerely,

Pierre Lapin
Sales Manager

PL/mg

Figure 6.8 Typical hotel group booking letter of confirmation. Many hotels send contracts or confirmation forms instead of letters.

Hotel Terms You Should Know

Most hotels will assume that travel counselors know their terminology. Here are some of the most frequently used phrases:

- ❑ **Rack rate**. The highest rate for a hotel room; the rate published on their public rate sheet and posted in the rack for the guest who walks in the door. As a group operator you should *never* settle for this rate! It is for the individual guest.
- ❑ **Gross**. The rate before commission has been deducted. A gross rate assumes that the hotel pays a commission, usually 10 percent—but always check. For example, in Germany the commission can often be only 8 percent; in some areas, when business is slow, it can be 15 percent; and there are still many hotels that pay no commission.
- ❑ **Net**. Rate after commission has been deducted.
- ❑ **Net net**. Rate after any commission has been deducted and any taxes or service charges have been added.
- ❑ **VAT (Value Added Tax)**. A government tax charged straight across-the-board on top of the rate quoted. It is not applicable in all countries, and it is sometimes called a "goods and services tax," as in Canada.
- ❑ **Run-of-house rate**. A flat rate for all rooms used by the group. Theoretically, the hotel is supposed to assign the best available rooms in the house at the time that the group checks in. This may mean that some members of the group get better rooms than others. Therefore, run-of-house should be avoided for groups.
- ❑ **Service charge**. Refers to a flat fee charged to cover gratuities to hotel staff-room maids, bellmen, telephone operators, and others. In many hotels this is a mandatory charge and theoretically is supposed to take the place of tipping (though many people still leave a small tip in addition).
- ❑ **European plan (EP)**. Rate for accommodations without meals.
- ❑ **American plan (AP)**. Rate for accommodation with three meals. Often the lunch and dinner will be restricted to a specific dollar amount, to meal coupons, or to a particular dining room.
- ❑ **Modified American plan (MAP)**. Same as American plan, but usually without lunch—born of beach resorts for guests who did not wish to come in from the beach and dress for lunch.
- ❑ **Full pension**. Full board, the European version of American plan. Usually implies continental breakfast (or breakfast as is the custom of the country concerned) rather than full American breakfast, plus lunch and dinner on a *table d'hote* basis (set menu). Often it is in a specified dining room and sometimes at a specified time when the group is served together.
- ❑ **Half pension** (also **demi pension**). Half board, the European version of modified American plan. Usually implies continental breakfast rather than full American breakfast, plus choice of lunch or dinner with the same restrictions as full pension.

Pricing Hotel Accommodations

The hotel may quote **gross rates** (commissionable) or **net rates** (non-commissionable). Regardless of which is quoted, it will be necessary to convert the rates into net rates, since net rates are the common denominator of the group tour business. Group tours are never costed on a gross basis. Three sample hotel rate quotations are outlined below.

Sample One. A hotel quotes a rate of $100 per night gross for a twin-bedded room, plus 10 percent tax and 15 percent service charge. They pay 10 percent commission. Therefore:

Basic gross rate for two	$100
10% tax on $100	+ 10
15% service charge on $100	+ 15
Total gross per night per twin	125
Less 10% commission on the basic gross rate	– 10
Net net rate per twin per night	115

The figure of $115 is divided by two in order to arrive at the per person cost of $57.50 per night. If the group were staying at this hotel for three nights, the per person cost would be $57.50 × 3 nights for a total of $172.50. Remember that this is net net; that is, what the tour operator will be charged for the client's hotel stay. This is not what the client pays your company. Note that in the United States neither the 10 percent tax nor the 15 percent service charge are commissionable. For more complete information on costing see chapter 7.

Sample Two. A hotel quotes you a net rate from the outset and, therefore, it is not commissionable. The hotel quotes a rate of $90 per night per twin room plus 10 percent tax and 15 percent service charge. Therefore:

Basic net rate for two	$90.00
10% tax on $90	+ 9.00
15% service charge on $90	+ 13.50
Total net net rate per twin per night	112.50

The figure of $112.50 is divided by two in order to arrive at the per person cost of $56.25 per night. If the group were staying at this hotel for three nights, the per person cost would be $56.25 × 3 nights for a total of $168.75. Here again, this is net net, what you pay the hotel and not what the clients pay your company.

As one can see from the examples, if you are quoted rates in gross, the client is costing you $57.50 per night. On the other hand, if you are quoted rates in net, the same client is costing you only $56.25 per night, which is a savings to you of $1.25 per night. It is always advantageous to secure quotations in net group rates whenever possible.

Many *experienced* tour operators may prefer to request quotations in the currency of the country concerned. That way, you can watch the dollar exchange rate and you can decide when the foreign exchange is advantageous to buy. (Note: This can be risky; foreign currency rates can just as easily move against you as in your favor. For this reason, most U.S. and Canadian operators prefer to be "safe than sorry" and get quotes in dollars from the outset to protect against currency fluctuations. However, many overseas operators may refuse to guarantee a quote in U.S. dollars.) A retail travel agency may not be accustomed to dealing with foreign exchange, since, for one or two clients, there rarely is sufficient profit to be made. But in dealing with groups, it is often possible to earn extra dollars just by carefully watching foreign exchange rates and buying foreign currency drafts at the appropriate time. Here is a sample quote in foreign currency.

Sample Three.   A French hotel quotes 1,000 French francs per twin plus 8 percent tax and 20 percent service charge. At the time of the quotation, the exchange rate is 5 francs to the U. S. dollar, therefore:

Basic net rate for two in French francs	fr 1,000
8% tax	+ 80
20% service charge on fr 1000	+ 200
Total per twin per night in francs	fr 1,280

To arrive at the per-person cost per night, the 1,280 French francs per room are divided by two, or 640 French francs per person. If the exchange rate were 5 francs to the dollar, the cost in U. S. dollars would be $128.00 net net rate per person per night.

If the group were staying at this hotel for three nights, the per person cost would be United States $384 net net.

BOOKING RECEPTIVE SERVICES

Once both the air reservations and the hotel space are confirmed, it is time to fill in the gaps, to add the missing ingredient, to consult that company whose services can make or break a tour; namely, the receptive services operator (i.e., a ground operator, inbound operator, land operator, or simply the initials RSO). This is the company on whom you will depend for good motorcoaches or bad, knowledgeable and helpful local guides or mediocre ones, gracious and personalized services or just average ones. This company will help the tour manager when there is a sick passenger, when someone has lost a tourist card enroute, or when the tour manager needs help in reconfirming air reservations enroute. Through this source, your company books sightseeing, transfers, local events, special motorcoach charters, cultural activities, special meals, visits to museums, and night life. In short, the day-to-day operation of the tour in the field will depend very much on the quality of the operator selected. So, the least expensive is not necessarily the best choice; anyone can bid low for the first chance to operate a tour. But experience and competence are necessary to handle emergencies and unforeseen events; and these attributes are worth paying for.

If you have not worked with such an operator previously, you might want to investigate the services of several operators in each city or country. Since it is often difficult to select an operator simply from a catalog listing or from a tariff, several sources should be checked.

The airline account executive may have useful information on the top operators. Consult particularly with the airlines that service the cities into which the group will be flying. KLM is certainly a better source of information on Dutch operators than Alitalia. The various government tourist offices can be helpful. Once a list of names and addresses of operators is compiled, your staff can contact these operators and request their tariffs and suggestions and ideas for the tour. Obviously, an operator who replies quickly and seems to be responsive is the kind of operator with which to work. Often, the tone of the operator's reply and the nature of the tariff will provide enough information for a decision. Did the company reply quickly? Did it provide easily understood rate breakdowns? Did it answer all the questions that were asked, so the tour planner can go on to cost and price the tour from the information sent? See Figure 6.9 for a sample excerpt from a receptive services operator's tariff.

An operator's tariff will outline specific services. However, existing services can be modified to meet the group's needs. There is no hard-and-fast rule that because Colonial City Tour No. 101 operates every morning at 9 A.M. that it cannot operate at 2 P.M. for your group. But there also may be a good reason why a tour operates at a specific time. Perhaps a certain museum on the tour is open only in the morning.

As in the letter or fax to the hotels, the name of the tour, arrival date (including year), flight, and maximum anticipated number of passengers should appear at the top of the letter to the operator. The letter should describe the day-by-day itinerary, outlining the services that the operator is to provide (i.e., transfers, city tours, package tours outside the city, meals, and other features such as baggage tips, social events or cultural activities). See Figure 6.10 for an example of a booking letter/fax to a receptive services operator.

It is essential to be explicit about what the RSO is expected to do, and what your company will be responsible for. For example, the operator should be told if the hotels have already been booked directly. Otherwise, the operator may assume that they are to book the hotels. Similarly, the operator needs to know which flights are being booked and ticketed as part of the international ticket that you are issuing and which flights, if any, the operator must ticket locally. The operator should also be told what information is expected in a reply letter, and on what number of passengers prices should be based. If your letter is not specific about numbers,

TREASURE TOURS
INTERNATIONAL

Government Licence n° A 447

Head Office : **PARIS**   15, rue de l'Arcade, 75008 Paris, France.
Telephone : (33) (1) 42 65 05 69 (nightline 42 65 61 17).
Cable : Treasure Paris. Telex : 290415 F Treas. Telecopier (Fax) : (1) 42 66 04 47.
Open 9:00 am to 6:00 pm Monday to Saturday.

Transfer Rates

All rates net per person, each way, in French Francs Fully inclusive of assistance and porterage at airport or station	INDIVIDUALS with private car or minibus and assistance of a multilingual chauffeur.					GROUPS with private coach, representative's assistance, porterage of 2 pieces of luggage per person at the airport or station. *One free leader for 20 paying.*					
Number of persons	1	2	3	4	5	6/10	11/15	16/19	20/29	30/39	40/48
Arrival or Departure (with assistance)						no supplement for Sundays and late or early flight					
City terminal/hotel or v.v.	395	230	178	168	160	198	141	112	96	78	70
Charles de Gaulle or Orly airport/hotel or v.v.	590	335	235	220	190	220	162	126	98	89	79
Charles de Gaulle airport/Orly airport or v.v.	840	480	335	310	270	310	220	175	152	125	116
Charles de Gaulle or Orly airport/station or v.v.	590	335	235	220	190	245	187	151	123	114	104

Half-Day Excursions

	INDIVIDUALS				GROUPS net per person			
	Private car (net per car) (admission not incl.)			Regular coach (net per person)	16/19	20/29	30/39	40/48
	Cat. 1	Cat. 2	Cat. 3					
Versailles Half-day + lunch, ending airport (Or vice versa) porterage airport incl. Description of the itinerary is the same as page 11 : Palace and Gardens (cost of lunch has to be added). * Rates include taxes for the Palace and a 2nd guide for groups from 31 to 60.	3110	2560	2125 *9:30 am daily except Mon.*	Not available.	364*	304*	304*	243* *9:30 am daily except Mon./public holidays.*
Fontainebleau and Barbizon Duration 4 hrs Drive through farmland (inspiration for such paintings as the Angelus, the Gleaners) to picturesque Barbizon, famous 19th Century art centre (studios of Millet, Rousseau etc.). Continue to Fontainebleau, with its 16th Century Renaissance palace built on the site of a medieval castle, containing collections of furniture, tapestries, porcelain etc., representing 700 years of French history. * Rates include a second guide for groups from 30 to 60.	2250	1800	1400 *150 km allowance daily except Tue. 9:00 am or 2:00 pm.*	229.50 *1:30 pm daily except Tue./Thu./ Sun./public holid. In Sum. 1:30 pm Wed./Fri./Sun. in Winter.*	260	216	204*	178* *9:00 am or 1:00 pm daily except Tue./ Sun. pm/public holidays, all year.*
Chartres Duration 5 hrs Drive via Sèvres and Ablis through rich farmland to the ancient city of Chartres. Visit the gothic cathedral – one of the finest in the world, and see the superb sculpture and stained glass windows (12th and 13th Centuries). See the graceful old houses, picturesque narrow streets, ancient town walls.	2750	2200	1700 *200 km allowance daily all year. 9:00 am or 2:00 pm.*	207 *Summer 1:30 pm Tue./Thu./Sat. Winter 1:30 pm Tue./Sat.*	244	195	184	160 *Daily 1:30 pm, all year.*
Giverny (Monet's Home) Duration 4½ hrs The Normandy Highway leads to Giverny, a charming village, located at the meeting of the Epte and Seine rivers. There, the artist Claude Monet decided to dwell and to satisfy his passions for painting, flower-growing and photography while living a country family life. In addition to Monet's home, skilfully restored to the state it was when inhabited by the artist, the guided visit will include the painter's workshop and a stroll in the exquisite garden. A thousand flowers, carefully chosen for their matching colours, the famous Japanese bridge and the ponds will restore to life the pictorial universe of the genial painter of water-lilies.	2750	2200	1700 *200 km allowance daily except Mon. from April to October. 9:00 am or 2:30 pm.*	243 *Summer only 2:00 pm Tue./Thu. from April 9 to Oct. 29.*	286	229	216	189 *Daily 8:00 am or 1:30 pm. Apr. to Oct. only, except Mon.*

Figure 6.9   Excerpt of tariff from a receptive services operator. (Courtesy Treasure Tours International.)

LSI Travel Agency
987 Park Drive #2A
Berkeley, CA 94704
Telephone Number: 510-555-2000
Fax Number: 510-555-7210

October 15, 19XX

Mr. Jean Claude Murat
President
Treasure Tours
15 rue de l'Arcade
Paris 75008, France

> RE: Rosemont Country Club
> "European Highlights Tour"
> Arriving Paris Sept. 08, 19XX
> Maximum 32 passengers

Dear Mr. Murat:

We would like to book the above-mentioned new tour with you. Kindly confirm arrangements and give us a cost quote on the following services:

Sept. 8   Meet and greet at Gare du Nord for arrival via train which leaves Amsterdam at 09:15 and arrives Paris 13:00. Immediately depart on your three-hour "Paris Complete Tour" and drop at Hotel Meurice at the conclusion. Include baggage transfer for maximum two bags per person. (We will instruct the group to have lunch on the train prior to arrival, so you will not have to make a lunch stop).

Sept. 9   Versailles morning tour inlcuding private motor coach and guide. Return drop at hotel in time for lunch on their own. Afternoon Paris Gastronomique Tour on an optional basis. Evening Lido tour—late show without dinner, including roundtrip private motor-coach transfers, champagne, entrance and tips.

Sept. 10   Morning walking tour of the Louvre including local guide. No coach transfer needed.

Figure 6.10 Sample booking letter to an RSO.

Sept. 11   Departure transfer Meurice/CDG Airport via private motorcoach, including baggage transfer, for AF 630 at 08:35 to Rome.

Please note we have booked the Meurice Hotel directly through CIGA's office in New York, so do not include hotel costs in your price quote. Similarly, we hold the air CDG/FCO and will ticket this sector here.

Although we hope to have 32 passengers, kindly quote with permutations of 15+1 and 30+2, specifying if quote is net or gross. The optional Gastronomique Tour should be quoted as a separate entity at 15+1. If you do not have your 19XX rates established yet, please give us this year's rates and we will add an anticipated margin for increase.

For continuity's sake, we would prefer to have the same guide assigned to our group throughout the Paris stay if possible. On our last group with you we enjoyed Monique Savin very much and would like to request her again if available.

Hoping to have your confirmation of services and price quotes as quickly as possible and looking forward to working with you again.

Cordially,

Marty Sarbey de Souto

Marty Sarbey de Souto, CTC
Group Manager

MFS/s

Figure 6.10 (Continued)

the operator will price the services based on the maximum number of passengers anticipated in the group. It is smart to ask for graduated prices (e.g., 20 + 1, 30 + 1, 40 + 2, and so forth). If the following year's prices are not available, the operator should be asked to quote in current prices, and a margin for increase will have to be included when costing the tour.

Once confirmations have been received from the various operators, the various review and payment dates should be noted on the master calendar. The correspondence then can be filed away.

The reputation that the receptive services operator maintains, in turn, with its own suppliers (e.g., local guides or hotels) will depend on the timeliness and accuracy of the information it receives from you. It is vital, therefore, that you make periodic progress reports with current booking status.

❑ SUMMARY

Negotiating and booking all arrangements for a tour is a detailed and time-consuming job. Some tour planners elect to do this themselves directly; others elect to work through a recognized wholesaler, thus devoting more of their time to the marketing and selling phase. The correct booking order is cruise, air, hotels, and receptive services operator. To eliminate misunderstandings, everything should be requested in writing (by letter or fax), and you should obtain written confirmation of all services before embarking on the marketing phase of a tour. All important review or payment dates, as well as dates on which you must submit final airline flight manifests and hotel rooming lists, should be entered onto a master calendar to be sure nothing is overlooked.

❑ REVIEW QUESTIONS

1. What is a receptive services operator and what sort of services does this type of company provide a group?

2. **What is the proper booking order?**

3. **Name three advantages and three disadvantages of cruises for groups.**

4. **What is CLIA and what can it do for you?**

5. **Define a "shell."**

6. What is the role of the coordinating (or sometimes called the originating) air carrier in a group tour?

7. Under what circumstances would you be most likely to get the best
deal from an airline for a group tour?

8. What do we mean by "surface legs" in an air itinerary?

9. Why are up-front promotional monies from a supplier more valuable than after-the-fact monies?

10. **Name three advantages and three disadvantages to booking your group hotel space directly with each hotel.**

11. **Compare Modified American Plan and Demi-Pension meal plans.**

❑ *ACTIVITIES*

1. Plan as though you were meeting with a cruise line representative to discuss putting a group aboard. Make a wish list of the special concessions you'd like to obtain from the cruise line for your group. Identify the items you'd be willing to forego if you can't get everything you want.

2. Select three possible hotels that you might like to use for a senior citizens group to London. Research them and then make up a chart comparing them in terms of price, central location, ambience, dining facilities, probable group-handling efficiency, and other similar factors.

3. Discuss the pros and cons of including most meals on a tour versus a tour with very few meals. Make a case for your position and be prepared to defend it against the opposite position.

4. Pretend that you are an inbound receptive services operator and that you have received a request from a foreign travel agent asking you to provide services to them for a group coming to your city. List what services you would provide them and what sort of review dates, deposits, and other data you would require of them.

▷ 7

COSTING AND PRICING A TOUR

LEARNING OBJECTIVES

After reading this chapter, you should:

❑ Know the basic points about costing that are common to the industry even though there is no standard costing method
❑ Learn to distinguish between variable costs and fixed costs
❑ Be able to make a checklist of items that should be costed into every tour
❑ Understand how tour operators make their profits through markups and profit margins, not through commissions
❑ Know where to look for cost reductions if it becomes obvious that your tour is priced too high

KEY CONCEPTS AND TERMS

Admission/Entrance Fees
Breakage
Charters
Costing
Fixed Costs
Forced Single
Gratuities
Per Diem
Pricing
Profit Margin
Pro-Rated
Risk Factor
Share-Room Basis
Single Room Supplement
Variable Costs

All the planning and negotiations described in the previous chapter will be wasted if one point is not kept in mind: *The purpose of a tour is to make money*! That may sound hard and cold, but it is true. Some companies may feel that a tour has one or more of the following purposes:

❑   A way to effect volume savings for a group, allowing members to travel less expensively than if they traveled alone
❑   A way to get public relations exposure in the community for their company
❑   A way to build a base of future clients who will return as individuals, or who will refer other business to the company
❑   A way to start an annual ongoing tour project
❑   A way to fill an otherwise slack period in the office.

Although all these purposes may be valid, the fact remains that unless a tour makes money, it is not successful. It may bring back a planeload of happy clients, promises of future business, and passengers who think very highly of the company, but this is not enough to justify the work of planning and handling the tour. If the tour was not profitable, it has failed—it is that simple.

It is likely that an unprofitable tour was incorrectly costed and priced from the outset. Effective costing and pricing are crucial to a successful group travel operation.

COSTING VERSUS PRICING

The discussion of costing versus pricing should begin with definitions of these terms. **Costing** is the laborious job of analyzing what each item on the tour will cost the company out of pocket. **Pricing**, on the other hand, is the process of determining what the company will charge the client for the tour. The difference between what the client pays (what comes in) and what the tour costs the travel company (what goes out) is earnings, or profit margin.

Costing might be considered an operational duty; the costing for a given tour may be prepared by the company's operations manager. Pricing, on the other hand, should be considered the duty of management after receiving costings and suggestions from those people involved in the operational details of the tour.

COSTING A TOUR

The travel industry has no sacrosanct method of costing. Ask one hundred different tour operators how they cost their tours, and there will be one hundred different answers.

Some tour operators use elaborate systems, charts, or percentages to calculate breakeven points. Others have been at it for so long that they can virtually calculate in their heads and come up with a figure so close to the real thing that it is uncanny. Still others are mispricing, and they have been doing so for years. The fact that they are still in business is purely a coincidence.

But here are some basic points about costing that are pertinent to any effective costing procedure and that are common to the industry:

- ☐ Tours should be costed in bottomline net figures with any commissions deducted, not in gross figures which have a commission in them.
- ☐ Tours should be costed on minimum enrollment expectations, not maximum.
- ☐ Most earnings come from markups, not commissions.
- ☐ A group tour project must be thought of as an entire unit, and earnings must be thought of in terms of per project rather than per client.

Figure 7.1 shows a sample costing worksheet. The following discussion tells what information is needed to obtain the figures that appear on such a worksheet.

VARIABLE VERSUS FIXED COSTS

Tour costs may be segregated into one of two major categories: variable costs and fixed costs.

Variable Costs

As the term implies, **variable costs** vary with the number of passengers in the group. These are best thought of as costs related to the individual passenger. Samples of variable costs are meals, hotel accommodations, taxes, tips, airfares, admission fees, and sightseeing tours. Note that these are items for which the company is not charged unless the passengers are present to use them.

Fixed Costs

Fixed costs do not vary with the number of passengers in the group. They are best thought of as costs related to the project as a whole. Some samples of fixed costs are promotional charges (e.g., brochures, printing, advertising, direct mail); free trips for the organizers; the tour manager's salary and expenses; and **charters** of planes, motorcoaches, or ships. Miscellaneous lump sum payments, such as a museum donation, would also fit into the category of fixed costs.

Many fixed costs, particularly promotional costs, are referred to as **upfront costs**; that is, costs that must be paid for in advance of the tour. Because these items are paid for before it is known whether the project will be a success or not, they are often thought of as risk factors.

Rosemont Country Club Europe Tour

LAND TOUR EXPENSES		VARIABLE (PER PERSON) EXPENSES	FIXED (PER PROJECT) EXPENSES
Quote from Amsterdam operator	$280.00		
Oneway rail ticket AMS/PAR	64.00		
Quote from Paris operator	367.00		
Quote from Rome operator	325.00		
Flight bag and departure packet	7.00		
Total per person land tour expenses		$1,043.00	

FREE TRIP FOR SPONSORING ORGANIZATION

Airfare for club president, as no comp air	$800.00		
Land tour expenses Amesterdam operator, comp	0		
Rail ticket AMS/PAR comp at 15	0		
Land tour expenses Paris operator, comp	0		
Land tour expenses Rome operator, comp	0		
Flight bag and departure packet	7.00		
Total expenses for club president			807.00

TOUR MANAGER EXPENSES

Salary, 11 days at $75 per day	$825.00		
Variable land tour expenses from above	1,043.00		
Single room supplement, net	130.00		
Airfare—no comp air	800.00		
Miscellaneous—extra meals etc.	300.00		
Total expenses for tour manager			$3,098.00

PROMOTIONAL EXPENSES

Brochure, 3000 copies	$975.00		
Direct mail	2,006.00		
Promotional evening	595.00		
Advertising	925.00		
Total estimated promotional expenses			$4,501.00

TOTALS		$1,043.00	$8,406.00

Figure 7.1 Sample costing worksheet, page 1.

RECAPITULATION

Per person variable expenses	$1,043.00
Fixed expenses per project of 8,406 divided by 15 persons minimum in group	+ 560.40
Total net land costs per person	1,603.40
Profit margin—to make 25% profit on the gross, divide net 1,603.40 by .75 = gross land price	2,137.87
Plus gross airfare	+ 800.00
Total retail price, land and air	$2,937.87

PROFIT PICTURE AT 15 PARTICIPANTS

Retail land price per person	$2,137.87
Less net land costs per person	− 1,603.40
Per person land profit	534.47
Per person land profit of 534.47 per person × 15 persons minimum in group = per project land profit with minimum 15	8,017.05
Plus commission on airfare, 11% on $800 gross fare = $88 per person × 15 persons minimum anticipated participants = total airfare profit	+ 1,320.00
Total profit at 15 persons (8,017.05 land plus $1,320 air)	9,337.05

PROFIT PICTURE AT 30 PARTICIPANTS

Retail land price per person	2,137.87
Less net land costs per person	− 1,603.40
Per person land profit	534.47
Per person land profit of $534.47 per person × 30 persons in the group = per project land profit when group reaches 30 passengers	16,034.10
Plus commission on airfare, 11% on $800 gross fare = $88 per person × 30 persons	2,640.00
Plus savings on fixed expenses for 15 passengers (that is for passengers #16 through #30), since the project's fixed expenses have already been covered by passengers #1 through #15. $560.40 × 15	8,406.00
Total profit at 30 persons ($16,034.10 land plus $2,640.00 air plus $8,406.00 savings on the last 15 passengers to join the group)	27,080.10

** Note at 30 passengers, tour membership has doubled but profits have virtually tripled, since tour was priced on minimum expectations from the start.

Figure 7.1 Sample costing worksheet, page 2.

SPECIFIC VARIABLE COSTS

Hotel charges, meals, tips, sightseeing tours, entrance or admission fees, and airfares are example of specific variable costs.

Hotel Charges

Whether hotel reservations are booked through a wholesaler in the United States or through a receptive services operator overseas, the hotel accommodations will be included in the total package price quote to you. However, if hotel accommodations are booked directly with the hotels, it will be necessary to calculate those costs on a night-by-night basis. This is fairly easy for a short, single-destination tour. However, if the itinerary is fairly long and complicated with many different hotels being used, costing hotel charges becomes a lengthy process.

Most advertised tour prices are based on a **share-room basis**—half the twin-bedded-room rate. The quoted per night twin-bedded room rate should be divided by two to arrive at the per person nightly rate. If working with student groups or ski packages based on minimum-share dormitory or share chalet accommodations, it may be preferable to cost the tour on three or even four to a room.

As an added check, a mental walkthrough of the trip night by night ensures that sleeping accommodations have been costed in for each and every night (except when spending the night on planes, ships, or trains).

Single-Room Supplements. Although most tours are priced on the share-room basis, it is also common practice to publish in the brochure the tour price of a single room. This is frequently called the **single-room supplement**; that is, the additional amount a passenger must pay to have a room for single occupancy. This is usually shown in the brochure as:

Tour price, per person, from New York, share-room basis	$2,995.00
Single-room supplement	389.00

Or, it may be expressed as:

Tour price, per person, from New York, share-room basis	$2,995.00
Single-room basis	$3,384.00

The amount of the single room supplement night by night must be calculated, or a quotation requested from a wholesaler, if one is being used. It is usually possible to obtain the single room supplement quotation in net figures, which then must be marked up to give you your profit margin.

Of course, there may be tours to certain destinations where single rooms are not offered or cannot be guaranteed. There also may be tours on which a tour operator does not wish to offer passengers traveling alone the option of sharing with a stranger, thus forcing such passengers into singles at the higher fare (termed a **forced single**). Such decisions are strictly management policy decisions; they vary from company to company.

Taxes, Service Charges, and Foreign Currencies.   National or regional governments may impose taxes on a variety of services, such as hotel accommodations, meals, and other items. In some cases, these taxes may be included in the quotation. In other cases, the taxes may be quoted as a flat amount or as a percentage. In this case, the actual amount must be calculated. For example, a hotel may quote a twin room rate of $100 plus 10 percent tax and a 15 percent service charge. That total of 25 percent on top of the $100 makes the room rate $125.

Any quoted taxes and service charges should be added to the hotel charges, because these costs can be sizable in many countries. In the best circumstances, hotel rates will be quoted on a net (non-commissionable) basis. But if they are quoted gross (commissionable), the net figure can be found by deducting the commission. The net per person figure is then entered on the costing sheet. When deducting commissions, keep in mind that commissions are not paid on taxes or service charges.

When foreign currencies are involved, they should be converted into U.S. dollars at the exchange rate of the day. It is a good idea to jot down the exchange rate used and the date when the hotel calculations were completed.

Meals

The variable individual cost of meals may be handled in a number of ways. In some cases, meals will be included with the hotel accommodations, as when booking American Plan, Modified American Plan, Full Pension, or Demi-Pension meal plans (see glossary for explanation of each). However, the budget may still be augmented by costing in for extra tips to waiters and the *maitre d'* or for additional meal items not included in the hotel meal plan. In other cases, it may be decided to keep the tour price low by omitting all meals. On more deluxe, all-inclusive tours, all meals may be included, either on a set menu *table d'hote* basis or on *à la carte* basis. In this case, an estimated per meal or **per diem** figure can be used, based on what the current rate is in the various countries or cities concerned. *À la carte* meals that passengers do not eat, or that they undereat (not spending as much as budgeted) constitute a savings to the company and are what is called **breakage**, which is an item budgeted for but not used.

Tips

Tips, or **gratuities**, come in all forms: those to waiters, maitre d's, or wine stewards; those to local sightseeing guides; those to porters for luggage handling at airports, piers, and trains; and those to bellmen at hotels. It is important to determine specifically what tips already have been covered in the services quoted, what

MONTE CARLO

A classic Cote d'Azur resort surrounded by picturesque countryside . . . palaces, casinos, rich villas, luxurious shops and flowered terraces.

Departure Dates:

Pre	Post
Jul 19	Jul 29
Jul 26	Aug 5
Aug 2	Aug 12

Your land arrangements include:

▶ Three nights accommodations at the Loews Monte Carlo in Monte Carlo.

▶ American breakfast daily.

▶ Service of local Olson-Travelworld agent.

▶ All applicable taxes and gratuities.

Package Price:* $830.00

6-NIGHT CITY PACKAGES

ROME AND VENICE

The Eternal City . . the ancient Colosseum and modern Via Veneto . . . the splendors of the Vatican. Romantic gondolas, the Piazza San Marco . . . the Cathedral of St. Mark.

Departure Dates:

Pre	Post
Jul 16	Jul 29
Jul 23	Aug 5
Jul 30	Aug 12

Your land arrangements include:

▶ Three nights accommodations at the Cavalieri Hilton in Rome.

▶ Three nights accommodations at the Hotel Danieli in Venice.

▶ American breakfast daily.

▶ Service of local Olson-Travelworld agent.

▶ All applicable taxes and gratuities.

Package Price:* $1770.00

MADRID AND SEVILLE

Sophisticated city highlights paired with the ancient city of Seville . . . museums and palaces offset by lazy afternoons at a cafe.

Departure Dates:

Pre	Post
Jul 16	Jul 29
Jul 23	Aug 5
Jul 30	Aug 12

Your land arrangements include:

▶ Three nights accommodations at the Eurobuilding Hotel in Madrid.

▶ Three nights accommodations at the Hotel Sol Macarena in Seville.

▶ American breakfast daily.

▶ Service of local Olson-Travelworld agent.

Package Price:* $1920.00

---

* Package and tour price based on per person double occupancy rate. Single, triple or quad rate available upon request.

Moscow

11

THE SOVIET UNION & EASTERN EUROPE

Rewarding but Different

A trip to the Soviet Union and Eastern Europe is a highly satisfying travel experience but it is also one for the most adventurous traveler.

The Soviet Union, in particular, does not have hotels and services of the same standards as Western Europe. Indeed, the accommodations can be rather austere. Therefore patience and understanding can sometimes be the order of the day!

At Olson-Travelworld we have contracted with Intourist, the government tourist office of the Soviet Union, for accommodations and services that Intourist designates as First Class. The meal plan is that which Intourist describes as deluxe. However, they should not be compared to similarly described hotels and restaurants in Western Europe.

Despite these difficulties, a trip to Eastern Europe is a deeply rewarding experience which will undoubtedly leave you with many lasting memories to be cherished.

7-NIGHT ESCORTED TOURS

MOSCOW AND LENINGRAD

St. Basil's Cathedral, the Kremlin and Red Square . . . Pushkin, Tolstoy and the Bolshoi Theater. The Hermitage Museum, St. Isaac Cathedral and the 18th-century Stroganov Palace.

Departure Dates:

Pre	Post
Jul 15	Jul 29
Jul 22	Aug 5
Jul 29	Aug 12

Your land arrangements include:

▶ Four nights accommodations in Moscow and three nights accommodations in Leningrad at deluxe and/or first class hotels.

▶ All transportation within the Soviet Union.

▶ Three meals daily exclusively from deluxe menus.

Figure 7.2   This page from a tour brochure shows the variable costs of meals handled in two different ways.   On the independent packages, breakfast only is provided.   On the escorted tours, three deluxe meals are included daily. (Courtesy of Olson-Travelworld, Ltd.)

additional tips must be costed in, and what tips the passengers must pay for out of pocket themselves. Again, a walkthrough of the tour day by day, move by move, meal by meal will ensure that no tips have been overlooked. Taking the word of your wholesaler or receptive services operators that "all tips are included" can sometimes result in a costing error of $50 or more per passenger. When this is multiplied by 40 passengers, it could be a disastrous $2,000 reduction in the tour's profit.

Sightseeing Tours

In many cities, your company will be contracting for city sightseeing tours. These may have been quoted as part of the overall per person package or they may have been itemized. This is another breakage item; if the receptive operator quotes sightseeing on a per person basis (not a chartered coach basis), your company should not be charged for passengers not present on sightseeing tours. To be safe, determine whether or not the quoted price is based on a stated minimum number of passengers.

Entrance or Admission Fees

Entrance or **admission fees** include fees charged by museums, castles, and other similar attractions on the itinerary; for special church donations to allow the tour into the inner sanctum; or for theatre and festival tickets, and so forth. Many tour brochures promise, "Today we see the XYZ Museum." And that is exactly what the travelers do. They see it—from the outside. If the tour leaves the motorcoach and goes inside, an entrance fee is paid. Be sure to determine if the quotation given includes the entrance fees, and if the guide actually escorts the group inside and explains what they are seeing (or hires a local guide to take the group around), or if the tour members are merely turned loose to explore on their own. There is a big difference in the cost of these two approaches.

Airfares

Airfares are usually quoted on a gross basis, and traditionally they are not marked up by the tour operator. Usually, the land portion is priced separately, net, then markup on the land tour is added, and last the gross airfare is added. Some airlines are changing this approach and are quoting tour operators net airfares. In this case, tour operators must mark up the airfares.

A CLOSER LOOK AT FIXED EXPENSES

Fixed expenses for a tour include the cost of printing a brochure, advertising, promotional evenings, direct mail, tour manager's salary and expenses, organizers, charters, and miscellaneous lump sum expenses.

Brochures

Producing a tour brochure is a fixed cost because the price of printing a certain number of them remains constant whether 13 people or 113 people join the tour. In fact, even if nobody joins the tour, the cost of producing the brochure remains. Production costs include typesetting, layout, pasteup, art, photography, paper stock, and printer's charges.

Advertising

The cost of an advertising campaign for a tour project is also considered a fixed cost. Here again, the charges are not related to the number of people who join the tour. Advertising costs are constant, and they are related to the project as a whole. This category of costs includes production costs for the ads, such as typesetting, art, layout, and pasteup, as well as the actual publication costs.

Promotional Evenings

Another fixed cost of the tour is a promotional evening. This category includes such things as invitations and postage, room rental, food and drink, and miscellaneous costs such as slide projector rental and paying for the door prizes or gifts.

Direct Mail

No matter how small the mailing list, direct mail promotional costs are considered fixed costs. This would include the cost of envelopes, cover letters, postage, and labor charges for stuffing and sealing envelopes, running off and affixing address labels, and bundling and delivering the envelopes to the post office.

Tour Manager's Salary and Expenses

Still another major fixed cost is the cost of the tour manager. Obviously, if the tour organizer is qualified, experienced, and willing to act as the tour manager on tour, that will keep the tour cost down, since such an individual will usually accept the responsibility in exchange for nothing more than a complimentary trip. On the other hand, it is unrealistic to expect to have a professional tour manager without being willing to budget properly for such an individual. Most smoothly operated tours budget for a real "pro," and they cost in accordingly for the tour manager's salary and enroute expenses.

A tour may carry both a professional tour manager *and* an organizer who earned a free trip. There will not be enough complimentaries from the hotels, airlines, and other suppliers to take care of both individuals; therefore, it will be necessary to use the complimentaries accrued for one of these individuals and pro-rate the full cost of the other individual's trip over the amount charged to members of the group.

Organizers

Free trips for tour organizers (i.e., Pied Pipers) are fixed costs. In some cases, the organizer can be unreasonable. Spouse, children, and secretary may be expected to travel on a complimentary basis. Never say no! Just point out that as many free trips as desired can be costed in simply by pro-rating them over the amount charged to the other members of the group. When the organizer realizes that the tour price is increasing by $300 or so for each free trip, he or she will understand the economics of the situation, which requires that the tour price remain competitive so that it will sell. Otherwise, there is no tour and no free trip for anyone. Usually, organizers want one free trip for 15 paid passengers and two for 30, but hotels rarely give one for less than 40, and many airlines do not give any free air tickets anymore—at least not when the lower priced promotional airfares are used. Check with your air carrier.

Charters

Whether it is a chartered airplane, boat, motorcoach, or villa, the fact remains the same: the entire entity must be paid for whether or not it is filled. Charters may be considered the ultimate fixed cost. The airline that charters its aircraft to a company is not interested in whether that plane is filled or not; the charge will be exactly the same amount whether there is one passenger aboard or 300. Most tour operators who handle charters frequently figure their costs on the assumption that they will only partially fill the plane. They never pro-rate the cost of the aircraft over the 100 percent occupancy figure—that is too risky.

Not only is there a risk factor of filling the plane, but there are also stiff payment deadline dates that must be met. These are often dates after which the flight cannot be canceled, even if the tour membership falls off. Or, if the flight is canceled, the agency may risk incurring sizable financial penalties. Therefore, charters should be **pro-rated** on a minimum or average membership expectations, not on maximum. The same would be true for motorcoaches, chartered yachts, and so forth. If the motorcoach holds 43 passengers, pro-rate over 25 or 30 passengers.

Miscellaneous Lump Sum Expenses

A multitude of miscellaneous expenditures are usually costed on a group project basis, rather than on an individual passenger basis. An organization might have been promised a $1,000 donation. Or perhaps there will be a large reception on tour, with 50 foreign guests invited to meet the tour group. Maybe there was an agreement to buy a certain painting for the museum sponsoring the tour.

One tour operator specialized in tours to remote South Pacific villages. He budgeted whole village projects, such as a new town sewer, into the tour costs, since the villagers would not accept payment for home hospitality offered to his group tours. These items, whether gifts or donations or goodwill social gestures, must ultimately find their way into the costing of a particular tour or series of tours. They are considered lump sum expenditures in the category of fixed expenses.

MARKUPS OR PROFIT MARGINS

Markups are no great mystery. They are the lifeblood of any tour. There is no right or wrong amount of markup. Perhaps we should say that the right amount is a markup that allows the company to make a reasonable profit to justify the time, expense, and risk. The wrong amount of markup is one that is either so low as to have inadequately compensated all involved, or so high as to make the tour non-competitive and nonmarketable. A markup may also be so low that it does not give the operator any room to move, any room to do what is right by a group to cover an error, or to surprise them with a nicety. Some operators may mark up the net land cost as little as 10 percent; some as much as 40 percent. But a 25 percent profit margin is usually adequate to cover your company, while still being fair to the client.

To understand profit properly, it's important to understand terminology. It's a terminology that many in the travel industry may not understand themselves and still use incorrectly.

The term **markup** means, as the word implies, increasing something, working from the bottom *up* to the top. For example:

$1,000	Net tour costs
+250	Mark*up* of 25% of the net figure of $1,000
$1,250	Sell price

As you can see, the above example means putting a percentage of the bottom, net $1,000 figure on top of it to arrive at the higher sell price of $1,250.

Note, however, that this 25 percent markup on the net is not 25 percent of the $1,250 sell price. The $250 markup is only 20 percent of the sell price figure $1,250. In other words, to be accurate, you have marked the net *up* 25 percent, but you are making 20 percent profit on the sell price $1,250 figure. This 20 percent figure is properly referred to as **profit margin**. The profit margin is the difference between what you take in on a tour project and what you pay out. As you can see, the dollar figure hasn't changed; it's still $250. But that same $250 represents 25 percent of the net and 20 percent of the sell price.

Many retail travel agents when first entering the group travel field make this mistake. They are accustomed to working with gross prices, commissionable at 10 percent. So, if they suddenly find themselves working with net figures, they simply add 10 percent and assume they are making 10 percent. For example:

$1,000	Net tour costs
+100	Markup of 10% on the net figure of $1,000
$1,100	Sell price

But 10 percent of the $1,100 sell price is $110, not $100, so they are really only making about 9 percent on the $1,100 sell price.

A more correct way to price a tour is to forget about marking up the net. Instead, work with the profit margin method. In this method, you determine what percentage of profit on the sell price you wish to make, but you don't know what the sell price should be.

Perhaps, for example, you are quoted a $1,000 net price. You wish to make 25 percent to wholesale the tour, keeping 15 percent for your company and passing 10 percent on to others selling the trip for you. You want to know what price tag to put on the tour to do that. *That formula is to divide the net price by a percentage, which is 100 percent minus the percentage you wish to make.* To make 25 percent, divide the $1,000 net by 75 percent to arrive at a sell price of $1,333. For example:

Step 1	Step 2
100%	$1,333 Sell Price
-25%	.75)$1,000 Net Price
75%	75
	250
	225
	250
	225
	250
	225

The $1,333 sell price would be broken out as follows:

$1,000.00	Net tour costs to be paid out by your company to operate the trip
133.30	Commission payable to your selling source (10% of $1,333)
199.70	Profit margin retained by your company (15% of $1,333)
$1,333.00	Total sell price

In this sample, the sell price of $1,333 is a figure arrived at mathematically. However, once that mathematical figure has been determined, it may prove desirable to round up or down. For example, the price $1,339 may prove more marketable than $1,333. In fact, a savvy decision maker might decide to drop the price to $1,325, even down to $1,299, and to delete a tour activity to bring the price down in line with the desired sell price.

Of course, any figures you wish can be plugged into the formula. If you wish to make 35 percent, you would deduct the 35 from 100 to arrive at 65 percent. Then, divide the 65 percent into the $1,000 net price to give you a sell price of $1,538.

Remember, it is not customary to mark up gross airfares. Therefore, the earnings of a tour come from the markup or profit margin on the land portion of the tour, plus whatever commissions and overrides are received from the airlines.

Estimating When Prices Are Not Known

There may be occasions when the actual costs for a particular item on the tour are not available. For example, a hotel may not have next year's rates established and may quote this year's rates. Often, it is not possible to hold up the promotion on the tour while waiting for that one hotel to make a decision. In this case, it may be necessary to take this year's rate and pad a reasonable amount, say 15 percent. This is the "pad and pray" method. Never price a complete tour this way; it is far too risky. However, occasional items within the framework of the tour may have to be costed on this basis when nothing more accurate is available.

Noncommissionable Items

Note that because the tour operator's earnings are not premised on commissions, rather on markups over the project as a whole, you are free to utilize noncommissionable resources and services. For example, university dormitories, private homes, country inns, theatre performances, lectures, cooking demonstrations, and fashion shows could be components of a fine tour. Yet, none of these pays commission. One company turned down a group that was to utilize university accommodations overseas because "they couldn't make any commission on it." Obviously, this company was thinking individual client handling, not group handling. Subsequently, a local university bought the idea of doing an overseas summer campus program based on this very concept; that is, utilizing university dormitory accommodations, which were not normally in use during the summer months. The project spawned several such far-flung campuses, at a profit to the tour company behind the idea.

SAMPLE TOUR SCENARIO

The following is a sample tour that demonstrates how the costing and pricing theories work. Please note that the figures in this sample are for demonstration purposes only.

A company is planning an 11 day, 10 night tour to Europe for the Rosemont Country Club (see chapter 5 for details of the itinerary and conditions). Although the tour has been booked for a maximum of 40 passengers, the company has decided to price it on a minimum of 15 passengers and has guaranteed to operate it if the club has at least 15 paying adult participants. The club president has been offered a free trip for herself at 15 paying passengers; but since she is not an experienced tour manager, the company has offered to send a professional tour manager along. All promotional expenses will be paid by the company.

The airfare selected is the Advance Purchase Excursion (APEX), on which the airline does not grant a complimentary air ticket. A sample costing sheet for this tour is shown in figure 7.1. As figure 7.1 shows, the airfare is not entered into calculations until the end, as it is a gross airfare and is not marked up. Note that the receptive services operators in Europe have quoted their prices on the basis of 15 + 1; that is, one complimentary for 15 paying participants. If the one complimentary is used to give the president of the country club a free trip, it means costing in the trip for the professional tour manager, since the suppliers do not give enough complimentaries to pass along two free trips (i.e., one to the club president and one to the professional tour manager).

Another solution might have been to ask the European receptive operators to quote on 15 + 1 and 30 + 2. In that case, the first complimentary accrued at 15 could be used for the professional tour manager, and the country club could be told that their president would receive a complimentary trip at 30 tour participants.

OTHER COSTING CONSIDERATIONS

The costing sample shows a basic tour with no complicated factors to be costed into the tour price. Remember that each custom-designed tour may have its own needs. If the company is required to make large deposits in advance to hold reservations, it might be necessary to cost in interest on borrowed money. If sending a member of the company staff as tour manager instead of hiring an outside professional, it might be necessary to cost in the fee for hiring a temporary worker in the office while the regular staff member is out on tour.

In addition to looking at other miscellaneous cost factors like those mentioned, you should also look at other sources of profit potential for every group. These could include commissions to be made on domestic air reservations to connect to the group flights, sale of travel insurance; and most importantly, additional commissions called **override commissions** from airlines, cruise lines, or other suppliers.

EVALUATING THE PRICE

Once the tour is costed and a price has been decided upon, it might be wise to review a number of competitive tours in the marketplace to see how pricing compares. Undoubtedly, yours will be more expensive. Major tour wholesalers with multideparture programs have certain savings not available to smaller *ad hoc* operators. Major tour wholesalers buy on a volume basis and probably receive lower wholesalers' rates. Many of their fixed expenses, such as advertising and brochure publishing, can be pro-rated over a series of monthly tours instead of being absorbed by one single tour departure. In addition, perhaps they keep tour managers stationed overseas and do not have to pay air transportation to send them back and forth.

On the other hand, you should not feel obligated to meet the price of these giants. If a small operator is offering a product that is unique to the marketplace, and if this product includes special features such as a renowned leader or private entrée to peoples and places to which the average traveler does not have access, then the price cannot even be compared.

Ways to Reduce the Price

If it appears that the tour price is totally out of line and that it must be brought down, the planner faces a number of choices. Obviously, it is necessary to settle on less earnings to the company or to bring costs down. The following are a few alternatives:

- ❑ Consider shortening the tour by a few days or simplifying the itinerary. Make part of the tour the "basic tour" and the balance a "post-tour option" at a separate supplemental price.
- ❑ Cost the tour on a higher minimum expectation. If it was previously costed on 15 passengers, consider redoing it based on 20 (thus operating it with a minimum of 20 instead of 15).
- ❑ Go back to the bargaining table. Can lower rates or higher overrides be negotiated from any suppliers?
- ❑ Consider using a tour manager who lives overseas.
- ❑ Convince the sponsoring organization that its demands for complimentaries are unrealistic, and that they are forcing the tour price up into a non-saleable price bracket.
- ❑ Lower the hotel category by one level throughout. (Do not lower some hotels and not others.)
- ❑ Drop all meals except perhaps a welcome and farewell meal function.
- ❑ Plan on a less-expensive tour brochure, flyer, or other promotional piece.
- ❑ Look at other profit possibilities surrounding the project (e.g., sale of optional tours, travel insurance, or pre-tour and post-tour arrangements).
- ❑ Piggyback the mailing if doing direct mail. Can the brochure be mailed in the same envelope along with another brochure to a different, noncompetitive destination? Although this divides the reader's attention, it also divides the postage and other mailing expenses.
- ❑ Publish more than one tour in the same brochure and thus pro-rate the cost of the brochure over more than one tour. For example, if the company is selling three winter programs—a Caribbean cruise, a golf week in Hawaii, and a Mexico tour—package them all in one brochure under one umbrella theme such as "Winter Sun Getaways."

Usually, the major price savings are found in the fixed costs (i.e., brochures, promotional costs, complimentaries, and leadership), rather than in the variable cost category.

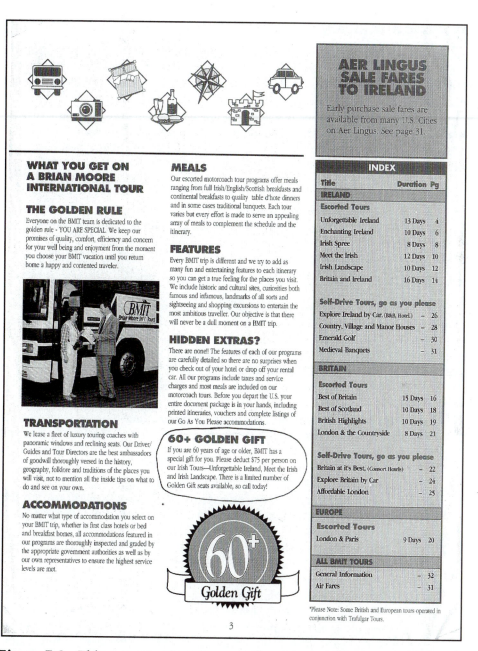

WHAT YOU GET ON A BRIAN MOORE INTERNATIONAL TOUR

THE GOLDEN RULE

Everyone on the BMIT team is dedicated to the golden rule - YOU ARE SPECIAL. We keep our promises of quality, comfort, efficiency and concern for your well being and enjoyment from the moment you choose your BMIT vacation until you return home a happy and contented traveler.

TRANSPORTATION

We lease a fleet of luxury touring coaches with panoramic windows and reclining seats. Our Driver/Guides and Tour Directors are the best ambassadors of goodwill thoroughly versed in the history, geography, folklore and traditions of the places you will visit, not to mention all the inside tips on what to do and see on your own.

ACCOMMODATIONS

No matter what type of accommodation you select on your BMIT trip, whether its first class hotels or bed and breakfast homes, all accommodations featured in our programs are thoroughly inspected and graded by the appropriate government authorities as well as by our own representatives to ensure the highest service levels are met.

MEALS

Our escorted motorcoach tour programs offer meals ranging from full Irish/English/Scottish breakfasts and continental breakfasts to quality table d'hote dinners and in some cases traditional banquets. Each tour varies but every effort is made to serve an appealing array of meals to complement the schedule and the itinerary.

FEATURES

Every BMIT trip is different and we try to add as many fun and entertaining features to each itinerary so you can get a true feeling for the places you visit. We include historic and cultural sites, curiosities both famous and infamous, landmarks of all sorts and sightseeing and shopping excursions to entertain the most ambitious traveller. Our objective is that there will never be a dull moment on a BMIT trip.

HIDDEN EXTRAS?

There are none!! The features of each of our programs are carefully detailed so there are no surprises when you check out of your hotel or drop off your rental car. All our programs include taxes and service charges and most meals are included on our motorcoach tours. Before you depart the U.S. your entire document package is in your hands, including printed itineraries, vouchers and complete listings of our Go As You Please accommodations.

60+ GOLDEN GIFT

If you are 60 years of age or older, BMIT has a special gift for you. Please deduct $75 per person on our Irish Tours—Unforgettable Ireland, Meet the Irish and Irish Landscape. There is a limited number of Golden Gift seats available, so call today!

Golden Gift

*Please Note: Some British and European tours operated in conjunction with Trafalgar Tours.

3

Figure 7.3 This operator is using an effective marketing technique by offering seniors a $75 discount on the land tour. This discount must be subtracted from the anticipated profit at the time the tour is costed. (Courtesy of Brian Moore International Tours/Aer Lingus).

Decision Making Based on Costing

As sometimes happens, closer toward departure date it may become apparent that the tour is not going to "make it." Perhaps it was costed based on 20 passengers, but only 17 have enrolled. At this point, it becomes necessary to make a quick decision whether to operate the tour or cancel.

Such a decision should be reached by going back to the drawing board, reviewing cost sheets, and reconstructing the tour price from scratch, based on 17 passengers instead of the hoped for 20. Never make an emotional decision to operate or cancel a tour without looking at the total financial picture.

Of course, there are considerations other than financial ones, such as:

❑ Loss of credibility with passengers
❑ Possible loss of the sponsoring organization as a future client for a future tour program
❑ Loss of credibility and reputation with suppliers
❑ Low staff morale at failure of the project.

As a rule of thumb, if a great deal of money has already been spent on promotion (e.g., several thousand dollars on the tour brochure, advertising, and direct mail) it is probably best to operate the tour. Even if you only break even, the books will not show a large loss for promotional expenses already paid. However, if operating the tour puts you further into the red, that is another matter.

If it is a losing proposition, here are some alternative suggestions:

❑ Cancel the tour and protect the people on an existing tour departure of another tour operator—as close in dates and itinerary as can be found. You will receive commission on these sales, which may partially offset your losses to date.
❑ Raise the tour price and operate it without diminishing the features promised the tour members. They will not be happy if they arrive abroad to find that hotels were changed to a lesser category to save money because the group was small.
❑ Change from a fully escorted tour to a locally hosted basis in each country or city. Advise passengers about this ahead of time, however.
❑ Consider operating by van or minibus instead of a large coach. (In this case it may be necessary to stop promoting and selling to fit the group into the confines of the smaller van. Also, limit luggage to fit.)
❑ If your company is airline-appointed through the ARC/IATAN (and, therefore, has access to agents' 75 percent discount air tickets), consider sending a company full-time employee as a tour manager instead of an outsider.

❏ *SUMMARY*

The costing and pricing facet of the tour preparation is probably the single most important facet, since the purpose of a tour is to make money. If this phase is not successful, then the whole tour is not successful. It's important to break costs into two prime categories—variable and fixed—and then to pro-rate the fixed expenses over the minimum number of passengers you anticipate, not the maximum. It's also important to realize that profit does not come from commissions, but rather from markup. All costing should be done in net figures, adding appropriate markup to form adequate profit margin.

This list of do's and don'ts recapitulates the important points to be remembered when costing a tour.

Do's

❏ Do cost the tour on the minimum number of participants anticipated, not the maximum.

❏ Do include a safety margin to cover errors, increases, or simply maneuvering room, if needed.

❏ Do keep good, clean records as to how figures were calculated, especially if staff members have to refer to them months later. If converting foreign currencies, jot down the exchange rate, the source, and date. Similarly, on airfares, keep track of airline, fare quote number, and date. Better still, have it in writing from the airline.

❏ Do walk through the tour mentally, day by day, tour feature by tour feature, to be sure that something important has not been forgotten.

❏ Do cost in adequately for good tour leadership; it can make or break a trip.

❏ Do calculate up-front risk monies that will be lost if the tour fails to materialize. Do the potential earnings warrant the financial risk?

❏ Do consider the up-front time expenditure that the company will lose if the tour fails to materialize. Do the potential earnings warrant the time invested? Could the time be better spent on some other, more profitable venture for the company?

Don'ts

❏ Don't quote a firm price to an organization until you have had time to price the tour accurately, based on actual confirmed services. If giving an advance quote, be sure that it is understood by all concerned that it is only a ballpark figure.

❑ Don't be too optimistic on sales and promotion results. Budget more than enough time for these items to ensure the tour's success.

❑ Don't forget the unseen costs, such as interest on borrowed money, loss of sales revenue from the sales staff who may be taken out of the office to operate the tour in the field, and so forth.

❑ Don't be afraid to compensate your company adequately by providing a large enough profit margin.

❑ *REVIEW QUESTIONS*

1. **Why are fixed costs often thought of as risk factors?**

2. **Name four examples of variable costs.**

3. **Name three examples of fixed costs.**

4. **What is the difference between costing and pricing?**

5. Why are tours costed on minimum enrollment expectations instead of maximum?

6. What is the purpose of a tour?

7. What are some attractive noncommissionable items that might be included in a tour very successfully?

8. What do we mean by the term single-room supplement?

9. What is a "piggyback" mailing?

10. Give three suggestions for lowering a tour price if it is too high.

❑ *ACTIVITIES*

1. Plan a two-day tour for a senior citizens' center in your town. Cost it out to include a complimentary trip for the center's president and one for you, acting as enroute tour manager. Determine the price you will charge if you operate the tour based on 15 passengers, the profit you will make at 15, and the profit you will make at 30.

2. Cost a fictitious tour. Upon completion, you decide the price is too high and you must somehow bring the tour cost down. Reprice on this new lower basis, showing where the savings are located.

3. Obtain a number of tour brochures from different tour companies and locate a tour that is similar in several different brochures, although the prices may vary radically. Analyze why on similar itineraries you think there may be such a disparity in tour price.

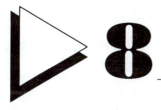 **8**

THE TOUR BROCHURE

LEARNING OBJECTIVES

After reading this chapter, you should:

- ❑ Know why it's necessary to publish a brochure
- ❑ Know when to write a brochure "from scratch" and when to use a supplier's partially prepared "shell" brochure
- ❑ Know where to turn for art and layout assistance
- ❑ Learn how to get a bid from a printer before you start writing
- ❑ Know what "musts" need to be included in a tour brochure
- ❑ Get ideas for clip art, photos, maps, and other design aspects
- ❑ Know the legal statement which all brochures should contain

KEY CONCEPTS AND TERMS

Color Key
Brown-Line
Blue-Line
Dylux
Four-Color Process
Galley Proof
Graphic Artist
Halftone
Layout
Line Art
Mockup
One-Color Job
Page Proof
PMS System
Screened
Shell
Spec Sheet
Two-Color Job

Once the tour has been planned, booked, and costed, it is time to publish the tour brochure. "Nothing to it," says the unwary planner. "I'll just get a shell from the airlines and get together with the printer." (A **shell** is an empty brochure that contains illustrations only. You fill in all the type.)

The planner who believes there is "nothing to it," when it comes to creating the tour brochure may not be creating a brochure that presents the best visible proof of the tour product. After all, clients are expected to pay thousands of dollars for a product that they cannot see, touch, or take home. They cannot even be sure that it really exists until they first hold their air ticket in their hand or first taxi down the runway. Why should they trust you? Why should they be convinced that all the promised services will be provided; that is, the transfers, hotels, social events, good times, camaraderie, experienced tour manager?

Clients are entitled to more than just vague promises. They're entitled to more than just a hastily thrown together itinerary and responsibility clause, and more than pretty pictures of glamorous hotels with sparkling swimming pools and bi-kini-clad girls beckoning them to warm waters. They are entitled to a complete, clearly written, no-nonsense brochure.

If clients do not know that they are entitled to this kind of brochure, the courts certainly do. More and more, when a tour company is brought to court by dis-gruntled clients, judges are looking at the tour brochure for honesty and forthright-ness, rather than for the intricate interpretations of the responsibility clause. For these and other reasons, it is essential that you take the time (and the money) to produce a thoroughly professional brochure.

REASONS FOR PRINTING A BROCHURE

A brochure should be produced for travel projects because:

- ❑ It forms a contract between the agent and the client
- ❑ It standardizes the sales presentation by assuring that each client in the group receives exactly the same information
- ❑ It gives the client a product that can be seen, touched, taken home, ana-lyzed, and shown to family and friends. It makes an intangible, tangible.
- ❑ It may be required by the airline that you are using in order to publish an itinerary (IT) number and thus qualify for an additional airline commission. Check if your sponsoring air carrier still requires this.
- ❑ It gives the airlines, hotels, and other suppliers proof of the operator's professionalism and an indication that the company's promotional efforts are serious and that space blocked with these suppliers is not unduly speculative.

The brochure does not have to be expensive, glossy, or a full-color job. It is quite possible, with the help of a good layout artist and some effective graphics, to pro-

U.S. General Sales Agents:

Rhine Cruise Agency
J.F.O. CruiseService Corp.

Eastern U.S.A.
170 Hamilton Avenue
White Plains, New York 10601-1788
Tel.: (914) 948-3600, (800) 346-6525
Telex: 6818192, Fax: (914) 948-1078

Western U.S.A.
323 Geary Street
San Francisco, California 94102-1860
Tel.: (415) 392-8817, (800) 858-8587
Telex: 470409, Fax: (415) 392-8868

See your professional travel agent
for details and reservations.

Croton Travel Service, Inc.
25 SO. RIVERSIDE AVENUE
CROTON-ON-HUDSON, N.Y. 10520
(914) 271-2144

Picture: The "Bastei-Bridge" in the Elbe-Sandstone Mountains

KD
German Rhine Line
Köln-Düsseldorfer Deutsche Rheinschiffahrt AG · 15 Frankenwerft · 5000 Cologne 1 / Germany
Tel.: 0221-20880 · Telex: 08882169 · Fax: 0221-2088229

Printed in Germany · Imprimé en Allemagne

Figure 8.1   Even the back cover of this brochure features an attractive photograph! It also gives complete information about the company and its U.S. sales agents. There is a blank box where the retail travel agency can stamp its own agency name and address (Courtesy of KD River Cruises of Europe.)

duce a visually attractive and well-written product without going to the expense of full-color process. Generally, the average retail travel company or small tour operator can afford a full-color brochure (called **four-color process** in the printing trade) only if a shell is used. Producing such a full-color brochure from scratch, using color transparencies, is usually financially viable only if you are a major operator planning to print 40,000 copies or more. But if you're printing small quantities (between 1,000 and 20,000 copies), the full-color process will be well beyond the budget. See Figure 8.2 for an example of an effective one-color brochure cover.

TO SHELL OR NOT TO SHELL

The basic decision is whether to use an existing shell or whether to produce an original brochure. A shell certainly has advantages. Primarily, it offers the simplicity and the availability of an attractive full-color product at low cost. A shell can be obtained from airlines, cruise lines, government tourist offices, wholesalers, and several other sources.

In some cases, however, shells can turn out to be more expensive than an original brochure done from scratch, and they can be extremely restricting. The following questions should be considered:

❑ Which method is most advantageous to you? Is the supplier charging you for the shell? If so, which will be less expensive—paying for good graphics/art and layout for an original brochure or buying the shell? For small quantities (i.e., 2,000 or so), buying the shell is probably less expensive. But if 10,000 or more copies need to be produced, pro-rating the cost of a good art/graphics/layout person is probably the better investment.

❑ Is the shell suitable? Does it have enough white space to allow for your needs or is a whole column devoted to describing the wonders of the sponsoring airline? Does the theme coincide with the image that you want to portray? A cover showing a couple with champagne glasses in hand may not be appropriate for a tour to the Girl Scouts' World Leadership Conference. And a shell with beach and bikini scenes may not be business-like enough for a travel seminar project intended to be tax deductible and having to pass the scrutiny of the Internal Revenue Service.

❑ Are enough shells available? Often a supplier can provide 2,000 to 5,000 shells, but if larger quantities are needed they may not be available, even if one is willing to pay for them.

❑ Can more shells be ordered later? If it later becomes necessary to reprint midstream in the promotion, can more of the same shell be obtained? Usually not.

Golfing in Scotland

May - November, 1992

Your Tour Price Includes:

- Hotel accommodations with private bath at deluxe properties as indicated in the itinerary;
- Full breakfast daily and table d'hote dinner each evening;
- All hotel taxes and service charges;
- Transportation and sightseeing with private motorcoach and driver throughout. All expenses for the vehicle and driver, who works an eight-hour day;
- Airport transfers;
- Greens fees for two rounds at Muirfield; two rounds at Old Course, including resident fee; two rounds at Kings and Queens in Gleneagles; and two rounds at Ailsa and Arran, at Turnberry; *
- Planning, handling and operational charges. The price is quoted on the rate of exchange and tariff as of March 1992; in the event of a marked increase in foreign currency rates or tariffs, the cost is subject to revision.

Your Tour Price Does Not Include:

- Any airfares;
- Meals except where specified;
- Admissions and entrance fees for sightseeing stops suggested on the itinerary;
- Baggage handling;
- Costs of obtaining passports or other types of required passenger documentation;
- Items of a purely personal nature, such as alcoholic beverages, laundry charges, telephone/fax/cable charges, or gratuities to driver.

Registration:

A non-refundable deposit of $250 per person is required at the time of booking and is applicable to the tour cost. Full payment is due 60 days prior to departure.

Cancellation:

In the event of written cancellation up to 60 days prior to departure, the deposit will be forfeited.

Cancellations received 59-30 days prior to departure will be subject to a 35% of the tour cost.

Cancellations received 29 days or less prior to departure will be subject to a 100% of the tour cost.

ABERCROMBIE & KENT STRONGLY RECOMMENDS THE PURCHASE OF TRIP CANCELLATION INSURANCE.

* Please note that A&K will make all arrangements for tee times, based on your travel date, except for those at St. Andrews (both Old and other courses). Those must be made direct by you over the telephone (44-0334-75757), or by letter with the golf club well in advance of your planned arrival. Also, a lottery for unallocated slots takes place each afternoon for unassigned tee times the next day; this avenue should only be utilized if the direct approach has not been successful. A written certification of handicap from your home club must be provided for each course.

Tour Price
(based on number of passengers travelling together)

# Pax	Golfer	Non-Golfer
8	$3,875	$3,395
6	$4,075	$3,595
4	$4,355	$3,875
2	$5,075	$4,595
Single Supplement	$520	

Abercrombie & Kent International, Inc.

1520 Kensington Rd., Oak Brook, IL 60521 • (800) 323-7308

printed on recycled paper

Figure 8.2 Brochures do not have to be full color to be effective. This brochure for Golfing in Scotland shows that one-color art can have a special quality and style. (Courtesy of Abercrombie & Kent International, Inc.)

Figure 8.3 This is the shell of an accordion fold brochure with six panels. While the cover shows the airline name, trademark, logo, and art related to the destination, the other five panels are blank, except for very small areas of art on each one. Travel agents can use the blank space to print tour information for members of a group. (Courtesy of Delta Air Lines, Inc.).

❑ Do you mind not having exclusivity? Remember that others may very well be using the same shell for other tours.

❑ Is the shell's layout easy to work with? Or is it necessary to adopt an unnatural layout, squeezing some subjects to fit and expanding others to fill white space?

CREATING THE BROCHURE

Although brochures *can* be any shape and size, when first learning to write a brochure, it is wise to keep to a standard size brochure instead of going into exotic formats. One standard size brochure is 9" × 16" flat and folds to 9" × 4" to fit a No. 10 size business envelope. If several brochures will be mailed in one enve-

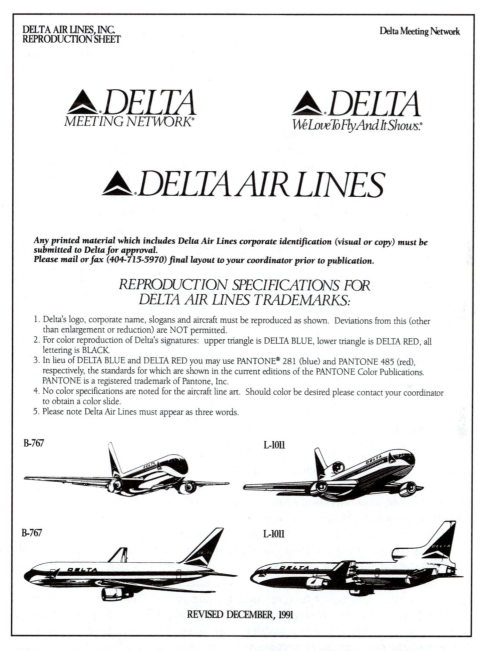

Figure 8.4   **Travel agents who use shells must follow guidelines concerning the reproduction of the company trademarks. In addition, the text and layout of the brochure must be approved by the carrier before printing.** (Courtesy of Delta Air Lines, Inc.)

lope, cut the brochure size down to 8 7/8" × 4" to have a little extra clearance at the end of the envelope. Another easy, standard size is 11" × 17" flat and folds to 8 1/2" × 11", a size which may be mailed flat in a 9" × 12" envelope or folded again in thirds to fit a No. 10 envelope.

Planning the Layout

Once it has been decided whether to use a shell or to do an original piece from scratch, it will be necessary to plan a **layout** (sometimes called a **mock-up**) and then write the copy to fit it, not the other way around. If an eight-panel brochure is planned (i.e., four panels on one side, four on the other), the panels will probably be used as follows: one panel for the cover, one for a reservation form, three for the itinerary (with photos interspersed), and one for the tour costs (and what is included/not included in that cost). A panel will also be needed for general information such as deposits, cancellation policy, clothing, baggage, passports, and so forth The last panel (usually the back page) will be for the responsibility clause. This eight-panel layout should work well for a tour of two weeks or less. For a longer tour, the next size will probably be necessary—a ten-panel brochure (five panels on each side) to provide room to write a longer itinerary.

Remember—be sure to plan how the brochure will fold and check the fold with the printer before completing the layout. Be sure the fold desired can be handled by machine. I once mistakenly had 13,000 copies of a brochure printed and then discovered that it had to be folded by hand. The bill was well over budget, to put it mildly.

Getting a Printer's Bid

Once a decision has been reached on whether to use a shell or not, and once the size, folds, and number of panels have been decided, it is time to approach a printer (or several printers) for a bid. It is also possible to put it out to bid through a printing broker, who will shop printers, their costs, and press sizes for you; but, of course, printing brokers add on a service fee for doing so. In order to quote a price, the printer will need to know the following: number of copies to be printed, number of **halftones** (printer's term for photos), number of maps or drawings (**line art**), and weight and color of **stock** (paper). Figure 8.5 is a **spec** or **specification sheet** showing the information the printer will need. Brightly colored paper stocks, imported papers, and fancy textures increase the price. The two main expenses are the typesetter's time and the paper stock, so small printing runs of several thousand brochures will be disproportionately expensive. The more copies printed, the less expensive each brochure becomes.

Another important factor is the number of colors—the least expensive is termed a **one-color job**; that is, one color ink and one color stock. Black is considered a color, so black ink on white stock is a one-color job just as is blue ink on yellow stock. If a second color ink is added, for example, both red and black ink on white

LSI Travel Agency
987 Park Drive #2A
Berkeley, CA 94704
Telephone Number: 510-555-2000
Fax Number: 510-555-7210

SPEC SHEET FOR PRINTER

NAME OF PRODUCT/JOB NO:	Travel brochure
QUANTITY:	3,000 copies
SIZE, FLAT:	9" x 16"
FOLD:	To 9" x 4", to fit a #10 size envelope
STOCK:	Coated, white, 70 pound, Flokote or similar
INK:	Two colors: Black and red PMS 199
ART:	One map, two line drawings, two halftones
PROOFS REQUIRED:	One blueline
PREPARATION:	You are to provide typesetting, pasteup, art and all separations.
	or
	Typesetting, pasteup and art being done elsewhere. You will receive mechanicals camera-ready.
DELIVERY:	100 to our office
	2,900 to our mail house: Best Mailing Services, 1234 Seventh Street, Anywhere, U.S.A.
SPECIAL NOTES:	Please advise if quote includes any delivery charges and taxes, or not.
	It is understood that all boards, negatives, art, and photos remain the property of LSI Travel Agency and will be returned to LSI Travel upon completion of the job and receipt of payment in full.

Figure 8.5 Sample spec sheet for printer.

stock, this is termed a **two-color job**, and the added color will mean about a one-third increase in the cost of the brochure. (Be sure that the ink is sufficiently dark to form a strong contrast on the paper. Black ink on pale yellow stock is fairly easy to read, but red ink on yellow becomes difficult to read if there is a lot of small type.)

Be specific about the colors of ink. There is a standard system called the **PMS system** (Pantone Matching System). Each color has a code number, making it easy to instruct the printer about the *exact* shade desired. These PMS colors may be **screened** (shaded), so that, for example, a navy blue could also appear as a medium blue and as a lighter blue, giving variety of tone but still using only one color ink. The very dark blue would be considered a 100 percent screen; a very pale blue, at the other end of the spectrum, would be considered a 10 percent screen.

Even after obtaining a firm price quote from the printer, it is a wise precaution to add a margin to the printing budget to allow for error, misunderstandings, and ac's (author's corrections). Printers do not charge when they make a mistake and have to correct it, but when the customer changes copy, changes layout, or changes his or her mind, printers *do* charge—and on an hourly basis.

Also, allow extra time in the schedule. If a printer promises that a brochure will be off the press in two weeks, add at least two weeks more to allow for holidays, paper delivery delays, strikes, and so forth. Usually 30 days is the shortest period in which one can expect a truly professional-looking brochure to be completed; I usually allow 60 days. Besides, there should be time to read at least three sets of printer's proofs. The first set, called **galley proofs**, are long strips of type that are read just for content and spelling errors but without headlines or layout. Second proofs are called **page proofs**; that is, proofs submitted after the corrected type has been pasted onto a layout page complete with headlines, borders, and so on. The third and final proof is usually called a **brown-line, blue-line, dylux, color key,** or other such term, and it is presented after all the pages have been photographed and negatives have been made. Corrections should be made at stages one and two and *never* at stage three; it is costly to change once film has been made because it means rephotographing the entire page. (See Figure 8.6 for most frequently used proofreader marks and see Table 8.1 for frequently used printing terms.)

Obtaining Art and Layout Assistance

If a shell is to be used, an artist or layout person will probably not be needed. All that is necessary is to block out the appropriate panels, measure the amount of copy that will fit, and, in consultation with the typesetter, select proper typefaces and sizes. It is best to keep to a simple, readable typeface for the body type, saving any fancy styles for headlines. For continuity and visual clarity, stick to one type style throughout the brochure; do not jump from one style to another. Also, be sure to select a typesize large enough for easy reading.

If the brochure is being produced from scratch, an artist/layout person will probably be needed. Such charges should be costed into the tour price from the

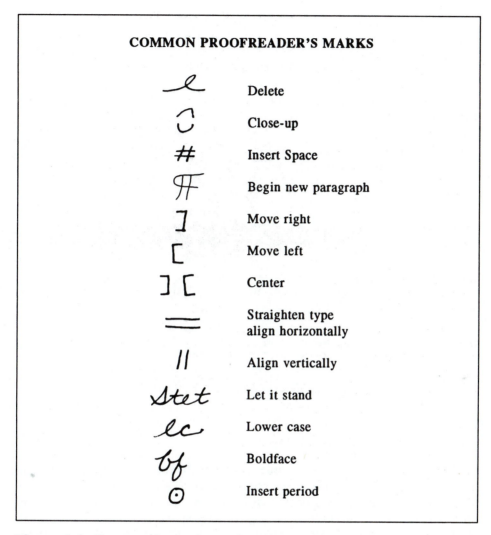

Figure 8.6 Frequently-used proofreading marks.

outset. Some full-service printers have such a person on the staff or available on a freelance basis. If not, an independent **graphic artist** should be consulted. A graphic artist will not only provide art, but he/she will also act as a project coordinator for you. He or she will design the layout, specify the typefaces and sizes, select and crop the photos, and prepare the final pasteup with instructions to the printer. If such a professional is not available, or if you are attempting the do-it-yourself approach, stay with a simple layout, an attractive type style, a couple of good photos, and decorative line drawings or silhouette art.

TABLE 8.1   Printing Terms

These terms are used frequently when dealing with printers, typesetters, and graphic artists. They are in addition to the terms that are defined in this chapter. The definitions of each of these terms may be found in the glossary on page 403.

Accordian fold	Finish
AAs (Author's alterations)	Flop
Bid	Flush
Bleed	Flyer
Blowup	Lowercase
Body copy	Matte finish
Brochure	Montage
Camera-ready	Opaque
Caption	Quote
Clip art	Responsibility clause
Color key	Stack
Copy fitting	Stock
Crop	Uppercase
Desktop publishing	Velox
Dummy	

Using Desktop Publishing

Another alternative to using a typesetter and graphic artist is to do it yourself via desktop publishing. This method is recommended *only if you are already adept at this* and can turn out a truly professional-looking brochure. If you are still in the learning phase and your brochure will look "homemade," leave it to the experts until you have had more experience. Of course, it is possible nowadays to do the typing directly on a computer or word processor, producing a disk that may then be converted to type, thus saving the expense of typesetting. If using this technique, check with your graphic artist to be sure that your disk and software are compatible with his/her system.

Locating Photos

Probably the most difficult job will be locating good photos. Although sources such as airlines and government tourist offices may be able to supply photos of buildings, ships, and planes, it is sometimes hard to find good human interest photos. Your tour managers should start carrying cameras on tour to establish a library of good human interest and action photos. In the past it was necessary to have black-and-white glossy photos. Recent techniques now make it possible, in *some* cases, to use color prints or transparencies, converting them to black-and-white for use in a one-color or two-color brochure. Be sure to check with your printer or graphic artist before assuming they can use your color shots. Color photos never convert clearly to black-and-white.

Using photos of recognizable people requires their written permission. If photos are obtained from outside sources, a credit line must be published with each photo. A credit line identifies the individual photographer or organization that gave, sold, or lent the photo. Photos should reflect actual destinations on the tour; to do otherwise is considered misleading.

Do not rely solely on travel-related organizations as a source of good photos. Commercial photo houses or museums are good sources. I once obtained permission from the Norton Simon Museum of Art in Pasadena for one-time reprint rights to a black-and-white photo of a Paul Gaugin painting in their collection; it was used as the cover of a Tahiti brochure. The search for good photos requires creativity. Photos for brochure use must be distinct, focused properly, and not too dark. This is particularly important when using textured papers, as they tend to absorb a lot of ink and thus darken photos.

Using a Map

A map is a *must* in any brochure, because many clients may not have a good idea of where they are going or where "there" is in relation to "here". Many clients are amazed to find that South America is actually southeast of North America, not due south, or that Hong Kong is far south of Japan, hence the difference in weather and clothing requirements. A map will help the potential client to understand the itinerary, the routing, the distances, and the flight times involved.

A sample map outline or silhouette can be drawn by a commercial artist, and the printer can then typeset and position the names of cities in their proper location on the map. But one cannot simply reproduce an existing map in an atlas. Some basic silhouette maps may be available in clip art catalogs.

Designing the Cover

Remember that the cover of the brochure is the gateway to the tour. Be sure that it *attracts* the client and that it will draw one to open and read the brochure. The cover need not give the full story—just enough to answer the basics: where, when, and with whom (i.e., the agency? a local club? a famous tennis pro?). Do not forget the year. The price of the tour doesn't have to be on the cover, unless it is such a low price that it's an outstanding feature that should be emphasized.

If the tour is going to be wholesaled through retail travel agents and displayed in a travel agency's brochure rack, the cover should be visually bold and simple, and easy to pick out from among other brochures on the rack. If, on the other hand, it is going to be merchandised primarily by direct mail, perhaps it can be a bit daintier or designed to be pulled out of an envelope easily. As a direct-mail piece,

FALL 1992, MS WESTERDAM

Vancouver

San Francisco

Los Angeles

Cabo San Lucas · Nassau · St. Thomas

Acapulco · Antigua

Curacao

Panama Canal

Ft. Lauderdale

12-19 DAYS				FROM $2,915
DAY	DATE	PORT	ARRIVE	DEPART
MON	OCT 5	VANCOUVER, BRITISH COLUMBIA		5:00PM
TUE	OCT 6	Wake up to the joys of luxury cruising		
WED	OCT 7	SAN FRANCISCO, CALIFORNIA	NOON	4:00PM
THU	OCT 8	LOS ANGELES, CALIFORNIA	NOON	5:00PM
FRI	OCT 9	At sea with every activity under the sun		
SAT	OCT 10	Cabo San Lucas, Mexico	NOON	5:00PM
SUN	OCT 11	A festive day cruising the Mexican Riviera		
MON	OCT 12	ACAPULCO, MEXICO	8:00AM	
TUE	OCT 13	Acapulco, Mexico		1:00AM
WED-THU	OCT 14-15	At sea, relaxing, playing, learning about the exotic ports to come		
FRI	OCT 16	Enter Panama Canal at Balboa / Daylight transit Panama Canal / Leave Panama Canal at Cristobal	7:00AM	4:00PM
SAT	OCT 17	At sea enjoying the good life		
SUN	OCT 18	Willemstad, Curacao	8:00AM	11:00PM
MON	OCT 19	At sea cruising the blue Caribbean		
TUE	OCT 20	St. John's, Antigua	8:00AM	6:00PM
WED	OCT 21	St. Thomas, U.S. Virgin Islands	7:00AM	5:00PM
THU	OCT 22	Cruising along, everything's fine		
FRI	OCT 23	Nassau, Bahamas	1:30PM	7:30PM
SAT	OCT 24	FT. LAUDERDALE, FLORIDA	8:00AM	

SAILING DATES TO FT. LAUDERDALE

Oct 5, 1992	From Vancouver	19 days	from $3,675
Oct 7, 1992	From San Francisco	17 days	from $3,420
Oct 8, 1992	From Los Angeles	16 days	from $3,220
Oct 12, 1992	From Acapulco	12 days	from $2,915

BOOK EARLY & SAVE 10%

Save 10% if you make your reservations and are on deposit by June 15, 1992. Early Booking prices start at **$2624**, with savings as much as **$683** per person.

MORE SPECIAL OFFERS ON PAGE 31

	TO FT. LAUDERDALE			
DOUBLE STATEROOMS	FROM ACAPULCO	FROM LOS ANGELES	FROM SAN FRANCISCO	FROM VANCOUVER
	12 DAYS	16 DAYS	17 DAYS	19 DAYS
OUTSIDE				
S Suites	US$5,040	US$5,975	US$6,350	US$6,825
A Staterooms Deluxe	4,395	5,230	5,565	5,980
B Deluxe	4,195	4,990	5,310	5,705
C Deluxe	3,995	4,750	5,055	5,430
D Large	3,885	4,590	4,885	5,250
E Large	3,755	4,420	4,705	5,055
F Large	3,645	4,240	4,510	4,850
G Standard	3,540	4,060	4,320	4,640
H Standard	3,430	3,940	4,190	4,505
I Economy	2,990	3,320	3,535	3,800
INSIDE				
J Standard	3,430	3,940	4,190	4,505
K Standard	3,325	3,760	4,000	4,300
L Standard	3,215	3,580	3,810	4,095
M Standard	3,065	3,400	3,615	3,885
N Standard	2,915	3,220	3,420	3,675
Each Guest Sharing Stateroom with Two Full-Fare Guests	1,245	1,535	1,605	1,765
Children Under Two Years Old Accompanied by Two Full-Fare Adults	250	250	250	250
Cruise Only Credit	300	300	300	300
Port Charges & Taxes	99	109	119	119
Deposit Requirements	400	400	400	400
Cancellation Fees Waiver	129	129	129	129

Refer to deck plans on pages 40 and 41 for specific facilities in each stateroom.

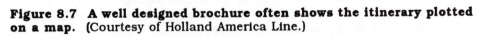

Figure 8.7 A well designed brochure often shows the itinerary plotted on a map. (Courtesy of Holland America Line.)

it could be designed to be sent through the mail without an envelope. If being planned as a self-mailer, check with the post office first to be sure the size and format comply with postal regulations.

Writing the Itinerary

Nothing sells as does a day-by-day, blow-by-blow, well-written itinerary that shows the clients all of the features that they will be getting each day. Beware of overblown terms such as "beautiful," "gorgeous," "unbelievable," and "unforgettable." Why is San Francisco beautiful? Because the itinerary keeps saying so? Or because a picture is formed for the reader, letting one visualize San Francisco's steep hills, shrouded in fog, and streets lined with brightly colored Victorian houses?

Write the itinerary in the language of the potential customer. An educational study tour to London with class sessions in the morning and afternoon sightseeing might more accurately refer to "afternoon field trip to Windsor Castle and Runnymeade, site of the signing of the Magna Carta," than "afternoon sightseeing tour." Teachers and students take field trips, not sightseeing tours. A program for the local dental association to the annual meeting of the American Dental Association could refer to "morning session of essays and table clinics" instead of "morning convention session."

Certainly, that entire alphabet soup of travel industry terms, such at GIT, APEX, and FIT, should be avoided unless they are spelled out for the reader.

Standardize the itinerary presentation. If hotels are listed by name, list them in all cities in the itinerary, not just in some. Do not jump from "you" to "we" do such and such. And above all, avoid being too specific. It is okay to say "afternoon departure by Air France jet to Paris." But saying "We leave via Air France flight number 5 at 2:00 p.m. for Paris," could back you into a corner if, by the time the tour leaves, both the flight number and flight time have been changed.

Indicating the Tour Price

Adequate space should be allowed for information concerning the tour price, for a full itemization of what is included, and for what is not included in the price. Prices may be indicated from more than one city, and they should be shown for both share-room and single-room basis. In some cases, the triple-room rate can be listed, as well as special family rates and children's rates.

The type of airfare on which the tour is priced, such as APEX, GIT, or ITX, should be specified, and the restrictions governing the particular fare noted. Indicate the minimum number of passengers on which the tour is priced, and stipulate the publication date on which the airfare and the foreign currency exchange rates are based. If the airfare is restricted to a specific air carrier, this should be so specified.

The brochure should have a paragraph that lists all services included in the tour price—airfare, hotels, meals, sightseeing, gratuities, and surface transportation. The more specific the better. For example, instead of just stating that meals are included, you might say "three meals a day, *table d'hôte* basis, in accordance with local custom in the country concerned." Specify if breakfasts are continental or full American style and if lunch and dinner are *à la carte* or *table d'hôte*.

Conversely, there should also be a paragraph listing services not included in the tour. These things include connecting airfare to the published gateway city; personal expenses such as liquors, wines, mineral waters, or laundry; and increases in airfares or currency exchange rates after date of publication. Also not included would be items such as passports and inoculations, travel insurance, services apart from the group, expenses due to flight delays, strikes, or other irregularities, meals not stipulated—in effect, any item not included in the tour price. This information gives the passengers an accurate way to budget for the out-of-pocket expenses they will incur. It also gives the tour brochure an aura of plain speaking.

Writing the Reservation Form

To encourage quick and easy bookings, have a good reservation form in the brochure, thus getting all the information needed from each client at one time. This eliminates needless telephoning or corresponding back and forth with each tour participant. The reservation form may be one panel in the brochure itself; or, if space is in short supply, it could be a loose insert panel. Figure 8.8 is a sample reservation form.

The form should ask the basics: client's name and name of accompanying family members, home and business addresses, telephone numbers, and occupation. If accepting children, ask for their ages. There should also be a place where the client can indicate a choice of either a twin-bedded or single room, smoking or nonsmoking section of the aircraft (for preassigned seating), and decisions on any optional tours that may be offered within the basic tour package or as post-tour optional features. When selling a cruise, be sure that space is provided for the client to indicate choice of cabin category and corresponding price. There may even be a place for first and second choice of cabin category in case the first choice cannot be confirmed.

Reserve a place for the client's signature and a spot at the bottom of the reservation form to indicate the amount of deposit that should accompany the reservation form, to whom it should be payable, and the exact address to which it should be mailed. If, by any chance, there is any extra space left on the reservation form, a good marketing technique is to ask the client for the name and address of any friend(s) who might also be interested in the tour or in being placed on the mailing list to receive information on future tours.

```
┌─────────────────────────────────────────────────────────────────────┐
│                                                                       │
│                          RESERVATION                                  │
│                                                                       │
│                      Rosemont Country Club                            │
│                   19XX European Highlights Tour                       │
│                                                                       │
│  NAME (please indicate full name) _____   │
│  ADDRESS _____  │
│  CITY _____  │
│  STATE _____  ZIP CODE _____   │
│  TELEPHONE    Area Code _____  Number _____   │
│  ACCOMPANYING FAMILY MEMBERS (if children, state ages)                │
│  _____  │
│  _____  │
│                                                                       │
│  PROFESSION _____  │
│  PLEASE ARRANGE FOR MY AIRLINE TRANSPORTION FROM                      │
│  _____  │
│                     airport nearest my home                           │
│                                                                       │
│  I/WE WOULD LIKE THE FOLLOWING HOTEL ACCOMMODATIONS (check one)        │
│      ___  Twin/share at basic tour price    ___  Single room at supplement │
│                                                                       │
│  WHERIN POSSIBLE TO PREASSIGN SEATS ON AIRCRAFT, I/WE WISH TO BE       │
│  SEATED IN  (check one)                                               │
│      ___  Non-smoking section        ___  Smoking section             │
│      ___  Aisle seat                 ___  Window seat                 │
│                                                                       │
│  AT THE END OF THE TOUR, I/WE WISH TO (check one)                     │
│      ___  Return directly home with the group from Rome September 16  │
│      ___  Remain in Europe independently and return on _____   │
│                                              specify date             │
│  I HEARD ABOUT THIS TRIP THROUGH (check one)                         │
│      ___  I am a member of the Rosemont Country Club and received direct mail notification │
│      ___  Through a friend who is a member of the club               │
│      ___  Through an ad (specify publication if possible) _____  │
│      ___  Other, specify _____    │
│                                                                       │
│  PLEASE SEND INFORMATION ABOUT THIS TOUR TO THE FOLLOWING PERSON(S)   │
│  WHO MAY BE INTERESTED (indicate name and mailing address)           │
│  _____  │
│  _____  │
│                                                                       │
│  THIS IS TO CERTIFY THAT I HAVE READ THE BROCHURE AND RESPONSIBILITY  │
│  CLAUSE AND AGREE TO THE CONDITIONS OUTLINED THEREIN                  │
│  _____    _____   │
│      signature                              date                      │
│                                                                       │
│          DEPOSIT:   Make deposit check for $100 per person            │
│                     payable to "Rosemont Country Club"                │
│                                                                       │
│          MAIL TO:   Rosemont Country Club, 1234 Willow Road,          │
│                     Berkeley, CA 94704                                 │
│                                                                       │
└─────────────────────────────────────────────────────────────────────┘
```

Figure 8.8 Sample reservation form.

Writing the Responsibility Clause

All brochures should include a complete responsibility clause—a clause which may be written by the agency staff and then reviewed by the company attorney, or a clause which is prepared from scratch by the attorney. An example of a responsibility clause will be found in the sample itinerary in Chapter 5.

Of particular importance is a statement allowing one to decline to accept a tour applicant or to drop a tour member if need be. (See Chapter 13 for a discussion of why a tour manager might find it necessary to drop a member enroute.) A proper statement on this subject might be "The right is reserved to decline to accept or retain any person as a member of the tour at any time."

Another very important inclusion in the responsibility clause is one related to foreign currency fluctuation and fare changes. Since the tour will be costed many months in advance, there will undoubtedly be changes in airfares, hotel rates, motorcoach costs, and other pertinent components between the date on which the tour was costed and the date on which the tour actually departs. In some cases, suppliers may have agreed to honor their original price quotes and not pass increases on to the tour operator once a price has been quoted and a brochure published.

In many cases, tour operators protect themselves by building in a financial margin to allow for such increases; thus, they avoid having to advise tour members of a price increase later on. In other cases, particularly if suppliers' increases prove to be steep, the tour operator has no alternative but to pass the increase on to the tour members in the form of a surcharge. For this reason, a statement in the brochure such as the following is helpful: "The price of the tour is based on tariffs and exchange rates in effect at the time of printing the brochure and is subject to change in the event of any changes in tariffs and exchange rates."

It is suggested that the planner read a variety of responsibility clauses in a variety of tour brochures on the market today; it will become apparent that virtually no two are exactly alike—each one is slightly different as interpreted by each company's ownership and its legal advisors. One clause that is standard throughout, however, is the airline clause portion, which is a portion that must be printed verbatim and that will be verified by the tour's sponsoring air carrier before approval for the final publishing of the brochure.

Final Touches

Remember to put the publishing date on the back of the brochure (i.e., actually the date on which the tour is priced, not the date that the brochure comes off the press). And, if your sponsoring airline requires it in order to grant you an additional airline commission, be sure to obtain the itinerary (IT) number from them and publish it in your brochure. Airlines will sometimes insist on seeing the printer's proof of a brochure before assigning the IT number, and may perhaps even send the proof to their head office for approval. Therefore, be sure to allow sufficient time for this in the overall time frame.

The final tour brochure can act as a true showcase for you; and, if slick and professional in appearance, the additional sales that a good brochure provides should more than warrant the time and money expended on it. If your first brochure does not turn out perfect, consider it a learning experience and make the next one even better. It is a good idea to run a supply of extra copies and use them as marketing tools when making sales presentations to other groups and potential new tour sources. This will show the type of brochure that you are capable of producing.

Alternative Sources of Brochures

It is occasionally possible to have what appears to be a customized brochure without having to create it yourself. If your company is booking a group onto an existing tour or cruise of a supplier, perhaps that supplier has already produced a master brochure. In this case, your group's name can simply be printed on the front cover. Perhaps an enrollment coupon on the back page can be personalized to reflect the group's name and address, indicating where the client should mail the enrollment coupon and trip deposit check (See Figure 4.2 on page 62 as an example of this type of brochure).

In other cases, sometimes a large operator will custom-write and print a brochure for a client organization or for a retail travel agency. Figure 16.3 on page 392 is an example of this type of customized brochure. In this case it was custom-written and produced in-house via desktop publishing for the Asia Society by the operator, Abercrombie and Kent. One panel of the brochure is devoted to information about the Asia Society. The remaining panels describe the itinerary, terms and conditions of the tour. Expenses for producing, printing and mailing such a product are usually part of the initial negotiation between the parties concerned. Operators who have indulged these client organizations and travel agencies in the past by absorbing these promotional costs and by taking financial risks on behalf of such client organizations are becoming less and less willing to do so. In today's economic climate they expect the retail travel agency and/or the sponsoring organization to share in or be totally responsible for the financial risk of such a promotion.

☐ *SUMMARY*

A tour brochure is the best possible way to present a travel product. If properly prepared, both from a creative perspective and from a business/legal perspective, it can best serve your purposes. It can act as a legal contract and as an attractive promotional piece to create sales. Since a brochure is the showcase of a tour, sufficient time and attention should be allotted to this important phase of the tour preparation process.

❑ *REVIEW QUESTIONS*

1. **Give three reasons why it is important to publish a tour brochure.**

2. **If selecting a supplier's shell rather than preparing a brochure from scratch, name at least four things to ask yourself about the shell before reaching your decision.**

3. **What are two standard size brochures?**

4. **Name the principal things that should be on a "spec sheet" that you send to a printer for a printing quote.**

5. Compare the terms four-color, two-color, and one-color printing jobs. Include in your comparison a discussion of the number of colors of paper, number of colors of ink, and relative costs. When would you use four-color process? When would you use only one-color or two-color process?

6. What are some of the services a good graphic artist will provide you?

7. Why is a map so important in most travel brochures?

8. Discuss the purpose of the brochure cover and what items should always appear on it.

❑ *ACTIVITIES*

1. Contact several international airlines serving the same destination and ask for samples of shells they may have available. Compare the shells for suitability. Then select the one you feel most appropriate and give your rationale for your selection.

2. Design an eight-column layout for a tour brochure you would write from scratch (flat size 9"x16", folded size 9"x4"). Indicate what will go in each column, how it will fold, and where you would place art and photos.

3. Write the reservation form to appear in a fictitious tour brochure. Lay it out to fit within one column.

4. Cut out the responsibility clauses from a number of tour brochures on the market. Compare them. Then write a responsibility clause that you would like to use in your fictitious tour brochure.

5. Write the brochure clause "What's Included in the Tour" for a fictitious tour. Then think of all the things which were *not* included in the tour and write a separate paragraph entitled "What's Not Included in the Tour." Be sure to cover thoroughly all facets which may or may not be included: air, hotels, sightseeing, social events, land transportation, sightseeing, transfers, baggage handling, tips, taxes, meals, cocktails, local guides, and tour leadership.

▷9

MARKETING THE TOUR

LEARNING OBJECTIVES

After reading this chapter, you should:

❑ Develop a marketing plan for your tour
❑ Plan the budget that your marketing plan will require and that you must cost into your tour
❑ Understand the advantages and disadvantages of direct mail
❑ Understand the pros and cons of working with a tour organizer (i.e., Pied Piper) to recruit your tour members
❑ Plan a successful promotional evening for a group tour or cruise
❑ Decide when to use an advertising agency
❑ Assess media possibilities for your advertising—newspapers, magazines, radio, TV
❑ Track results from your ads to determine actual acquisition costs for each tour inquiry you receive from these ads
❑ Get free publicity by effective use of press releases

KEY CONCEPTS AND TERMS

Acquisition Costs
Advertising Slicks
Co-op Advertising
Coupon Coding
Direct Mail Marketing
Marketing Plan
Marketing Mix
Media Release
Press (News) Release
Promotional Evening
Sales Organizer
Specific Market Segment

The term "marketing" may conjure up the image of interviewers in shopping malls, new soap product samples left on the doorstep, or telephone surveys asking for preferences in television shows.

This image is partly true, since marketing does include research into demographics and buying habits. But marketing also includes many other components, such as direct mail, public relations, sales efforts, a cruise night or similar promotion, use of a well-known celebrity as tour leader, news releases to the media, and advertising. Advertising contains still more components, such as newspapers, magazines, radio; and on rare occasions television, billboards, and posters.

However, despite the seeming complexity of the subject, the process of marketing a tour does not have to be intimidating. It is not necessary to hire a $100-an-hour expert to market a tour properly. When all the Madison Avenue mystique is stripped away, *marketing a tour simply means getting the tour to market.* The combination of how the tour gets to market and what it costs to do so is the **marketing plan**.

DEVELOPING A MARKETING PLAN

A realistic marketing plan and budget are essential and they should be developed before the tour is priced, not after. Special group tours are generally not included in a company's overall annual promotional budget. That budget covers the usual institutional marketing, such as Yellow Pages advertising, newspaper advertising, newsletters, and so forth. A special separate promotional budget should be established for each tour that you operate, and this budget can then be built into each tour's costing formula.

The Market Mix

A good marketing plan uses a variety of components, not just one. The particular combination of components selected for a particular tour is termed the **marketing mix**. The mix selected may vary from tour to tour. One tour might need a mix of direct mail to a club's membership and a cruise evening. Another tour might be marketed through paid advertising, a local celebrity, and news releases to the press to generate free publicity.

The selection of components will depend on the type of itinerary, the desired clientele, the best means of reaching that clientele, and the promotional budget that can realistically be incorporated into the tour costing. Figure 9.1 shows a sample budget, based on marketing plan decisions for a specific tour project.

Selecting a Specific Market Segment

It is important to research the various promotional avenues carefully, and then choose those that will be most effective in generating interest in a particular travel

---

SAMPLE BUDGET BASED ON MARKETING PLAN

(1) PROMOTIONAL EVENING, maximum 100 guests

    (a) Wine and cheese estimate (including paper plates, napkins, table decor, etc.) $600.00

    (b) Films—no charge, complimentary from sponsoring airline. However, contingency for rental of film projector if necessary   30.00

    (c) Door Prize, if not donated   50.00

    (d) Room rental, if necessary   300.00

    (e) Tips, associated with room rental, waiter, etc.   30.00

    (f) Invitations for 200 to assure 100 in attendance   50.00

    Estimate total budget for promotional evening $1060.00

(2) PAID ADVERTISING

    Three consecutive monthly ads in the Club's magazine, one quarter page, at $275 per issue × 3 $825.00

(3) DIRECT MAIL to 2,000 member club list. Initial announcement mailing.

    (a) Postage at 19.8¢ bulk × 2,000   733.00

    (b) Printing cover letter from club president   85.00

    (c) Mailing house charges—folding, stuffing, sealing, sorting, taking to post office, etc.   210.00

    Total estimate for initial announcement mailing $1,028.00

(4) TOUR BROCHURE, 3000 copies (2,000 to mail out, 1000 to keep for inquiries and miscellaneous purposes)   750.00

(5) SECOND FOLLOW-UP MAILING if necessary to boost sales

    (a) Postage at 19.8¢ bulk rate × 2,000   733.00

    (b) Reminder letter from club president   85.00

    (c) Mailing house charges   150.00

    (d) Enclosure flyer or perhaps an additional 2,000 brochures   400.00

    Total estimate for follow-up mailing $1,368.00

(6) CONTINGENCY FEE, for late "boost" if necessary $100.00

    GRAND TOTAL MARKETING PLAN AND BUDGET FOR THIS PROJECT $5,131.00

Figure 9.1 This is a sample marketing plan budget. Each tour's budget should be costed using specific quotes for that job from printers, mail houses, and so forth.

product. The trick is to direct all promotional efforts to a **specific market segment**. A ski tour would best be promoted by advertising in ski magazines, mailings to ski clubs, and so forth. An expensive advertisement in the Sunday travel section of the *New York Times* would be wasted, because only a small percentage of readers would be skiers.

Deciding on a Promotional Budget

Not only is it necessary to select the promotional avenues that lead to the desired clientele, but it is also necessary to estimate the cost of acquiring clients for a tour. One can then decide whether the potential for profit on the tour warrants the promotional risk investment. If the profit is projected to be only $100 per client, you will probably not risk $80 per client on promotional expenses. On the other hand, if the per client profit is projected to be as high as $500, perhaps a promotional investment of $80 per client is justified.

The following discussion looks in more detail at various means of marketing.

DIRECT MAIL

Direct mail is a form of advertising that reaches potential clientele through the postal service. Although an expensive method of marketing, direct mail certainly can bring results and may, in the long run, prove to be the most cost effective. Tour planners always ask "What percentage of return can I expect?" The answers to this question depend on the validity of the mailing list, the tour product itself, its price, and the income level of those on the list. Probably of prime importance is how closely knit is the group on the mailing list. A list of members of an upper-income private organization, solicited by letter from the organization's president for their officially sponsored tour, might draw as high as five percent. On the other hand, using a commercial purchased list and solicited by an outsider, one might be lucky to draw 1 percent.

Assume that you have presold a trip to an organization—a church, tennis club, Chamber of Commerce, or professional group. The directors have been convinced that they should sponsor an official trip for their organization next year. They have accepted the proposed itinerary, you have booked it, and now you hold confirmed space with all hotels, airlines, and so forth.

The directors of the organization may already have made advance teaser announcements to their membership in publications or at meetings. However, the first official announcement should be via direct mail to each family in the organization to assure total coverage. It is best to have the mailing go out in the sponsoring organization's envelope rather than in yours. The brochure describing the tour in detail should be customized to the organization, so that it appears to be *their* tour, not yours. Of course, your company's name will appear in the brochure, but it should be played down, with full buildup given to the sponsoring organization. A letter of invitation from the organization's president should accompany the brochure, and to facilitate reservations, the brochure should include a reservation form to be completed and returned with the deposit.

If possible, the reservation form should be returned to the sponsoring organization, which will then endorse the check and forward it to you with the reservation form for handling. This procedure will keep most of the workload in your office and out of the sponsoring organization's office. At the same time, members feel more comfortable sending initial monies to their own organization rather than to a travel agency or tour company with which they might not be familiar.

Assume that you are working with an organization that has 3,000 members. A direct-mail budget might look like the following sample.

Sample Direct-Mail Budget

Envelopes, 3,000 including printing with club's return address and logo on them	$120.00
Letters, 3,000 from the club's president announcing the trip, including printing and folding	$155.00
Brochures, 3,000, size 9" x 16" (8 panels). Based on buying shells from the airlines at 5 cents each, plus printer's charges for typesetting, printing layout, and folding	$975.00
Postage, at bulk rate of 19.8 cents each for 3,000	$594.00
Mailing house charges	
Minimum setup charges	25.00
Affixing address labels at $15 M	45.00
Stuffing envelopes at $20 M	60.00
Sealing, metering, at $7 M	21.00
Tying and sacking at $10 M	30.00
Delivery to post office	20.00
Total mailing house estimated charges	$201.00
Total direct-mail budget	$2,045.00

The estimates in this sample budget are based on the assumption that the club does not charge for use of its membership list. If an outside list must be purchased, estimate at least five cents a name for one-time use, perhaps more. Also, even if the club allows free use of its membership list, there still may be a charge for a printout of the address labels.

The above $2,045 total must be costed into the tour as promotional expenses (see chapter 7, Costing and Pricing a Tour). Ultimately, these expenses are paid for by the passengers as part of their tour cost. However, note that these direct-mail costs are an up-front expense for your company. If, for any reason, the tour should fail to operate, they are nonrecoverable expenses—to be looked at as a risk investment in the project.

A Few Hints for Direct-Mail Marketing

Host Club Arrangement.   If the organization is not large, consider a host club arrangement. In this arrangement, one organization sponsors the tour, handles all the decisions, and works with you but opens the trip to related clubs. Rotary clubs frequently do this. One club sponsors a trip, opening it to other Rotary clubs in the same Rotary district. Quite often, an organization may be overly optimistic about the numbers that it can generate from a small membership list, so it is wise to discuss this at the outset and perhaps cost in for direct mail to affiliated organizations at the time the tour budget is drawn up.

Use a Personalized Envelope.   The more personalized the direct-mail approach, the better the result. If the list is small, a hand addressed envelope with a first-class stamp instead of a metered envelope will ensure the recipient's opening it because it will not appear to be junk mail. Of course, in dealing with large lists, this personal touch may not be feasible.

Aim for Sole Occupancy in the Envelope.   A direct-mail piece will receive greater attention if the envelope is not stuffed with a multitude of pieces. On the other hand, it is possible to cut down the cost of the mailing by offering two non-conflicting tours in the same envelope and splitting the promotional costs of the mailing between the two tour projects.

Plan for Several Mailings.   One mailing alone will not be enough. Most likely it will be necessary to do a follow-up mailing and perhaps even a third "last call." (See Figure 9.2 for a follow-up flyer.) Be sure to budget accordingly. Once the tour is announced and has sold out, a second or third mailing can be eliminated if not needed, thus effecting a savings on promotional expenditures. But the reverse is not true. If just one announcement mailing has been budgeted but it is later decided that the tour needs a boost, you cannot then accommodate the unexpected additional expense. It is not necessary to let the organization know that a second mailing has been costed in to the project. Later, when you offer to make a second mailing, you can suddenly appear as a knight in shining armor, rescuing the project.

Combine Direct Mail with Other Marketing Methods.   Do not expect direct mail to succeed all by itself. It probably works best in conjunction with reminder advertising in the organization's publication, and with a sales organizer inside the organization working toward the complimentary trip.

Check with a Professional Mailing House.   Consult carefully with the post office and a professional mailing house before beginning. It is important to discuss such things as bulk mail permits, zip code sorting, size and dimensions of mail pieces, standardized sizes for mechanical folding and stuffing machines, delivery timing, and other matters.

Use Nonprofit Postage.   Check to see if the organization sponsoring the tour has nonprofit status. If so, it will have a nonprofit mailing permit that they may elect to use for this project, thus keeping postage costs down. In this case, the brochure,

Figure 9.2 Sample follow-up flyer. (Courtesy of Golden Bear Travel.)

cover letter, and envelope will have to comply with certain requirements to qualify for nonprofit mail, so this should be decided before the brochure is prepared.

USING A SALES ORGANIZER

One of the most effective methods of forming a group is by using a **sales organizer** (i.e., Pied Piper or draw). This person's name, when affiliated with the project, ensures that people will be drawn to the tour. It could be the minister leading his congregation to the Holy Land, a renowned writer or lecturer speaking to the group during the tour, the golf "pro" forming a group from his or her country club, or an outstanding businessperson promising to open import/export doors overseas.

Use of such a person can be an advantage because this person can serve as a focal point around whom people will gather. In short, this person can provide built-in publicity. People who may not have thought of traveling in a group may be motivated to travel as part of this group for a number of reasons, such as the following:

❑ Respect for the leader
❑ Desire to be a member of the "in group"
❑ Entrée to people and places overseas not generally available to the individual traveler or even to the average group
❑ Assurance of travel companions of similar tastes and interests.

If your organizer truly has a "name," this means that less publicity will be needed, or that the publicity that is needed will get more attention. For example, a news release to the local newspaper using the name may have a better chance of being published, and the brochure that is printed with a famous name on the cover may have a better chance of being read.

However, for all the advantages that name recognition can bring to the travel project, there also can be some disadvantages, or at least some factors that should be considered.

Things to Consider When Using a Name Draw

❑ Free trip(s). Usually such an individual will require a free trip (sometimes two, to include the spouse). Lesser known individuals might be willing to receive one free trip for a given number of passengers booked—perhaps one with 15, the spouse with 30, and a cash payment (less blatantly referred to as an honorarium) with 45 and above. On the other hand, certain well-known individuals may require a guarantee of the free trip or trips up-front, without sales volume prerequisites. In other words, conceivably you could be placed in a risk position so that if the tour did not sell well, the complimentary trip(s) would still be required as agreed upon in exchange for use of the draw person's name. In this event, you might have to pay out-of-pocket for complimentary air tickets, hotel rooms, and so forth if insufficient complimentaries were forthcoming from suppliers due to low sales figures.

❑ Some name draw persons may act as salespersons and actually work at helping to fill the tour. Others may simply lend their name to the project but expect you (or the tour's sponsoring organization) to do all the work. They are, in this case, a "silent draw."

❑ A name draw person or organizer may be an excellent public relations person or salesperson, but may not have the personal qualities necessary to act as the real working tour manager enroute. Such a case requires putting on a professional tour manager in addition to the draw person and costing this person in as well. (See chapters 12 and 13.)

❑ You should take the responsibility of reminding your tour organizer to be sure that important deadlines are met. You will have to make sure that he/she is adhering to a strict schedule if the trip is to be a success.

Letter of Understanding

It is important to have a contract, or at least a letter of agreement (see Figure 9.3) between your company and your organizer clarifying areas of possible misunderstanding. This letter should mention the following:

❑ Complimentary trips—will they be up-front or as earned, for one or for two?

❑ Additional remuneration—will there be a salary, a speaker's fee, or honorarium?

❑ What does the complimentary trip include? What meals, what sightseeing, or what shore excursions will be included? Will lodging be on a share basis or single-room basis?

❑ What expenses are not covered in the complimentary trip? Must the individual remain with the group throughout? What duties are expected of this person? (Many times one may lead the organizer to believe that the position involves nothing more than a little public relations. Once out on tour, it becomes obvious that there is a great deal that needs doing, such as reconfirming air tickets, assisting ill passengers, tracing lost passports, acting as host at parties, and so forth.)

❑ Will you have use of the organization's mailing list or a list of the organizer's personal following? Often, you may want to stipulate that the offer depends upon this person providing one-time access to a specific mailing list for promotion of the project. Granted, the mailing will cost money, but it might reach clients to whom you would not otherwise have access. A minister, for example, might agree to circulate a brochure not only to his own congregation, but also to affiliated congregations. A university alumni association might promise to

LSI Travel Agency
987 Park Drive #2A
Berkeley, CA 94704
Telephone Number: 510-555-2000
Fax Number: 510-555-7210

June 23, 19XX

Dr. Elaine Whittaker
Archaeology Lovers Assn.
167 Rose Court
Kansas City, Missouri 64106

Dear Mrs. Whittaker:

This will reconfirm our discussion today regarding your participation in our July 11 cruise to the Baltic with Royal Cruise Line.

(1) The cruise described is RCL's Mediterranean Highlights July 11-25, 19XX as described on page 17 of their brochure.

(2) It is agreed that you will be entitled to one complimentary air/sea cruise round-trip from Kansas City with a minimum of 30 adult air/sea passengers joining this project and a second similar complimentary when the group reaches 45 adult air/sea passengers.

(3) The complimentary will consist of the same services as included in the cruise for other members of this group. Conversely, any service not included for other members of the group are not included for you.

(4) You will agree to give a minimum of four shipboard lectures exclusively for our group, subject matter and brief description of each to be made available to us no later than January 1, 19XX. No honorarium will be paid for these lectures.

(5) You will agree to allow your name to be listed as group leader in all promotional materials published on this project.

(6) You will travel on air tickets accrued through volume bookings and issued by Royal Cruise Line. Travel will be via economy class air and choice of airline, flight schedule and other flight matters will be as designated by Royal Cruise Line.

(7) Complimentary cruise accommodations will be on a share-cabin basis and will be in a category which is an average of categories purchased by participants in this group. Final assignment of cabin will be at the discretion of Royal Cruise Line.

(8) You will agree to make available use of the special mailing list of the approximate 8,000 member "Archaeology Lovers Association" with which you are affiliated.

(9) LSI Travel Agency, Inc. agrees to provide a professional tour manager for this project to handle all behind-the-scenes business details. No tour managing duties are to be expected of you while on the cruise.

(10) All expenses related to promotion and sales of this project shall be at the expense of LSI Travel Agency, Inc. No sales efforts are expected of you.

(11) You will agree to participate with us in one pre-trip promotional evening, the date of this event to be cleared with you first.

Signature: _____   Signature: _____

Figure 9.3 Sample letter of agreement with the name draw, Elaine Whittaker, Ph.D., President, Lovers of Archaelogy Association.

mail to all alumni who were graduated within a particular time period. A celebrity might have a list of his or her personal "following."

❑ If bookings are coming in on this tour from more than one source, how will the source of each booking be identified? Will the organizer's initials be on the reservation form? Will different color reservation forms be assigned to different organizations? Will you rely on the passenger's word? (These details should be clear so that there is no infighting over a client by different outside salespeople.)

❑ Will free airfares be given from the home city or the gateway city?

PROMOTIONAL EVENING

If the potential tour participants are in a reasonably close geographical area, a promotional evening could be an effective way to generate interest, as well as enrollments for the tour. On the other hand, if the tour is being sold nationwide or even statewide, it probably will not be possible to get sufficient attendance in one locale.

Assume, however, that the tour is being marketed locally and that 90 percent of the tour participants will come from the local community. In this case, a promotional evening can be quite effective without being unduly expensive. This gathering is not to be confused with a pre-departure party or briefing. The purpose of a **promotional evening** is exactly that—to promote the tour. The success of such an evening is not measured by how many attended, how many glasses of champagne were consumed, or what a wonderful time was had by all. The success of such an evening is measured by how many tour bookings it generated—either with enrollments that very night or shortly thereafter. So, it is important to be sure that invitations are issued to the following:

1. Those who already are enrolled in the tour. They will generate enthusiasm.
2. Friends of those enrolled in the tour. Why not ask each person already under deposit on the tour to bring or send a friend?
3. Those whom you and the organizer believe are "on the fence"—people who have called to inquire about the trip or who have said that they are considering the trip but who have not yet signed up.
4. Other potential travelers whom you, your company, and the organizer carefully cull from lists.

If this is a private club's tour, the promotional function will have to be open to all members of the club; it is not possible just to pick and choose which members to invite. However, double-check to be sure that those in the above four categories are especially encouraged to attend.

Of course, the function does not have to be held in the evening. If appealing to a senior citizens' group whose members might not want to go out at night, or to

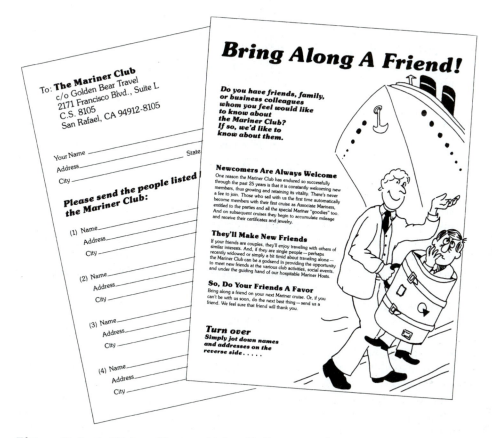

Figure 9.4   A "Bring Along a Friend" flyer can be a successful marketing tool to attract new people to a promotional evening or a trip. (Courtesy of Golden Bear Travel.)

a clientele that is not employed during the day, it may be more appropriate to schedule an afternoon function, perhaps a tea.

Pre-Planning

The first thing is to establish the date of the promotional function, making sure that there is more than enough lead time to plan the function properly, get the invitations out, and be assured of a good turnout. Clear the date first to avoid conflict with other functions the target group might be expected to attend. You will probably want to avoid holidays or long weekends when many people may be out of town or may have conflicting plans. Then pick the location. It is a good idea to have a second choice for a date just in case the chosen location is not available on the date selected.

After the date and the place are confirmed, be sure to reserve any films, speakers, or other programming that are planned. Get the participating airline or cruise line involved. Often, they will give financial help or will provide films or props. Group operators have known air and cruise lines to supply everything from engraved matchbooks to a Japanese torii gate.

Checklist

As does any good host or hostess, it is wise to have a checklist to be sure that everything goes smoothly. Points to check include the following:

1. **Invitation RSVP control**—a system to keep track of how many people are attending; how many people have not answered the invitation and need follow-up; and how many people have declined. Knowing the anticipated turnout makes it easier to plan for refreshments, seating, and other items. Be sure to allow for last-minute cancellations due to illness, bad weather, and so forth; invite twice as many guests as needed. It is also a good idea to call those who RSVP'd and remind them a day or two prior to the event.
2. **Refreshments** that are attractive and generous but do not overshadow the program itself. Emphasis should focus on program content and on building interest in the trip. Wine and cheese or coffee and tea with finger desserts are particularly appropriate.
3. **Equipment check** or trial run on such equipment as the public address system, movie projector, tape recorder, light-dimmer, draw draperies, and extension cords. There is nothing more embarrassing than having a hundred people sitting quietly waiting for the film to roll and having the projector break down or showing the wrong film.
4. **Miscellaneous details**—arrangements for greeting people at the door, handling coats, name tags, parking, and other seemingly extraneous details that can help make the evening a success.

Promotional Evening Format

A successful promotional program will not be overly long. It should incorporate a film or two of the area(s) to be visited. It should be a film that is up-to-date and slick. Any film should be previewed before it is shown to assure that it is appropriate, in good condition, and will generate excitement. Slide shows, unless professionally done, may tend to appear homemade. Few people truly enjoy sitting through a slide show of someone else's trip.

Music is one of the greatest catalysts in the world. When promoting a trip to the Adriatic, a strolling Greek bouzouki player during refreshments would be appropriate. Or, if the evening is designed to promote a trip to Latin America, perhaps a local college would have a student salsa band or guitarist for hire. Plan for music that is appropriate to the destination; a Mexican mariachi band would not do much to promote a trip to Spain.

Handicrafts, posters, artifacts, and costumes can add to the color of the evening. I have led a Greek folk dance to promote a Greek Islands cruise, worn an alpaca poncho to promote a trip to Peru, shown off my favorite Japanese wood-block prints, and even woven artificial cherry blossoms up an entire staircase for a Night in Japan.

And, if the guests' senses have been stimulated both visually and aurally, why not provide a taste treat as well? Many finger foods suggest foreign countries—miniature Italian pizzas, French petit fours, Chinese egg rolls, or Argentinian empanadas, and so forth.

After the film has been presented and refreshments have been served, allow a period for questions. You can plant one or two friends in the audience, prepared with a couple of good questions in case people are shy about starting the question-and-answer period. Everyone present should be given another copy of the tour brochure. Do plan to make a sales pitch that night, referring to the brochure and the reservation form therein. State that reservations are being accepted that evening. You might, at this point. State that the tour is already more than half-filled and there is room for only a limited number. If people do not have their checkbooks with them, you can suggest that they complete the reservation form and turn it in that evening, and ask them to forward the check in a day or two. Writing out something that night makes clients feel committed to taking the tour. You might wish to grant a discount to those who enroll that evening.

Giveaways

Giveaways or door prizes, although sometimes gimmicky, can be fun and can ensure that the audience will stay until the drawing at the end of the evening. Tapes, videos, picture books of a foreign country, or travel calendars are often appreciated. Gift certificates to a popular department store are welcome prizes also. Of course, a free around-the-world trip could be raffled off, but the local rules on raffles, lotteries, and the like should be checked first. Sometimes suppliers will help out, depending on how rich they are feeling at the time. Perhaps local merchants could help with luggage, a travel diary, or a foreign cookbook. Ask! If not, buy one impressive door prize and cost it into the promotional budget for the tour.

Wrap-Up

It is helpful to know exactly who was present at the promotional event and how to reach them later. An elegant way to find out is to have each guest sign a guest book on arrival with name, address, and telephone number. At the end of the program, remind the audience to sign on the way out in case they did not get to do so on the way in. Another way to know the name, address, and telephone number of each person present is to use the cards collected for the door prize drawing.

After the festivities are over, it is time to take stock—pay the bills, see how much the event finally cost, and how many bookings resulted. It is also considerate to send thank-you notes to all those who helped, such as the guest speaker, the airline sales representative, and the hotel banquet manager. In a week or two, you will also want to do a followup mailing or phone blitz to those people who attended but did not yet enroll in the trip.

ADVERTISING

Undoubtedly, you will want to use advertising in some form for promotion of a tour product. Even if the tour is for a private organization, which would not require public solicitation of tour membership, it still may be necessary to advertise in the organization's newsletter or to augment the tour membership formed by a strong nucleus from the organization by advertising to outsiders from the general public.

In some cases, you may simply be putting together a tour on speculation, hoping to promote it in the community or within a certain profession. In this case, it will most surely be necessary to plan an advertising campaign.

Advertising Agencies

If you plan to use nationwide advertising or if you have a fairly large advertising budget, it may be possible to consider using an advertising agency. Advertising agencies, like retail travel agencies, work on a commission basis. Their suppliers are the media they use—the newspapers, magazines, radio and television stations, and so forth. These media usually pay them 15 percent.

So, if the media selected will pay the advertising agency a commission, it probably will not cost you any more to work through an advertising agency than to go direct to the publication. On the other hand, if the media selected will not pay a commission to the advertising agency, the agency undoubtedly will charge a service fee. This is a situation similar to a client asking to be booked into a pension or small hotel that does not pay a travel agency or tour company a commission. Usually, newspapers do not pay commissions to advertising agencies for local advertising. Most magazines and radio and television stations do. If in doubt, ask!

Whether or not they receive a commission, advertising agencies will charge production costs for such things as typesetting, art, layout, and photos. Many agencies are full-service agencies offering a complete range of services, including market research, public relations, advertisement preparation and placement, advertisement clipping service, and coordinated billing. This is similar to the full-service travel agency that sells everything from a two-day local bus tour to an around-the-world cruise. Other advertising agencies are smaller operations, or agencies that elect to handle only specific services in a selective fashion. This is much like some travel agencies that elect to handle only certain cruise lines or tour operators whom they know are reputable, or to specialize in certain kinds of travel such as business travel for commercial accounts, adventure trekking, and so forth.

Dealing with only one or two publications may be relatively simple to do. However, running advertisements in a wide spectrum of publications may become totally unwieldy. It requires juggling different deadline dates, varying advertisement sizes and dimensions, and billings. In such cases, it may be worthwhile to work through an advertising agency just to keep visits from advertisement salespeople, phone calls, and the work load within reason.

Just as it is important for the traveler to have a good relationship with a travel counselor, so it is important to have a good working relationship with the advertising agency selected. Shop around. Ask questions. Does the advertising agency really want your account? Is the account big enough to interest them? Can their copywriters write about travel? Have they handled any other travel accounts? Are their artists creative? Ask to see some of their work—particularly travel-related campaigns. Expensive four-color process slick catalogues with professional color photos will not show what an advertising agency can do on a small budget for a tiny, black-and-white ad.

Many travel companies find that their advertising account is not large enough to warrant an advertising agency, meaning that they have to learn to do it themselves. This requires learning how to work with a typesetter and a freelance commercial artist (or using desktop publishing skillfully), probably writing the headlines and copy, and selecting media on a trial-and-error basis. You might start with newspaper advertisements and then graduate to magazines (and perhaps radio occasionally as skills improve). Here are some of the advantages and disadvantages of the different media.

Newspapers

Newspapers are one of the most effective media, because newspapers are heavily read by the public and the cost of advertising in them is relatively low compared to the costs in magazines, radio, and television. Newspaper rates are based on circulation, so the greater a newspaper's readership, the higher the rates. Do not overlook the small weekly papers; many of them are less expensive than the dailies, and they may even reach a targeted local market more effectively than the higher circulation dailies. It is fairly easy to schedule advertisements in newspapers because of frequency of publication and short lead time (e.g., advertisements do not have to be scheduled months in advance). However, newspapers are read by all—rich and poor alike, tour prospects and not—so a tour advertisement may be wasted on armchair travelers.

Magazines

If a magazine is directed to a specific market segment, that is, photographers, single working women under age 35, the male *bon vivant*, or any specific type of reader—it will be more beneficial to direct advertising to this specific clientele rather than

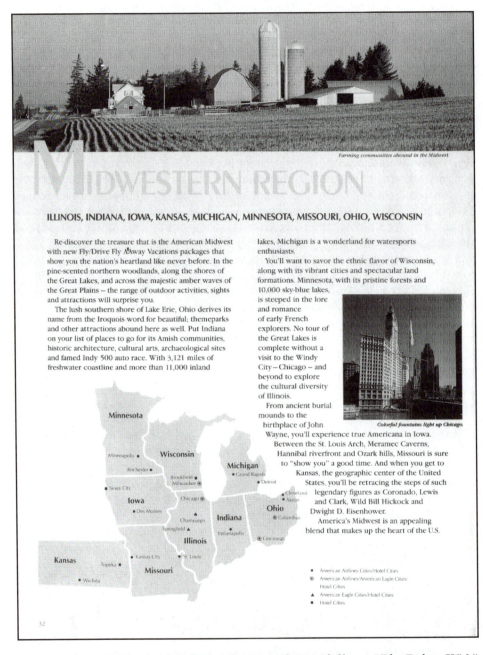

MIDWESTERN REGION

ILLINOIS, INDIANA, IOWA, KANSAS, MICHIGAN, MINNESOTA, MISSOURI, OHIO, WISCONSIN

Farming communities abound in the Midwest

Re-discover the treasure that is the American Midwest with new Fly/Drive Fly A Away Vacations packages that show you the nation's heartland like never before. In the pine-scented northern woodlands, along the shores of the Great Lakes, and across the majestic amber waves of the Great Plains – the range of outdoor activities, sights and attractions will surprise you.

The lush southern shore of Lake Erie, Ohio derives its name from the Iroquois word for beautiful; themeparks and other attractions abound here as well. Put Indiana on your list of places to go for its Amish communities, historic architecture, cultural arts, archaeological sites and famed Indy 500 auto race. With 3,121 miles of freshwater coastline and more than 11,000 inland lakes, Michigan is a wonderland for watersports enthusiasts.

You'll want to savor the ethnic flavor of Wisconsin, along with its vibrant cities and spectacular land formations. Minnesota, with its pristine forests and 10,000 sky-blue lakes, is steeped in the lore and romance of early French explorers. No tour of the Great Lakes is complete without a visit to the Windy City – Chicago – and beyond to explore the cultural diversity of Illinois.

From ancient burial mounds to the birthplace of John Wayne, you'll experience true Americana in Iowa. Between the St. Louis Arch, Meramec Caverns, Hannibal riverfront and Ozark hills, Missouri is sure to "show you" a good time. And when you get to Kansas, the geographic center of the United States, you'll be retracing the steps of such legendary figures as Coronado, Lewis and Clark, Wild Bill Hickock and Dwight D. Eisenhower.

America's Midwest is an appealing blend that makes up the heart of the U.S.

Colorful fountains light up Chicago

Minnesota
Minneapolis •
Rochester •
• Sioux City
Wisconsin
Brookfield ◉
Milwaukee ◉
Iowa
• Des Moines
Chicago ▲
Champaign ▲
Springfield ▲
Illinois
Michigan
• Grand Rapids
• Detroit
◉ Cleveland
• Akron
Ohio
◉ Columbus
Indiana
Indianapolis ▲
◉ Cincinnati
Kansas
Topeka ■
• Kansas City • St. Louis
Missouri
• Wichita

• American Airlines Cities/Hotel Cities
◉ American Airlines/American Eagle Cities/Hotel Cities
▲ American Eagle Cities/Hotel Cities
■ Hotel Cities

32

Figure 9.5 This is a page from the American Airlines "Fly Drive USA" brochure that was created by an advertising agency. It has a clean attractive layout, includes a map of the region, and the copy mentions many points of interest. (Courtesy of American Airlines).

to the general public. Special-interest magazines of this nature, instead of general-circulation magazines, are the trend nowadays. Magazines reach more affluent readers than do newspapers, and they stay around the house longer than the daily newspaper. Therefore, an advertisement might be read several times and by several different people. However, magazines require a longer lead time than newspapers. This requires that advertisers place the order for space and then submit the advertisement several months in advance to meet the magazine's publication schedule.

Radio and Television

Just as some magazines specialize in certain markets, radio stations appeal to specific audiences—those who enjoy country and western music, soul, rock, the classics, and so forth. Radio stations will be happy to send you a media kit, providing details on who is listening and when. Drive time during commuting hours usually is most expensive time to advertise. Radio advertisements do not need to be just a straight message. They can combine music and sound effects along with the message. But it is important that the message be short (i.e., usually 30-second spots) and easy to remember. Most listeners are not just sitting with pencil and paper in hand, poised to write down a telephone number; it is necessary to repeat it over and over, slowly, so that they can retain it in their mind long enough to get a pencil.

Television is rarely used for tour promotion by the small-to-medium-sized travel agency or tour operator, due to high costs and the need to produce a truly professional advertising spot. It is now being used successfully by some cruise lines, by Club Med, and by some large wholesale tour companies with large budgets.

Some Hints for Using Print Media Effectively

Note the following guidelines when preparing ads:

Continuity. One advertisement in one issue of a magazine or newspaper will not bring the desired results. Plan and budget for a series of advertisements to improve the chances of success. Many readers do not clip the coupon and send in for the tour brochure the first time that they see the advertisement. However, by the second or third week, they begin to assume that a company must be solid if it can continue advertising week after week. A minimum of three advertisements will be needed. Stay with the same style of advertisement (same typeface, same artistic appearance), even if the copy changes each week. Readers will begin to recognize the style when they see it.

Also note that publications give a better rate if a series of advertisements is reserved in advance—they have a one-time rate, three-time rate, and so forth.

Focus. An advertisement cannot tell the entire story of the tour. It should focus around the major points, both visually and in words. Think of different approaches; then emphasize one. When planning an advertisement, ask: Are we selling price?

Elegance? Unusual itinerary? A sun break from rotten winter weather? A learning experience? Camaraderie? In selecting the approach, remember that the ultimate purpose of the advertisement is not to sell the tour. It is to get the reader to call or write in for the brochure.

Simplicity.   The best advertisement is probably the simplest. An advertisement can be clever and different in order to stand out from others around it, but it does not have to be complicated or overly elaborate. An advertisement that incorporates one piece of dominant art with good headlines and a small amount of body copy probably works best.

Borders.   An advertisement does not appear alone. It usually appears on a page surrounded by articles and other advertisements competing for the reader's attention. Something should set an ad off from the surrounding clutter. A border, dotted lines, or art forming a natural barrier can indicate where one advertisement ends and the next one begins. Theme borders can enhance the feeling of a certain country.

White Space.   There is nothing more valuable than white space; that is empty, uncluttered, perfectly blank space. Often, the more elegant the ad, the more blank the space. Since advertising space is expensive, there is a tendency to fill it. But an advertisement that is too full and too busy simply confuses the reader. Also, white space can act as a buffer that forms an undeclared barrier around the advertisement, onto which neighboring copy cannot encroach.

Think Double Duty.   Often an advertisement can be used later. It can be blown up and reprinted as a flyer that can be used as a reminder insert in a mailing. When paying for original art or graphics, encourage the artist to produce a design that can also be used for the cover of the tour brochure, for another advertisement, and for invitations to promotional evenings.

Coupons

A reply coupon included in an advertisement serves two purposes. First, it gives the reader something physical to cut out and to send in, requesting information about the tour, thus providing the interested reader's name and address for further follow-up. Second, it helps you to track which publications are bringing results and how much these results are costing you. This is termed **acquisition costs**. Reply coupons should be coded. For example, the code CPD71193 might be used for an advertisement in the July 11, 1993 issue of the *Cleveland Plain Dealer*. The same advertisement on the same date in the *San Francisco Chronicle* could be coded SFC71193. These codes, typeset on the advertisement itself, provide a record of the number of responses each advertisement generates. If an advertisement costing $300 brings in 100 inquiries, it is costing $3 per inquiry, or what is called a $3 per inquiry acquisition cost. By running exactly the same advertisement—same size, same tour product—in different publications, and by tracking the number of

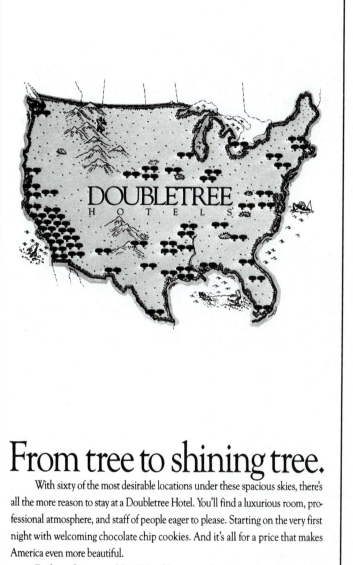

Figure 9.6 This ad for Doubletree Hotels uses several techniques for communicating effectively in print: an attention-getting headline and a dominant visual. (Courtesy of Doubletree Hotels and Doubletree Club Hotels.)

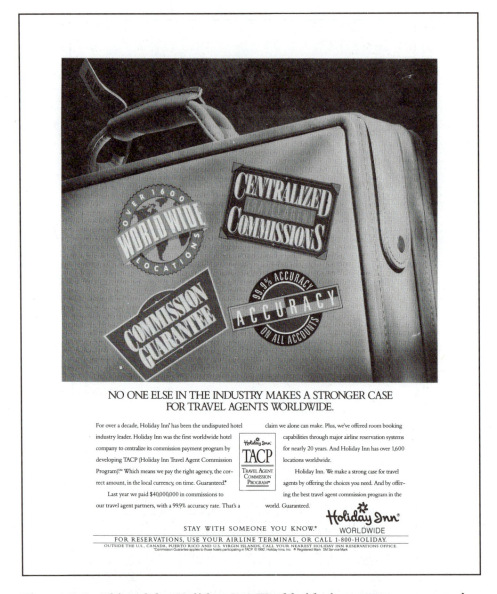

Figure 9.7 This ad for Holiday Inn Worldwide is a strong communicator because its bold visual, clever headline and body copy speak directly to its target market—the travel agent. (Courtesy of Holiday Inn Worldwide; Advertising agency, Tucker Wayne/Luckie & Company.)

Figure 9.8   This ad uses white space to give a clean, uncluttered look and to focus the eye on the copy in the center.   The white space also serves as a barrier against other ads or copy on the same page.   (Courtesy of Kahala Hilton.)

inquiries that result from each, you can easily determine which publications are most effective. Note that these acquisition figures are per *inquiry*, not per booking. What is equally important is how many inquiries are then successfully converted into bookings by effective sales personnel.

When first reserving advertisement space with a publication, indicate if the advertisement will have a coupon. This will help prevent two coupons from being printed back to back. Ask for an "outside position"—that is, the outside edge of the page. It is much easier to cut out a coupon if it is not in the center of the page. The coupon should also be large and clear enough to permit the reader to write on it easily. See Figure 9.9 for a sample coded coupon.

Co-op Advertising

The possibility of **cooperative (co-op) advertising** should not be overlooked. This is advertising in which the costs are shared with a supplier. Sometimes several stores in one city suddenly seem to be advertising Wrangler Jeans instead of Levi's, or Martex towels instead of Cannon, in a particular week. It may be because the jeans company or towel company had offered to share the cost of the advertising

```
Mail coupon to        T&LF93
Holiday Air
P.O. Box 555
New York, NY  10055


Name _____
Address _____
State _____ Zip _____
CALL YOUR TRAVEL AGENT OR:

    HOLIDAY AIR
 1-800-123-5555
```

Figure 9.9 A coded coupon. This code indicates that the coupon was prepared to run in *Travel and Leisure Magazine,* **February 1993.**

campaign with the department stores that particular week. You can look to travel suppliers for similar help.

If you are selling a cruise or an existing tour package "as is," the supplier should have **advertising slicks** for that particular product available. A slick is a pre-prepared or partially prepared ad usually on glossy "slick" paper (hence the name) You can then simply drop in your company's own name, address, logo, and phone number. In many cases, the supplier will share the cost of the advertisement with you upon receipt of proof that the advertisement actually ran. This proof can be a sample tear sheet from the publication and invoice. Check first with the supplier to make sure this arrangement is acceptable. In other cases, if the supplier already has agreed to pay you an override commission, it may be assumed that the override is paid to cover promotional expenditures of this nature; therefore, the supplier may not be willing to spend additional monies on co-op advertisements.

When a tour package is put together from scratch, the availability of co-op advertising funds is strictly a negotiable item between your company and the sponsoring airline or other suppliers (see Chapter 6 regarding negotiations with suppliers). It would be considered part of the total negotiated package. If you are planning to use a supplier's ad slicks, note that they may be generic, and therefore not really appropriate for a custom-designed tour product. Also the supplier's slicks may project the image of the supplier and its product, rather than the image of your company, the sponsoring club, or other entity that you wish to project.

PRESS RELEASES

In the past, getting one's name in the paper was a sure route to social ruin. Influential families paid to keep their names out of the press. Today, as a cafe society and the jet set have replaced the old society, at least in the public eye, people are more and more assured that they are somebody if their name appears in print. Many people pay to see that it does. The public wants to read who vacationed where and what new far-flung corner of the world is in fashion today. Many people enjoy traveling vicariously through the society pages, or through a relatively new phenomenon—the travel section of the newspaper or the travel columns of leading magazines.

Although a tour may not make the pages of *Vogue,* perhaps it is possible to get a mention in the hometown newspaper or in a specialty magazine. The average retail travel agency that may be large enough to have a tour department or the small tour company or independent tour planner still cannot afford to retain a full-scale public relations company or professional press person. Once again, it is a matter of the do-it-yourself approach by learning how to get the tour into the press.

The usual vehicle for placing an article in the print media is what is termed a **press release** or sometimes a "news release." (The more generic term is "media release" which would encompass not only newspapers and magazines, but also the electronic media—radio and television). This is a short, punchy article that is sent to various editors. (See Figure 9.10 for an example of a press release.) It should be sent to a specific editor (e.g., Travel Editor or Theatre Editor). Many theatre tours may be better promoted in the Sunday theatre section or Superbowl tours on the sports pages than in the travel section. If it is possible to get the name of the editor and to address this individual personally, so much the better.

Press Release Format

The usual press release format is to type the release double-spaced, on plain white bond paper with your company name, address, telephone number and fax number in the upper left-hand corner. Also include your name or the name of a contact person. This lets the recipient know immediately who sent it and how to reach that person quickly and easily for further information or a telephone interview. The release should be dated, and it should also indicate when the "news" may be released. Note the term news; it should be worded carefully so that it *is* news. If it is the same old tour repeated every year, a new angle should be stressed. A publication needs a new "peg" on which to hang the article; it needs a reason to justify publishing the article. It cannot appear that they are just giving away free advertising in the form of an article.

If possible, keep the release to one page. The essentials should be in the first paragraph—where the tour goes, dates, highlights, name of leader if a known name, and any unique angle. Remember, the editor is inundated with similar press releases for many tours every week. So anything unusual about this tour that might catch the editor's eye should be mentioned early in the release. Is the tour sponsored by a local college for academic credit? Does it feature behind-the-scenes visits to private homes? Perhaps the tour is sponsored by a local museum and raises money for the museum. Whatever the local or unusual angle, stress it.

Most importantly, news should be told in a straightforward, simple manner. A release is not an appropriate place to write poetic descriptions of the scenery. Accuracy and credibility are important. If the tour stays at first-class hotels, say so; do not inflate them to deluxe. If the tour is open to the public and if there is still space available, say so. Many readers assume that a private-sounding tour is just that—private. At the end of the release, put the journalistic sign: -30-. Then, check the release for errors, misspellings, and misunderstandings. If clients' names are mentioned in the release, be sure you have their written permission. Let the release set for a day or two and then reread it. Does it still sound as good as it did when you wrote it? Are all those extra words necessary, or can you tighten it?

LSI Travel Agency
987 Park Drive #2A
Berkeley, CA 94704
Telephone Number: 510-555-2000
Fax Number: 510-555-7210

March 1, 19XX

<u>For Immediate Release</u>

TO: Sunday Travel Editor
Your local newspaper
Address

FALL TOUR TO EUROPE SCHEDULED
BY ROSEMONT COUNTRY CLUB

An exciting eleven-day trip to Europe will depart on September 4, sponsored by the Rosemont Country Club.

The itinerary includes Amsterdam, Paris and Rome. Highlights include a cruise along Amsterdam's canals, a full-day excursion to the Hague and Delft to see the world-famous blue Delft-ware china, and an evening at the Lido Night Club in Paris. Other features are a personally-escorted tour of the Louvre, an afternoon at the Vatican Museum and Sistine Chapel while in Rome, and a full-day Sunday excursion with country lunch to the Villa d'Este outside of Rome.

The trip is via Trans World Airlines and is operated by LSI Travel Agency, Inc. of Berkeley, California. It is fully escorted and includes deluxe hotels, air fare, full program of sightseeing and social events, many meals, taxes, tips, and all tour services.

Although planned by the Rosemont Country Club for its members and their friends, other interested members of the community are welcome to join the tour. To obtain full details including a day by day itinerary and prices, contact LSI Travel Agency, Inc. at 891 Park Drive #2A, Berkeley, California 94704 or call toll-free: 510-555-2000 or FAX 510-555-7210.

-30-

Figure 9.10 This sample press release follows the standard form and content of information released to the press. The main theme is expressed in the headline and the copy tells the who, what, where, when, and why of the story.

Photos

Sometimes a photo may be included with the press release. The newspaper may not have room to run both the article and the photo, but the photo at least draws the editor's attention to the release. If the photo and the release are good enough, the editor just might make room for them. Of course, it can be costly to send photos if releases are sent simultaneously to a large number of publications. Photos for a newspaper's use have traditionally been black-and-white glossies, not color. However, today with new techniques, many publications can accept color transparencies or prints. It is suggested that you check with the publication by telephone first, if in doubt. Photos should be well focused and not too dark, since newsprint paper tends to absorb ink and darken photos. Be sure that the photo carries a caption, and if necessary, a credit line recognizing the photographer or source of the photo. Subject matter can be a destination scene of an area the tour will visit or it can be the tour organizer with several of the tour members together packing a suitcase or discussing the trip (they should not look too posed). Be sure to obtain written permission from those in the photo before using it.

The press release and accompanying photo should go out some months before the tour's departure, since the newspaper may not find a place for it until later, and since it should appear early enough to bring in some sales. The release will not do much good if it appears three weeks before the tour's departure when unsold air and hotel space had to be released 30 days prior.

Do not be disappointed if the paper does not use the release. They are not obligated to do so. Advertising is paid space and, therefore, guarantees that a paid advertisement will appear. But a press release is not paid space. If it is published, it is simply free publicity, a bonus, but not something to be counted on. The editor may choose to use it or not, to rewrite it, or to chop it, as more important competing news or a large advertisement comes along to compete for space in the publication. An article will have a better chance of being published if it is news, if it has a local angle (e.g., a local organization sponsoring it or a local name escorting it), and if it has a local price. The price out of New York is not really relevant to a reader in Des Moines.

Press Release Do's and Dont's

Do continue to send releases to publications even if they do not publish them at first. *Don't* threaten to withdraw advertising if they will not run a story. *Do* try to develop a rapport with the editor, if possible. And *don't* forget the rural or residential weeklies, where there may be a better chance for publication than in a big-city daily newspaper and where news or feature articles are often needed. *Do* always remember to include contact name, telephone number, and fax number on every media release should the publication wish to reach you. And *do* remember to be considerate. Even the most callous big-city editor appreciates a gracious "thank you."

❑ *SUMMARY*

Every tour should have its own marketing plan, which is drawn up with accompanying budget before the tour is priced. The most cost-effective plan is to direct your promotion to a specific market segment. A variety of promotional avenues are available to you: direct mail, use of an organizer as a recruiter, a promotional evening, press releases; and paid advertising in magazines, newspapers, private publications, or on radio and TV. Most tours will require one or more of these in combination. The sum of these is known as the "marketing mix." Each method has its pros and cons and should be assessed before deciding on the final marketing plan. Since the success or failure of a tour may depend on its marketing, it's important to budget adequately for this phase and to include a contingency fund for extra promotion if deemed necessary. Readers interested in learning more about travel marketing may wish to read Delmar Publishers' *Travel and Tourism Marketing Techniques* by Robert T. Reilly.

❑ *REVIEW QUESTIONS*

1. **Why is it important to develop a marketing plan for a tour *before* you price the tour?**

2. **Name three items that might be included in your "marketing mix."**

3. **What do we mean by a "Pied Piper"?**

4. Name five points that should be covered in a letter of understanding between yourself and a tour organizer.

5. If you were planning a promotional evening, to whom would you send invitations?

6. What are some of the pros and cons of placing your tour ad in daily newspapers?

7. What are the pro and cons of placing the same ad (as in No. 6 above) in magazines?

8. **If you ran an ad three consecutive weeks at $300 each week and received a grand total of 100 inquiries, what would be your per-inquiry acquisition cost? If you ran the exact same ad in another publication three consecutive weeks at $200 each week and received a grand total of only 70 inquiries, what would be your per-inquiry acquisition cost? Which is the better buy for you?**

9. **What is co-op advertising? Who co-ops with you?**

10. **Why is it important to use borders around an ad?**

❑ *ACTIVITIES*

1. Contact your local post office to determine the difference in mail costs between first class and bulk rate for a mailing you plan to do to 2,000 potential tour prospects. Decide if the difference in price warrants using first class and how much the additional expense might raise the tour price to your passengers.

2. Clip several ads from the Sunday travel section of your metropolitan newspaper. Select examples of ads that demonstrate: (a) use of strong graphics and simple concise copy; (b) use of borders; (c) plenty of white space.

3. Write a sample press release for your local newspaper describing a fictitious group tour of your choosing. Keep it terse and factual.

4. Plan a fictitious promotional evening to be held at a hotel in your town. Contact the banquet manager of your selected hotel and query the prices of a function room, refreshments, and audiovisual equipment for your party.

▷ 10

CLIENT HANDLING

LEARNING OBJECTIVES

After reading this chapter, you should:

❑ Be able to handle tour inquiries and convert them to sales
❑ Learn what to include in information bulletins for your tour members to help them prepare for the trip
❑ Know how to invoice tour members properly for final payment
❑ Learn what travel insurance you should be offering group tour clients
❑ Know how to handle cancellations and refunds for those tour members who cancel their tour participation
❑ Be able to keep wait-listed passengers happy while they standby for space on tours that are fully booked
❑ Know how to prepare a final document package for group members prior to their departure

KEY CONCEPTS AND TERMS

Billing
Cancellations
Cancellation Waiver
Clients' Final Payments
Confirmation of Tour Space
Final Documents
Final Payments
Information Bulletins
Option Offer
Tour Questionnaire
Travel Insurance
Waiting Lists

Once the promotional material on the tour is published, the first thing that may happen is that prospective clients will write or call for information. Someone has to answer those questions, so the week that the promotion breaks is not the week for the person or persons responsible for the tour to be on vacation. Staff should be carefully briefed in advance on the tour so that they can sound knowledgeable (and gracious) when telephones ring or when letters arrive. This will be the client's first contact with the company, so be ready to make it a favorable first impression.

INQUIRIES

Be prepared with a standard letter to answer inquiries. (See Figure 10.1.) This standard letter should accompany the brochure because it is impersonal to send a brochure alone in an envelope. This letter can be preprinted if a large volume of inquiries is anticipated, or it can be typed and be on line in a word processor, personalizing each letter. The letter should convey personal warmth and friendliness, and the closing should urge some action. Keep a record of the names and addresses of those who inquire, so that a follow-up letter can be sent to those who do not enroll. (See Figure 10.2 for a sample of a followup letter.)

Many group operators make an **option offer** to a client if it appears that there is real interest. To do this, offer to hold a firm place on the tour for a certain limited period. This limited period is usually ten days or so. By the predetermined date, the client must submit the required deposit and registration form to formalize and enroll. (See Figure 10.3 for a sample of an option offer letter.) Never include in your booking totals those people who have said that they are joining but who have not sent in a reservation form and deposit. Without a deposit they cannot be considered firm bookings.

RESERVATIONS AND DEPOSITS

As bookings start arriving they should be acknowledged immediately. Clients want to know that their reservation and deposit have been received. They are anxiously waiting to know if their space is confirmed. Try to make it a rule to acknowledge all bookings the same day they arrive. The acknowledgment need not be a lengthy and complicated letter. It can even be a preprinted thank you card of some sort. (See Figure 10.4.) But promptness is important.

If you are selling a cruise and cannot immediately confirm the cabin category of space that the client requests, that thank-you should simply acknowledge the booking but not use the word "confirm." That way, if clients request category "E" on the ship (an outside twin), and only an "F" (inside twin category) can be confirmed, they cannot later quote the letter to say that the request had been confirmed.

If a client is enrolling in the tour through a club or organization that, in turn, is forwarding the booking to your company, have an acknowledgment letter

LSI Travel Agency
987 Park Drive #2A
Berkeley, CA 94704
Telephone Number: 510-555-2000
Fax Number: 510-555-7210

Date

Dear Friend (or personalize):

We are so pleased to know of your interest in our tour program.

Enclosed is the brochure you requested, giving full details and including a day-by-day itinerary that will give you an idea of the many exciting activities planned.

Please refer particularly to the paragraph entitled "Tour Price Includes." You will note our price is virtually all-inclusive—airfare, top hotels, many meals, a full program of sightseeing and social activities, baggage handling, even tips—thus enabling you to plan ahead and budget accordingly, knowing you won't have lots of unexpected expenses along the way.

Most of our tours do fill up well in advance, so if you are serious about joining us, we would urge that you submit your reservation quickly to assure you of a place. We like to keep our groups to a fairly small, friendly size, so once our space is sold, we close out the tour rather than trying to secure additional reservations.

If you have questions before enrolling, do feel free to call us collect at 510-555-2000 or FAX 510-555-7210.

Cordially,

Marty Sarbey de Souto

Marty Sarbey de Souto, CTC
Group Manager

MS/s
enclosure

Figure 10.1 Sample inquiry reply letter.

LSI Travel Agency
987 Park Drive #2A
Berkeley, CA 94704
Telephone Number: 510-555-2000
Fax Number: 510-555-7210

Date

Dear Friend (or personalize):

We recall that earlier you inquired about our tour program. (Or, you can individualize it to the fall tour to Europe with the Rosemont Country Club). To date, we have not heard from you further and we wonder if you are still hoping to travel with us.

This is simply a courtesy note to let you know that the tour space is selling rapidly and that if you are still considering going, we must hear from you quickly. Enclosed is a duplicate copy of the tour brochure in case you may no longer have the one sent you earlier.

Would you be kind enough to give us a call or drop a line and let us know of your plans? If you have questions not answered in the brochure, feel free to call and chat with us.

Awaiting word . . . .

Cordially,

Marty Sarbey de Souto

Marty Sarbey de Souto, CTC
Group Manager

MS/s
enclosure

Figure 10.2 Inquiry follow-up letter.

LSI Travel Agency
987 Park Drive #2A
Berkeley, CA 94704
Telephone Number: 510-555-2000
Fax Number: 510-555-7210

Mrs. Merle Davis
2433 Beaver Place
Briston, IN 46507

Dear Mrs. Davis:

It was nice chatting with you today and we are looking forward to having you and Mr. Davis join us on the European Highlights Tour sponsored by Rosemont Country Club.

To reconfirm our telephone converstaion, we are holding two places for you under option for ten days. We will need to receive the reservation form from the brochure along with a $400 deposit by then in order to secure these reservations.

If you have any more questions, do feel free to give me a call. In the meantime, I'll be on the lookout for your reservation in the mail.

Sincerely,

Marty Sarbey de Souto, CTC
Group Manager

MS/s
cc: Mrs. Charles Goodwin-Rosemont Country Club

Figure 10.3 Option offer.

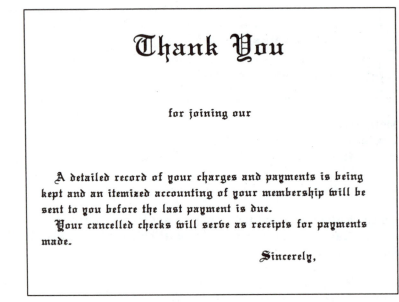

Thank You

for joining our

A detailed record of your charges and payments is being kept and an itemized accounting of your membership will be sent to you before the last payment is due.

Your cancelled checks will serve as receipts for payments made.

Sincerely,

Figure 10.4 Standardized acknowledgment card. (Courtesy of Howard Tours Inc.)

preprinted on the club's letterhead so it can send the letter to the applicant when it receives the reservation. (See Figure 10.5.) This letter should advise the applicant that the reservation form and check have been received and have been forwarded to LSI Travel Agency, Inc., the official business agent for the project. The clients should also be assured that they will be hearing directly from LSI Travel.

INFORMATION BULLETINS

Between the time when members join the tour and when they depart on the trip, they should receive a minimum of three mailings and **information bulletins**. The first one goes out immediately after they enroll, perhaps along with their welcome or acknowledgment letter. (See Figure 10.6.) This first bulletin should be the most complete. The second bulletin should go out with the members' bills at invoice time. This is a short update bulletin. The third bulletin is the departure bulletin, which goes out with the final documents a couple of weeks before departure. These information bulletins have to be written from scratch and then photocopied or printed. Bulletins serve five basic purposes.

1. Information bulletins give the tour members a feeling of confidence and of well-being; they show that your company has anticipated many of their questions as they prepare for the trip.

Rosemont Country Club
1234 Willow Road • Berkeley, CA 94704 • (510) 555-6000
Fax Number: 510-555-1212

Dear Friends: (or personalize to individual names)

This will acknowledge receipt of your application and deposit for member-ship in our exciting tour to Europe this fall. We are pleased that you have decided to come along!

As you may know, we are working in cooperation with LSI Travel Agency here in town. As travel professionals, they are handling all the business details of the program for us. Therefore, your reservation request has been given to them, and very shortly you should be hearing from the tour manager in their office in charge of our trip.

You will also be receiving a great deal of background information that should help you in your pretrip planning and that should answer a number of ques-tions one always has before such a trip . . . information on things like pass-ports, luggage, appropriate clothes for the various functions we'll be attend-ing, and so forth.

We at the Rosemont Country Club know it's going to be a wonderful vaca-tion. We look forward to traveling with you.

Sincerely,

Marian Goodwin

Mrs. Charles Goodwin
President

MG/mfs

Figure 10.5 Sponsoring club's acknowledgment letter.

LSI Travel Agency
987 Park Drive #2A
Berkeley, CA 94704
Telephone Number: 510-555-2000
Fax Number: 510-555-7210

Date

Mr. and Mrs. Elliott Wing
2433 Brown Derby Road
El Cerrito, CA 94530

Dear Mr. and Mrs. Wing:

We have been advised by the Rosemont Country Club that you are applying for participation in their tour to Europe this fall. As I believe they may already have advised you, we are the agency working with them in handling all the business details of the trip. Therefore, we wanted to get in touch with you right away to say "Welcome Aboard" and to let you know that your space on the tour is definitely confirmed.

To assist you in your pre-trip planning, we are enclosing an information bulletin that should answer a number of questions that may occur to you. Please read it carefully and if there are any things of concern to you, feel free to call us collect.

If you do not already have a passport, or if your present one has expired, may we urge you to begin passport proceedings right away. The U.S. Passport Office can get terribly backlogged sometimes, so it is urgent that you not delay. Full instructions on how to apply for a passport are enclosed.

You probably will not be hearing from us again until late in June, when we will be in touch with you with any new tour developments. At that time we will be sending your itemized bill for balance of payment, which, as indicated in the brochure, is due July 6. You might wish to flag that date on your personal calendar so you plan and budget accordingly.

One last word—the tour is filling rapidly, so if you know others in the Club who are planning on going or if you have friends who would like to join you, do tell them to send in their reservations quickly while space remains.

With all best wishes, and again Welcome!

Cordially,

Marty Sarbey de Souto

Marty Sarbey de Souto, CTC
Group Manager

MS/s
enclosures
cc: Mrs. Charles Goodwin-Rosemont Country Club

Figure 10.6 Company's acknowledgment letter.

2. Information bulletins answer many questions that could not be covered adequately in a tour brochure. For example, in the brochure it may be possible to have one short paragraph on clothing, packing, and wardrobe selection. However, it is not possible to give a complete list of wardrobe suggestions in a brochure, nor would it really be appropriate there. The main purpose of the brochure is to sell and to move the reader to enroll in the tour. The bulletins have room for more information; this is their purpose.

3. Information bulletins standardize information, ensuring that all group members receive exactly the same answers.

4. Information bulletins reduce the number of letters and phone calls to your office, allowing staff more time to deal with operational problems, volume of bookings, and the true management of the tour. Of course, personal contact with tour members should not be eliminated, but the time spent with them should be quality time, not time spent in showing them how to fill out a visa form.

5. These written bulletins form a strong legal basis against possible claims. The client who later says, "I didn't know I had to cancel by July 1 to avoid a penalty" can be told, "Sir, you were told, in writing, not only in the original brochure on this project, but you were also reminded again in our first information bulletin."

Learning to Prepare Bulletins

One of the most difficult transitions for a retail travel counselor converting from individual client handling to group handling is converting from the spoken word to the written one and from personal counseling across the desk or by telephone to mass counseling via written publications such as brochures or bulletins.

When first starting in the group business, the tendency is to think of local groups, to encourage the participants to feel free to call at the office, and to have a group gathering at which they receive verbal instructions.

As a company expands its group business, however, this method quickly outlives its usefulness, particularly if business depends on group volume. It soon seems more practical to turn to suppliers for prepublished pamphlets and instructions (e.g., cruise lines). However, although some of that information is helpful, much of it is not pertinent to the group and, in fact, may even give conflicting information to your tour members. For example, a cruise line's preprinted literature may instruct passengers to fill out a dining room seating request form and return it directly to the cruise line. However, you may have selected late meal sitting for the entire group, and you may have arranged with the cruise line to have the group seated together at tables of eight. Therefore, these cruise line instructions would only confuse tour members. In fact, one problem faced in putting a group on an existing travel package, such as a cruise or another company's tour, is eliminating information that is not pertinent to your group.

As your company handles more and more groups, you are eventually going to handle statewide or even nationwide groups rather than local ones. At this point, it is essential to master the art of most client counseling via the written word rather than via telephone or in person. This can be done by learning to prepare effective written pieces such as information bulletins, letters, departure instructions and so forth, thus preparing and printing your own tour information bulletins and not depending on outside sources.

Of course, there will be occasions when clients need to speak with you for special help on an individual matter not covered in your written material. Your company should have a WATS toll-free telephone line for these calls.

First Information Bulletin

The first information bulletin will be quite lengthy, and will take a good deal of time to prepare. It should cover the numerous subjects about which the tour members are anxious, such as passports, inoculations, visas or tourist cards, rooming arrangements, airport security checks, cameras and film, travel insurance, and seating on motorcoaches or airplanes. Other subjects to cover are cancellations and refund policy, smoking/nonsmoking, airfare restrictions, tipping, use of credit cards, and spending money. First bulletins are also concerned with foreign currency, appropriate clothing, luggage and packing, care of valuables, customs, and duty-free shops. If the trip is a cruise, the first bulletin includes information on optional shore excursions and special social events on board. Tour participants also appreciate background reading recommendations, information on shopping enroute, and advice on how to handle special diet restrictions or certain health limitations. Let us look at some of this information in detail.

Passports. If a passport is needed on the trip, the bulletin should let the tour member know it immediately. This is particularly important today, with delays at some United States passport offices during peak periods. If visas must be secured, remember that they cannot be obtained until after receiving the passenger's *valid and signed passport.* If there is a deadline date for receiving the passport, be sure to advise clients of that deadline date at once and urge them to begin passport proceedings immediately. Often, older people have trouble getting a birth certificate; the courthouse burned down, they have to obtain an affidavit of birth instead, and so forth. All of these possibilities further delay the proceedings. Try to avoid losing a tour participant at the last minute for lack of a passport. To expedite matters, include passport application forms and a separate "how-to" instruction sheet. The instruction sheet will have details on number and size of photos, required acceptable identification, and cost. If passports are not required but some sort of proof of citizenship *is* mandatory, be sure participants are advised what proof is acceptable by the authorities. Also, if participants are not U.S. citizens, be sure they are properly notified as to correct documentation—both for entry into foreign countries they will be visiting and for reentry into the United States.

Figure 10.7 Pre-trip information booklets are a great help to travelers. The booklets in this illustration were published by the U.S. Customs Office and U.S. Department of State, but many tour companies and cruise lines publish their own. (Courtesy of U.S. Department of State and U.S. Customs.)

Inoculations.   Advise clients as to which inoculations are required and urge them to consult their physician. Advise them also of inoculations that are recommended but not required, again referring them to their own physician. (If you are in doubt as to what inoculations are required, you may wish to contact the Centers for Disease Control in Atlanta, Georgia.)

Visas/Tourist Cards.   The passport represents permission from one's own country to travel, while visas or tourist cards represent permission from other nations to visit them. It is important to check each country on the group's itinerary carefully to verify if a tourist visa or tourist card is needed (either in addition to or instead of a passport). Then, advise each passenger formally of what must be done. The first information bulletin is an ideal place to do this.

If visas or tourist cards are required for any of the countries on the itinerary, it is necessary to obtain a supply of visa or tourist card applications from the particular consulate(s) concerned, or perhaps to work through a visa service that will handle this for a fee. A visa service will charge the consular fee for issuing a visa, if any, as well as a service fee and a fee for registered mail or overnight express delivery charges. (Be sure these total charges are budgeted into the tour costs at the outset.)

Your company will have to give tour members detailed written instructions on how to complete the forms and what type of photos are needed. If tour members know this in advance, they can obtain visa photos at the same time that they obtain their passport photos. To avoid confusion in filling out the visa or tourist card applications, many tour operators fill them out for their passengers, simply instructing the passengers to sign by the "X."

Rooming Arrangements. Although the tour brochure probably stipulates that accommodations are share twin-bedded room basis or single-room basis, this bulletin is an excellent place to elaborate on such things as class of hotels. Many inexperienced travelers do not understand what is meant by hotel terminology such as "first class," "deluxe," "five-star," and so forth. Many Americans who assume that first class in Europe is the same as first class in the United States become angry upon finding that the accommodations are much more modest than they thought.

The first information bulletin is also the place to discuss single-room supplements and share-room with strangers. It is helpful to include a sentence to the effect that "Paying a single-room supplement ensures privacy but does not necessarily guarantee superior accommodations." Many knowledgeable tour operators know that single rooms are often the worst rooms in the house; they are located under stairways, next to elevator shafts, and in other undesirable locations.

This bulletin should also state the company's policy on sharing a room. Will the tour operator team up roommates? If there is a "leftover" passenger at the end with no potential roommate, will this person be forced to pay the single-room supplement or will your company absorb that cost? Tour participants are entitled to know the company policy, particularly since, in some cases, people traveling alone may withdraw from the tour if they have to pay the differential for forced single-room occupancy. Conversely, some clients will refuse to enroll on the trip unless they can be guaranteed single-room occupancy. In either case, it is wise to include a statement that the agency cannot assume responsibility for the compatibility of share-room arrangements and that if individuals move out of a shared room midtour, such additional charges are at their own expense.

Airport Security. Passengers should be advised that even as part of a tour group that they still have to go through an individual airport security check (i.e., by metal-detection device or by hand search). They should be reminded not to carry pen-knives or other things that can set off the metal detectors and delay the entire group.

Cameras and Film. It is best to alert people to the cost and occasional scarcity of film in some overseas areas. Let them know that they should carry an adequate supply of film with them, and not depend on buying it enroute. Holding up an entire tour bus while one passenger goes out in search of film is not fair to the other passengers. This first bulletin is also the appropriate place to remind passengers that a small camera is allowed as carry on luggage. However, large cameras, cases, flash equipment, tripods, and so forth are weighed and/or counted as part of their tour luggage allowance. Remind them not to let film go through the x-ray equipment, even with a shield on it. They should hand carry it and pass it around the

FINAL PAYMENT

Please refer to your tour brochure for final payment date. You will receive a fully itemized statement from us shortly prior to that date. It is suggested that you now "flag" your calendar or make a mental note of payment date so that you may budget accordingly.

AIRPORT SECURITY

Most airports here at home and abroad nowadays have an airport security force which will X-ray your hand luggage or physically search it. If you have not traveled by air in recent years, this may prove a new experience for you, but please do not be alarmed. It is to be expected.

CAMERAS AND FILM

Part of the fun of your trip will be recording your enjoyable hours on film and then reliving them months later at home. Remember that a small camera, which you carry in your hand or around your shoulder, probably will not be weighed in by the airlines as part of your luggage allowance. However, all large cameras, cases, flash and additional equipment may be weighed in as part of your allowance.

Although many types of film are available in major cities, we urge you to take a *full* supply with you, as in most cases it is much more expensive than at home. Have your film developed upon returning home, not enroute.

Please be aware that at most airports nowadays, both your hand baggage and your checked baggage are subject to X-ray devices used at airport security checks. Therefore, you may wish to inquire about a shield for your film at your local camera store.

Figure 10.8 Airport security and cameras and film are good topics for a pre-trip information booklet. (Courtesy of Harvest Travel International.)

x-ray equipment whenever possible. Many tour members, who have returned home with film totally ruined, have blamed the tour manager or the tour company for not issuing a warning.

Travel Insurance.   It is probably best to send detailed information and application forms for travel insurance in a later special mailing. However, this first information bulletin can allude to the fact that full information on this subject will be arriving later, so that passengers do not worry and start asking for it or buy it elsewhere.

Airplane and Motorcoach Seating.   Passengers should be reminded that your company needs to know if they wish to be seated in the smoking or nonsmoking section of the aircraft. (When such a choice is possible,) you can request preseating assignments from the airline, and the group can be appropriately divided. Of course, many flights today are totally nonsmoking. This is also an opportunity to advise that even if their preference is known, there is no guarantee that the airlines will comply. There are some airlines and some countries where this division is not followed as rigorously as it might be in the United States.

Motorcoach seating is another subject that needs mentioning. Perhaps, it should just be mentioned at first, then reinforced later by the tour manager at the tour briefing once the tour is under way. Your company should establish a policy on whether smoking will or will not be allowed on the coach. For a large group, you might have one bus for smokers; for a smaller group, perhaps limit smoking to rear seats only or forbid it totally. Most tour companies today simply state that there will be no smoking in the coaches but that there will be occasional stops for rest rooms, smoking, camera buffs, and so forth.

It is helpful to mention now that motorcoach seats will be rotated. This pre-tour warning (also reinforced later by the tour manager enroute) helps to deal with difficult tour passengers who want to establish squatter's rights on the front seat for the entire trip. Another very helpful suggestion is that anyone who suffers from motion sickness be prepared with a supply of Dramamine or something similar. Some tour operators like to mention whether the motorcoach has a lavatory aboard.

Cancellations and Refunds.   Although the tour brochure should give specific details on cancellation dates, penalties, and refund policy, this first information bulletin is the place to reiterate those details. If nothing else, the bulletin should remind passengers to refer to the company's policy as stated in the brochure. One might use a statement such as, "While we certainly hope you will be able to travel with us as planned, sometimes illness or family emergency or unexpected events can force one to cancel travel plans. Therefore, we urge you to reread the Cancellation/Refunds clause in your brochure to understand how late you may cancel without any penalty. If you have questions, please ask now."

Tipping.   It is appropriate in this first information bulletin to reiterate what tips are included so that passengers may budget accordingly. Be specific. Which of the following are or are not covered:

❏ Airport porters
❏ Hotel bellboys from the motorcoach into the hotel lobby and from hotel lobby into the passenger's hotel room
❏ Dining room waiters
❏ *Maitre d'*
❏ Room maids
❏ Bus drivers
❏ Local guides
❏ Tour manager?

For cruises additional tips have to be considered. Which of the following are or are not covered: room steward, dining room waiters, *maitre d'*, and wine steward? Where tips are not included, what are some guidelines for the appropriate amount: 15 percent, so much per day, or so much per person?

Credit Cards.   Credit cards are so widely used in the United States that many tour members assume that their cards will be readily accepted everywhere overseas. No matter how wealthy the clients may be, they often fail to bring sufficient funds in travelers checks with them; they plan to rely entirely on credit cards. This assumption is a mistake. It's a mistake that, unfortunately, the credit card companies do little to remedy, since they want to convey the impression that their card is accepted at the far corners of the earth. Often this is true; more often, it is not. For example, even some cruise lines do not accept credit cards for enroute passengers, although many will accept a personal check. A large number of the better hotels and restaurants will accept them, but small out-of-the-way country inns, trattorias, or small-town shopkeepers will not. Many tour managers have had to spend the better part of a day in a city overseas trying to get a check cashed for a tour passenger or assisting the passenger in cabling home for funds.

Also, if traveling in countries where there is an official bank exchange rate of the dollar to local currency and also an unofficial street rate or "gray market," passengers who pay by credit card will usually not be able to take advantage of the better rate. Credit card transactions are generally at the official bank rate. Surprisingly, many merchants would prefer a personal check to a credit card transaction, since they do not have to pay a percentage to the credit card company.

Spending Money.   At the time clients buy the tour, they may be overwhelmed with everything that is included in the tour price. It sounds so all inclusive. Many of the more deluxe, quality tours are just that—virtually all inclusive. However, some of the moderate-priced tours (and certainly the no-frills, stripped package type of tour) cannot claim to be all inclusive. The passengers will have to pay a number of expenses out-of-pocket as the tour moves along. It is only fair that they be prepared, so that they have a rough idea of what to budget.

It is probably not advisable to recommend a dollar amount, since there may be a great difference in spending habits among tour members. But it is legitimate to remind them of what is not covered, so that they can mentally calculate how much extra money to take. Items to mention might be:

- ❑ Cocktails
- ❑ Wines
- ❑ Souvenirs
- ❑ Shopping
- ❑ Postcards and stamps
- ❑ Some tips
- ❑ Baggage overweight
- ❑ Meals not in the tour
- ❑ Optional tours or shore excursions not included in the basic prepaid trip
- ❑ Laundry
- ❑ Telephone
- ❑ Illness and other emergencies
- ❑ Snacks and room service.

Foreign Currency. Tour members seem to worry unnecessarily about purchasing foreign currency. They fail to realize that on a prepurchased group tour that most of their major expenses are already prepaid. Their expenditures overseas will be primarily for incidental expenses not covered by the tour. This situation contrasts with the independent traveler who, indeed, needs to have available a sizable amount of funds.

Therefore, the principal things that the information bulletin should tell tour participants about foreign currency are: (1) that your company does not recommend carrying large amounts of cash, in any currency; (2) that you urge them to carry all funds in travelers checks; (3) that if they do wish to exchange fairly large amounts of currency enroute, they will get a better rate at a bank than from a hotel cashier. However, point out that often it is not convenient to break away from planned tour activities during local banking hours, and they may spend more on a taxi to and from the bank than they lose exchanging with a hotel cashier; (4) that if they are going to be in any country for a fairly lengthy period, they might consider buying travelers checks at home directly in the currency needed (e.g., English pounds, Swiss francs, or whatever). These travelers checks usually can be purchased at many American Express offices, foreign banks in the larger cities in the United States, or through exchange houses. If dealing through a branch bank or small-town bank, it is best to do this well in advance, because such U.S. banks do not stock supplies of foreign currencies and are not yet geared to handling foreign currency quickly (if at all).

Baggage. Passengers should be advised about what kind of luggage and how much to take. Usually, hard-sided luggage is recommended instead of the new popular soft-sided lightweight luggage. Thieves can easily slash soft luggage. On tours, baggage receives heavy use—going in and out of hotels, on and off luggage trucks, and in and out of airports. In short, it takes a beating. Passengers should realize this and perhaps not take their very best matched Gucci luggage this time. Of course, specific tours may have specific needs—particularly adventure tours, which may require backpacks, duffle bags, or other equipment. Special arrangements can be made with the airlines on ski tours to allow one suitcase and one set of skis instead of two suitcases. A similar arrangement is popular for golf tours; that is, to accommodate a bag for golf clubs in lieu of one suitcase.

Your company may wish to limit passengers to one or two suitcases, depending on the length of the trip and on whether the tour is costed on handling and tipping for two suitcases per person or one. Regardless of costing and regardless of airline regulations, certain limitations are necessary in certain areas of the world. For example, a trip such as the Chilean Lakes crossing from Puerto Montt, Chile, which includes numerous boats and buses enroute to Bariloche, Argentina, would be an exercise in madness if a tour manager were expected to safely shepherd 40 passengers, each with two bags, through to the end. Getting 80 bags off the bullet train in Japan during a 60-second station stop is not exactly easy. Most boats in the Galápagos Islands restrict each passenger to one fairly small suitcase. In this situation, it is better for passengers to bring two small suitcases rather than one large one, so that they may take one with them on the boat, while leaving the other at a hotel on the mainland.

Those people who travel frequently within the United States but infrequently internationally are under the impression that two suitcases, regardless of weight, are the rule; this is true in most areas. However, on some flights in many countries the old 44-pound limit (20 kilos) still holds, particularly for smaller airlines flying within a particular country.

Also, those people who travel frequently on business in the United States may be accustomed to traveling with garment bags, which are not suitable for touring. Probably the best kind of bag, in addition to being hard-sided and sturdy, is the kind with dividers and pockets so that the passenger can devise a system for finding things. It is one thing to pack solidly for a single destination and then unpack on arrival (or pack for a cruise and then unpack totally once you are aboard). It is quite another to live out of a suitcase during a series of one-night stands. Personally, I prefer to travel with a suitcase with wheels, since there are so many areas today where porters are not available, even if you are willing to pay for porterage.

Luggage Tags.   Along with final documents, your company will want to send luggage tags to the tour members. Tell the tour members that these will be coming with their final documents. It is also a good idea to suggest that they put their name and address somewhere inside each suitcase in case the outer luggage tag tears or wears off.

Packing Suggestions.   Although many tour members are experienced travelers and have learned a number of tricks of travel for packing, undoubtedly the novices in the group will appreciate hints. Remind them to pack around one basic color, leaving things that cannot be worn with that color at home. Warn them to use plastic

LUGGAGE IDENTIFICATION

Please have a personal identification tag with your full name and home address on each and every piece of luggage you are taking with you. The airlines now require this, and should you check in at the airport without such tags on your luggage, the airline will supply you with tags and require that you complete them and attach them to your luggage before they will agree to check the luggage. Please help to avoid such confusion and delay at the airport by having your I.D. tag on your luggage before you arrive at the airport.

In addition to this personal I.D. tag, shortly before departure you will receive our identification tags. These tags identify our group luggage and enable airport and hotel porters to easily pick it out from other passengers' luggage.

Name _____

Address_____

Country_____

Figure 10.9 Luggage identification is a small but important part of traveling. This page shows that one can provide interesting visuals for such a pre-trip information brochure. (Courtesy of Harvest Travel International.)

bottles for all liquids, and to plan clothes for multi use (a raincoat that can double as a bathrobe, separates that can be mixed and matched, and sandals that can be used as slippers). Warn them about the perils of air-conditioning on planes and in hotels (and subsequent traveler's bronchitis), of the practicality of drip-dry fabrics (except in the tropics, where they are too warm because polyesters do not "breathe"), and of the need for good walking shoes (broken in, not new). Suggest a travel alarm (to ensure their promptness for morning departures).

People usually want to be dressed appropriately, so they will appreciate advice about where formal wear, or at least coat and tie, is expected. Local customs that affect clothing are important to mention. For example, in Japan, where you take your shoes off and then put them on a dozen times a day while entering and leaving temples and shrines, passengers might like to wear slip-on shoes such as moccasins rather than tie shoes.

Discuss electric plugs and converters and the use of hair dryers and electric shavers. Certainly, if there are any special functions requiring certain attire, such as a costume party aboard ship, or a formal reception with business colleagues, your tour members would like to know in advance. You might even wish to make up a suggested wardrobe checklist for men and one for women. For certain countries, they might be advised to take along some small token gifts to give to local friends that they might make enroute. These token gifts might be things typical of their home state or city.

Those who plan to carry a prescription drug should be warned to carry it in the original bottle with the pharmacy's label on it. They should also carry all medicines with them and not pack them in checked luggage. There is nothing more frightening for a tour manager than to have a tour member announce that her blood pressure medicine, which she must take within the next four hours, is packed in a lost suitcase. Knowledgeable travel counselors also advise their clients to pack a small folding tote bag in order to pack purchases they may buy on the trip.

Care of Valuables. Passengers should be urged to be prudent while traveling. Women should carry a purse that zips closed, and men should carry their wallets inside their jackets, not in a rear pocket that's readily accessible to a pickpocket. Also, remind them that good jewelry, cameras, travelers checks, tickets, and passports must be handcarried and watched, and that they should never be packed in their checked luggage. Tour participants sometimes see a trip as a festive occasion, perhaps as a chance to show off new clothes and good jewelry. Therefore, they often need to be urged to leave expensive furs, valuable jewelry, antiques, heirlooms, or priceless photos at home. Simply tell them not to take anything on this trip that they cannot afford to lose. The tour manager should reinforce all this later enroute, but it is also best to tell tour members before they start planning their wardrobe so that they can shop and pack accordingly.

Shopping on Tour. Advise passengers about good buys in the country that they will be visiting, so they can plan ahead. This is a good time to let them know that your company is not pushing shopping stops and cannot assume responsibility for their bad buys nor assist them in tracing lost shipments. One problem that plagues tour operators is the passengers who write to them several months after a tour. They complain about the now broken cuckoo clock that they bought at the cute little shop where the tour manager had taken them in the Black Forest or about the tile coffee table that had been shipped from the factory in Mexico but has not arrived. In short, they're asking that someone from your company follow up the next time he or she is in that area. A suitable statement to include in this first information bulletin would be, "We urge you to be cautious and discriminating in your purchases. We regret that we cannot be responsible for any shopping activities and are unable to intervene on your behalf in the event that merchandise does not live up to your expectations or if merchandise that you may ask to be shipped home does not arrive."

Health Problems.   It is important to obtain information on any health difficulties that passengers have that could be a problem enroute. The tour manager needs to know about passengers who have potentially dangerous health conditions, such as high blood pressure, heart disease, or diabetes. In addition, if the tour visits areas at high altitudes, it might be wise to require that tour members with a history of heart disease or high blood pressure obtain a physician's written permission to travel. The first information bulletin provides the opportunity to discuss this matter and to impress upon passengers the importance of revealing pertinent medical information. It is difficult for the tour manager who discovers at an altitude of 11,000 feet that a tour member has a heart problem, or only finds out on departure day at the airport that a tour member is in a wheelchair.

Suggested Background Reading.   Some tour members like suggestions for pretour reading about the countries and cultures that they will be visiting. It should never be implied that this is required reading, but merely suggested as enjoyable reading. I once had a gentleman cancel from a tour, saying that he was frightened by the reading list and that he had joined the tour thinking it would be a vacation, not a study tour.

In making reading suggestions, give no more than three or four possibilities. One book might be an overview of a country, one might be on history, perhaps another might be on arts and crafts, or another might be something for light reading. Consult with the local library, bookstore, or university for suggestions.

Airfare Restrictions.   If the group is traveling on a special airfare, participants should know the kind of fare and what restrictions apply. Although this may have been mentioned briefly in the brochure, the first bulletin is the place to give further information. For example, if the tour is traveling on the Group Inclusive Tour (GIT) airfare, a statement might be "Passengers are advised that this tour is based on a special 14/35-day Group Inclusive Tour airfare, which requires a minimum of 15 passengers and that passengers travel together as a group on all international flight segments of the trip."

United States Customs. Discuss duty-free airport shops and mention the $400 per person limit on duty-free items that U.S. residents may bring back. Also, alert passengers to the fact that items shipped and not accompanying them will be subject to duty. Discuss written versus oral customs declarations and the $50 gifts that may be sent free of duty. Your company may wish to obtain supplies of the U.S. government publication, "Know Before You Go," (figure 10.7) to include in the mailing.

Members visiting developing countries may particularly like to know of the U.S. Customs Service's program permitting returning residents to bring in duty-free handicrafts under a provision known as the General System of Preferences (GSP). This information may be obtained for your clients from the U.S. Customs Office.

Standardizing Bulletins

The material presented in this first information bulletin is quite comprehensive. Writing it and presenting it in a professional manner can be very time consuming. In fact, it may take several days to prepare this information bulletin the first time.

As your company develops more and more tours per year, bulletin preparation can become quite a chore and it will become obvious that much of it is repetitious. Large tour companies solve this by writing different standardized bulletins for different programs. For instance, they write one for their South Pacific tours, one for the European tours, and so forth. Of course, in this age of computerization, one solution is simply to store all the paragraphs in a word processor. In this way, for each tour you can pull up the master paragraphs and then customize them for the particular tour in question, thus publishing a "new" information bulletin for each tour.

Another solution for small to medium-sized companies is to write one standardized bulletin that is suitable for all tours anywhere in the world, augmenting it with supplemental short bulletins pertinent to a specific area or to a specific subject. For example, discussions of clothing and wardrobe checklists would be standardized, with no comments about the tropics or skindiving or ski clothes or winter rains. Any discussion of special wardrobe needs, other than those listed in the standardized bulletin, can be covered in a supplemental bulletin. Similarly, information on visas for specific countries, flight schedules, names of tour managers, time of year, and climate could be deleted or generalized in this standardized bulletin.

In fact, if your company is operating a large number of tours per year, this lengthy first information bulletin might be typeset and printed instead of photocopied. It can be done nicely in pamphlet form, perhaps with some attractive or humorous illustrations. Then it can be used for a number of years and supplemented each time by a short bulletin that touches on subjects pertinent only to the particular tour in question at that time. Before investing in printing such a pamphlet, however, it might be a good idea to use just the photocopied one for a year or two in order to "live with it" and be sure that it really is working as anticipated.

This first information bulletin has one additional function. It can also be an effective sales piece. If a client is undecided, or is asking a great number of detailed questions before joining a tour, a good sales counselor can volunteer, "Mr. Jones, I have an information bulletin we normally don't send out until someone has joined our tour. But it sounds as though you're really seriously interested in traveling with us, and I think if I sent it to you now ahead of time it might answer a lot of your questions."

Tour Questionnaire

A considerable amount of information will be needed concerning each passenger as the company begins final preparation of flight manifests, hotel rooming lists, passengers' travel documents, and materials for the tour manager who will escort the tour enroute. Probably the simplest way to obtain all this information is to develop a **tour questionnaire** (see Figure 10.10) that can be enclosed with the first information bulletin; each passenger must fill it out and return it with the final payment or earlier. Like the information bulletin, this questionnaire may be standardized to work for all tours. The following is a list of needed information:

1. Name of tour on which member is enrolled.
2. Legal listing of member's name (to match name as listed on passport—not nicknames).
3. Home address and telephone numbers including area code.
4. Business name, address, and business area code and telephone number. Fax number if they have one.
5. Citizenship (important to know if there are people in the group traveling on foreign passports; visa and immigration policies vary for them).
6. Passport number, date, and place of issue (or other proof of citizenship if not a U.S. citizen).
7. Birthplace (city, state, country).
8. Birth date (including year and thus age).
9. Emergency contact—name, address, telephone number, and relationship to tour member.
10. Any health or diet history—particularly diabetes, heart disease, high blood pressure, difficulty in walking, respiratory problems.
11. Smoker or nonsmoker.
12. Any special interests or requests.
13. Names of those with whom they would like to be seated on flights or have adjoining hotel rooms wherein possible.

Name of Tour: _____

TOUR QUESTIONNAIRE
(one per person required, not one per family)

Mr.
Mrs.
_____   Ms.   _____
Last Name   First Name

_____
Home Address   City   State   Zip Code

_____
Name of Business   Business Address   City   State   Zip Code

Home Phone ( )_____   Business Phone ( )_____
        Area Code   Number   Area Code   Number

Birth Date _____   Birth Place _____
        Month   Day   Year   City   State   Country

Present Nationality_____   Former Nationality, if any_____

If a naturalized citizen, date and place of naturalization _____

Passport Number_____   Date of Issue _____   Place of Issue_____

Occupation/Position _____

Special interests? _____
_____

Do you smoke? __ Yes   __ No

In case of emergency during the trip, whom do you wish us to contact?

_____
Name   Relationship

_____
Address   (   )   City   State   Zip Code
                                                     (   )
Home Phone _____   Business Phone _____
        Area Code   Number   Area Code   Number

Please indicate how you wish your name badge to read (we usually show your first and last name)

_____

Confidential Information For Tour Manager

Do you require special medical attention or diet?   ___ Yes   ___ No
Heart Problems?   ___ Yes   ___ No   Respiratory ailments?   ___ Yes ___ No
Diabetes?   ___ Yes   ___ No
Difficulty walking long distances and/or climbing stairs?   ___ Yes   ___ No
Further details on above health _____
_____

Use reverse side if you need additional room

Figure 10.10 Passenger tour questionnaire.

Prepacking Envelopes

Once all the materials are prepared for this first mailing, it expedites things to prepack them into large envelopes ready to mail as bookings arrive by simply adding the personalized acknowledgment letter and putting a label on the envelope. If it is a party of two, you need only one confirmation bulletin and welcome letter, but two passport application forms, two tour questionnaires, and so forth. Therefore, it is handy to prepack envelopes ready for parties of one and parties of two. Also, remember to put one master set in the file for later reference to show what was sent to everybody and to show a sample to the tour manager.

Interim Mailings Between First Bulletin and Billing

Some tour companies believe that three mailings (welcome mailing, billing mailing, and final document mailing) are more than adequate and, in fact, are trying to find ways to cut down on these. Other tour companies believe that it is important to keep in touch with the tour members so that they will not lose interest and perhaps cancel. These operators send out what they call "keep the interest" mailings (i.e., additional mailings in between the three basic ones) to ensure that the customer remains excited about the trip.

Sometimes this can be a postcard mailed from a city that the client will be visiting on tour. Sometimes it is a little booklet or news item. Perhaps these "keep the interest" mailings are most valid if there is a long time span between the date that the client enrolls in the tour and the date that the bill is mailed out. For example, if a client enrolls in January for a late September tour and would not hear from the company between January, when the booking is acknowledged, and July, when the invoice is mailed, it might be effective to design a mailing piece to go out around April or May.

BILLING

Approximately two weeks before final payment is due into the company office, it is time to start the billing process. If the brochure states that final payment is due 90 days before departure, it will be necessary to bill by 104 days before departure, to ensure that all payments are in on time. If the brochure states that final payment is due 60 days prior, bills should go out 75 days prior. A master control calendar should be flagged accordingly, and it is also helpful to flag the week before as a reminder, if it will be necessary to bring in temporary office help to prepare the bills.

It is important to send out bills sufficiently early for two major reasons:

1. If tour members are going to cancel, most likely they will do so when final payment is due. It is best to find this out early and not to receive these cancellations as a late surprise.

2. A company needs turnaround time—the time between when all payments are received in the office and when it is time to pay suppliers—cruise lines, hotels, and others. Always leave a sufficient time gap; never set the final payment date from passengers as the same date when you must pay your suppliers.

Billing Format

There are many different ways of billing passengers for a group project. If the group is relatively small, it is possible to type individual invoices for each family. (See Figure 10.11.) If the group is quite large, more sophisticated methods such as computer billings are available. Some companies simply bill by photocopying the client's master control card. Whatever the method selected, remember that the bill must be *understandable from the client's point of view*. Although your company may know that the airfare has gone up $140 since the brochure was printed, the client may not. You may understand that a YLAP airfare is an economy class, low season, advance-purchase airfare, but the customer probably does not. In addition, of course, more complicated tours will require more detailed bills to cover such items as single-room supplements, convention fees, pre- or post-tour independent travel arrangements, and so forth.

Whether the initial deposit was sent directly to your company or to the sponsoring club, it is best for final billing to be from the company directly to the client. By now the client should know that your company is handling the club's trip and will feel comfortable paying the bill directly.

Accompaniments to the Bill

Sending a bill out by itself seems cold and impersonal. Although the bill must not be lost in a sea of information stuffed into the envelope, a short cover letter (see Figure 10.12) and a second brief information bulletin are appropriate accompaniments. The tone of the cover letter should be warm and friendly; it should excite the passengers about the trip but at the same time gently remind them that payment is due shortly.

The second information bulletin could touch on new tour developments—something upbeat. This might include the news that a particular celebrity is going to meet with the group while in Rome, that a restaurant where the group will be dining has just won a Michelin star rating, or that the exchange rate between the French franc and the dollar has improved.

Also, this bulletin should give any update information, even if negative. This includes information about certain visas being required or about cholera inoculations being suggested because of a recent outbreak. This is also the time to advise passengers about airfare increases since the publication of the brochure. How much is the increase? How does the agency plan to protect them against any future possible increases, especially if they pay quickly so their air tickets can be issued immediately?

LSI Travel Agency
987 Park Drive #2A
Berkeley, CA 94704
Telephone Number: 510-555-2000
Fax Number: 510-555-7210

June 21, 19XX

Mr. and Mrs. Merle Davis
2433 Beaver Place
Oakland, CA 94611

For Rosemont Country Club European
Highlights Tour. Basic tour at $2985 per
person × 2 persons ....$ 5,970.00

Increase in air fare since publication date of
brochure . . . $140 per person × 2 (see enclosed
Information Bulletin #2 for details) 280.00

Optional Purchases
  Half-day Paris Gastronomique tour Sept. 11,
  Mrs. Davis only at $24 × 1 ....24.00

  Airport Inn Sept. 3, confirmed at $68 for
  two plus 6% tax 72.08

Total Charges $6,346.08

Less deposit on account $400.00

Balance Due and Payable $5,946.08

PAYMENT DUE NOW BUT NO LATER THAN JULY 4
PLEASE MAKE CHECK PAYABLE TO LSI TRAVEL AGENCY, INC.
LAST DATE TO MAKE ANY CHANGES—JULY 1

Tour Accounting Code #576

Figure 10.11 Sample simple invoice.

LSI Travel Agency
987 Park Drive #2A
Berkeley, CA 94704
Telephone Number: 510-555-2000
Fax Number: 510-555-7210

June 17, 19XX

DEAR FRIENDS:

September and departure day for the Rosemont Country Club tour to Europe may seem like a long way off! But it's closer than you think. As mentioned in the tour brochure, final payment is due 60 days before departure, so I'm afraid payment date is upon us shortly.

Therefore, enclosed is an itemization of your charges. Please review them carefully. Payment is due in our office by July 4. A stamped self-addressed envelope is enclosed for your convenience.

We are including some supplemental information bringing you up to date on a few new developments. Also enclosed is full information and an application form for optional travel insurance—medical, baggage, and trip cancellation. We urge you to give it your serious consideration, particularly the trip cancellation coverage due to the heavy cancellation penalty that goes into effect 60 days before departure.

May we also point out that July 1 is the last date you may make any changes in your travel plans or request additional pre-trip or post-trip arrangements.

This is going to be an exciting trip for all of us and as departure time draws near you may have questions on matters we have not covered in our information bulletins. If so, do feel free to call and chat with us.

Sincerely,

Marty Sarbey de Souto, CTC
Group Manager

MS/s
cc: Mrs. Charles Goodwin-Rosemont Country Club
Enclosures: Information Bulletin No. 2
               Invoice
               Return Mail Envelope
               Insurance Information Bulletin
               Insurance Application Form

P.S. Reminder. Anyone who has not yet turned in his or her tour questionnaire, please do so quickly. We need the information therein to finalize your tour arrangements, preregister our group at all the hotels, and so forth.

Figure 10.12 Sample invoice cover letter.

It is a nice touch to include some giveaways, such as a map, a book, or some background reading. The U.S. State Department publishes excellent pamphlets entitled "Background Notes" on each country; they can be ordered from the Bureau of Public Affairs. They give information on the country's history, population, economy, agriculture, educational system, and so forth. The U.S. Department of State also publishes a series of pamphlets called "Tips for Travelers to...". Brigham Young University in Provo, Utah, has an excellent series. Also, try other organizations such as the United Nations, the Organization of American States, the Pan American Union, and the Pacific Asia Travel Association (PATA), or perhaps magazines such as *National Geographic*. Although government tourist offices and airlines of the countries concerned may be helpful, sometimes their materials are merely pretty pictures and sales pieces, rather than solid background information. Do not overlook novels or popular nonfiction such as Michener's *Iberia*, de Gramont's *The French—Portrait of a People*, or Magner's *Men of Mexico*. Of course, giveaways should be costed into the tour price from the outset and should be ordered early in order to arrive on time for inclusion in the billing mailing.

Travel Insurance

One of the things that a company should definitely offer all trip participants is optional **travel insurance**. The information and application form for this insurance can be included in the billing mailing; or if preferred, it may be a separate mailing.

Some insurance plans are usually a package of a variety of coverages: accidental death, emergency assistance, medical expense, theft or mysterious disappearance of baggage and travel documents, and trip cancellation/interruption.

A number of insurance companies now offer this insurance, so you may wish to review the plans of several companies before deciding which insurance company your travel company wishes to represent and sell. (You must get an "appointment" from the insurance company to sell their product.) You should compare plans carefully. Some are "pick-and-choose" policies, wherein each passenger may select the amounts of coverage desired in each category. Other plans are prepackaged so that passengers don't have the flexibility to modify them.

When comparing plans, particularly notice the clauses on pre-existing medical conditions. Check to see if the policy includes default coverage to protect your passenger if any of your suppliers default. (Read "To Go Bankrupt or Go into Chapter 11 Reorganization and Not Provide Services".) Also double-check to see if it includes what is called "medical evacuation" coverage, since this is very costly for a tour member should he/she have to be flown home on a stretcher accompanied by a full-fare attendant.

If you are not designing your own tour, but placing your group on a cruise or an existing tour of another tour operator, this supplier may be offering what is termed a **cancellation waiver**. Please note this is not true insurance. It is simply the supplier agreeing to refund your clients their monies if they cancel. No insurance company is behind it. Therefore, if the supplier defaults and does not provide services to your clients, they would have no protection. A much safer suggestion is to sell true third-party insurance, underwritten by a separate insurance company.

Emphasize how important it is for tour members to consider the insurance; on the other hand, do not oversell and insist that they purchase something that they do not really need. Often, it is best to suggest that they check their existing insurance and then augment it. For example, if their personal medical insurance covers them for claims incurred overseas, perhaps they do not need the supplemental medical coverage. However, if their present medical coverage does not protect them while traveling overseas (e.g., as the case with Medicare), undoubtedly they will appreciate having this brought to their attention.

Many tour passengers erroneously assume that since your company is handling baggage throughout the tour that it is legally responsible for loss or damage to luggage or personal effects. This is not the case, and it is important that the client be reminded of this—first in the brochure and second in the information bulletins that follow. A suggested statement to appear in the second information bulletin might be:

> As stated in the brochure describing the tour project, LSI Travel Agency, Inc. shall not be responsible for loss, theft of, or damage to baggage or belongings, and we highly recommend that you double-check your personal insurance and/or purchase the optional baggage insurance offered. Valuables such as jewelry, cameras, travelers checks, tickets, passports, and so forth always should be hand carried, never checked in your luggage. This is simply a courtesy reminder of this matter so that you now may enroll in the appropriate insurance coverage for your baggage and personal effects if you so desire. A descriptive bulletin and application form are enclosed for your convenience.

It is also a good idea to advise tour members what the Warsaw Convention insurance coverage is under the contract of their air ticket. Liability for loss, delay, or damage to baggage is limited unless a higher value is declared in advance and additional charges are paid. For most international travel (including domestic portions of international journeys), the liability limit is approximately $9.07 per pound for checked baggage and $400 per passenger for unchecked baggage. For travel strictly between U.S. destination points, (not continuing to an international destination) federal rules require any limit on an airline's baggage liability to be at least $1,250 per passenger. Tour members should be reminded that these provisions cover baggage only while in the care of the airline. Warsaw Convention protection does not cover luggage if it is lost in a hotel or baggage truck enroute to the airport, and so forth.

The existence of nonrefundable air tickets on the market has prompted many travel industry professionals to require that their clients sign a statement that they have been offered travel insurance and have turned it down. You may wish to consider such a step.

Return-Mail Envelope

It is helpful to enclose a stamped, self-addressed return-mail envelope in the billing mailing. This expedites payment, and for the cost of a first-class stamp, appears gracious.

CANCELLATIONS

It is important to be prepared for **cancellations**. Although it is difficult to predict numbers, probably an estimate from 17 percent to 20 percent would be accurate. If the tour has a high percentage of couples, cancellations may be more, since if one becomes ill and has to cancel, the partner usually cancels as well. If the tour is a short and inexpensive tour with a small deposit—under $100—cancellations may be higher than if there is a large deposit of $400 to $500 per person. Usually, if clients have to pay a large deposit, they think about the trip carefully at that time, whereas if they have to deposit only $50 or so, they may have enrolled on impulse without really thinking it through.

The brochure should have an explicit cancellation clause outlining cancellation dates, refund policies, refund penalties, and specifying that cancellations must be in writing, via letter or fax. This protects your company against clients who cannot really make up their minds whether they are officially canceling or not, or couples who cannot come to an agreement.

Once your company has received a written cancellation notice from a tour member, the cancellation should be processed immediately and the refund made as quickly as possible. Of course, if there is any possibility of salvaging the booking, it might be advisable to call the client first to express regrets about the cancellation and to see if there is anything that can be done to retain the client. It is not a good idea to try to hang on to a client by delaying the refund; this will incur nothing but ill will. An immediate refund with a short accompanying note of regret will do wonders to establish a company's reputation as a serious tour operator, and one to be considered in the future. If it is not possible to get the refund into the mail by the end of the same week, or if the company, in turn, has to apply to someone else for the money (e.g., a cruise line), at least process the refund request and acknowledge the cancellation in writing the same week that it is received. (See Figure 10.13.) Explain the circumstances and advise the client that the refund will follow as soon as it is received from the pertinent source.

WAITING LISTS

One way to protect against cancellations is to maintain a **waiting list** of people ready and eager to go the minute an opening occurs. Do not offer to put people's names on the waiting list without a deposit. If the tour is sold out and people call or write in for space, add a paragraph to the usual sales letter advising them:

LSI Travel Agency
987 Park Drive #2A
Berkeley, CA 94704
Telephone Number: 510-555-2000
Fax Number: 510-555-7210

June 30, 19XX

Mrs. Louis Seidman
10035 Gardenside Drive
Hayward, CA 94544

Dear Mrs. Seidman:

We were sorry to receive your note advising us that Mr. Seidman will have to go into the hospital for surgery and that you, therefore, must cancel your participation in our European Highlights Tour for the Rosemont Country Club this fall. We have a nice group making the trip and you two will be missed!

Here's hoping that Mr. Seidman recuperates quickly and that perhaps you can make the trip with us next year instead, as this is an annual tour and we will be offering it again next year.

There well not be any cancellation fee since your cancellation was received prior to the 60-day cut-off date. Your refund is being processed and you should be receiving a check from our accounting department in about ten days.

With all best wishes. . .

Cordially,

Marty Sarbey de Souto

Marty Sarbey de Souto, CTC
Group Manager

P.S. We're enclosing a calendar of our future tours . . . for Mr. Seidman's bedtime reading while he's recuperating!

Figure 10.13 Cancellation acknowledgment letter.

At present, the tour is fully booked. However, since we always receive a certain number of cancellations due to illness or last minute emergencies, we will be happy to put your name on our waiting list and advise you as openings develop. To establish your waiting list priority, kindly complete the reservation form in the brochure and return it along with your deposit in the amount of $000.00 as indicated on the reservation form. Of course, if for any reason we ultimately cannot accommodate you on the trip, your money will be totally refundable. We regret that we cannot accept wait list applications without a deposit.

It is also a good idea to service the waiting list passengers just as one does the confirmed passengers, sending them information bulletins, visa applications, and so forth. It keeps their spirits up and makes them feel that their chances of getting on the trip are good.

Of course, as "D" Day (i.e., departure) draws near, it is only fair to these people to give them an honest assessment of the situation. If all final payments have been received from all passengers, the chances of there being many cancellations are fairly slim. At this point, cancellations would be bona fide emergencies—illness, death in the family, and so forth. On the other hand, before final payment date there probably will be a number of cancellations—those who overplanned, underbudgeted, were not really sure in the first place, have had business reversals, and have court dates. So the biggest drop in passengers will be around final payment date—90 days prior, 60 days prior, or whatever date is specified in the tour brochure as final payment date. Plan accordingly!

Acknowledging Final Payments

Once billings are mailed, anticipate that **clients' final payments** will come in fairly quickly and be prepared to handle them. Also, be prepared to follow up those few who do not pay on time. If they do not pay on time, it may mean they are canceling and the company should be concerned. You may wish to acknowledge final payments as they come in with a thank-you letter, thus assuring tour members that their file is in order and advising them when their final documents will be mailed. This is also an excellent time to review the clients' files and to remind them if anything is missing, such as their tour questionnaire, their passport data, their decision on whether they want to take insurance, any decisions on their pre-tour or post-tour optional tours, or any decisions on their domestic flight connections to and from the gateway airport. In short, if there is any piece of information missing from their file, the time to handle it is *now*. Do not discover it later while preparing the final documents.

FLIGHT BAGS

Some companies like to give out complimentary flight bags—either airline bags that they purchase from the air carrier or their own tour company bags. They believe that passengers appreciate receiving them and that they serve as free advertising for the tour company. In some instances, organizations that repeatedly do tours have their own flight bags. A number of university alumni groups do this; in fact, some have developed their travel program to a science and travel with their own flight bags, T-shirts, pre-trip bulletins, and other items.

If you elect to send flight bags, they can be mailed separately—perhaps right after final payment is received. A major problem with flight bags is storing, packing, and shipping. It can be unwieldy and time consuming. Be sure to budget for flight bags in the tour costing if planning to purchase them.

FINAL DOCUMENTS

Three to four weeks prior to departure, package the departure materials to be sure that they reach tour members at least two weeks before departure. Nothing is more surely the sign of a careless tour operator than sending out final departure materials just before departure day. And nothing is more likely to upset participants and start them out on their trip on the wrong foot than not getting their documents in time. After all, so far they may have paid out several thousand dollars, but have nothing to show for it. The participants want time to receive everything, read it over carefully, savor it, and be sure that they understand it.

Therefore, it will be necessary to work backward. Plan far enough ahead to have everything that is needed on hand and ready to mail out on schedule. Allow extra time for holiday mail delays. This means, in turn, that items that come to your company from elsewhere (e.g., tickets from a cruise line, vouchers from a wholesale tour operator, and so forth) must be ordered early. Plenty of time must be allowed to check each air ticket, each cruise ticket, and each voucher. Be sure that they are issued correctly and at the rate charged to the customer and that the customer's name is spelled properly. If there is an error, the items must be returned to the supplier for exchange. If your company and the supplier are in the same town, errors may be corrected quickly. However, if your company is in Iowa and you have purchased the ground arrangements through a wholesaler in New York, extra time must be allowed. You must plan ahead and insist that suppliers do likewise. Sometimes suppliers are not cooperative in this endeavor.

The following is a checklist of **final documents** and other items your company might send out to clients:

1. Passport billfold or decorative document envelope of some sort to hold all final materials (do not just throw them loose into a mailing envelope).
2. Air tickets in appropriate airline ticket jacket, with individual flight itinerary tucked inside the jacket.
3. Cruise tickets in appropriate cruise-line ticket jacket.
4. Departure bulletin giving final instructions.

5. Lapel name badge to be worn on the day of departure (and perhaps throughout the tour) so that the tour manager and others can identify the group members.

6. Baggage tags—one per suitcase to be checked in or handled by hotel bellmen and porters. (Do not include baggage tags for hand-carried luggage; they confuse the porters and might cause them to pick it up by mistake.)

7. Supply of mailing instructions (see Figure 10.14) to leave with friends, family, and office colleagues that show hotel names, addresses and emergency telephone, fax, or cable contacts where tour members may be reached while traveling.

8. List of tour participants (home addresses at your company's discretion; you may wish to obtain participants' permission).

9. Map of departure airport, indicating meeting place. Not mandatory, but helpful.

10. Vouchers, if necessary, for basic tour package. Also vouchers for any independent pre-tour or post-tour services, such as airport hotels and so forth.

11. Insurance policy or certificate if purchased by the passenger, with instructions to take the number of the policy on the trip but to leave the policy itself at home in a safe place.

12. Passport, if precollected for obtaining visas, with visas stamped therein.

13. Miscellaneous items, if desired or if not sent earlier, such as phrase books, currency exchange charts, and so forth.

14. Bon Voyage cover letter (see Figure 10.15) attached to the front of all this material.

It is important to send final documents via certified mail (since air tickets are negotiable). Or, if passports are enclosed, send via registered mail with return receipt requested; you may prefer to use a delivery service such as Federal Express and cost such service into your tour. Accurate records of certified or registered number, date mailed, and exact address on the mailing label should be kept. This will help in tracking a lost envelope in case a client calls in to say that final documents have not been received.

CONTENTS OF DEPARTURE BULLETIN

The departure bulletin should be short and to the point. It should give the passengers the essentials of what they need to know in order to get packed and onto the plane. Points to cover in this bulletin should include the following:

❑ Where and when to meet—specify airline, flight number, departure time, airport check-in place and time, whether to check in as independent traveler at the airport or look for someone special.

❑ Tour manager—name of manager and exactly when and where the manager will be greeting the passengers.

INSTRUCTIONS FOR ADDRESSING MAIL TO PARTICIPANTS
OF ROSEMONT COUNTRY CLUB TOUR OF EUROPE 19XX

This list is furnished you to give to your family, friends, and business contacts who may wish to contact you while you are on tour.

ARRIVAL DATE	DEPARTURE DATE	HOTEL AND ADDRESS	FAX
September 5	September 8	Hotel Krasnapolsky Dam 9, 1012 JS Amsterdam The Netherlands	020-6228607 Country code: 31
September 8	September 11	Hotel Meurice 226 Rue de Rivoli 75001 Paris France	44581015 Country code: 33
September 11	September 14	Hotel Ambasciatori 70 Via Veneto 00187 Rome, Italy	06-4743601 Country code: 39

Please allow at least one week transit time to all places and be sure that you have sufficient postage on all letters. The cost of airmail to all of the above destinations is fifty cents PER HALF OUNCE. We suggest that you address your envelope per sample below. If contacting by fax, note you must use the international code 011 first plus the country code.

Your return address   50 cents per half ounce

        Your Name
        Rosemont Country Club Group
        Ambasciatori Hotel
        70 Via Veneto
        00187 Rome, Italy

Please hold for group
arrival September 11   AIR MAIL

Figure 10.14 Mailing instructions.

LSI Travel Agency
987 Park Drive #2A
Berkeley, CA 94704
Telephone Number: 510-555-2000
Fax Number: 510-555-7210

August 20, 19XX

DEAR FRIENDS:

Very shortly you will be leaving on our exciting Rosemont Country Club European Highlights Tour. Enclosed are all necessary final materials for the trip. Please review all items enclosed to make sure they correspond to the check list below. If anything has been omitted inadvertently, <u>call us right away</u>—do not wait. You should find the following:

(1) Your air tickets, in the airline ticket jacket, with a flight schedule inside.
(2) Departure instruction bulletin—important.
(3) Name badge.
(4) Baggage tags (see departure bulletin for instructions on use).
(5) Supply of mailing instructions (to leave with family and friends).
(6) List of tour participants
(7) Vouchers for any independent pre-tour or post-tour hotel reservations or other services you may have asked us to arrange for you.
(8) Your insurance policy (if you have purchased this optional coverage).
(9) Miscellaneous items—currency converter, phrase booklet and so forth.

Your tour manager, Mrs. Margaret Kimberly, will meet you at the TWA check-in counter at O'Hare International Airport when you arrive the afternoon of September 4; please be on the lookout for her.

We know that you must be very busy getting ready for the trip, but please take the time now to read the enclosed departure bulletin carefully. It should answer most questions you may have, but if not, feel free to call us. May we also remind you that your passport is valuable and the enclosed air tickets are negotiable, so please put them all in a safe place.

Bon Voyage!

Cordially,

Marty Sarbey de Souto

Marty Sarbey de Souto, CTC
Group Manager

Enclosures

Figure 10.15 Sample passenger bon voyage letter.

❑   Baggage tags—how to fill out baggage tags and the importance of having them on the bags when they check in at the airport.

❑   Baggage check-in—instructions as to what airport passengers should check baggage, whether to interline luggage through to the final destination or just check it to a certain point and reclaim it; the importance of holding the luggage stubs and turning them over to the tour manager later.

❑   Name badge—the importance of wearing it on departure day so that the tour manager can identify people.

❑   Last minute reminders—to be sure that they have passport, tourist cards or visas, air tickets, cruise ticket, travelers checks, and any medication with them, not packed in checked luggage or left at home.

❑   Emergency instructions—what to do if there is a last minute emergency, if they miss their plane, and so forth—around-the-clock telephone contact, particularly if on a weekend or when your office is closed.

With this much information and attention prior to departure, participants should leave on tour in a favorable mood, anticipating the tour with excitement, and convinced that your company has done a good job so far and that the trip will live up to their expectations. Now, it is up to the enroute tour manager to take the trip to the next stop along the road to success.

❑ *SUMMARY*

Handling clients, from the time they first inquire about a tour until the date they depart on the trip, is an acquired skill. Good sales letters and an organized method of follow-up to ensure enrollments are necessary. Effective handling keeps clients informed and enthusiastic and gives them confidence in your company. Much of this handling is via the *written* word, so it is important to develop good research and writing skills in order to prepare the many pre-trip information pieces that will be needed. A minimum of three information bulletins and mailings will be necessary: on receipt of the booking, with the invoice, and with departure materials. Such effective pre-trip client handling sets the stage for the tour manager and a successful trip enroute.

❑ *REVIEW QUESTIONS*

1. **What is an option offer and what is its purpose?**

2. What are the five basic purposes of detailed information bulletins that are sent to clients after they enroll in a tour?

3. Name some of the subjects that you would cover in information bulletins for your clients.

4. Why is it to a client's disadvantage sometimes to pay for enroute purchases by credit card?

5. What are some of the incidental enroute expenses for which a tour member should budget —expenses not usually covered on the prepaid tour?

6. What is the best type of luggage to take on a traditional international tour?

7. How would you advise tour participants about enroute care of valuables, precautions against theft, and the like?

8. What is the purpose of a tour questionnaire?

9. How can you guard against too many cancellations on a tour?

10. If your tour were full and you were still receiving inquiries and bookings, how would you handle these?

❑ *ACTIVITIES*

1. Review several different travel insurance plans you might recommend that your tour members purchase to cover such things as baggage and personal effects loss or damage, cancellation penalties, overseas medical emergencies, and supplier defaults. Compare prices and coverage to determine which company's offering is the best for your clients.

2. Obtain information and a sample passport application form from your nearest U.S. passport office and then write a paragraph for a first information bulletin advising participants on how to obtain a passport.

3. Write a fictitious departure bulletin for a group. Include such instructions as where and when to meet, how to mark luggage, how to locate their tour manager, and last-minute reminders of what they should have on them when they check in at the airport.

▷ 11

IN-HOUSE OPERATIONS AND DEALING WITH SUPPLIERS

LEARNING OBJECTIVES

After reading this chapter, you should:

- ❏ Understand the importance of proper ongoing communications with your suppliers
- ❏ Know the purpose of 90-, 60-, and 30-day reviews and what is expected of the tour operator on each of these reviews
- ❏ Learn how to calendar properly the various duties of a tour operator related to each tour so that all tour duties may be performed in a timely fashion
- ❏ Learn how to keep succinct client records
- ❏ Be able to review suggested forms you might use or modify to your needs to properly control a tour through all its pre-departure phases
- ❏ Know how to finalize a tour with all suppliers prior to tour departure

KEY CONCEPTS AND TERMS

Calendaring
Client Records
Control Forms
Finalizing with Suppliers
Final Tour Roster
Flight Manifest
Float
No-Name Seats
Review Dates

The single most important mark of a professional tour operation is the operations department behind it. Promotional material may be beautiful. Sales may be fantastic. But if the operations department does not come through with the product that the client expects, all other efforts have been useless. Both the client and the suppliers have every right to expect reasonable efficiency with a feeling that the company is in control. This control can come only through organization and by attention to the most minute details.

But how do you achieve this control? What contributes to the assurance that important dates will not slip by, that deposits will not be overlooked, and that promises will be kept and deadlines met? When a large number of tours must be juggled at once, each with its own set of dates, how do you avoid sleepless nights spent worrying whether anything important has been overlooked or whether some deadline has been missed?

CALENDARING

The secret to the control of any travel project is **calendaring**. This means keeping a meticulous *visual* calendar of what must be done on each tour or cruise project. Many large tour companies keep such a calendar on the wall and plot the progress of a tour for everyone to see. Others keep a desk calendar and enter each duty on the appropriate date. Whichever method is selected, the trick is to write the information on the calendar and then adhere to the schedule by planning ahead and, when necessary, by hiring temporary, part-time help to keep work on schedule. Many professional tour operators not only calendar the exact date that a given task is to be done, but also calendar a reminder the week before. For example, if June 18 is the date to invoice tour passengers for final payment, they will put on their calendar for June 11: "Bills out June 18. Hire typist." This way they are a week ahead of the problem, instead of a week behind trying to catch up. Some operators like to enter key dates in their airline computer queues, but others prefer the old-fashioned method of using a large visual wall calendar to see the year at a glance. (See Figure 11.1.)

Typical Dates to Calendar

In entering important dates on the calendar, the usual procedure is to work *backward* from departure date. For example, if September 4 were tour departure date, the following might be entered:

August 4	30-day review and finalization
July 4	60-day review
	Final payment due from clients
June 17	Billing date (in order to get payment in by July 4)
June 4	90-day review

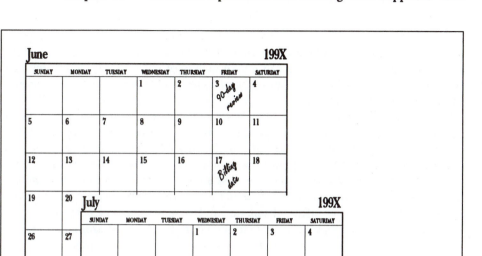

Figure 11.1 These are the typical and important dates to calendar.

If hotels have given specific dates by which time reports or deposits must be made, these dates should be entered as well. If there are any cancellation penalty dates (i.e., dates by which clients lose their money or dates by which the company might lose deposits to cruise lines or hotels), these dates should also be entered, perhaps in big red letters.

Certain promotional dates should also be included on the calendar. These would include advertising deadlines, date to submit press releases, date for a promotional evening (including such things as date to mail invitations, catering deadline, and so forth), date to do a "last call" follow-up mailing to fill remaining spaces on the tour. *In short, the year should be plotted on paper from tour conception to departure.* Of course, as you calendar for many tours, the calendar will reflect many different stages of many different tours all in the same week, or perhaps even on the same day. June 17 may be the date to send out bills for the Europe tour leaving on September 4, but it also may be the date to do the 30-day finalization wrap-up on a July 28 Orient tour. If you can graphically see this pileup occurring on June 17, something can be done about it by bringing in extra help or by doing some of the work in advance during a relatively slack period.

REVIEW DATES

Review dates are dates on which suppliers will ask to review the inventory of space a tour operator is holding and perhaps take back part or all of the space if it is not being sold quickly enough. One of the most important factors in a company's growth as a successful tour operator is its credibility and professionalism, not only as perceived by clients, but also *as seen from within the travel industry*. It will be crucial to your continued success as a group operator that a good reputation be built with suppliers.

Suppliers are quick to judge. They watch to see how a company measures up in professional behavior and dealings with them. If suppliers constantly have to contact you to see how the tour is doing (and if you are not prepared to give them the answers they need when they call), they will have doubts about your company's success and productivity.

There probably will be five important times to contact overseas hotels, receptive services operators, airlines, and other major suppliers:

1. When first booking—asking for space confirmation and rates.
2. When your tour brochures come off the press—sending them a courtesy copy and inviting them to check it over to pick up any discrepancies (many errors have been caught this way!).
3. The 90-day review—that is, 90 days before tour departure, just a note letting everyone know how the tour is selling. This is mostly for public relations purposes. If it is obvious that all the space held is not going to be filled, it is considered more ethical to drop some of it 90 days before departure rather than closer to departure date, when perhaps it is too late for the suppliers to sell it elsewhere. (See Figure 11.2 for sample 90-day review.)

LSI Travel Agency
987 Park Drive #2A
Berkeley, CA 94704
Telephone Number: 510-555-2000
Fax Number: 510-555-7210

June 4, 199X

Mr. Hans Van der Hooten
Sales Manager
Hotel Krasnapolsky
Dam 9, 1012 JS
Amsterdam
The Netherlands

RE: Rosemont Country Club
European Highlights Tour
Arriving: Sept. 05, 199X
90-Day Review

Dear Hans:

As you know, you are holding 14 twins and 4 singles for us on the above-mentioned tour group.

This is just a courtesy report to advise you that the tour seems to be selling well and to ask you to continue to hold all space. We will be reporting to you again at 60-day review time, at which time we will be able to give you a further booking picture.

You may be interested in the attached photocopy of our advertisement on this tour, which is currently running every Sunday in the travel section of our local newspaper. We are also enclosing a sample copy of the tour brochure which we published and mailed to 2,000 members of the Rosemont Country Club.

Thank you for your continued cooperation. We look forward to having our group at your property next September.

Sincerely,

Marty Sarbey de Souto, CTC
Group Manager

MS/s
enclosures: 2

Figure 11.2   90-day review letter to hotel.

4. The 60-day review—that is, 60 days before tour departure, giving everyone a realistic look at numbers, cutting back on space that probably will not be filled in the next 30 days. (If 60 days is also the date by which the clients had to make final payment, there should be a fairly accurate picture of booking numbers by this time.) However, you might still want to retain a few unsold spaces in order to accept late bookings within the next 30 days. (See Figure 11.3 for sample 60-day review.)

5. The 30-day review—that is, 30 days before the tour departure, giving a final report. At 30 days, you cancel all unsold space and finalize with suppliers, submitting rooming lists, flight manifests, and all other necessary final information. (See figure 11.4 for a checklist of things to be done at 30-day review time.)

The checklist in Figure 11.4 is a rule of thumb. In some cases, you might skip the 90-day review. In domestic tours, it is possible that many hotels do not require final rooming lists until 15 days before arrival, not 30, which gives your company a little more leeway. Conversely, when working with cruise lines, it is usually necessary to finalize much earlier and release unsold cabins considerably earlier, depending on the cruise line and on the popularity of the particular sailing. But the 90-day, 60-day, 30-day reviews are fairly standard in the industry, and they should be used as a base plan, adjusting as necessary around the constraints of specific suppliers. Obviously, with Carnival in Rio or Christmas in Hawaii, suppliers are going to hold a much tighter rein than they would on a Caribbean tour in a slack season.

Although these five contacts with each supplier for each tour may sound like an overwhelming amount of correspondence, a great deal of it can be stored in your word processor and personalized, as necessary, for each tour and its pertinent suppliers. For protection, these five contacts should be made by letter or fax (i.e., in writing) not verbally.

However you make these frequent contacts with suppliers, whether by letter, telex, or fax, the important point is that you *take the initiative, both in plotting these dates into your calendar and in contacting the suppliers* rather than waiting until the suppliers contact you. After working with a particular airline or hotel on several tours, your company will earn a reputation for taking the initiative and for automatically contacting suppliers with a progress report. The airline or hotel will begin to feel at ease working with your company and will respect it.

CONTROL FORMS FOR OPERATIONS

Many times it is necessary to make quick decisions. You may need to decide whether to continue to promote a tour or cancel it, whether to release certain flights or retain them, or whether to schedule more advertising or not. But these management decisions are not made in a vacuum. They are made on the basis of information on the current status of the travel project. How is that information acquired? It is acquired with the proper tools. In this case, the tools are office **control forms** developed to help keep track of all essential information.

LSI Travel Agency
987 Park Drive #2A
Berkeley, CA 94704
Telephone Number: 510-555-2000
Fax Number: 510-555-7210

July 4, 199X

Mr. Hans Van der Hooten
Sales Manager
Hotel Krasnapolsky
Dam 9, 1012 JS
Amsterdam
The Netherlands

RE: Rosemont Country Club
European Highlights Tour
Arriving: Sept. 05, 199X
60-day Review

Dear Hans:

You are currently holding 14 twins and 4 singles for us on the above-mentioned tour group. We have sold 8 twins and 2 singles for a total of 10 rooms (18 persons) in our group so far. Unfortunately, a few of the participants found it necessary to cancel.

We are continuing our advertising and other promotional efforts for the next 30 days, so we are hopeful to be able to sell up to a maximum of 28 persons. Therefore, kindly:

Continue to hold: 13 twins, 2 singles
Cancel now: 1 twin, 2 singles

We will finalize with you 30 days prior to the group's arrival. At that time we will send final rooming list, prepayment, and other last-minute details. In the meantime, if you have any questions, feel free to contact us.

Sincerely,

Marty Sarbey de Souto, CTC
Group Manager

MS/s

Figure 11.3   60-day review letter to hotel.

CHECKLIST 30-DAY TOUR FINALIZATION*

☐ **Make final master tour roster** showing names, addresses, passport data, hotel rooming status and roommates, flight assignments, and any optional tours.

☐ **Finalize all air** with controlling airline. Send final flight manifests showing breakdown of smoking/nonsmoking passengers, friends traveling together, and any special in-flight meal requirements. Request any special handling at departure airport. Release any unsold air.

☐ **Finalize with all hotels,** sending final tour roster which shows rooming breakdown. Prepay or send sizeable deposit (unless you have made other credit arrangements). Release any unsold rooms.

☐ **Finalize with all receptive operators,** sending final tour roster, verifying arrival/departure flights. Prepay or send sizeable deposit. Recap services expected, advise name of tour manager, and outline any special requests. Release any unsold space.

☐ **If cruise is involved, finalize with cruiseline*,** recapping total numbers, cabin assignments, meal sitting, any special requests such as parties, meeting rooms, presold shore excursions, and who is using the cruiseline's group air blocks.

☐ **Request all complimentaries** formally in writing, even if agreed to previously. Specify names and itineraries of those who are to utilize the complimentary tickets or accommodations.

☐ **Prepare departure materials** for clients, to include final itinerary, air tickets and flight schedule, list of tour participants, departure instruction bulletin, mailing lists, voucher(s) for ground services if needed, cruise tickets, baggage tags, name badge, and any special materials (such as special convention materials, for example).

☐ **Prepare tour manager's materials** and set date to meet with tour manager for final briefing.

---

* Finalization on most tours is at 30 days prior to departure. However, when a cruise or convention is involved, it may very well be required as early as 90 days prior. Be sure to double-check the requirements for each particular tour in question.

Figure 11.4 Checklist—30-day finalization.

One such form might be a weekly office booking report that shows how many new bookings were received on each tour that week, how many cancellations, and the current net standing. (See Figure 11.5 for a sample weekly booking report.) Another typical form might be a control sheet for hotel space on a tour that shows at a glance how many twins or singles have been sold, how many rooms remain unsold, and how many share-rooms are open for roommates. Similar forms can be developed to show how many passengers are on which flights, how many are signed up for an optional tour, or who is a smoker and who is a nonsmoker.

These forms can be as simple or as complicated as desired, depending on how large a tour is anticipated and on the number of variables. It is not too difficult to keep track of a one-week Hawaiian tour for 30 people, especially if they are all staying at the same hotels, if they're all flying out of a Los Angeles gateway on the same flight, and if they have the option of returning with the basic group at the end of the tour or of staying on for a two-day Kauai option.

It is quite another feat to know the status at any given moment of a meeting for 120 passengers divided into three motorcoaches going to three different Waikiki hotels, originating in a choice of three West Coast gateways (Seattle, San Francisco, or Los Angeles), and having a choice of four post-meeting optional tours from which to choose.

One simple manual method for a fairly small tour is to keep one master control sheet (See Figure 11.6) and add each client's name to the sheet as he or she joins the tour. Put a check mark in various columns under different headings next to the client's name (e.g., under gateway city selected, under special optional tours selected, and so forth). Instead of everything on one master control sheet, another system involves a separate control sheet or index card for each variable. This system allows one card for the San Francisco/ Honolulu flight, another for the Los Angeles/Honolulu flight, and so on. In this case, it is necessary to enter each client's name on each of these pertinent cross-reference cards.

These methods show at a glance what is selling and what is not. If you anticipate 30 passengers, you may have initially booked 15 seats out of Los Angeles and 15 out of San Francisco. But if a disproportionate number of passengers are enrolling for the Los Angeles flight, you can adjust the flight request by asking the airline to change to 20 seats from Los Angeles and only 10 from San Francisco. This early change is better than waiting until the 60-day or 30-day review later. You do not want to be surprised suddenly to find that the Los Angeles flight is oversold and the San Francisco flight is undersold.

A master control system also permits keeping track of totals to be sure that no one has been lost. If your booking sheet indicates that bookings have been received from 24 participants, but there are records of only 14 on the Los Angeles flight and 9 on the San Francisco flight, somebody is missing. Perhaps somebody has not been listed on the flight. Here again, with a small group of 30, it is possible to locate the missing name and balance fairly quickly. However, with large groups and manual control sheets, hours can be spent searching for the lost participant whose name was inadvertently omitted from the flight.

WEEKLY BOOKING REPORT

WEEK ENDING   December 6, 199X
TOTAL BOOKING THIS WEEK 72
TOTAL CANCELLATIONS THIS WEEK ...... −12
NET GAIN THIS WEEK .... +60

Project	Accounting Code Number	Dates	Under Deposit Last Week	New Bookings This Week	Cancelled This Week	Net Status As of Today	Total Space Held	Space Open For Sale
Europe Rotary Tour 1	805	Feb. 08– Feb. 28	31	8	2	37	80	43
Europe Rotary Tour 2	806	Feb. 25– Mar. 17	18	8	1	25	40	15
Roundhill Country Club Hawaii Golf Tour	901	Feb. 28– Mar. 08	121	12	3	130	160	30
Mississippi Cruise	917	Apr. 09– Apr. 16	13	8	0	21	32	11
Aspen Spring Ski Week	933	Apr. 16– Apr. 23	81	11	4	88	100	12
Omaha Garden Club Japan Spring Tour	937	Apr. 17– May 05	14	4	0	18	32	14
Pearl Cruises China	942	Jun 04– Jun 20	24	4	2	26	40	14
Alaska – Westours Tour/Cruise	948	Jul 07– Jul 21	13	2	0	15	32	17
Rosemont Country Club European Highlights	956	Sep. 04– Sep. 14	0	11	0	11	32	21
Stella Solaris Xmas– New Years Cruise	972	Dec. 17– Jan. 04	0	4	0	4	40	36
University Xmas in Oaxaca Tour	979	Dec. 21– Jan. 06	0	0	0	0	40	40
TOTALS			315	72	12	375	628	253

Figure 11.5 Weekly booking report.

TOUR NAME AND DEPARTURE DATE: ROSEMONT COUNTRY CLUB. SEPTEMBER 4, 19XX

NO.	NAME	SHARE	SNGL.	OTHER	BLOCK AIR SFO	BLOCK AIR JFK	OPTIONAL TOUR	COMMENTS
1.	DAVIS, Mr. Merle	X				X		Prefer king-size bed if available
2.	DAVIS, Mrs. Annie	X				X	X	See above
3.	GOODWIN, Mr. Charles	X			X			
4.	GOODWIN, Mrs. Marian	X			X	X	X	VIP. Club President
5.	WILSON, Mr. Craig		X					
6.	HOLMES, Mrs. Winifred	X				X	X	Willing to share
7.	~~SEIDMAN, Mr. Louis~~	X				X	X	~~Cancelled 6/24/XX~~
8.	~~SEIDMAN, Mrs. Helen~~	X				X	X	~~Cancelled 6/24/XX~~
9.	KNOWLES, Mr. George			X	X			Party of 4. Two adjoining twins,
10.	KNOWLES, Mrs. Nancy			X	X		X	or suite arrangement OK.
11.	KNOWLES, Miss Melanie (18)			X	X		X	
12.	KNOWLES, Miss Jane (16)			X	X		X	
13.	PICKETT, Mr. James	X			X			Leg injury. Aisle, bulkhead
14.	PICKETT, Mrs. Elaine	X			X		X	
15.	NEFF, Mr. Charles	X			X			
16.	NEFF, Mrs. Ruth	X			X		X	
17.	MARTIN, Miss Adele	X			X		X	Shares with Roswell

Figure 11.6 Master tour control sheet. Note that names are entered in the order they are booked. Passengers keep their tour number for the life of the project. Cancellations are not erased until finalizing the tour so agents can track cancellation percentages.

CLIENT RECORDS

Not only is it necessary to keep track of what each tour member is doing and to enter the name on the proper operational records so that suppliers are kept accurately informed, but it is also necessary to know what each tour member is doing so that staff can sound knowledgeable about the file when the client calls. In addition to operational control records, therefore, it will also be necessary to maintain some sort of individual tour member control record. A variety of systems can be devised, ranging from rather sophisticated computer programming for large conventions or incentive groups, to a homemade shoe-box file system for small, simple groups.

Whatever system is ultimately used, the idea is to have a synthesis of each tour member's travel plans readily available and visible. If clients call and want to know how much they owe, or want to know if they are registered for a certain optional tour, or if their final payment has been received, it should not be necessary to read through an entire file to locate the answer. Files are for storage only. It's a good place to keep the participant's letters to the company, copies of the company's reply letters, and copies of invoices or reminder notes to the file following telephone conversations. The file is not the place to locate quick answers or to have a quick visual grasp of that individual's trip.

Instead, a concise recap should be available separately. Some companies have the front cover of the tour member's file printed with such a chart. Other companies keep a card index and complete a master client control card for each new member as booked. These cards are then kept alphabetically in a card box for each tour and are readily accessible to the tour counselor when calls arrive. These cards are never taken out of the box; they are not filed in the client file. Still other companies develop a computer program to handle this.

Most retail travel agencies utilize their airline computer system (Sabre, Apollo, or whatever system they subscribe to) to build a Master Tour Profile for each tour. From that they then build individual participant profiles as each new participant joins the tour. This permits the agency to issue computer-generated receipts, invoices, and so forth. Agencies will also build individual passenger name records (PNRs) from the group block of air space so that the air tickets can be computer-issued just as they would be for individual clients. These air tickets may be issued at the time of finalizing the tour, or they might often be issued considerably earlier to "lock in" a certain airfare and ticketing-date deadline.*

---

*These are all airline profile systems (such as a "star" in American Airlines' Sabre system). These systems were designed for handling individual clients' air, not for groups. However, many agents use them for groups by modifying them to their needs on a tour-by-tour basis. Those agents who have United Airlines' *Focal Point* system can write their own script rather than having to adapt the script already programmed therein. It is expected that each airline computer system will eventually come out with its own program for handling groups.

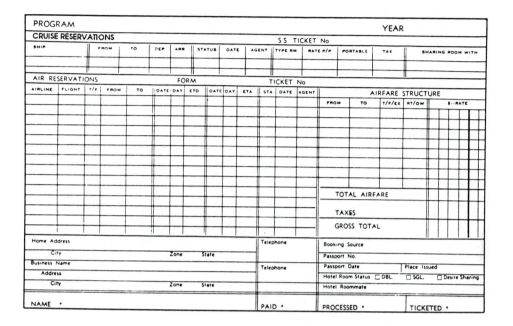

Figure 11.7 Manual client control system designed for a visible card index.

HANDLING OF MONIES

As deposits and subsequent monies arrive, they should be deposited and acknowledged. To ensure accurate profit-and-loss figures on completion of each tour, *be sure to assign an accounting code number to each tour project.* Subsequently, all payments arriving for that tour should be credited by the company accountant to that specific tour. Any checks that are issued for expenses against the tour should also carry that accounting number.

If the company is just beginning in group business, a meeting with the company accountant is recommended. At this meeting the accounting codes can be discussed, so that there is a thorough understanding of your goal, which is to have an accurate and *separate financial picture of each tour or cruise project.* Achieving this goal may require that some changes be made in the accounting system or that the accountant may have to do additional work so that the company can obtain the figures quickly and easily.

TRACKING INQUIRIES

In addition to keeping track of bookings and participants' records, it is a good idea also to keep track of bookings that do *not* come in. The staff should keep a record of every inquiry arriving concerning a tour. If the inquiry converts into a booking, the original inquiry can be pulled out and filed with the client file. With such a system, all inquiries remaining in the inquiry file will be from people who did not book and thus need follow-up. Inquiries that arrive by letter are easy to keep track of; you have the letter in the file. However, inquiries that come in verbally, either by telephone or in person, are not as easily controlled. Often sales counselors receiving the initial phone inquiry are rushed; they may jot down only the bare essentials. They may send out a brochure and do nothing else.

To assist sales counselors taking these calls, it is helpful to develop a small card and to leave supplies on each counselor's desk to be completed each time a query arrives. The card should have a place for the date of the call, the caller's full name, address, telephone, and the source (how he or she heard of the tour). Knowing the source is helpful in determining which advertisements or promotional efforts are bringing results and which are not. (See Figure 11.8 for a sample inquiry record card.)

FINALIZING WITH SUPPLIERS

Approximately 30 days before departure, you will finalize with the airlines, hotels, receptive services operators overseas, and cruise lines.

```
┌─────────────────────────────────────────────────────────────────┐
│                        INQUIRY RECORD                           │
│                                                                 │
│   DATE OF INQUIRY _____ │
│   TOUR BROCHURE _____ │
│   NAME _____ │
│   ADDRESS _____ │
│   CITY _____ │
│   STATE _____   ZIP CODE _____   PHONE_____  │
│   SOURCE OF INQUIRY _____  │
│   DATE BROCHURE SENT_____   │
│                                                                 │
└─────────────────────────────────────────────────────────────────┘
```

Figure 11.8   Inquiry record card.

The Airlines

Normally, at 30 days before departure, a final report must be made to the airlines involved in the tour. This report gives them passengers' names and final details. This is done with the originating (controlling) air carrier, who, in turn, passes the information downline to other airlines involved in the onward air space. It is not necessary to contact every air carrier on the group's itinerary. Although it may be easier to finalize by telephone, this should be followed up *in writing* by submitting a flight manifest and a cover letter by mail or fax.

Flight Manifest.   The flight manifest should be numbered for the total count of passengers. Anyone in the group who uses a seat gets a number. An infant, carried on a parent's lap and not assigned an individual seat, is listed by name on the manifest but on the same line next to the parent's name. An older child occupying a seat is listed on a separate line and with a corresponding number. Remember, the airlines are counting seats, not couples, families, or hotel rooming units. For a domestic tour, last name and first initial may be all that the airline requires. For an international tour, the usual procedure is to list the full, legal name exactly as it appears on the passenger's passport (or other legal document that he or she is carrying as proof of citizenship). If a man goes by the name of "Buzz" Jones but his real, legal name is Mortimer Alfred Jones on his passport, list him as: "Jones, Mr. Mortimer Alfred." The manifest should be divided into smokers and nonsmokers to help the airlines and the tour manager in seat assignments.

If the group is traveling together as a unit from beginning to end, only one master flight manifest is necessary for the entire trip. If, however, members are dropping in and out of the group tour flights, so that the name list is not standard for each flight on the itinerary, separate manifests will be needed for each flight leg where the list varies. The tour manager's name should be at the bottom and should be listed as the manager for easy identification by the airline. Be sure to photocopy a supply of extra lists for the tour manager so that a separate one is available for check-in at the airport on each flight sector, and for presenting to the airlines for flight reconfirmation overseas at each stop. (See figure 11.9 for a sample flight manifest.)

Cover Letter to Controlling Airline.   The flight manifest should be submitted to the controlling airline with a cover letter (Figure 11.10). The cover letter might touch on the following:

- ❑ Formal release of unsold flight space. (You may wish to ask for permission to retain a few unsold seats, referring to them as **"no-name" seats** for late sales, if you honestly believe that there is the potential for late sales.)
- ❑ Recap of total number of smoking and nonsmoking seats needed and grand total.
- ❑ Indication as to how seating reservations should be handled.
- ❑ Any special group requests or reminder of things promised earlier, such as use of the VIP departure lounge, a special group check-in lane, and special group baggage marking.
- ❑ Any special individual requests that certain passengers may have made, such as diet meals or seating with extra leg-room.
- ❑ Name of the tour manager and contact prior to flight time.

The Hotels

Normally, at 30 days before departure, a final report is made to each hotel involved in the itinerary if hotels have been booked directly. If hotel accommodations were booked by a wholesaler or by an overseas receptive services operator, there is no need to contact the hotel directly, but the wholesaler or overseas receptive services operator must be given the same information that would have been sent directly to the hotels. This procedure should be done in writing, by mail, or fax, with a rooming list and with a cover letter, just as with the airlines.

Rooming List (Confidential Tour Roster).   Whereas the flight manifest was listed alphabetically by name, one name to a line (since airlines count seats), the rooming list should be prepared by rooms. One method is to list twin-bedded rooms first, then singles, and last triples or suites or other special rooming arrangements. At the bottom should be a recap, indicating totals; that is, total number of twins, singles, and triples being used, grand total number of rooms, and grand total number of people.

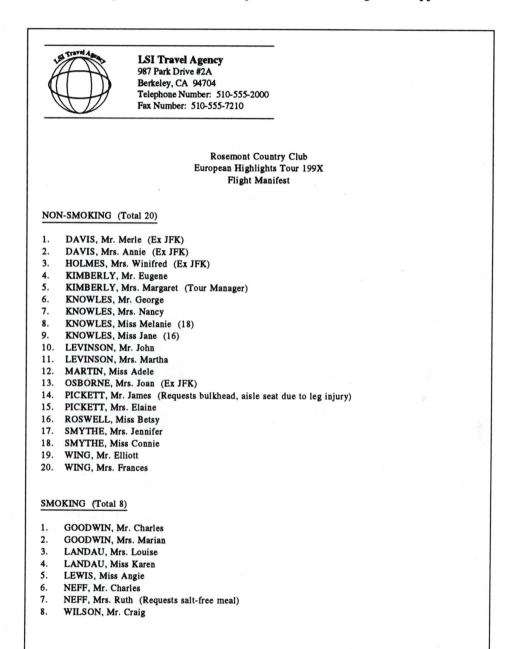

LSI Travel Agency
987 Park Drive #2A
Berkeley, CA 94704
Telephone Number: 510-555-2000
Fax Number: 510-555-7210

Rosemont Country Club
European Highlights Tour 199X
Flight Manifest

NON-SMOKING (Total 20)

1.   DAVIS, Mr. Merle (Ex JFK)
2.   DAVIS, Mrs. Annie (Ex JFK)
3.   HOLMES, Mrs. Winifred (Ex JFK)
4.   KIMBERLY, Mr. Eugene
5.   KIMBERLY, Mrs. Margaret (Tour Manager)
6.   KNOWLES, Mr. George
7.   KNOWLES, Mrs. Nancy
8.   KNOWLES, Miss Melanie (18)
9.   KNOWLES, Miss Jane (16)
10. LEVINSON, Mr. John
11. LEVINSON, Mrs. Martha
12. MARTIN, Miss Adele
13. OSBORNE, Mrs. Joan (Ex JFK)
14. PICKETT, Mr. James (Requests bulkhead, aisle seat due to leg injury)
15. PICKETT, Mrs. Elaine
16. ROSWELL, Miss Betsy
17. SMYTHE, Mrs. Jennifer
18. SMYTHE, Miss Connie
19. WING, Mr. Elliott
20. WING, Mrs. Frances

SMOKING (Total 8)

1.   GOODWIN, Mr. Charles
2.   GOODWIN, Mrs. Marian
3.   LANDAU, Mrs. Louise
4.   LANDAU, Miss Karen
5.   LEWIS, Miss Angie
6.   NEFF, Mr. Charles
7.   NEFF, Mrs. Ruth (Requests salt-free meal)
8.   WILSON, Mr. Craig

Figure 11.9 Flight manifest.

LSI Travel Agency
987 Park Drive #2A
Berkeley, CA 94704
Telephone Number: 510-555-2000
Fax Number: 510-555-7210

August 4, 199X

Mr. Jeffrey Whelan
Trans World Airlines
680 Market St.
San Francisco, CA 94108

RE: Rosemont Country Club
European Highlights Tour
Departing: Sept. 4, 199X
30-day finalization

Dear Jeffrey:

We are now ready to finalize the above-mentioned tour. There are a total of 28 in the group (27+1), per the attached passenger manifest. Since you are holding 32 seats, you may now release any unsold space. Note that of the 28, 24 board at SFO and we pick up four at JFK for a total of 28 out of JFK.

May we remind you that TWA earlier offered use of the VIP departure lounge at San Francisco International and a special group check-in lane. We will appreciate your reconfirming that these two requests are in order.

The tour manager's name is Mrs. Margaret Kimberly. I will be mailing the formal request for her ticket in a day or two. She will check with your counter two hours prior to flight time at SFO and will be present to assist as our passengers arrive. They will be carrying their own tickets and will be checking in for this initial flight individually.

Please arrange to have the group seated as a block and to have the seats pre-assigned with boarding passes ready to expedite matters. We have indicated on the attached flight manifest smokers/nonsmokers for seat assignment purposes. Also please note that there are two special client requests for seating and special meals on the attached manifest. Please assign Mrs. Kimberly to an aisle nonsmoking seat.

Many thanks for all your help, Jeffrey, in seeing this tour through to fruition. You've been great to work with!

Cordially,

Marty Sarbey de Souto, CTC
Group Manger

MS/s
enclosure: flight manifest

Figure 11.10 30-day finalization with airline.

Some tour companies prefer to have the rooming list to be just that—rooming lists only. Then, they provide backup information such as passengers' passport numbers, addresses, and so forth on a separate sheet. Others prefer to put everything on one master tour roster that is broken down by rooming arrangement but also lists all the backup information on the same sheet. (See Figure 11.11 for a sample final roster.)

Under this arrangement, items that should appear on this tour roster sheet would be the following:

❑ Each passenger's full, legal name, shown with his or her roommate. (Therefore, the list may not be alphabetical.)
❑ Each passenger's home address.
❑ Each passenger's passport data—number of passport, date of issue, place of issue. This information often is required by the hotel because local police or immigration authorities, in turn, require that hotels submit this information to them.
❑ Each passenger's full birthplace and full birthdate. Here again, this is often information that the hotel must have on its records if requested by local law enforcement authorities.
❑ Options—a column for pre-tour or post-tour optional tours that passengers may have elected to take or not to take—and a total at the bottom showing how many are on each optional tour.
❑ Smoking/nonsmoking column. Although this information is not necessary for the hotel (unless the hotel is one of those nowadays which may have no smoking rooms), it should appear on the master tour roster for other purposes: the airline's information, the tour manager's information in assigning smoking or nonsmoking motor-coaches, and so forth.
❑ Comments—a special column to indicate such things as passengers traveling with friends, or a passenger who may have difficulty in walking.

Remember, this list is *confidential*; it is used by the company and the tour manager with hotels and other suppliers only. It is *not* given out to the passengers. Many passengers are sensitive about their ages and other personal data, and they do not want this information distributed to the other tour members.

One of the principal purposes of this detailed list is so that the hotels may *preregister* the members of the group. If the hotel has done so, when the group checks in, rooms should be preassigned, with keys laid out for passengers to pick up, after which they can go to their rooms. In some cases, particularly if the group is arriving early in the morning when all rooms are not cleaned or available, this may not be possible. But 90 percent of the time, submitting a detailed list such as this enables an efficient hotel to work ahead. When the group arrives, the passengers simply sign the hotel registration card and do not have to fill in name, address, passport data, and so forth as do independent hotel guests.

FINAL ROSTER—ROSEMONT COUNTRY CLUB EUROPEAN HIGHLIGHTS TOUR

No.	Name	Address	Birthdate and Place	Passport No. Expiration	Block Air ORD	JFK	Gastr. Option	Comments
1.	DAVIS, Mr. Merle	2433 Beaver Pl Oakland, CA 94611	9/06/31 Plains, GA	D62386938 7/15/9X		X		
2.	DAVIS, Mrs. Annie	Same as above	4/15/33 Reno, NV	D62386937 7/15/9X		X	X	
3.	GOODWIN, Mr. Charles	625 Oak View Dr. Rosemont, CA 94526	2/06/28 Buffalo, NY	B23695849 9/03/9X	X			
4.	GOODWIN, Mrs. Marian	Same as above	4/16/32 Akron, OH	J23975927 6/02/9X	X		X	President of Rosemont Country Club
5.	HOLMES, Mrs. Winifred	4600 W. Whitesbridge Danville, CA 94526	6/20/19 Erie, PA	C54769392 8/16/9X		X	X	
6.	OSBORNE, Mrs. John	1591 Palmetto Lane San Jose, CA 95720	10/09/21 Erie, PA	C29358939 4/30/9X		X	X	
7.	KIMBERLY, Mr. Eugene	% LSI Travel Agency 987 Park Drive #2A Berkeley, CA 94704	10/06/21 New York, NY	B29396029 5/16/9X	X			
8.	KIMBERLY, Mrs. Margaret	Same as above	7/08/24 Boise, ID	B69293809 6/03/9X	X		X	Tour Manager
9.	KNOWLES, Mr. George	12 Eton Place Alameda, CA 94501	9/30/41 Joliet, IL	B69939292 9/15/9X	X			Family of four. Two adjoining twins or suite arrangement.
10.	KNOWLES, Mrs. Nancy	Same as above	5/16/45 Chicago, IL	B69939291 9/15/9X	X		X	
11.	KNOWLES, Miss Melanie	Same as above	2/24/67 Joliet, IL	B69939293 9/15/9X	X		X	
12.	KNOWLES, Miss Jane	Same as above	9/01/69 Joliet, IL	B69939294 9/15/9X	X		X	
13.	LANDAU, Mrs. Louise	3201 Longwalk Dr. Rosemont, CA 94526	7/13/33 Bisbee, AZ	C59392299 10/02/9X	X		X	
14.	LANDAU, Miss Karen	Same as above	3/06/57 Rosemont, IL	C92239021 11/16/9X	X		X	

Continued . . . .

Figure 11.11   Final roster.

No.	Name	Address	Birthdate and Place	Passport No. Expiration	Block Air ORD	Block Air JFK	Gastr. Option	Comments
15.	LEVINSON, Mr. John	2617 Le Conte Ave. Rosemont, CA 94526	10/05/22 Miami, FL	B29395983 7/16/9X	X			
16.	LEVINSON, Mrs. Martha	Same as above	12/02/24 Chicago, IL	B29395984 7/16/9X			X	
17.	MARTIN, Miss Adele	2093 Cedar Ave Kensington, CA 94707	1/13/18 Roswell, NM	D39295083 11/04/9X	X			
18.	ROSWELL, Miss Betsy	Route 1, Box E Millbrae, CA 94030	11/19/22 Chicago, IL	B39602397 12/03/9X	X		X	
19.	NEFF, Mr. Charles	5909 Gloucester Pl San Carlos, CA 94070	5/23/21 Ames, IA	B39672093 1/06/9X	X			
20.	NEFF, Mrs. Ruth	Same as above	9/22/25 Chicago, IL	B39672094 1/06/9X	X		X	Salt free menu
21.	PICKETT, Mr. James	379 Lyman Circle San Jose, CA 95720	10/16/22 Dallas, TX	B39270963 7/15/9X	X			Requests aisle/bulkhead seat due leg injury
22.	PICKETT, Mrs. Elaine	Same as above	12/02/55 Dallas, TX	B39270965 7/15/9X	X		X	
23.	SMYTHE, Mrs. Jennifer	1168 Parkside Drive McHenry, CA 94526	6/12/41 Raleign, NC	C39276092 9/03/9X	X			
24.	SMYTHE, Miss Connie	Same as above	12/02/64 McHenry, IL	C39276093 9/03/9X	X		X	
25.	WING, Mr. Elliott	2433 Brown Derby Rd Rosemont, CA 94596	11/16/52 St. Louis, MO	C36923792 10/13/9X	X			
26.	WING, Mrs. Frances	Same as above	6/17/55 St. Louis, MO	C36923793 10/13/9X	X		X	
27.	LEWIS, Miss Angie	617 Broadmore Apt. A Sacramento, CA 94596	6/19/21 Atlanta, GA	B3926709 11/03/9X	X		X	Requested single; paid supplement
28.	WILSON, Mr. Craig	1501 15th Ave. Oakland, CA 94611	12/01/29 Evanston, IL	B5920762 12/03/9X	X		X	Forced single
					24	4	18	

RECAP
13 Twins, 2 Singles = 15 Rooms = 28 Persons   Block AIR JFK: 4
Optional Paris Gastronomique Tour: 17+1   Block AIR SFO: 24

Figure 11.11   (Continued.)

Cover Letter to Hotels.   When the tour roster is sent to each hotel, a cover letter recapping arrangements should accompany it. (See Figure 11.12.) Some of the things that this cover letter might touch on are as follows:

❏ Recap of arrival date, flight number, and approximate time. Name of receptive services operator in that city transferring the group in from the airport to the hotel (so the hotel has a local contact to find out what has happened to a group if they do not arrive on time).

❏ Recap of departure date and approximate time. (The departure flight may be late in the day, which would mean that passengers have to check out of their hotel at the hotel's regularly posted checkout time and then wait in the lobby with their luggage until time to transfer to the airport.) Never assume that rooms may be kept past checkout time. Always ask. If the hotel is not heavily booked, they may permit it. On the other hand, if the hotel is booked solid, it probably will not be possible unless the company offers to pay a day rate—if there is one—or the extra night—an item that should be thought of when costing the tour, not later! Some deluxe operators do cost in for the extra night, particularly if the departure flight is leaving in the middle of the night, as often is the case in tours to India. (Once out on tour, an experienced tour manager may ask the hotel manager to provide one or two courtesy rooms for changing clothes and storing luggage after checkout hour. If a hotel is not full, management may often extend this courtesy to a group at no additional cost.)

❏ Resumé of total rooms to be used—twins, singles, and triples.

❏ Release of any unsold rooms, or request to retain one or two no-name rooms for late sale.

❏ Recap of any special arrangements. This would include meals, special dinner parties or receptions, rooms set aside for briefings and meetings, special dining room hours, and extra bellmen on duty at arrival and departure times.

❏ Recap of finances and payment, showing rates for each type of room, totals, complimentary rooms, taxes, and deposits. This can appear in the cover letter itself, on a separate calculation sheet, or on the check if space permits. Normally, the company will prepay at 30 days prior, less any early deposits that may have been made.

However, some tour operators arrange to have the tour manager pay by company check as the tour moves along. Some volume operators work from a **float**, which is a large, rotating fund left on deposit with a particular hotel. Others, who may have preestablished credit, arrange to have the hotel bill the agency later. This decision is between the company and each individual hotel, depending on a number of factors.

❏ Name of the tour manager and an indication to the hotel as to what his or her role is. For example, instructions as to what may be charged to the master account and what the tour manager or the individual passengers must pay for directly at the time. Putting this in writing helps to limit the company's finan-

LSI Travel Agency
987 Park Drive #2A
Berkeley, CA 94704
Telephone Number: 510-555-2000
Fax Number: 510-555-7210

August 4, 199X

Mr. Hans Van der Hooten
Sales Manager
Hotel Krasnapolsky
Dam 9, 1012 JS
Amsterdam
The Netherlands

RE: Rosemont Country Club
European Highlights Tour
Arriving September 5, 199X
30-day review

Dear Hans:

We now wish to finalize the above-mentioned tour with you. We have sold a total of 28 (27+1), so our final needs are:

13 twins
2 singles

Full details of rooming arrangements are on the attached roster.

The group arrives September 5 via TWA 814 at 07:05 from New York and departs September 8 for Paris via morning train. We wish to hold a briefing at 5:00 p.m. on September 5 followed by a cocktail party/welcome dinner. Kindly reserve a small suitable room, and send us suggested menu and prices, including tax, tip, and domestic liquor/wines.

Enclosed is our check #0217 in the amount of $0000, with breakdown of charges on the check. This is your original quote, including daily accommodations, 4% tax and 15% service to hotel personnel. It is understood that meals are not included in the rate. The welcome party will be paid for by our tour manager upon check-out. Any other charges are to be billed to the individual folios of the passengers concerned.

Mrs. Margaret Kimberly is the tour manager in charge. Should there be any questions, please feel free to query her.

Cordially,

Marty Sarbey de Souto

Marty Sarbey de Souto, CTC
Group Manager

MS/s
enclosures: Check #0217
Roster of Members

Figure 11.12 30-day finalization with hotel.

cial liability if there is a problem in this regard later. Some companies permit their tour managers to charge almost anything to the master account; others restrict them severely.

All of the above information can be synthesized in a cover letter and mailed or faxed to each hotel with the rooming list (tour roster) and payment. If the hotel space was booked initially through a hotel chain sales office in the United States, such as Sheraton, Westin, Hilton, or other, the considerate travel company will copy in that hotel office chain's sales as a courtesy. Then the chain office knows that the agency has complied with the hotel in finalizing. However, the actual letter, rooming list, and check should go directly to the hotel property, either to the attention of the sales manager or to the front-office manager. The original should not be sent to the hotel booking office in the United States unless they have specifically instructed that this be done.

Receptive Services Operators Overseas

At 30 days before departure, the company should finalize with each receptive services operator handling the tour enroute. (See Figure 11.13 for a suggested 30-day finalization letter to a receptive services operator.) (If the land tour was booked through a wholesaler in the United States, this step is not necessary; the retail travel agency finalizes with the wholesaler, who, in turn, notifies its overseas branches or representatives.)

If these operators are to do a good job on your behalf, it will be necessary to give them full information, as follows:

❑ Several copies of the **final tour roster**, showing all necessary data, such as rooming arrangements, passengers' names, addresses, birth data, passport data, optional tours, and comments.

❑ Resumé of total passengers, total rooms, and total on optional tours.

❑ Verification of arrival and departure flights, and a request that the local receptive operator call the departing airline in their city at this time to verify that the group is, indeed, holding reservations, and to verify departure time. Many a group has left home with signed and sworn confirmations of onward flights, only to be bumped or to have local airline employees inform them that there was no local record of the booking. This can be avoided by having the flight checked locally a month ahead of time.

❑ Name of tour manager and any necessary explanation as to this individual's financial limits, and other matters.

❑ Brief recap of services you expect the receptive operator to provide your tour.

❑ If receptive operators are handling the hotels, each operator should be reminded to tell the hotels everything that you normally would have told them directly. This includes information about preregistering the group, meal arrangements, parties, briefing rooms, arrival and departure times, and request for adequate baggage assistance at those appropriate times.

LSI Travel Agency
987 Park Drive #2A
Berkeley, CA 94704
Telephone Number: 510-555-2000
Fax Number: 510-555-7210

August 4, 199X

Mr. Jean Claude Murat
President
Treasure Tours
15 rue de l'Arcade
Paris 75008, France

RE: Rosemont Country Club "European Highlights Tour"
Arriving Paris September 5, 199X

Dear Mr. Murat:

We are now ready to finalize the above-mentioned tour. Final total are 27 paying passengers plus the tour manager (27+1) for the basic tour, and 17+1 for the optional half-day Gastronomique Tour Sept. 7. A copy of the group roster is enclosed. Also enclosed is our check # 6372 in the amount of $0000 in prepayment for services, as itemized on the check.

There have been no changes in arrival or departure. The group will still arrive Sept. 5 via the train which leaves Amsterdam at 09:15 arriving Paris 13:00, and will depart Sept. 9 via AF 630 for Rome.

Mrs. Margaret Kimberly is the tour manager in charge. She will be paying entrance fees at the Louvre and at Versailles directly, as well as gratuities on behalf of the group to the local guide, the bus drivers, and the hotel porters.

We have finalized with the Hotel Meurice directly. However, we would appreciate your double-checking with them that all is in order. Should you find that by doing the city tour enroute from the rail station to the hotel there may be a problem with late arrival at the hotel, I would suggest you pull the room keys earlier in the day and distribute them in the coach.

Should there be any questions, let us know. Trusting that all is in order and that everything will go smoothly.

Cordially,

Marty Sarbey de Souto

Marty Sarbey de Souto, CTC
Group Manager

MS/s
enclosure: Check # 6372
Final Tour Roster

Figure 11.13 30-day finalization letter to receptive operator.

❏   Any special requests (e.g., a particular guide, a specific restaurant, and a reminder regarding a tour participant with a health problem.)
❏   Recap of finances and payment, showing breakdown of rates, complimentaries, and credit for any deposits already paid on account. This can be done in the cover letter, on a separate calculations sheet, or on the check itself, space permitting. If you have established credit with these companies, it may be possible to have the tour manager verify and initial the bill locally on site and have it sent to the company office for later payment. *Never assume*, however, that this arrangement will be satisfactory; always ask. The tour world is full of stories of embarrassed tour managers who were forced to pay by their own personal credit card before leaving.

The primary advantage of not paying in advance (other than cash flow) is that there is no risk of overpaying in case of a late cancellation or when some passengers do not show up for certain tour activities. In these cases, the receptive operator owes the company money, and must send a refund check or, as often happens, issue a credit memo and retain the monies toward a future tour. This occurs particularly if local currency restrictions or exchange problems make it not worthwhile to refund relatively small amounts.

Cruise Lines

If there is a cruise within the tour, or if the entire project is a cruise, finalize with the cruise line just as you did with the receptive services operator by sending a tour roster and cover recap letter.

The Cruise Roster.   The final roster for a cruise has much the same information on it as a roster for a tour; namely, passengers' full names, home addresses, passport data, and birth data. However, a cruise roster has some special requirements all its own.

❏   Cabin numbers, listed next to passengers' names.
❏   Pre-purchased shore excursions, if any.
❏   Dining room seating (early or late seating) if participants were given a choice.
❏   Flights on which passengers are flying, if the cruise line is handling the air and/or transfers as part of an air/sea cruise.

Sometimes the cruise line keeps its internal records by booking number, and each passenger is assigned this number when the booking is recorded. When this is the case, adding those booking numbers to the list assists the cruise line in locating the booking.

Cover Letter.   The cover letter that accompanies a cruise roster should recap all arrangements and previous discussions or promises. (See Figure 11.14.) For example, the cover letter should include the following:

❑   Total number on the cruise, on each flight, on pre-purchased shore excursions, at meal sittings—recap of figures on the accompanying roster.

❑   Name of tour manager and reminder of his or her cabin arrangements, if not reserved previously. Formal request to send tour manager's cruise ticket.

❑   Special requests on behalf of group (e.g., meeting room for a briefing, welcome party, special use of the theatre for seminars or lectures, observance of any birthdays or anniversaries, wine, and tour of the bridge or the ship's galley).

❑   Special requests on behalf on individuals—any with particular health problems or walking difficulties, special menu requests (if possible).

❑   Reminder of any item still outstanding, such as a passenger still on a waiting list.

APPLYING FOR TOUR MANAGER'S TICKET

When using an airfare that permits a complimentary air ticket, you must formally apply to the airline for this ticket. It cannot be issued in-house in a travel agency, and it does not just automatically arrive at your office from the airline. This application is made in writing on company letterhead, and it should follow specific wording. (See Figure 11.15.) Accompanying the letter of application must be the flight manifests. (This is where the manifests that were prepared earlier can also come in handy).

Note that the letter must indicate exactly how many passengers are accompanying the manager on *each* leg. Also, note that when it comes to issuing tour manager tickets, the airlines are concerned with how many *adult* fares are accompanying him or her, so two children's half fares count as one full fare, even if the children occupy two seats. If the tour includes children, you should always indicate the age of each child next to the name on the airline manifest.

The air complimentary policy of a particular tour should be thoroughly understood *before* the tour is priced. It is no longer safe to assume that a ticket is received free for every 15 passengers as it was prior to airline deregulation. This is still true with some fares to some areas of the world. However, on many fares to many areas there are no automatic complimentary air tickets anymore, and the tour manager's airfare must either be negotiated or costed into the tour as a fixed expense so that each tour participant is, in effect, paying part of it.

LSI Travel Agency
987 Park Drive #2A
Berkeley, CA 94704
Telephone Number: 510-555-2000
Fax Number: 510-555-7210

August 25, 1992

Ms. Jane Jones
Royal Cruise Line
One Maritime Plaza
San Francisco, CA 94111

RE: 90-day finalization
"Lovers of Archaeology" Group
Mediterranean Highlights Cruise September 25, 199X
Crown Odyssey

Dear Jane:

Enclosed is our check #0000 in the amount of $0000 representing final payment for the above group. Please see breakdown attachment to the check for details.

Also enclosed is our final roster. Totals are as follows:

Total Passengers:	40+1
Meal sittings:	Early sitting 16, late sitting 25
Options:	Pre-cruise London package 16
Your block air:	SFO 31; JFK 10

By way of wrap-up, please implement the following points which we discussed previously:

1. Mrs. Elaine Whittaker of the "Lovers of Archaeology" organization is our name draw and guest speaker. We would appreciate her receiving VIP handling. She is currently holding cabin C-15; if you can upgrade her, great! Do note she is not the tour manager; we have Mrs. Sandy Johnson aboard for this purpose.

2. RCL is to host a welcome party on board. We would prefer this the second night out, if possible. Kindly request now and Sandy will reconfirm this after boarding. Also recall that you have offered a $25 per person bar/boutique credit and one bottle of wine per cabin.

Figure 11.14 Finalization letter to cruise line.

3. Note from the attached list that we have several special requests—one diabetic and one salt-free diet. Kindly alert the dining room.

4. Do recall that Mrs. Whittaker will be giving two lectures during the days at sea and you indicated that you would make meeting room space available to the group for this purpose. Please now advise us time and place so we may notify her accordingly.

We are now returning all unsold space, as required by RCL. This is with the understanding that we may continue to promote for late sales on a space-available basis only. Important—since many of these people live in rural areas out of state, we will be mailing final documents September 8, so must receive tickets well in advance of that deadline.

Sincerely,

Marty Sarbey de Souto

Marty Sarbey de Souto, CTC
Group Manager

MS/s
enclosures

Figure 11.14 (Continued.)

LSI Travel Agency
987 Park Drive #2A
Berkeley, CA 94704
Telephone Number: 510-555-2000
Fax Number: 510-555-7210

August 4, 199X

Mr. Jeffrey Whelan
Trans World Airlines
680 Market St.
San Francisco, CA 94108

RE: Rosemont Country Club
European Highlights Tour
Departing Sept. 4, 199X

Dear Mr. Whelan:

In accordance with existing IATAN Regulations and terms of the tariff rules, we hereby request Tour Conductor transportation as follows:

Names of Tour Conductors:	Mr. Eugene Kimberly
	Mrs. Margaret Kimberly
Title of Advertised Tour:	Rosemont Country Club "European Highlights Tour 199X"
IT Number:	TW1CHI385
Type of Journey:	Roundtrip

From/To	Carrier	Flt.#	Date	No. Pax	Rebate
SFO/JFK	TW	746Y	Sept. 04	22	One at 100%; one full-fare
JFK/AMS	TW	814Y	Sept. 04	26	One at 100%; one at 50%
AMS/CDG	———	——	Surface		———————
CDG/FCO	AF	630Y	Sept. 11	26	One at 100%; one at 50%
FCO/JFK	TW	845Y	Sept. 14	26	One at 100%; one at 50%
JFK/SFO	TW	757Y	Sept. 14	26	One at 100%; one full-fare

Attached is a list of the names of members of the group and two copies of the promotional material used for this tour which has been distributed to the interested public.

In consideration of the granting of this Tour Conductor transportation, we agree that it will in no way be used to rebate any part of the cost to any or all individual members of this tour.

Figure 11.15 Tour manager's ticket request.

We confirm that the conditions attached to the fare paid by the passengers in the group do not prohibit the application of the tour conductor rebate.

We understand that in no case shall a tour conductor's reduced rate ticket, issued by a Member to a tour conductor, be sold to the tour conductor, directly or indirectly, at more than its face value, nor shall such ticket be resold.

We certify that the above application is true and correct in every respect, and all arrangements will have been paid for in full prior to commencement of travel.

Sincerely,

Marty Sarbey de Souto, CTC
Group Manager

MS/s
enclosure: Passenger Manifest

Figure 11.15   (Continued.)

Those fares that still *do* allow for a complimentary may be 15 + 1 free, 25 + 1-1/2 free, 30 + 2 free, and so forth. Note that some stop there with a limit of two free for 30 passengers. Even if a group continued growing to 100 or more, the tour would still be limited to two complimentaries. On the other hand, other fares may allow you to continue to accrue complimentaries to infinity (e.g., 30 + 2, 40 + 2-1/2, 45 + 3, 60 + 4, and so forth). Be sure to ask from the outset and get a commitment. If the limit is two complimentaries per group, it may be more advantageous to book the trip as two separate groups from the beginning, even though the two groups just happen to be traveling together on the same flights

READY TO GO

When all of the above tasks have been completed, the tour is ready to go. It now remains to make copies of the above materials for the tour manager and to get ready to brief that very important individual who will be responsible for the success of the tour henceforth.

❑ *SUMMARY*

While the planning, designing, and marketing are the more glamorous duties of preparing a tour, the in-house operations that follow are equally important. This stage of the tour requires firm operational control. This is achieved by calendaring all important duties, payment dates, and deadlines so that nothing is overlooked. A number of helpful forms may be used to keep control of a tour. By following this carefully planned schedule and using necessary forms to keep control of the tour, it should be possible to finalize all pre-tour materials for the clients and all operational materials for the suppliers in a timely and efficient manner.

❑ *REVIEW QUESTIONS*

1. What do we mean by "calendaring" a tour?

2. **What are some of the data that you would list on each client's tour record?**

3. **What are "no name" seats on a flight?**

4. **How does a hotel use the 30-day tour roster?**

5. **What can tour operators do in their relationships with suppliers to assure a company's credibility and professionalism as perceived within the travel industry?**

6. **What is the purpose of the 60-day review with suppliers?**

❑ *ACTIVITIES*

1. Prepare a year's calendar for a fictitious tour, working backwards from departure date. Enter all important dates: 90, 60, and 30-day supplier review dates, date of promotions (e.g., ads, direct mail, promotional evening, etc.), date for brochure completion, date to complete costing, etc.

2. Prepare a 30-day list of duties for finalizing and dispatching your own fictitious tour.

3. Write a 30-day recap letter to an airline finalizing a fictitious tour with them and to the other downline airlines involved. Cover all important points that the airline(s) will need to get this tour on its way.

12

TOUR MANAGER PREPARATION AND DISPATCH

LEARNING OBJECTIVES

After reading this chapter, you should:

- ☐ Know what qualities to look for in hiring an enroute tour manager (or assess your Pied Piper or yourself for this job)
- ☐ Know the six roles a tour manager must play on the road
- ☐ Be able to draw up a written agreement with a potential tour manager
- ☐ Know what materials to have ready to give the tour manager at the pre-trip briefing
- ☐ Know how to brief the tour manager prior to tour departure

KEY CONCEPTS AND TERMS

Foreign Language Ability
Incoming Tourism
Independent Contractor
Leadership Ability
Local Guides
Master Flight Itinerary
No-Go Date
Outgoing Tourism
Pre-Tour/Post-Tour Flights
Pre-Trip Briefing
Pre-Trip Briefing Materials
Reconfirm
Record Locator Number
Rooming List

Supplier Payment Methods
Tour Manager Agreement or Contract
Tour Manager Job Description
Tour Manager (Escort, Leader, Director, Courier)

After the pre-trip arrangements for the tour are completed, the dealings with all suppliers are finalized, and the final documents have been sent out to passengers, one last thing must be done before the group leaves. The tour manager (also known as tour director, tour leader, or tour escort) must be briefed and given all necessary materials for the trip. But first, let us look at this person, because this manager will determine the success or failure of the tour project. Has the tour manager been selected carefully? Do you and the tour manager know what is expected? (For more indepth coverage of tour escorting, see Chapter 13 and also *Handbook of Professional Tour Management*, by Robert T. Reilly, Delmar Publishers, Inc.)

THE TOUR MANAGER

Managers come with all sorts of titles: tour escort, tour leader, tour organizer, courier, tour guide, and the current term—tour manager. What do these terms have in common? What is the role associated with each title?

The term **tour manager** is the important one for our purposes. It means the person who actually leads the group from point to point, usually from the gateway city. In some cases, however, the group may fly as a group, but unaccompanied (or as individuals on different flights from different gateways), convene overseas, and meet the tour manager there at a prearranged assembly point.

"Tour manager" is the current term in Europe, and this nomenclature now is being recognized in the United States, together with the new, upgraded title of "tour leader" or "director." However, in many offices, the term tour manager still refers to the individual in the tour office handling the tour inside, not outside in the field. Perhaps in the future, this confusion of terms will be clarified; in this text, we will use tour manager to mean the person who handles the group enroute.

This individual, no matter what title is bestowed on him or her, should not be confused with a guide. The tour manager is not a local city guide and is not expected to know the year that every cathedral was built nor is expected to speak the local language of each country visited. Those details are left to local city guides receiving the tour at each stop. However, the tour manager does provide continuity and carry-through from one city to the next and from one country to the next. The tour manager also acts as overall coordinator as the tour moves along.

Contiki **the world**

A major part of the success of Contiki is due to our worldwide team. Carefully selected, highly *professional* - their training really puts them through their paces. Made up of hard working, loyal, totally fun-loving individuals, the Contiki team are completely committed to your vacation enjoyment. A **fantastic experience** in the company of like-minded people your own age, you'll always find our team wherever and whenever you need them... teaching sports... helping you discover what's where... joining you for meals... driving... Quite different from conventional staff, the Contiki team make you feel *welcome wherever you are* with a willingness to help whenever you need a hand. Keeping things running smoothly. Holding out for **hassle-free** vacations.

Check-out these introductions to some of the Worldwide Contiki Team.

'bj' - brett jakes

At home behind the microphone, BJ has been a Tour Manager with Contiki since completing his training in time for the 1990 season.

Aged 30 and born in New Zealand, Brett has a **degree** in marketing and worked as an Account Director for Ford motors for 7 years. From there the travel bug bit and before joining Contiki he travelled through Canada, the USA, Asia, Greece and Kenya. Sport plays an *important* part in BJ's life and he's keen on rugby, cricket, squash, jogging and sky diving.

phil hutson

The experience of a Contiki holiday whilst in the army convinced Phil there was **more to life** than armoured personnel carriers. Turning down a promotion he joined the Contiki team and soon found himself leading the ▮▮▮▮▮ way in one of Contiki's air-conditioned coaches. New Zealand is the *perfect place* for outdoor hobbies and that's ideal for Phil who spends most of his **leisure** time bungee jumping, skiing and scuba diving.

julie hanham

Four years working for Contiki in Europe and New Zealand make Julie an old hand even though she's only 24. The constant company of people her own age who want to really get *involved* in the **experiences** that Contiki offer makes the job worthwhile. Julie loves skiing, sailing and white water rafting on NZ's fantastic rapids. She's often found leading the way on one of the many excursions that Contiki offer on their NZ adventures.

6

Figure 12.1 America Contiki Holidays, a wholesale tour operator, uses its tour managers and other trip personnel as a selling feature. This ad describes Brett Jakes "bj's" qualifications for being a good tour manager. (Courtesy of America Contiki Holidays.)

Who Is This Manager?

The tour manager may be a member of a travel agency or tour operator's staff. He or she may be the Pied Piper (i.e., the organizer who sold and recruited the group). Or perhaps it could be an outside professional manager, whose salary, as a professional, has been costed into the trip.

Whoever it is, it is important to select this person carefully, since the failure or success of the trip may depend on its tour manager. It is amazing how many companies spend tremendous amounts of time, money, and energy on a tour, only to send it out with a totally inexperienced, unqualified individual. They tell the person not to worry and that he or she does not have to do anything except to act as social director! Many times a professional tour manager is not used because the company is trying to save money and make the tour less expensive and thus, more competitive with other tours on the market. In other cases, a professional tour manager is not used simply because the company staff does not realize the importance of good management in the field or because the staff believes that "anyone" can manage a tour.

Qualities to Look for in a Tour Manager

Choosing your tour manager carefully is important; it requires both logic and common sense. The person responsible for this choice cannot give the job to a friend, to the office manager who has not been on a trip in a long time, or to a former Spanish professor because he or she speaks the language well. Most of us know individuals who are marvelous friends and colleagues but who have made terrible tour managers. I had a friend who taught Spanish, who spent every summer in Spain, and who had been wanting for some years to be selected as a tour manager. However, she is totally disorganized. What is worse, she hates groups! Obviously, this person would be totally inappropriate as a tour manager.

Although choosing the right person is always difficult, there are a few guidelines; that is, qualities to look for in a tour manager:

❑ *Outgoing personality*—someone who is not shy and is able to mix socially, to speak in public, and to approach strangers—these are often the same qualities most prevalent in a good sales recruiter or Pied Piper.

❑ *Common sense*—someone who can handle emergencies well, deal with enroute problems sensibly, and think quickly. Often maturity is an advantage here; an older person, just by virtue of having lived longer and having dealt with life's problems, may be better qualified than a young person. Age, however, is no automatic guarantee of common sense.

❑ *Organization*—the kind of person who can plan ahead and always be prepared for the next day's activities. Those who cannot get themselves to a plane on time will never be able to get 40 people there on time. The organized person is one who has pulled all the flight coupons prior to flight check-in, who has secured the right amount of change for departure tips to hotel bellmen and has it ready in an envelope, and who is down in the lobby early on departure day checking on the bell captain to be sure that the baggage gets down on time, and so forth. This attribute of organization is often the area where many sales recruiters are lacking. It is important to analyze your Pied Piper. If it appears that he or she is a real sales dynamo, a public relations person who may, however, be weak on details and organization, use this individual for what he or she is best at—sales and public relations. However, hire a real, behind-the-scene working manager as well. Your Pied Piper can act as host/hostess while the working tour manager handles the business details of the tour (e.g., baggage, air tickets, tipping). If each is properly briefed from the outset on the other's role, the two can work together effectively and smoothly as a team.

❑ *Empathy*—the kind of person who truly cares about other people. This means truly liking people, not in the backslapping, salesperson way but in a selfless, caring, human way. This is the tour manager who gets up at 2:00 a.m. to tend a sick tour member and the tour manager who goes out of the way to take a passenger shopping or to help him or her place an international telephone call home. Tour managing means intimate contact with a group of individuals for an extended period. The tour manager becomes emotionally involved in the members' lives by force of circumstance, since they may view him or her as a confidant in whom they entrust their hopes, aspirations, and tragedies. (As a tour manager, I have had to tell a couple that their son had been killed in Vietnam. I have been go-between in some on-tour romances and have been invited to the wedding later. I have encountered tour passengers with severe emotional, sexual, and psychological problems.) Although the person chosen as tour manager need not be a registered psychologist, he or she must have a humane, empathetic quality necessary to handle such situations.

❑ *Extreme tact*—the ability to handle people, to work well with others. These others are not just the tour participants; they are also the local guides, bus drivers, waiters, customs officials, receptive services operators, and local hosts overseas; that is, people of various nationalities, educational levels, ethnic backgrounds, and motivations.

❑ *Even-tempered personality*—the kind of person who does not fluster easily and does not lose his or her temper easily. This is not to say that a tour manager never shows anger, but, when he or she does, it should be done cooly for effect, not just because the manager has lost control.

❑ *Commitment*—the person who does not have a nine-to-five mentality, who understands that tour managing is not an eight-hour-day job, and who is willing to invest extra time, energy, and personal involvement as needed. The tour manager who deposits the group at the hotel and says, "I'll see you all tomorrow at 9:00 a.m." will never be successful. Although everyone needs a night off now and then, it should be understood that one of the tour manager's functions is to fill in those time gaps when the group is not accompanied by a local sightseeing guide (e.g., the Dutch-treat dinners, the shopping expeditions, and the free time). Therefore, if the manager wants to take this trip as a way to visit friends overseas or do research or business for some reason other than dedicating time, attention, and energies to the group, then you have the wrong person.

❏ *Leadership qualities*—probably this is the important characteristic to look for. **Leadership ability** is that nebulous, charismatic quality of leadership. It is always a plus to find someone who has had experience in a leadership position, whether as president of the local Parent-Teachers Association or officer of a private club. A true leader is more qualified to be a tour manager than the person who may know the country and speak the language fluently but who cannot lead.

❏ *Balanced personality*—the person with a sense of fun and a serious side It's a person who is part intellectual and part social. After all, a trip is not all one thing or another; it is not all historical lectures and not all a big party. If it were, it would not be a success. The operator who puts together and carries out a balanced itinerary—one with some learning (e.g., cathedrals, museums), some fun (e.g., dining around, partying), some relaxation (e.g., beaches, sports)—seems to have the best prospects for success. So it would seem with tour managers also. If they emphasize socializing and ignore intellectual depth, they may fail. Conversely, if they see the trip as one vast classroom from which they may teach their specialty with no light touch or fun, they will lose their passengers.

❏ *Good health*—simplistic though it may sound, it is important that tour managers be in good health at the outset and maintain it through the trip. While on a trip, they are under stress with less sleep and less time for themselves and their own needs than at home. Managers often find it difficult to stay on a restricted diet, to remember to take medication, or to rest when overtired. They cannot schedule their own day or put their own interests first.

❏ *Control and firmness*—the person who can keep a tight rein on a group and not let his or her leadership be eroded by passengers or local guides. There is a fine line between the ability to be firm without being a dictator. Many people assume that teachers or ex-military personnel make good tour managers. This is not always the case, since sometimes they tend to treat their tour members like students or recruits rather than as equals.

The Importance of Experience

Previous Travel to the Country. It's also important to assess the needs of a particular itinerary. If many tour activities are already included and if local bilingual guides will be with the group a large percentage of the time abroad, then your tour manager's knowledge of the country is not so important.

If, on the other hand, your itinerary has a lot of free time with no activities planned and if local bilingual guides will be with the group only briefly, then your

Come to a Place Where
Learning and Laughter
Go Hand in Hand

Figure 12.2 Successful tour managers are ready to go out of their way to make their tour members happy, like arranging visits to special attractions for the children. (© Premier Cruise Lines, Ltd.)

tour manager's knowledge of a particular country, city, culture, and customs will prove more important. Obviously, even if **local guides** are being used frequently, your tour manager can fill in on long drives or on free days. It should be noted that in many countries and specific cities, only local licensed guides are permitted by law to take groups through certain museums and historical sites. In these cases, your tour manager may be fined if observed performing as a local guide.

Foreign Language Ability. Similarly, how important is it for the tour manager to have **foreign language ability** in the country or countries to be visited? If you speak foreign languages, so much the better. I speak Spanish fluently. I probably do a better job as a tour manager in a Spanish-speaking country than if I did not. However, many of my colleagues without this language skill have led tours to Spanish-speaking areas quite successfully. Similarly, I have led tours to Germany, Japan, and other countries where my vocabulary is limited to "Good Morning" and "Where is the bathroom?" Language ability alone is not a reason to select someone as tour manager.

However, in **incoming tourism** the tour manager must be totally fluent in the language of the incoming group. Preferably he or she should be a native speaker, because the members of the group are totally dependent on this person for translation and for an understanding of what is happening day to day. In **outgoing tourism**, however, there are English-speaking local guides overseas in addition to your own English-speaking tour manager traveling with the group.

Job Description

The previous discussion has made it clear that the **tour manager's job description** is a complex one. It could be described as six professions in one:

- ❑ *Housemother (father) figure*—the person everyone in the group looks up to.
- ❑ *Business manager*—handling the day-to-day business of running the tour: checking in for flights, locating lost baggage, reconfirming onward reservations, tipping, handling hotel check-ins and check-outs, paying bills enroute, and checking that buses and guides are on time and that itineraries are fulfilled as promised.
- ❑ *Social director*—setting up special meals and parties, observing birthdays and anniversaries, acting as host or hostess, introducing people, and acting as a social catalyst.
- ❑ *Psychologist*—serving as a shoulder to cry on (i.e., a good listener).
- ❑ *Internationalist*—tying the countries together, comparing the country just left with the next one on the horizon, and explaining cultures and customs different from those to which the passengers are accustomed.
- ❑ *Teacher*—pointing out new things, giving clients an educational experience, (however subliminal), and giving people a good time.

WHERE TO LOCATE TOUR MANAGERS

Professionally trained tour managers are usually independent contractors who do not work solely for one company, but are available on a per-tour contract basis. They are generally paid on a per-day salary plus expenses. Veteran tour managers expect between $75 and $150 per day (1992 rates), and some newcomers may charge considerably less. Those with foreign language ability will often charge higher rates than those who only speak English, and those working conventions or incentives may charge more than working a relatively simple ad-hoc tour.

Your nearest Convention and Visitors' Bureau may be a source of local contacts. Some community colleges offer one-day training and may have a list of those who took the class and may now be working as tour managers. There are also excellent in-depth private courses whose graduates are available, for example, the International Tour Management Institute (ITMI) based in San Francisco but offering classes in other cities as well. Some major cities have local guide associations, for example, the San Francisco Tour Guide Guild. Although geared to local guides for incoming tours, many of its members are also available for hire as tour managers for outgoing tours.

WHEN TO SELECT THE TOUR MANAGER

Most decisions on leadership should be made before the tour is priced. The actual individual does not have to be selected at that time, but it is necessary to select the category of person. That is, if a professional, salaried leader will be used, this person's trip, salary, and expenses must be costed-in to the tour before the tour price is established and the brochure printed. It is not necessary to make a commitment to use a certain manager until it is definite that the tour has materialized, say 60 days in advance. The danger is to work in reverse; that is, to assume that the manager will be someone from the company staff already on salary or a Pied Piper who just wants a free trip and no salary—only to find out later that this individual does not have the qualifications to perform as a real working tour manager, or that the staff person suddenly cannot get away, has left the company, or is eight-and-a-half-months pregnant.

AGREEMENT WITH THE TOUR MANAGER

Regardless of tour manager, it is wise to have a **tour manager agreement or contract**. Some of the things to agree upon are:

❑ *Salary*—if any. If so, how much (per day? per trip?). And when is it paid? (Some managers are paid part in advance and part on completion of the tour; others are paid totally on completion.)

❑ *Free Trip*—from what city? What is included in the free trip? All meals? Tips? Dutch-treat events if accompanying the group? Extra spending money for taxis, phone, baggage insurance, laundry, miscellaneous? Single room or share? Be specific!

❑ *Responsibility*—is this tour manager totally in charge? Or will there be an assistant or overseas leader traveling with the group as well? Will the group be large or small? Will the person be a titular tour manager or a real working one? Must the person travel outbound and return on the group flights?

❑ *Gratuities*—can the manager expect to receive additional remuneration through tips or not? Is tipping encouraged, discouraged, or forbidden by the company?

❑ *No-go Date*—by what date would the prospective tour manager be told if the tour were being canceled? It is not fair to have a manager hold certain dates open and then be dumped at the end.

See Figure 12.3 for a sample contract for this important person.

THE PRE-TRIP BRIEFING WITH THE TOUR MANAGER

Shortly before departure, the tour manager should be asked to come in for a **pre-trip briefing**. This should be done early enough to review all materials, read the files, and then ask questions on things not fully understood. No manager can do a good job when receiving departure materials the day of departure at the airport or in a mad rush the night before. The manager needs to feel well informed, totally in control, and self-confident.(By contrast, some extremely experienced tour managers who work extensively for major U.S. wholesale tour companies simply receive their departure materials by mail. They never go into the headquarters office for a pre-trip briefing; in fact, they may not even live in the same state as the company hiring them.)

Materials for the Pre-trip Briefing

To prepare for the briefing session, make sure that the following **pre-trip briefing materials** are ready A checklist such as shown in Figure 12.4 is helpful:

❑ *Supply of flight manifests*—if everyone is traveling together at all times on all flights, one master list will do (but give the tour manager plenty of photocopies so that a clean list may be presented at the airline check-in counter for each separate flight sector). If people are joining and leaving the group block air space at various points, separate flight manifests may be needed for each sector. It is helpful to have the list divided into smoking and nonsmoking sublists.

❑ *Supply of master rooming lists/tour rosters*—at least two for each city to be visited plus some extras.

TRAVEL COMPANY/TOUR MANAGER AGREEMENT

Agreement made this __30th__ day of __November__, __199X__, by and between LSI Travel Agency, Inc., a California corporation with principal office at _____ __891 Park Drive #2A   Berkeley, CA__, (hereinafter referred to as "LSI") and Roberta Miller (hereinafter referred to as "Roberta");

Whereas, LSI is engaged in the travel agency and tour operator business; and

Whereas, LSI desires to engage Roberta to assist as a tour manager;

Now, therefore, in consideration of the mutual benefits to them accruing, the parties hereto agree as follows:

1.   LSI engages the services of Roberta to escort vacation groups.

2.   Roberta shall be paid a fee of Eighty Dollars ($80.00) for each day of service including day of departure and arrival.

3.   LSI will reimburse Roberta for all costs incurred in her duties, including, but not limited to, meals, baggage insurance, accommodations, laundry, telephone calls, cables or wires, and tips.

4.   LSI will advance One Hundred Dollars ($100.00) per program for out-of-pocket expenses, which will be deducted from the expense report which must be submitted within thirty (30) days from the completion of the trip.

5.   Roberta is an independent contractor and agrees that she is not to be covered by any employment compensation, workmen's compensation, or other health insurance, which LSI may provide for its employees. Roberta is not to participate in any pension or profit-sharing plan, nor will there be any payroll deductions for state or local wage tax, social security tax, unemployment compensation tax, or federal withholding tax. All fees will be reported on IRS 1099 MISC. form for federal income tax purposes.

6.   Roberta shall be entitled to twenty-five (25) percent of her estimated fee prior to departure with the balance to be paid within fourteen (14) days subsequent to the completion of the trip.

7.   LSI reserves the right to cancel this agreement for any specific tour without penalty up to four (4) weeks prior to departure. Any cancellations within four (4) weeks of departure will result in Roberta receiving her entire fee but no reimbursement for expenses.

8.   This agreement may be terminated by either party hereto at any time upon ten (10) days written notice to the other party.

9.   This agreement contains the entire understanding of the parties and supercedes all previous verbal and written agreements. There are no other agreements, representations or warranties not set forth herein.

In witness whereof, the parties hereto, intending to be legally bound thereby, hereunto set their respective hands and seals the day and year first written above.

LSI Travel Agency, Inc.

	By	
_____		_____
Witness		President
_____		_____
Witness		Roberta Miller

Figure 12.3 Sample contract with a tour manager. (Reproduced with permission of Jeffrey R. Miller.)

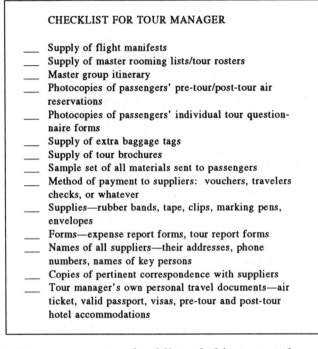

CHECKLIST FOR TOUR MANAGER

___ Supply of flight manifests
___ Supply of master rooming lists/tour rosters
___ Master group itinerary
___ Photocopies of passengers' pre-tour/post-tour air reservations
___ Photocopies of passengers' individual tour questionnaire forms
___ Supply of extra baggage tags
___ Supply of tour brochures
___ Sample set of all materials sent to passengers
___ Method of payment to suppliers: vouchers, travelers checks, or whatever
___ Supplies—rubber bands, tape, clips, marking pens, envelopes
___ Forms—expense report forms, tour report forms
___ Names of all suppliers—their addresses, phone numbers, names of key persons
___ Copies of pertinent correspondence with suppliers
___ Tour manager's own personal travel documents—air ticket, valid passport, visas, pre-tour and post-tour hotel accommodations

Figure 12.4 Tour manager's checklist of things to take.

❑ *Master group flight itinerary*—one copy. The **master flight itinerary** should show airline, flight number, airport (not just city), estimated time of departure and arrival (ETD/ETA), and meal service for each flight sector. The tour manager should know the name of the controlling airline and that airline's **record locator number** to **reconfirm** the air reservations for the tour, if any. This helps the manager in the field, if, when reconfirming onward air reservations, a carrier says that it has no record of the group's reservations. It is then possible to refer the overseas airline personnel to the controlling air carrier that originated the booking.

❑ *Individual air reservations*—photocopies of tour members' **pre-tour and post-tour flights**, so that the tour manager knows how each passenger is arriving at the assembly point and, how each is continuing on after the tour terminates.

❑ Tour *questionnaires*—a photocopy of each of those personal questionnaires that the passengers sent in to the office, indicating their health problems, special diet requirements, personal interests, emergency contacts, and so forth.

❑ *Baggage tags*—supply of extra baggage tags, the same style and color as those distributed to passengers with their final documents. These are used to replace passengers' tags that fall off with wear and tear as the tour progresses or used as samples to give to porters and bellmen to identify the group's baggage.

❑ *Sample set of passenger materials*—one complete set of everything that the passengers have received so far, from the tour brochure and initial offer to the information bulletins and departure materials. The tour manager should know everything that the passengers were told in order to continue in the same vein and not contradict something that they were told previously.

❑ *Method of payment to suppliers*—whether the **supplier payment methods** include vouchers, company checkbook, travelers checks, or whatever mode used for payment. If the tour is completely prepaid, the tour manager should carry copies of checks or proof of payment. Even so, he or she may need to carry monies for emergencies, tips, and other items. Some foreign currency should be considered also—at least for the first overseas arrival in the event that the greeter does not show up at the airport and the tour manager is forced to move the group to the hotel in taxis.

❑ *Care package of supplies*—a small envelope of rubber bands, cellophane tape, paper clips, black marking pens, and expense report forms.

❑ *Tour manager's own documents*—air ticket, pre-tour or post-tour hotel vouchers, baggage insurance policy, baggage tags, name badge.

❑ *Information on suppliers*—photocopies of pertinent correspondence with each supplier, particularly the original commitment letters and the agency's finalization wrap-up letter. The manager should have the name, address, telephone number, and key person contact for each hotel and for each receptive services operator along the line. If the tour manager is a member of your staff or someone who leads tours for you frequently, a relationship of trust probably has been established and you will not mind this individual having copies of confidential correspondence with suppliers, particularly information on the net prices that are being charged. On the other hand, if the manager is a Pied Piper representing a sponsoring client organization (e.g., club, church, or business entity for whom a private trip has been arranged), you may not want that individual to have access to confidential information and prices. Therefore, use discretion. However, the more information the manager has, the better job he or she can do overseas if a problem arises. If the hotel tries to put the group into rooms overlooking the garbage cans and you were guaranteed ocean-front rooms, the tour manager cannot do as good a job getting what was promised if he or she doesn't have a letter signed by the hotel's sales manager guaranteeing ocean-front rooms.

Briefing the Tour Manager Before Departure

When the tour manager arrives for the pre-tour briefing, all of the materials discussed previously should be ready for review. After he or she has read through everything and has made notes on questions of concern, a discussion clarifying certain philosophies is essential. This is the time to discuss how to handle certain kinds of situations in line with company policy. Obviously, every circumstance that could possibly arise cannot be anticipated and covered in this discussion. (That is why common sense is an important qualification for a tour manager.) Yet, philosophies do vary from company to company, from tour to tour within a particular company, and even from individual to individual within the company. Therefore, it is not fair to expect the tour manager to second guess someone else's wishes. Points of policy that might be helpful to discuss are:

❑ *How bills are to be settled*—does the tour manager pay enroute? Is everything prepaid and, if not, specifically what has not been paid? Has the tour manager been given more than adequate funds to meet these needs? If he or she is merely to sign bills, should the bills be analyzed and compared with the original quote given the company? Or is the tour manager merely to verify that the services were provided and the number of passengers present at each activity? Is the manager perhaps to pay by voucher?

❑ *How the tour manager is to handle emergencies*—how should he or she handle death of a passenger, severe illness, or political upheaval? Most professional tour managers have had experience in this regard, but a Pied Piper or even a member of the staff who is not an experienced tour manager might not know company policy, what expenses are authorized, or what legal procedures should be followed.

❑ *Airfare*—what kind of airfare is being used? If the group members' air tickets are issued using a special fare, such as a Group Inclusive Tour (GIT) fare, an Advance Purchase Excursion (APEX), or other restricted fare, the tour manager should know the rules and regulations covering that fare. When out in the field with a group, you should know whether there can be a change of air carriers, whether an ill passenger can travel apart from the group and catch up later, whether a passenger can change homeward travel plans without incurring an extra charge, and so forth. This will help the tour manager deal with passengers' questions, rather than being at the mercy of a local airline clerk's interpretation of a fare generated in the United States.

❑ *Changing arrangements*—to what extent, if any, is the tour manager authorized to make changes in the published itinerary as the tour goes along? (Remember—the tour brochure is a legal/moral commitment to the passenger.)

❑ *Lost or damaged luggage*—how should the manager deal with this thorny problem, other than try to locate the missing luggage and try to get the airlines to assist the passenger? Is the tour manager authorized to spend any money on the passenger?

❑ *Celebrations and entertaining*—should the tour manager celebrate group members' anniversaries, birthdays, and other festivities? Should anyone be entertained enroute? If so, is this expense budgeted?

❑ *Emergency expenses beyond the budget*—in case of an emergency causing the group to be rerouted, thus incurring additional airfare or additional ground expenses, is the manager authorized to pay this? Or is each passenger to pay at the time?

❏   *The company's attitude toward this tour*—is this a deluxe tour on which the manager should spend a little, if necessary, to keep everyone happy? Or is this a tightly budgeted tour on which the manager has little financial leeway?

Special Thoughts for Cruises.   For a cruise (or if a short cruise is included as an integral part of the trip), the tour manager should be especially informed about the following:

❏   *Meal seating*—has it been arranged for the group to sit together, and, if so, at an early or late seating? Or have the passengers selected individual meal seating, perhaps at different times and at different tables?

❏   *Welcome-aboard party*—does the budget permit one? If so, has it been prebooked or is the tour manager to set it up with the ship's cruise director after boarding? Is it paid by the cruise line as an additional amenity for the group or is the manager to pay for it on his or her shipboard bill and tip the waiter out-of-pocket?

❏   *Shore excursions*—how are they being handled? Have they been prebooked (either for the group as a whole or for those individual passengers who have purchased these options)? Or are passengers to purchase their own shore excursions as the cruise moves along? What about the manager's own shore excursions—are they complimentary or is he or she to pay for them if the cruise line does not grant a complimentary at each port?

❏   *Wine or other festivities*—is any budget built in?

❏   *Cabin locations*—has the manager been given a deck plan to take along and a list of the passengers' cabin numbers?

❏   *Shipboard gratuities*—what arrangements have been made, if any, for gratuities to the shipboard personnel at the end of the cruise? Are passengers to tip on their own, and if so, have they been advised in the information bulletins as to the appropriate amount? Or have gratuities been costed-in to the cruise cost and is the tour manager to tip on behalf of the entire group at the end of the cruise? Either way, the manager's shipboard gratuities will have to be paid. Have they been costed-in to the trip? Or will the manager have to pay his or her own?

Special Thoughts for Motorcoach Tours.   Those who have escorted motorcoach tours effectively through the years find it helpful to plan ahead for those long periods of time on the road—times that might prove boring were it not for some fun or intellectual stimulation injected into the trip by the tour manager.

They bring with them a "bag of tricks," which may include song books, games, stories, jokes, prizes, candy, and so forth. Some even bring a guitar! Your "bag of tricks" or that of your tour manager can be as fertile as one's imagination. Time on the road is an excellent opportunity to move and mix passengers so they get to know each other or to plan impromptu stops to buy strawberries or chocolates. It's also a great time to have a route map and have tour members follow along with the

Figure 12.5 Cosmos is known for low-cost coach tours. During long drives, tour managers in charge must rely on their own "bag of tricks" (songs, games, jokes, prizes) to keep tour participants happy. (Courtesy of Cosmos Tourama.)

tour manager as he or she points out the various routes the group will be following. These and other similar hints might be discussed with your selected tour manager during the pre-trip briefing.

EVERYTHING IS READY

If everything listed here has been thought of, the tour manager has been prepared and briefed as well as possible. The manager has received all the necessary materials, and has been informed about the behavior appropriate to company policy in certain situations. The tour manager should now be able to go home, pack a suitcase, and prepare for departure, confident of fulfilling the company's expectations.

❑ SUMMARY

Selecting an individual with the right qualifications to act as your tour manager on the road is extremely important. You should understand this individual's roles and the personal qualifications necessary for the job prior to choosing the tour manager. A written agreement should be drawn up between the company and the tour manager to avoid any misunderstandings. All departure materials should be prepared in adequate time for the tour manager to review and a pre-tour briefing of the tour manager should be scheduled. Careful advance planning, early preparation of departure materials, and a detailed pre-trip briefing will help ensure the success of the tour in the field.

❑ REVIEW QUESTIONS

1. The term "tour manager" is the current term. What are some other titles for this same person?

2. In interviewing potential tour managers and assessing their personal qualifications, there are a great number of qualities for which we look. Name at least six that you would look for if you were assessing someone to manage a tour for you.

3. How would knowledge of a foreign language be an additional asset for a tour manager in outgoing tourism where you usually have local bilingual guides overseas?

4. Why is it important that a tour manager in incoming tourism be totally fluent in a foreign language?

5. You are meeting tomorrow for the pre-trip briefing with your selected tour manager. What are the things you will review with this individual at the briefing?

6. What entertaining would you authorize your tour manager to do enroute and how much would you budget per passenger?

7. Why do you think so many companies refuse to hire a professional tour manager and let the tour go out under the direction of a Pied Piper, even if that person may not be a professional tour manager?

8. Name an unforseen circumstance on tour where a tour manager might have to solve the situation by common sense.

9. Why is the ability to handle people tactfully such an important factor in tour managing? Who are the people you would have to handle, other than the tour passengers themselves?

10. When should the tour manager be selected—if not the exact individual, at least the category of individual?

❑ *ACTIVITIES*

1. Interview a friend or fellow student, assessing this individual's capabilities as a tour manager.

2. Locate an individual who has been a tour manager previously. Prepare a list of questions and interview this individual for hints and for suggestions as to how he/she handled specific difficult situations that arose on tour.

3. You have just been hired as a tour manager for a fictitious tour. Research at the library, government tourist offices, bookstores, etc., what materials you, as tour manager, might like to distribute to the tour passengers (i.e., in addition to the materials the company may already have sent them). Consider such things as maps, lists of restaurants, money exchange charts, suggested background readings, U.S. Customs regulations, and so forth.

4. Call five or six of the major U.S. wholesale tour companies across the United States and speak to the individual responsible for hiring their tour managers. Ascertain each company's hiring policies and salary levels.

13

MANAGING THE TOUR ENROUTE

LEARNING OBJECTIVES

After reading this chapter, you should:

- ❑ Know how to greet your first group at the airport and look like a "pro"
- ❑ Know how to give an orientation briefing to a tour group
- ❑ Be able to deal with enroute emergencies
- ❑ Learn how to handle hotel check-ins and check-outs smoothly
- ❑ Be able to work tactfully with local guides, drivers, immigration, and customs officials
- ❑ Be able to keep track of air tickets and baggage enroute
- ❑ Know what it takes to handle the special needs of groups on cruise ships

KEY CONCEPTS AND TERMS

Enroute Problems
Flight Check-In
Hotel Check-In
Hotel Check-Out
Leadership Hints
Local Guides
No Shows
Orientation Meeting or Briefing
Personal Comportment
Rules of the Road
Seat Rotation
Security of Valuables

When the tour manager has received all departure materials and instructions from the company early enough to allow time for careful review, any questions should be resolved with the company before departure. Now is the time to read any correspondence with suppliers, to check to be sure that all necessary materials and lists are available, and to spend a little time reading about the passengers (e.g., names, interests, health problems, and so forth). The tour manager might also check to see if any of the passengers have birthdays or anniversaries for a special celebration enroute. And, of course, the tour manager will want to do some background reading on the countries to be visited, if he or she is not extremely conversant with them. If the company has not sent out adequate preparatory materials to the group members, the tour manager may want to gather or make up handouts such as maps, currency converters, phrases in foreign languages, articles, and fact sheets on some of the countries to be visited.

Everything should be packed as efficiently and compactly as possible, and it should remain separate from personal apparel. It should not be necessary to search enroute for the Paris city maps among the dirty laundry. The tour manager will also want to call the departing airline to verify departure times and to check whether arrangements have been made for a group check-in lane, preassigned seats on the aircraft, and other special services.

AT THE AIRPORT

Before the Passengers Arrive

It is important for the tour manager to arrive at the airport *before* the tour members arrive. Therefore, if the passengers have been advised to check in one and one-half hours before flight departure, for example, it is best for the tour manager to be there at least two hours before flight time.

On arrival, the tour manager should go to the check-in counter and ask to see the flight supervisor on duty. After presenting a business card and a copy of the group's flight manifest, you can then discuss with the supervisor how **flight check-in** will be handled so that there is no chance of giving conflicting information to the passengers as they arrive for check-in. Here are some of the things that should be discussed.

❑ How seat assignments are being handled—are passengers in the group free to select their own seats throughout the aircraft? Or is a certain area blocked off for the group and are they to select their seats within that block? Or have seats been preassigned?

❑ How many people are in the group boarding this flight and of the total how many are to be in smoking (if permitted) and how many to be in nonsmoking sections of the aircraft.

❑ Whether there will be a special check-in lane for the group.

Figure 13.1   The International Association of Tour Managers, with head-quarters in London, is one of several organizations trying recently to bring professionalism to the position of tour manager with performance guidelines and ethical standards. (Courtesy of IATM, London.)

☐   Airport to which all luggage is to be checked. Are any interline tags needed? (If so, perhaps they can be prepared at this time to facilitate the entire process.)

☐   Full details of the flight itself; for example, boarding time, gate number and location, departure time, expected in-flight meal service and times, and in-flight movies, if any.

❏   Follow-through on any previous special requests such as use of the VIP lounge or special meals.
❏   Follow-through on any special needs for tour participants with disabilities.

Before the group's arrival, the tour manager should check in, selecting an aisle seat so that it is easy to get up to attend to the group without constantly having to climb over passengers. It is also a good idea to be prepared to answer typical questions that the passengers may ask such as where are the airport restrooms located, is there a duty-free shop and is it open, or where is the coffee shop?

As the Group Members Arrive

When the group members start arriving for flight check-in, the tour manager takes the initiative by approaching them and introducing himself or herself. (He or she should wear a name badge and perhaps carry a clipboard to look official.) Members of the group should be identifiable because they should be using the tour name badges and luggage tags. If several members of the group are standing around, the tour manager should again take the initiative and assume the role of host by introducing them to one another. If individual passengers are carrying their own air tickets, they should be alerted to get their air tickets and passports out and to go to the counter. In this case, the tour manager should not interfere between the tour members and airline personnel during the check-in procedure. The airline agent will handle the actual check-in—making seat assignments, tagging baggage, reviewing passports and visas, if any, returning air tickets to passengers, stapling baggage claim stubs into the ticket jacket, and issuing boarding passes. On the other hand, if the tour manager has the group's air tickets, he/she will need to handle or assist with the check-in.

The tour manager can then tell the group members that they are free to roam the airport, have a cup of coffee, or visit the duty-free shop, and that the group will reassemble at the boarding gate. Tour members should be reminded of boarding time and gate number and of the importance of proceeding to the gate sufficiently early to pass through security check. In some cases, passengers may check in and check their luggage at the counter but may still have to go to the gate to get their seat assignments and boarding passes. In such cases, it is important that they do so early. Do not assume that, because they have already checked in at the counter and because the tour manager knows that they are present, that they have been taken care of. *They are not really on board until they have a boarding pass and a seat assignment.*

As the group moves along from country to country, it will probably be best for the tour manager to provide group check-in for the entire tour at the airport. In this case, he/she can pull the flight coupons in advance, receive all the boarding passes and seat assignments from the airline, and subsequently distribute them to the individual passengers.

The basic idea of this entire predeparture procedure is to get each individual member checked in as quickly and efficiently as possible and then away from the check-in area. Tour members should know that they should board the aircraft as independent travelers even if they do not see the tour manager at the gate. The tour manager will find them later on board after takeoff. This frees the tour manager to wait for any last-minute passengers and to thank the airline personnel who have helped the group with check-in.

Passengers should be given or mailed their tickets beforehand so that they can bring them to the airport. The tour manager shouldn't carry the entire group's tickets to the airport. In this way, if the tour manager is delayed, passengers can check in on their own. Also, if passengers have their own tickets, and if they miss an inbound flight connecting to the group flight, they can go directly to the airline counter and ask airline personnel to rebook new flights or reissue a ticket as needed to catch up with the group.

No Shows

If it is departure time and a tour passenger has not arrived, there is no alternative but to go on without the passenger—a **no show**. The tour manager's basic responsibility is to the group as a whole and not to any one individual tour member. Quite frequently, when a passenger has not shown up, it turns out that he or she bypassed the lobby check-in counter and went directly to the gate, or perhaps checked in early before the rest of the group arrived and is browsing around the airport. On the other hand, the passenger may have called your office to advise you of an emergency, and the message may not have been passed on to the tour manager. If possible, the tour manager should try to call the passenger or should call the office (or the home phone of the office manager, if during off-hours) and advise them of the missing tour member. If it is so late that calling will cause the tour manager to miss the plane, you should give the airline flight supervisor the office phone number and ask him or her to call.

IN FLIGHT

On Boarding

Once aboard, the tour manager should introduce himself or herself to the inflight service manager/purser, sit down, see that the group settles in, and make sure that they stay seated until after takeoff. Inflight personnel will not appreciate a tour manager who blocks the aisles while socializing with tour members at this particular time. Of course, if it appears that there is a problem, the tour manager should be as quietly helpful as possible, asking the flight attendant for assistance if necessary.

After Takeoff

Once the flight is airborne and the seat-belt sign has gone off, it is then time to get up and circulate through the plane (being careful not to interfere with inflight personnel). Locate the tour members, reintroduce yourself, and chat with individual tour members. The tour manager is the host and should set the tone and take the initiative. He or she should not just sit and wait until someone comes by with a question. *Visibility is important*, particularly during the first 24 hours when tour members feel insecure.

At some time during the flight, depending on flight schedule and meal service, you may collect air tickets and baggage claim stubs from each member of the group. This can be done efficiently by going down the aisle with a list of tour members and with two manila envelopes—one envelope marked "Air Tickets" and one marked "Baggage Stubs."

Air Tickets. The tour manager should then strip down the air tickets and return to the passenger the ticket jacket and any typed flight itinerary or other miscellaneous loose papers. The tour manager should keep the air ticket only and check it off against the passenger's name on the manifest. Then after all tickets are collected, they can be alphabetized, counted to be sure that they are all there, and double-checked to be sure each flight coupon is intact at the time that each ticket is picked up.(This is a double check that a flight coupon has not been erroneously pulled by airline personnel at check-in or at the time the ticket was issued.) There is nothing worse than suddenly finding out, ten days later somewhere enroute, that a flight coupon is missing. In such a case, the passenger in question may not be allowed to board a specific flight without paying out-of-pocket for the missing sector. The group's air tickets should then be bundled together with a rubber band. The tour manager should carry them for the balance of the trip until just before the last flight home, when they should be redistributed to the tour members, who can then check in individually for their homeward flight.

Air tickets are negotiable and, if lost, may require payment for a replacement ticket at the time, since filing for refund of a lost ticket can take months to process. Therefore, it is important that tickets be guarded carefully. They shouldn't be left lying in an unattended briefcase or flight bag; they should be checked in a safety deposit box at the hotel each and every night enroute. If, at any time, the package of air tickets is turned over to airline personnel or receptive operator employees for the purpose of reconfirming onward flights, the tour manager should be sure to get a receipt for the number of tickets. When they are returned, they should be counted again to be sure that they are all there. Similarly, it is wise to check that all flight coupons are intact each time the tickets are returned. This should not wait until everyone is in the bus enroute to the airport to check the tickets; it is too late then to do anything if one is missing!

Baggage Claim Stubs. While chatting with the passengers, the tour manager should verify how many bags they checked through, write that number down next to their names on the flight manifest, and pick up the baggage claim stubs. The

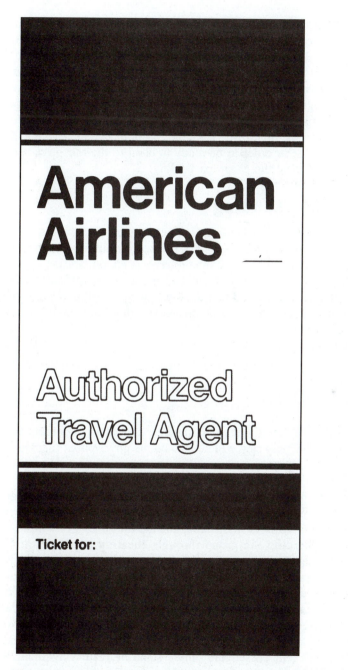

Figure 13.2   The tour manager may collect air tickets and baggage claim stubs from each member of the group.   (Courtesy American Airlines.)

passenger's last name should be written in black marking pen on each stub and then the stubs can be dropped into the manila envelope marked "Baggage Stubs." Hand luggage should not be included in the count. The count should include only those bags that the passengers actually checked in with the airline and for which they should have baggage claim stubs. After collecting all the stubs and adding the tour manager's own stubs, a total count should be made to be sure that the number of stubs in the envelope equals the total of the number written down next to each name on the manifest. Then the envelope can be sealed and the total written on the outside in order to be ready to hand to the receptive services operator, who will be meeting the group on landing.

Just Before Landing

About 30 minutes before landing (but before the plane begins its descent and before the seat belt sign goes on), it's time to circulate again and explain to tour members what documents they should have handy on landing such as passports or tourist cards. Members may also need assistance completing landing cards. The members should also be told that the tour manager will precede them to make contact with the operator meeting the group and that they should follow as individuals through immigration and out to the customs area on the other side, where they all will convene.

ON LANDING

Immediately after landing, the tour manager should go as quickly as possible ahead of the group. The next step will depend on the government regulations in the country concerned. Some countries will permit the receptive operator who is meeting the group to go inside the customs area and greet the group there. In some cases, the receptive operator might be permitted inside the immigration area to help the group through immigration and customs. Other countries will not permit anyone inside the immigration/customs area, and the tour manager will have the responsibility of shepherding the group through, locating porters, getting the luggage counted and loaded onto carts, and going through customs with the group and the luggage. In many airports, it may no longer be possible to locate porters and move the luggage as a group. In this case, it will be necessary for you and the tour participants to obtain individual baggage carts and caravan through customs inspection. In some cases, customs officials may wave the group on through or merely spot check the luggage. In other cases, all passengers may be asked to open their suitcases, so all tour passengers should stand by readily available with their luggage keys. Once through customs and immigration, the receptive operator should be waiting to direct the group to the motorcoach for loading. The tour manager should ask that all luggage be lined up on the sidewalk outside the coach and that all passengers check to see that their luggage is there as they board the coach. This may cause a short delay in departure while waiting for the luggage to be loaded after boarding, but it is the best way to be absolutely sure that no luggage has gone astray or, if it has, to determine at what point it may have disappeared.

While the passengers are boarding the coach and double-checking to see that their luggage is there, the tour manager should ascertain the name of the representative meeting the group and the name of the driver so that these individuals may be introduced to the group once everyone is aboard. The tour manager should also ask to see a copy of the local itinerary or any other material that the representative plans to hand out to the group to be sure that it agrees with what was promised. This is a good time to catch any errors before the material is distributed to the group. Sometimes these hand-out materials are standardized by the receptive operators and may mention things not pertinent to one's particular group. For example, they may mention that airport departure taxes or farewell tips to the local guides are not included in prepaid tour arrangements. In actuality, perhaps your tour company has costed-in for the tour manager to tip the guide on behalf of the group or to pay the airport tax. Quite often these standardized materials may try to sell optional tours that the tour manager does not want offered to the group. (Perhaps the options spend a great deal of touring time at stops to ensure commissions to the local guides. This is a financial fact of life in many countries where the local guides work on a miniscule base salary with the expectations of tips and commissions to augment their earnings. Or, perhaps the passengers are too tired and need some free time instead of additional tours. In addition, the tour manager may simply feel that the options offered are not a good value or are a duplicate of something that the group did in a previous country.)

After all passengers and luggage are aboard, the tour manager should board and do a head count to be sure that everyone is present. This is the time to take the microphone and formally introduce the driver and greeter/guide and then turn the microphone over for the greeter's welcoming comments. This makes it clear to the local company that the tour manager is in the leadership position and is in control, yet the local personnel are graciously invited to take over in the area of their expertise. If the tour manager simply boards the bus with the group and sits down, control has been automatically relinquished to the greeter guide.

ON ARRIVAL AT THE HOTEL

As the group arrives at the hotel, the tour manager should either ask the group to remain in the coach a minute (i.e., if traffic conditions permit) or ask them to proceed into the hotel and sit down in the lobby, perhaps asking one tour member to act as a focal point around whom the others should be seated. The idea is to make them feel comfortable but not to permit them to gather at the registration desk. The tour manager needs this freedom to speak with the hotel front-desk people in private without the pressure of the group standing impatiently nearby.

Figure 13.3 When the bus is loaded with tour members, the bus driver and tour manager take over. (Courtesy of America Contiki Holidays.)

The tour manager should present a business card and the tour/rooming roster at the desk and ask the hotel personnel how they plan to handle **hotel check-in**. The hotel check-in procedure will vary from hotel to hotel. Some hotels will have a special group desk where keys are laid out and ready in alphabetical order. Others may have the keys ready at the main desk and may ask the tour manager to distribute them. A few hotels may be totally disorganized and may not have the rooms assigned or the keys ready. In fact, the rooms may not even be cleaned and made up. It is important that the tour manager work with hotel personnel patiently and insistently until all rooms are assigned and all keys are ready. This is the time to check for any special needs; that is, any connecting rooms requested by families or friends traveling together, any room near the elevator for a passenger who has difficulty in walking, and any double beds mistakenly assigned instead of the twin-bedded rooms promised.

If there are any errors, or if room changes are necessary, they should be handled before handing out keys, if possible. Of course, there always may be the passenger who is dissatisfied with a room after seeing it and who comes down to the lobby afterward requesting a change. A few of these changes may be avoided by checking room assignments *prior* to the distribution of the keys. If two strangers are sharing a room (and particularly if this is the first night of the tour when roommates do not yet know each other), it is a nice gesture to formally introduce roommates and to ask the front desk for two room keys because usually hotels hand out only one key per room.

Before distributing the keys and dispatching people to their rooms, the group should be gathered for any announcements. One could say something such as "I'm going to hand out your keys now, folks. Please go directly to your rooms and carry your hand luggage with you; your big suitcase will be sent up just as quickly as possible but it may take some time, so please do not be concerned. Do not tip the hotel bellman when he brings your bags; we are tipping for you. If you wish to walk around the hotel you may do so; you do not need to wait in your room for the bellman. If you need me, I will be here in the lobby for a while until I get everything settled, and afterward my room number is 302. Remember, per your itinerary, we will all meet here in the lobby at 7:30 p.m. for dinner. Dress is coat and tie for the gentlemen, short dinner dresses for the ladies."

Wherever possible, the above speech (or any announcements at departure times) should be given over the microphone in the motorcoach. This is not only because the group is a captive audience at the time, but it is also for security reasons. There is no reason to announce to the whole world in a hotel lobby what time the tour members are leaving the hotel. This gives a listening thief the time that the tour group's rooms will be empty. For this same reason, it is not smart to post departure time announcements in hotel elevators or on lobby bulletin boards, as many tour companies seem to do.

As soon as tour members are on the way to their rooms, a number of things remain for the tour manager to do before relaxing:

❑ Help expedite the delivery of luggage to the rooms, perhaps translating foreign-sounding names to the bellmen or assisting them in marking room numbers on baggage tags.

❑ Take out a safety deposit box and place the group's air tickets and any other valuables there. (Double-check the access hours so that things can be taken out when needed, especially on departure day.)

❑ Get a list of the room numbers assigned to the group or work with the front-desk personnel in writing down on the master list each person's room number.

❑ Familiarize yourself quickly with the hotel in order to be knowledgeable when directing people in the group to the money exchange, pharmacy, coffee shop, and so forth.

❑ Check for mail for yourself and the tour members.

❑ Visit the coffee shop and dining room and note the hours that they normally serve. If possible, meet with the *maitre d'* and discuss the group's meal plan, how signatures and tips are handled, which meals are on the master tour account and which meals are on the clients' own personal accounts, and which meals they must clear individually when they check out of the hotel. If a meal plan is included for tour members, verify which meal items are in the meal plan and which are considered extra items that the passengers must pay for on their own. Some hotels restrict group meals to certain hours, certain dining rooms, or a certain monetary amount. Most tour passengers are understanding if they know about this in advance; if they find out after they have eaten the steak and received the bill, they are furious.

❑ Ask to meet the sales manager or front-office manager for public relations purposes and to be sure that instructions have been transmitted from the sales division to the hotel cashier about how the group's bill will be handled. It is important to avoid any financial surprises at check-out time. Such surprises might include the cashier not having a record of the deposit, or not having knowledge of a complimentary for the leader, or not providing a breakdown analysis of the total bill.

Once all of these items are taken care of and all luggage has been delivered to the rooms, you can relax. However it is important not to go off duty until personally seeing to the last of the luggage. Often, well-meaning bellmen will delay group luggage delivery to attend to new arrivals as they walk into the hotel; that is, unless the tour manager is there to watch them.

ORIENTATION MEETING

One of the first and most important events of any tour is a good **orientation meeting or briefing**. This is the time when the entire tour gets together for introductions and a discussion about how the tour will operate. It is the tour manager's opportunity to give members the "rules of the road." Some tour operators like to give a welcome cocktail party as a place for introductions and getting acquainted. Then, they often give a short briefing, followed by a period of hype and selling optional tours. Other tour operators prefer not to have a briefing after a cocktail party because they know it is important that the tour members be attentive. Later on, if certain passengers are consistently late and a sightseeing tour goes off one morning and leaves them behind, they may become angry and abusive. However, if the tour manager can say "Remember, I told you at the briefing that we would leave for sightseeing on time and I would not wait for latecomers," they will realize that everyone else heard it at the briefing and they are not being singled out for punishment. It is best to hold this briefing within the first 24 hours of the tour, if possible, because it sets the right tone. It is a good idea to wait until all tour members are present, although if some are joining the tour three days late this is not always feasible. If a problem develops with a passenger later on tour, often the one who did not attend the briefing is the culprit.

One of the best briefing times is a breakfast briefing. Passengers do not expect cocktails at that hour, and it starts the tour off on the right foot. If there isn't a budget in the tour for breakfasts, sometimes the hotel will grant a meeting room free of charge for an hour or so if you order coffee and sweet roll service. A nice icebreaker is to ask the tour members to stand one by one and give their names, hometowns, and the reasons they came on this tour. If there are people in the group who have made previous trips with the company, this is an excellent time to mention this and give them a bit of recognition. After introductions, it is nice for the tour manager to introduce himself or herself by providing some personal background information. Then the tour manager should introduce any VIPs or service personnel in the room, such as the local receptive services operator, guides, and hotel personnel. After these niceties, it is time to discuss important points of the tour—**the rules of the road**.

Points to Cover

❑ *Departure on time*—The group will not wait for habitual latecomers; it is the individual's personal responsibility to get up on time in the morning, get to breakfast on time, and so forth. The tour manager is not responsible for waking people or ordering group breakfasts. Stress that repeated tardiness is a discourtesy to the other passengers and indicate that breakfast service in the dining room may be slower than at home, so they should allow sufficient time.

❑ *Coach seating*—Everyone paid the same for the tour and therefore everyone is entitled to a chance at the front seats. Passengers are expected to behave as adults and observe **seat rotation**, automatically rotating their seating positions. They are also expected to follow any stated policy on smoking.

❑ *Courtesy to others*—Passengers are expected to be gracious and courteous to one another, no matter how tired or out-of-sorts they may be, and to the local people with whom they come in contact (e.g., guides, waiters, hotel personnel, customs officials, or immigration officials). Unkind behavior on the part of group members will not be tolerated no matter what the circumstances, even if the other person is wrong.

❑ *Attention to guides*—Local guides have a great deal of information to give to the group, and it will be appreciated if the group gives its undivided attention to the guide when he or she is speaking. A passenger should not chat with a seat mate or run off to take photos in the middle of the guide's presentation.

❑ *Appropriate dress*—Members will be advised adequately in advance about the expected dress code for a particular event, and they are expected to comply. There will be certain activities where coat and tie attire is appropriate or where Bermuda shorts are not acceptable.

❑ *Dissatisfaction on tour*—It is anticipated that there may be certain times in the coming days when some group members are upset or unhappy with something. They should go directly to the tour manager with the complaint, rather than internalizing it or circulating the complaint among the tour members. In this way the tour manager can handle complaints privately.

❑ *Reminder about security of valuables*—Passengers are urged to check their valuables in a hotel safety deposit box, to keep an eye on their cameras, to know where their passport is at all times, and never to leave watches or valuable jewelry in their hotel rooms or at the beach or pool. Men should keep their wallets inside their jacket, not in a rear pants pocket, and women should keep their purses zipped and worn close to the body at all times.

❑ *Luggage reminder*—The tour manager will always advise the group of what time to have their luggage ready for pick-up and will appreciate their complying. If a passenger should lose a baggage tag, the tour manager should be notified immediately, since the bellmen and airport porters are instructed to pick up only those bags with the company baggage tag. Members must be responsible for their own hand luggage. If they add or subtract a bag, they should advise the tour manager so there is no confusion over the count.

❑ *Review of tipping policy*—Tour menbers should be reminded of which tips are included in the tour and which are not, and suggestions should be made regarding appropriate amounts when the participants must do their own tipping. It is helpful to read out loud the tour brochure statement on tipping and then to explain it in more detail. Participants are entitled to know specifically which of the following tips are included: waiters, *maitre d'*, room maids, airport porters, hotel bellmen, local sightseeing guides, and, if a cruise is involved, cabin steward and dining room personnel.

❑ *Water and food*—The safety of local water and food, the advisability of buying bottled water, peeling fruit, and staying away from raw vegetables and salads should be discussed. Mention the local foods that are particularly good and that tour members may want to try. Remind them of the high cost of imported wines and liquors and suggest that they stick to domestic drinks. Mention local meal hours and any dining customs pertinent to the area. It's also wise to discuss in-room minibars and their high cost.

❑ *Hotel check-out procedure*—The importance of each tour member checking out of the hotel individually to clear any extra charges with the cashier and turn in the key should be stressed.

❑ *The tour manager's availability*—Some parameters of when participants may feel free to call the tour manager's room should be laid out. A good policy is for the tour manager to be available from 8:00 a.m. to 10:00 p.m., but if group members are ill or have a real emergency they should feel free to call any time, even in the middle of the night.

LEADERSHIP AND PLANNING

Leadership is not just a coincidence. Granted, there are some people who are better at it than others, but there are skills that a tour manager can develop to appear as a true leader. The following **leadership hints** outline crucial advice to tour managers:

❑ *Be visible*—look like a leader. If necessary, count, carry a clipboard or checklist, circulate, and oversee. Do not just sit and wait for things to happen.

❑ *Plan ahead*—has someone called ahead to the restaurant to remind them that the group is coming and to advise them about how many are in the party? Has someone double-checked that the coach will be on time? Is the right change available for the next day's departure tips? Has the bell captain been reminded of tomorrow's check-out time and been given an up-to-date list of room numbers? Think 24 hours ahead.

❑ *Be early*—do not be the last one down to the lobby. Be there ahead of the group. Check the following. Has the guide arrived? Has the motorcoach arrived? If so, where is it parked? Which hotel exit will be used?

❑ *Make announcements when the group is together*—preferably on the coach when all are "captive" and the microphone can be used. Do not wait until some participants have gone to their rooms and then ask others to pass the word. The "word" usually becomes garbled.

❑ *Anticipate problem situations*—announce them and ask for passengers' help. (If there is a particularly difficult passenger, put this individual to work assisting you.) People are usually cooperative if they know in advance of a problem. There is no need, however, to tell them of every little thing that is going wrong; many of these problems will be solved as the tour goes along.

❑ *Announce what is going to happen when leaving the coach*—always tell the group where and when they will be reboarding, whether the coach will be locked or not, and whether they may leave things on board or not. It is always a good idea to remind group members of the coach number and to tell them where the coach will be parked. If someone wanders from the group or does not feel well, it is possible to locate the tour manager back at the coach.

❑ *Circulate at group meals*—and see that everyone has ordered and is being waited on. Be aware of situations in which perhaps meal service could be expedited. Be sure that passengers know which items on the menu are included in their tour and which items are at additional cost to them. Many times a restaurant will offer a drink, wine, or coffee, only to present tour members with the bill afterward, much to their surprise.

❑ *Do not be afraid to enforce the rules of the road*—those that were outlined at the orientation meeting. Although speaking about the rules may anger the offending tour member, it will gain the tour manager the respect and support of the remaining tour members. Remember, the tour manager's main duty is to the group as a whole, not to any one individual, no matter how much of a VIP that individual may be.

Dealing with Local Guides

A **local guide** can be a real gem and can contribute immeasurably to the success of the tour. Conversely, an unsatisfactory guide can detract from the quality of the tour and can even cause a disaster, especially if you have to depend on this person for a long period of time. Therefore, it is wise to establish a good working relationship with the guides. Formally introduce them to the group, let it be known that they are appreciated, and try to bring out the best in each guide as the tour moves along. However, if despite all your efforts, a particular guide does not work out, a tour manager may feel free to tell the local receptive operator and ask for a replacement.

Guides come in all sizes, shapes, ages, and levels of competency and intelligence. In countries such as England, Greece, and Israel, most tour managers agree that the local guides are some of the most knowledgeable and educated individuals in the world. In other cases, you may work with guides whose only interest is getting the group into the carpet showroom. Over the years, however, experienced tour managers have developed their own personal expectations of a professional guide; these include the following:

❑ A guide who reports ten minutes or so before departure—not breathlessly at the last minute.

Figure 13.4 Tour members gather around the local guide to listen to his explanation on a city tour. (Courtesy of America Contiki Holidays.)

❑ A guide who has checked with the motorcoach dispatcher the night before to be sure that the order is on record and who checks again the next morning to be sure that the coach is ready and waiting.

❑ A guide who is neatly dressed and groomed.

❑ A guide who is organized, departs on time, and maintains the pacing of the day's activities to get in everything that was promised.

❑ A guide who supervises the coach and driver by checking that the driver knows the route, has sufficient fuel, and keeps the coach clean. A guide who makes sure that the public address system is working and assists passengers to board and alight.

❑ A guide who keeps control of the group, maintains their attention, and announces in advance what is going to happen.

❑ A guide who does not continually solicit for optional events, shopping, and other activities on which a commission may be made.

❑ A guide who can give more than just dates and historical facts, who has a good cultural understanding of a particular city, country, or era; who is attuned to the interest of the group, and who is sensitive to the amount of information that the particular group can absorb.

HOTEL CHECK-OUTS

One of the most difficult times for a tour manager can be the **hotel check-out**, which means getting out of a hotel and to the airport on time. The best procedure, of course, is to leave sufficiently early to allow extra time for the unexpected (e.g., the lost suitcase, the flat tire, the late bus, the bureaucratic airline check-in clerk, and so forth). It is helpful to start preparing for hotel check-out the night before by mentally walking through the next day's departure. Details that should be checked the night before might include the following:

❑ Does the bell captain have a list of room numbers and know what time all bags are to be pulled?

❑ Will the dining room be open sufficiently early for breakfast before departure? If not, is it possible to arrange for coffee and rolls at the hotel? Or can the group leave earlier and have coffee at the airport?

❑ Does the tour manager have correct change for tipping bellmen, the bell captain, *maitre d'*, or others who have been helpful to the group during their stay?

❑ Has the cashier been advised of the check-out time and alerted to present an itemized bill? (The tour manager should not accept a lump sum bill but a bill that breaks down the number of twins, singles, complimentaries, tax, and so forth.) Perhaps the hotel will permit the tour manager to settle the bill on the night before departure to alleviate the push in the morning.

❑   Has the group been properly advised as to baggage-call time? Have group members been reminded to have their passports on them, not locked in their luggage; to be sure to pay the cashier for any extras on their bill; and to turn in their keys?

❑   Is there an airport departure tax the next day? If so, who is paying it? If the tour manager is paying on behalf of the entire group, it is important to have the right amount of cash in local currency and in the right denominations. If passengers are paying individually, they should be so advised. If the local ground operator pays it, he or she should be reminded.

To be sure that things go smoothly on departure day, it is best for the tour manager to be visible down in the lobby ahead of the group. He or she should be sure that luggage is coming down and should do a bag count *before* it is loaded on the motorcoach or baggage truck. Everything should be taken out of the safety deposit box, including the group's air tickets; the coupons for that day's flight should be pulled, and they should be put together, ready to turn in at the airport. The tour manager should check with the cashier and settle the master bill (double-checking that all passengers in the group have paid their personal hotel bills and turned in their keys); should tip all the appropriate hotel personnel; should say goodbye; and should thank those who were helpful, such as the sales manager or front desk manager. If you are unable to locate them, it is a nice gesture to leave your business card with a personal thank you line or two. On boarding the coach, tour members should be reminded not to leave anything behind and to be sure that they have their passports. Last, but not least, before leaving for the airport, the tour manager should do a head count or roll call to be sure that everyone is on board!

PERSONAL COMPORTMENT OF TOUR MANAGER

One of the most sensitive subjects is that of **personal comportment**: the tour manager's behavior on tour. When are you working and when is your free time? What about friendships or personal involvements enroute? Should gratuities, gifts, or free drinks be accepted? In fact, should the tour manager drink at all? These questions and many others have plagued those in the travel industry for years. Most travel professionals have come to realize that there is a certain unwritten code by which to operate. Some elements of this unwritten code are:

1.   A tour manager should give equal time and attention to all, never playing favorites. This means dining, dancing, and sitting with all tour members, not just a select few (even if they are more fun, more enjoyable, more beautiful, more available).

Figure 13.5 A good tour manager will be a gracious host and sit with different tour members at each meal so no one will feel left out. (Photo courtesy of Frances Friedman.)

2. A tour manager is on the trip in a professional role; that is, working, not on vacation.
3. A tour manager should not upgrade some participants and not others on flights or designate certain passengers as VIPs. (However, if someone gets a bad room one night, it is a good idea to compensate the next night.)
4. A tour manager should go places with groups of people—never appear to be going off with just one person from the group. Others should be invited to participate.
5. A tour manager should not become personally involved with a tour member.
6. If the tour manager wishes to see local friends along the way, this should be done quietly and discreetly and away from the group, occasionally after the day's tour activities.
7. A tour manager should not hustle a group into stores or activities to make a personal commission.
8. A tour manager should have an understanding with the tour company before the trip begins as to whether it is acceptable to receive gratuities from the passengers at the end of the trip. If so, the tour manager should accept them graciously but not constantly remind the group as the trip moves along that a tip is expected.
9. A tour manager should feel free to accept small token gifts, poems, songs, and emotional protestations of undying loyalty and affection from tour members.
10. A tour manager should not drink to excess, but should feel free to have a before dinner cocktail or wine with meals if the group, or most of them, drink. If this is a nondrinking group, the tour manager should refrain.

SAFETY OF THE TOUR MANAGER

It usually comes as a surprise to first-time tour managers to learn that they are seen as potential crime victims. Yet, when tour managers get together, many can relate stories of attempted robberies, holdups, or rapes. As the leader of a group, a tour manager is seen by outsiders as the individual most likely to be carrying large amounts of cash, travelers checks, negotiable air tickets, and perhaps the group's passports (valuable on the black market in some countries). Once it is known that a group is in town, the tour manager may be approached by everyone from jewelry fences to black marketeers who are eager to buy dollars. To avoid unnecessary risks, a tour manager should dress with decorum, should not give out his or her hotel room number, and should scrupulously safeguard all tour documents and valuables.

SOME PROBLEMS ENROUTE

Many tours run smoothly with never a ripple on calm waters. These are the tours that almost anyone can escort, since the tour manager's expertise or lack thereof may never be put to the test. However, most tours do encounter some **enroute problems**. It is in these problem areas that true leadership ability comes to the fore. Small problems can be solved quietly behind the scenes without the group aware that there is a problem. But for larger, more obvious problems, the group looks to the tour manager to resolve these difficult situations; yet, he or she may not know any more about a problem than the group. It is here that common sense and the ability to think on your feet come into play.

Some problems might be passenger oriented, such as tour participants who are always late, who are complainers, or who are just generally unpleasant people. Also, passengers become ill or lose their passports or their money. Other problems may be operational in nature (e.g., the receptive operator who does not show up at the airport to meet the group, the lost or damaged luggage, the delayed flight, or the bad hotel room). Still another category, and a totally unforeseen one, is what is termed "acts of God" or *force majeure*—the typhoon, civil war, strike, or accident. You could write an entire book on handling enroute emergencies, but the following are a few of the most commonplace problems.

Problems with Passengers

Most of these problems are personality related that often involve personality traits or difficulties that cannot be solved during the duration of the tour. A tour manager probably cannot cure somebody of inconsiderate behavior, complaining, anxiety, kleptomania, alcoholism, hypochondria, or nymphomania in the course of a tour. What the tour manager must do, however, is *control* the problem. *Step One* is to give a good, strong briefing, outlining at the outset of the tour the behavior expected. *Step Two* is to call negative behavior to the attention of the offending individuals privately and quietly by drawing them aside from the group and reminding them. *Step Three* is to use the rest of the group as leverage; peer pressure often will bring an offender into line. Asking the entire busload to boo loudly when a tardy passenger boards the bus can work wonders. You can also appoint a "sergeant at arms" for the day. At the beginning of the day's tour, the tour manager announces on the microphone: "Since I don't like the image of a 'bad guy,' today I'm going to appoint you, Mary, as sergeant at arms. You have my permission to reprimand anyone who is tardy or who hogs the front seat or who talks while the guide is talking. Now, did you all hear me? I don't want any of you to get mad at Mary if she comes up and says something to you because she's doing it in my name."

Dropping a Tour Member. *Step Four* is to threaten to remove someone from the tour. A tour manager does this only after several warnings, and nine times out of ten such a threat usually will jolt the person into correcting their behavior.

Dropping someone from a tour is a serious matter, a matter that could bring a lawsuit against the company. It is not something that you do on a whim. If a tour manager does decide to drop a participant, he or she must be sure to be on strong legal ground. The company should have a statement in the brochure declaring that it does have the right to drop someone. The tour manager should document in a journal as the tour moves along the difficulties encountered with the passenger in question and the attempts that have been made to have him or her correct the offending behavior. Also, at the time the decision is made to remove an individual, a brief statement should be written as to what has occurred and why the individual is being removed from the tour. Then, the entire tour group should be asked to sign it. It is also a good idea to get any other witnesses, such as the hotel manager or local receptive operator, to sign the statement.

Dropping someone should be considered only for major offenses (e.g., stealing, repeated drunkenness, involvement in drugs, smuggling, or other behavior illegal under local law). Whether or not the passengers agree with a local law, they are expected to abide by it as long as they are guests in that particular country. You cannot afford to have the safety of a group and the reputation of your company jeopardized by one individual.

I once had two couples on tour in Spain who chartered a fishing boat for the day in Marbella and then refused to pay the full amount that they had agreed on, since at the end of the day they did not believe that they had received what they had bargained for. The entire group was horrified that night when, at their elegant farewell dinner at the hotel, the Spanish National Guard tracked the couple down and came to arrest them. They paid up quickly! You cannot afford to have incidents such as this happen.

Illness or Injury. It is a rare tour that makes it through to the end without some injury or illness. Of course, one of the best ways to avoid this is preventative care. Advise passengers about food and drink, warn them of the dangers of air-conditioning and subsequent travelers' bronchitis, and ask them to get enough sleep and to take care of themselves. Often they are so excited at being on vacation that they want to see everything and to do everything to the detriment of their health. However, despite care, there will always be the passenger with a gastrointestinal problem, a twisted ankle, or even a broken leg. In these cases, it is important that professional medical help be obtained immediately. Usually, the hotel's house physician is the first resource.

You should be wary of practicing home cures on the patient because there may be legal repercussions. It should be understood from the outset of the trip that any medical bills incurred enroute are to the passenger's individual account. Passengers are often surprised when they discover the charges for a doctor's call to their hotel room. In fact, one of the major problems that you may encounter is the passenger who refuses to see a physician, because he or she doesn't want to spend the money or disrupt the day's activities. Then later (usually in the middle of the night or in the middle of nowhere), they realize that a physician should have been consulted after all.

Of course, if an individual is seriously ill and needs hospitalization or surgery and must leave the tour, the matter takes on a new dimension. It is here that using a top-notch receptive operator can make all the difference in the world. Since the tour manager will have to continue on with the group to the next city or country, leaving an ill person behind, he or she must depend on the local operator to handle all the details, such as visiting the tour member in the hospital, arranging for follow-up care, packing up luggage and personal belongings, reissuing the air ticket (either to catch up with the group when recovered or fly home), notifying family at home, and so forth. When this happens, the tour manager should immediately contact the company at home regarding the circumstances, advising them that he or she is proceeding with the group and leaving the passenger in a certain hospital. Remember to give the name of the passenger's physician. I still have a strong sense of loyalty to a certain receptive ground operator in Bogotá who helped me through a difficult situation such as this. Even though other operators have since come to the fore offering very attractive and less-expensive receptive operator services, I have not switched my allegiance.

Lost Passports. A lost passport can be a frightening and disruptive experience and one that can be solved only by the consulate because the passenger cannot continue to the next country on the group's itinerary until a substitute passport has been issued. It may even mean the passenger's missing the group flight and remaining in the country independently until the new passport is issued. If the tour manager has the number, date, and place of issue of the missing passport, this will expedite matters. Even with this information, the individual will have to go to their consulate *in person* and, here again, the local operator can be of assistance in providing transportation and perhaps a guide to accompany the passenger. Of course, any such expenses will be on the individual's own account, and it may mean that the passenger might miss certain tour activities while attending to this important matter. If there were visas for upcoming countries stamped in the lost passport, it will be necessary to obtain new visas (from the consulates of the countries concerned) once the new passport has been issued.

Operational Problems

These problems occur between the tour manager or the group and those who are providing services (e.g., airlines, hotels, receptive operators, guides, and motorcoach companies). Since the tourism industry is basically a service industry, no matter how well things may be planned in advance, a great many things can go wrong in providing services. In fact, since the service depends on so many diverse people, from the manager to the busboy, it is often a miracle that things go as well as they do! A few areas in which problems can occur are the following:

Lost or Damaged Luggage. It is important that lost or damaged baggage be reported immediately to the airline or other source presumed to be responsible. Although this may delay the group slightly, it often is impossible to locate the bag and to service the claim unless a formal written claim form is completed right away. The tour manager should write down the name of the individual with whom the claim was placed and the telephone extension at the airport for follow-up phone calls later. This is another area in which the local receptive operator can be helpful. The tour manager may be busy with the group and not be able to call the airline repeatedly or drop everything to go to the airport. However, the tour manager and the passenger will have to stay in close touch, since it may be necessary for one of them to produce the claim check and the key and go to the airport personally to claim the bag if customs clearance is necessary. In other cases, the local operator may be able to arrange to have it delivered to the hotel.

If the bag remains lost, everyone on the tour will usually be willing to pitch in and lend the victim pieces of clothing from their wardrobes; however, some purchases of essential items will be necessary. If the bag does not arrive in short order, the tour manager should begin to pressure the airline to give the passenger immediate financial assistance. If the bag is merely damaged, it should be ascertained immediately from the airline as to the quickest procedure for repair and reimbursement, since the tour may not be staying in that city long and the suitcase may not hold up for the next flight unless it is fixed.

Delays. There are often delays in flights, trains, or other transportation—delays that are beyond the tour manager's control. They simply must be endured. When these delays occur it is (1) important to check periodically as to what is happening and report back to the group, keeping them informed; (2) work on the group's behalf in obtaining free meal or drink vouchers from the airline; (3) be sure that the group knows that if they are missing any tour activity because of the delay, their itinerary will be rearranged in the city to give them everything promised, or a substitute activity for anything missed. If it becomes evident that the delay may be lengthy, causing the tour to arrive at the next city extremely late, it is important to cable ahead to the hotel and to the receptive operator meeting the group, telling them that the group is going to be late but that they are surely coming. This may prevent the group's hotel rooms from being given away.

Strikes. Sometimes a strike will occur with absolutely the worst timing in the world; that is, just when the group arrives. Many tourists have had to make their

own beds when the hotel staff walked out or have had to make do with a cold dinner when the kitchen help closed down the kitchen. These situations try your patience and test your ingenuity, but it is amazing what can be done when you have
to. I have stopped the bus at a supermarket and staged an impromptu picnic. I have
paid private citizens to drive groups to the airport in their own cars when taxis
went on strike. Groups have made their own music with bottles, pots, and pans
when the band walked out. Other groups have gone from France to England via
Belgium when the French dock workers were on strike. These are situations in
which you must often solve the problem through quick thinking—and sometimes
with cash. A voucher or a company check means nothing, so tour managers must
have emergency funds available for situations such as these.

Non-appearance of Receptive Operator.   Occasionally a group will deplane, the
tour manager will go through immigration and customs, go out into the waiting
area, and discover that no one is there to meet them. The first thing to do in such
a case is to get the entire group to sit down in one area and remain there. The tour
manager then may ask airline officials if they have seen a representative from the
company that is supposed to meet the group. If not, the airlines may be asked to
page. Quite often the representative will be there but may have wandered off to
help a passenger or to get a cup of coffee on the assumption that the group would
take longer in clearing customs and immigration than was actually required.
However, if no one shows up, the next step is to call the company if they are open
(one reason to have the name and phone number handy when arriving, as well as
some change in local currency). Perhaps the person is on the way to meet the group
but has been caught up in a traffic jam or has been involved in an accident.

Whatever the case, if 15 minutes or so have gone by and the tour manager has
not been able to locate anyone, there is no alternative but to put the group into
taxis and get them to the hotel as quickly as possible. By now, the tour members
are tired and perhaps out of sorts, so it is best to consider their needs first. The
tour manager should try to treat the matter lightly and vent his or her anger on the
local operator later, not on the passengers. The tour manager should pay for the
taxis and get receipts from the taxi driver. It's smart to have sufficient money in
local currency to pay the various drivers and to pay tips to the airport porters and
hotel bellmen. After the group is settled into their rooms, you can then find out
what really happened.

When leaving this city, if the tour manager is paying the local operator for
services rendered or is turning in a voucher or is signing an invoice, it is important to make a notation that the group did not receive the arrival transfer service
and payment for it is not authorized.

Acts of God

Acts of God encompass a number of natural disasters, such as earthquakes or
storms, and man-made disasters, such as war, civil disturbances, or riots. Each
one has to be dealt with in the best way that you can at the time. When in doubt

as to the best procedure to follow, the tour manager may call the embassy and be guided by their advice. Often the group may be in a perfectly safe place but may have heard of a problem in the next country on the itinerary. The decision then is whether to proceed as planned or whether to try to avoid the affected area—perhaps overfly it or turn back. If, after consulting with the embassy and reaching a decision, the tour manager decides not to proceed, he or she may be faced with a passenger who says, "I'm going on in. I've spent all this money to come this far and all my life I've dreamed of going there and now, by God, nobody is going to stop me." In this case, the individual should be allowed to go, but the tour manager should ask for a signed statement to the effect that the individual is doing so as an independent traveler and against the tour manager's better judgement. The reverse may happen: the tour manager may have decided that it is safe to go on, but there may be an individual who feels uncomfortable doing so. A person should never be forced to accompany the group. Instead, the local receptive operator may be asked to rearrange the individual's itinerary to stay where he or she is for a longer period of time and then catch up with the group at a later stop. Of course, if the group is traveling on a group airfare, an individual wishing to deviate might have to pay the supplemental airfare involved, unless the airline will make an exception. If truly in doubt as to what to do, the tour manager may call the home office long distance. A call to almost anywhere in the world can be made for $12 or so, and having the backing of the company will reassure the tour manager about any decision.

DEALING WITH THE AIRLINES ENROUTE

On a lengthy trip involving 15 or 20 different flight legs, each of these legs must be reconfirmed as the tour goes along. In some cities, the tour manager may do this personally; in other cities, the receptive operator will offer to do it, with the tour manager turning the air tickets over to the local office and getting them back before the next flight. Whoever does the reconfirming, it is still up to the tour manager to be sure that it gets done! Reconfirming flights can turn up some amazing information—no record of the group's reservations, an oversold flight where the airline has arbitrarily bumped the group to another flight or even another day, changes of flight scheduling, and a number of other unexpected possibilities. Therefore, it is wise to reconfirm as early as possible to be assured that all will go smoothly and to provide ample time to do battle if it becomes necessary.

SPECIAL HINTS ON CRUISES

Escorting a group aboard a cruise ship is somewhat different than escorting an air/ land tour. Since virtually everything is done for the members by the cruise personnel or shore excursion operators, the tour manager's role is really that of a host or hostess. The tour manager follows up what the cruise and shore staff people are doing to be sure that the group is getting the best, getting efficient handling, and getting special service.

This, in effect, puts the tour manager in the position of go-between by relaying messages, instructions, tickets, and so forth between the group and the cruise staff. In one sense, it is easier than managing a regular tour with its daily traumas of flights, transfers, and guides. In another sense, it is more difficult, since the tour manager really has little decision power. If the sightseeing tour in a particular city spends three-fourths of its time in a shop buying emeralds, the tour manager cannot really say anything because it is not a private tour. However, there are a number of things that you can and should do to establish leadership, loyalty, and control of the group, such as the following:

❑ If you have not been on a particular ship before, immediately on boarding, make a quick tour in order to locate everything (e.g., the dining room, purser's office, pool, sauna, and so forth). You should have brought a deck plan from home and circled in red the cabin numbers of the group.

❑ Soon after boarding, you should go around and meet the key staff people, because developing a good rapport with them is all important in the success of the trip. These are the purser, the director of the shore excursion desk, the cruise director (social director), and the *maitre d'* (head dining room steward).

❑ It is a good idea always to hold a private welcome party and a briefing, even if there is not much on which to brief the group. It makes them feel special, apart from the regular passengers. This party is in addition to the captain's welcome party.

❑ Shortly after boarding, you should double-check seating arrangements in the dining room with the *maitre d'*. If the company has requested group seating ahead of time, it should be determined if this is being provided as requested. Some companies like to provide group seating. Others prefer to let the passengers select early or late seating and take their own chances on table mates. There are advantages and disadvantages to each approach. If possible, the single women should not all be seated together. If there are birthdays or anniversaries in the group, the *maitre d'* should be advised early so that a special cake or festivity can be arranged on the appropriate day.

❑ If you do not know all of the tour members well, ask them to wear their name tags—at least for the first few days. Sometimes it is difficult to recognize them the second day when they have changed clothes, and you end up greeting everyone on the ship for fear of snubbing one of the group. Once, in Yucatán, I spent an entire evening at dinner seated with a charming couple that I assumed was part of my group, only to find out over dessert and coffee that they were not on my tour at all. I had simply seated myself with them in the dining room assuming they were in my group.

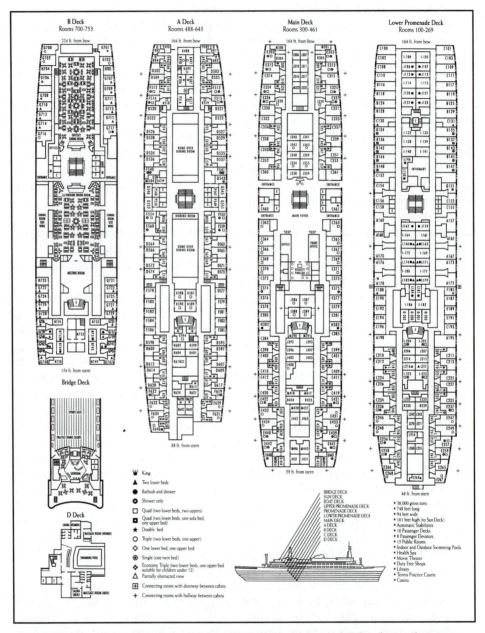

Figure 13.6 Tour managers should bring along a deck plan when operating a group tour on a cruise ship so they know where everyone in their group is located. (Courtesy of Holland America Line.)

❑ The tour manager should try to arrange special shipboard tours during days at sea (e.g., a tour of the bridge, the galley, or the engine room). Quite often this is done for the regular passengers. They may start talking among themselves, and the group members will wonder why it is not being done for them. To beat them to the punch, a tour manager may announce to the group at the briefing that he or she is working with the cruise staff to arrange special shipboard tours for their group, and they will be informed when these will take place.

❑ The tour manager should act as a catalyst to get people to know one another, to mix, and to enter into activities. Group members might be invited to join you in, say, a swim at 2:00 p.m. or bingo at 11:00 a.m.

❑ The tour manager may decide to talk up the usual cruise costume party—helping the reticent ones plan their costumes. Maybe a group theme could be worked out. For example, I once saw an entire group of thirty plus tour members from Salt Lake City twirl onto stage dressed in tiny white tulle skirts, billing themselves as the "Salt Lake Swan Lake Ballet."

❑ The tour manager may try to arrange with the shore excursion manager to assign the group together in one particular motorcoach for sightseeing. This is not always possible if different people in the group are buying different optional shore excursions. However, if the entire group is taking the whole package of shore excursions, sometimes it can be worked out. In this way, the group will not have strangers disrupting their good habits.

❑ The tour manager should circulate every day and should be visible, working, and available, perhaps carrying a notebook and pen even when on the sundeck in a bathing suit! One might consider stipulating a certain time and place on board to be found every day if needed.

❑ If the cruise line has a departure briefing on the last day to give passengers information on baggage pickup, transfers to the airport, and flight reconfirmation, the tour manager can expedite this for the group so that they do not have to stand in long reconfirmation lines. They may assume because they are in a special group that they should get this special service and may resent having to line up with everyone else.

❑ The tour manager should try not to spend a lot of time in front of the group with the officers or other passengers or groups. Your group may become possessive, convinced that they have paid for a tour manager, and some may resent the time and attention paid to outsiders.

As can be seen, the basic thought behind all of these hints is to make a group feel special so that if they book another cruise or tour they will want to book through the same agency. The cruise line will do everything possible to secure their loyalty and participation in future cruises aboard their ships; what a tour manager must do is augment that loyalty to book through his or her agency. After all, if group members are getting exactly—and only—what every other passenger is getting, they could just as easily have booked independently through any travel agency or tour operator.

THOSE LAST TWENTY-FOUR HOURS

Just as the first twenty-four hours were all important in setting the tone of a trip and pulling the group together as a unit, so the last twenty-four hours are important in leaving a good impression, warm feelings, and good friendships. If possible, and if the tour budget permits, it is a good idea to have a farewell party of some sort. If nothing else, perhaps an after-dinner drink and a few good songs and laughs can be shared together. I often write an epic poem about the group and read it at the last night's function, trying to bring in a verse about each of the individuals in the group. Here again, it is not always money that does the job—it is the feeling of personal warmth and togetherness. This farewell function is also an opportunity to give last-minute departure instructions and suggestions for money exchange, packing purchases, and completing U.S. immigration/customs clearance forms.

On that last flight homeward, it is preferable to have each person check in at the airport as an individual passenger (usually much to the dismay of the local receptive operator). This individual check-in is for two reasons. First, usually by

Figure 13.7 A farewell dinner party for the group on the last night of a tour is a nice way to end a trip. (Photo courtesy of Frances Friedman.)

the last flight home, the tour members have become pack rats and are carrying twice the luggage with which they started. If they all pool their luggage together and if the entire pool is over the allowable amount, the tour manager will be given the bill. However, if they check in individually, each pays for his or her own over-weight or perhaps teams up with someone in the group whose weight is under the limit. Second, when the group members arrive at the return gateway city, they can claim their luggage and go right on to their connecting flight to their home town. If, on the other hand, the tour manager has all the baggage claim stubs for the group and has to wait for the entire group to claim luggage and go through customs as a group, someone in the tour may miss a connecting flight. The tour manager should remain with the group members to the end, seeing to it that the last passenger has located his or her luggage, has gone through immigration and customs, has been given a farewell hug, and has gone happily into the night.

❑ SUMMARY

A tour manager's job in the field is a demanding and varied one. You should know how to handle flight check-ins, hotel arrivals and departures, and a broad variety of tour activities and social events. To start the tour off on the right foot, the tour manager should hold an orientation meeting to brief participants on the "rules of the road." A tour manager should plan ahead, should look and act like a leader at all times; and should know how to deal with local guides, other personnel, and problem situations which may arise in the course of any tour. The Golden Rule "Equal Time and Attention To All" is the best guideline in dealing with tour participants.

❑ REVIEW QUESTIONS

1. **Why is the tour manager's visibility so important at the outset of any tour?**

2. If a suitcase is lost enroute, what immediate action should the tour manager take?

3. Upon check-in to a hotel, after the members are dispatched to their rooms, name four or more duties left for the tour manager.

4. An orientation meeting with your tour members is an important kick-off to a successful tour, as the tour manager outlines the "rules of the road." Name at least six points you would touch on at such a meeting.

5. What are five things you have a right to expect of a good local guide?

6. **What do we mean when we say "think 24 hours ahead"?**

7. **If you were the tour manager, carrying lots of air tickets, travelers checks, and some cash, what would you do to ensure your own safety and the security of the valuables you are carrying.**

8. **How might you tactfully handle a know-it-all tour member who wants to play "tour leader" and run the show?**

9. **Why is it important to give extra service to a group on board a cruise when virtually all necessary services are already being provided by the cruise line?**

10. Why are the last 24 hours together so important on any tour?

❑ *ACTIVITIES*

1. Pretend that you are to give a tour orientation meeting at your first overseas stop. First, make an outline of the points you will cover. Then stand up and give the presentation to your family, friends, or class.

2. Imagine that you are out on tour and in the middle of the night that you are awakened by a tour member who is very ill. How would you handle it?

3. You and your group are scheduled to check out of a hotel and leave for the next city on your itinerary tomorrow morning. Make up a checklist of the things that you would do tonight to ensure a smooth on-time departure tomorrow.

▷ 14

POST-TOUR WRAP-UP

LEARNING OBJECTIVES

After reading this chapter, you should be able to:

☐ Understand the importance of properly debriefing your tour manager
☐ Know the importance of post-tour follow-up with tour participants
☐ Know what must be done to close the tour financially and ascertain the profit/loss status of the tour
☐ Know when to start discussing next year's trip

KEY CONCEPTS AND TERMS

Debriefing
Tour Manager's Expense Report
Welcome-Home Letter
Clients' Post-Tour Questionnaire
Profit/Loss Status

As soon as the tour returns, six things that must be taken care of before the project can be considered closed, as follows:

1. Debrief the tour manager.
2. Send the tour participants a welcome-home letter and a questionnaire to solicit their evaluation of the trip.
3. Close the tour financially, completing any unpaid bills, collecting any accounts receivable, and looking at a profit-and-loss statement on the project.
4. Pack away all operational files and client correspondence in an orderly fashion for future reference.
5. Add tour members' names and addresses to the company's permanent mailing list of clients.
6. Look to the future.

DEBRIEFING THE TOUR MANAGER

A tour manager will return weary at first, but then eager to talk at length about what went right and what went wrong on the trip. Whether the manager was a staff person, a paid professional, or the organizer, this person feels emotionally attached to the tour and is anxious to share with the company both the successes and the problems encountered along the way. On the one hand, the tour manager is looking for the company's support, a pat on the back saying "You did right" or "You did what we would have done in such and such a situation." On the other hand, if things went wrong, the tour manager is in a defensive position. He or she wants the company to know what transpired *before* passengers start to call in with complaints.

Therefore, it is wise to plan a **debriefing**—in short, an opportunity for you to listen. If other groups are leaving shortly, the tendency is to put the tour manager off or to speed up the debriefing session and perhaps not give him or her the time and attention deserved. This can be a mistake. Even if the tour manager is totally wrong in some aspects, this debriefing session can be a learning experience for you and your company. After all, the tour manager is the person who was closest to the tour, to the participants, to the hotels, and to the various servicing companies. This is the person who knows what was done well, what was lacking, and what improvements could be made if the trip is repeated next year. It is not enough just to elicit negative feedback, such as that a hotel was terrible. Can the tour manager make a positive recommendation as to a better one?

One of the best arrangements for a debriefing session is to invite the tour manager to the office in the morning and tell him or her that an hour will be spent with him or her in consultation. Then a desk should be made available for the balance of the morning so that he or she may complete an **expense report** form for reimbursement of out-of-pocket payments. A separate sheet would be used for each foreign currency, and receipts (numbered) attached for each item over U.S. $25. Hotels, motorcoaches, and local receptive operators are not listed, as they would probably be paid by voucher or company check or be prepaid. Type up the post-tour evaluation report. The tour manager will also want to meet with the accountant/bookkeeper to turn over the financial report and return any unspent monies.

This arrangement will ensure that the tour manager's report gets proper attention, that the financial report is turned in quickly after the tour rather than letting it drag on, and that a complete recap report is submitted in writing. Therefore, this is a report that can be referred to later as needed. This written report can be particularly important when booking next year's tour or if filing a claim with a supplier, or even in forming a base should a legal problem develop. The tour manager's final salary check should be ready to hand over at this debriefing session also. If the tour manager is an outside professional who is paid by the day, most better agencies pay the daily salary for both the pre-tour briefing day and the post-tour debriefing day and cost the two days' salary into the tour.

TOUR MANAGER'S EXPENSE REPORT

Name of Tour _____ Rosemont Country Club _____   Currency: _____ French francs _____
Departure Date: _____ September 4, 19XX _____   Number of Passengers in Group: _____ 27+1 _____
Tour Manager's Name: M. Kimberly

DATE	PLACE	EXPLANATION	REC. NO.	MEALS	TIPS	ENTRANCE FEES	MISC	TOTAL
Sept 8	Paris	Rail station porterage 56 bags × 3 Fr			168			168
"	"	Guide tip 27 × 5 Fr			35			35
"	"	City tour driver tip, 27 × 3 Fr			81			81
"	"	Extra driver tip, unloading bags			150			150
"	"	Meurice arrival porters, 27 pax × 2 bags						
"	"	× 2 Fr			280			280
"	"	Own dinner, service included		120				120
"	"	Own dinner, small extra tip			15			15
Sept 9	Paris	Upfront tip to maitre d'			60			60
"	Versailles	Entrance, palace, 27 × 8 Fr				216		216
"	Paris	Local guide tip half-day, 27 × 5 Fr			135			135
"	"	Driver tip, half-day, 27 × 3 Fr			81			81
"	"	Own lunch at cafe, incl. service		80				80
"	"	Small extra tip at lunch		10				10
"	"	Taxi to Air France to reconfirm, RT					60	60
"	"	Own dinner, incl. service		100				100
"	"	Small extra dinner tip			5			5
"	"	Lido. Maitre d' tip for good tables			90			90
"	"	Evening-Lido bus driver tip			60			60
Sept 10	"	Upfront tip to maitre d'			60			60
"	"	Louvre entrance fee, 27 × 8 Fr				216		216
"	"	Own lunch at hotel, incl. service		100				100
"	"	Small extra tip at lunch			10			10
"	'	Dinner including guests: Rosemont						
"	"	Country Club Pres & husband, incl. tip	1	400				400
"	"	Roundtrip taxi for above					40	40
Sept 11	"	Upfront tip to maitre d'			60			60
"	"	Meurice Hotel - incidentals bill	2				315	315
"	"	Meurice Hotel chambermaids 28 × 3 Fr			84			84
"	"	Concierge tip, flat amount			75			75
"	"	Hotel bellboys 28 × 2 bags × 5 Fr			280			280
"	"	Departure transfer tip to bus driver			60			60
"	"	Porters CDG Airport, 28 × 2 bags × 3 Fr			56			56
"	"	Misc. Newspaper, gum					50	50
TOTALS IN LOCAL CURRENCY				800	2,090	432	465	3,787

AT AVERAGE EXCHANGE RATE OF 7.90 PER U.S. DOLLAR, EQUIVALENT IN DOLLARS   U.S. $479.37

Figure 14.1 Sample of a tour manager's expense report form.

TOUR MANAGER'S POST-TOUR EVALUATION REPORT

NAME OF TOUR MANAGER _____

NAME OF TOUR _____

DEPARTURE DATE _____

1. ON AN OVER-ALL BASIS, How successful do you feel this tour was?

☐ Very Successful;   ☐ Successful: ☐ Moderate;   ☐ Poor;   ☐ Very Bad

2. AIRLINE(S). Give us names of airlines on which you flew and your opinion, good or bad of each.

_____

_____

3. HOTEL(S). Any hotels not up to par? Where and why? _____

_____

_____

_____

Any hotels particularly outstanding? Where and why? _____

_____

_____

_____

4. RECEPTIVE SERVICES OPERATOR(S). Specify wherein particularly good, wherein not up to par (in which case, how would you improve it?)

_____

_____

_____

5. LOCAL COURIERS OR GUIDES. Names of any couriers or local guides who were particularly outstanding and whom we should try to use again?

_____

_____

Any couriers or local guides who were not good and why _____

_____

Figure 14.2 Suggested tour manager's post-tour evaluation report form.

6. COMMENTS ON SPECIAL EVENTS. Any special tour events you would add or delete and why.

---

7. COMMENTS ON PASSENGERS. Any passengers whom you feel may prove to be potential problems for the company? Any who need post-tour follow-up servicing from our office?

---

8. ANY COMMENTS ON PRE-TOUR PREPARATION OF TOUR MANAGER'S MATE-RIAL? Were materials given you correct, adequate quantities, etc.? Any suggestions for improvement?

---

9. ANY MAJOR PRICING/BUDGETING ERRORS WE NEED TO KNOW ABOUT? Places wherein you found our anticipated expenditures too high or too low, for our planning purposes the next time 'round.

Figure 14.2 (Continued)

CONTACTING THE TOUR PARTICIPANTS

One of the things the company should do right after the group returns is to write to the members to welcome them home and to ask how they enjoyed the trip. This serves several purposes:

❑   It shows that the company is interested—not only in selling them a trip and taking their money before the tour leaves, but also in being sure that the trip lived up to expectations.

❑   It makes them feel needed, that their opinions are valuable and helpful in improving the trip for future travelers.

❑   It gives the company a reason to keep the relationship open—it is hoped with an eye to future business.

❑   It may provide referrals—friends or organizations who might travel with the company in the future.

The **welcome-home letter** should be warm and friendly. (See Figure 14.3.) Enclosed with the letter should be a questionnaire about the trip with a stamped return-mail envelope, or it might be designed as a self-mailer. (See Figure 14.4 on page 348–349.) A nice gesture is to send everyone a group photo of their tour (if the tour manager took such a photo). However, if getting the photo developed and copies made for everyone is going to delay the letter, the photo can wait until later, because it is important to get the welcome-home letter out quickly.

The letter should indicate that the company would appreciate their taking a few minutes to fill out the enclosed questionnaire, since their opinions are valuable in planning future trips. The **post-tour questionnaire** should be fairly specific if specific answers are wanted. For example, instead of asking "How was the airline service?" You might ask "Which airlines do you believe did the best job? The worst?" In short, guide and direct them into being specific.

Sometimes the tour participants will not answer certain questions for fear of hurting someone's feelings or getting someone into trouble, particularly if a question pertains to the tour manager or organizer. They may be afraid that if they make a negative comment about someone that the person may see their complaint and be angry with them. One effective way of getting around this is to have the welcome-home letter go to the passenger directly from the company president with the return-mail envelope marked "Personal."

Of course, this all assumes that travel professionals have broad shoulders and can take a certain amount of criticism. Anyone who has ever organized or managed tours in the field has been criticized—sometimes unjustly by an impossible-to-please or misinformed tour participant. Professionals must expect this, learn from it, but not let it totally undo them.

If you already know of a problem that occurred on the trip, perhaps the best solution is to mention this in the letter. For example, if the flight home was delayed six hours, bringing everyone in late and disagreeable, you might say "We

LSI Travel Agency
987 Park Drive #2A
Berkeley, CA 94704
Telephone Number: 510-555-2000
Fax Number: 510-555-7210

Date

Welcome Home!

We presume that by now you have had time to "settle in" . . . to unpack, catch up on jet lag and adjust to life at home again . . . reality.

However, while your travels are still fresh in your mind, could we ask you to spend a few minutes and give us your opinion of the trip? Our staff does travel frequently to keep up to date, but it simply is not possible for us to be everywhere at all times, so we particularly value the suggestions of tour participants like yourselves.

A questionnaire is enclosed along with a postage-paid return-mail envelope. You will note it is to be returned to me personally, so you may feel free to make whatever comments you wish with the assurance that they will be con-fidential.

You have now joined the ever-growing family of LSI travelers and we hope to see you on many a future tour with us. To that end, we are placing your name on our permanent mailing list to receive notices of new trips as they develop and first offerings of exciting tours and cruises.

Thank you for traveling with us, and I look forward to hearing from you shortly.

Sincerely,

Frederic Schmidt

Frederic Schmidt, CTC
President

FS/s
enclosures: Questionnaire
                Postage-paid envelope

Figure 14.3 Suggested welcome home letter.

LSI Travel Agency, Inc.

POST-TOUR QUESTIONNAIRE

NAME _____

ADDRESS _____

TOWN _____ STATE _____ ZIP CODE _____ TELEPHONE _____

NAME OF TOUR _____

1. WHAT PROMPTED YOU TO JOIN THIS TOUR? _____
   _____

2. ON AN OVERALL BASIS, HOW WOULD YOU RATE THIS TOUR?

   ❏ POOR　　❏ LESS THAN AVERAGE　　❏ AVERAGE　　❏ GOOD　　❏ SUPERIOR

3. WHAT DID YOU ENJOY THE MOST? _____
   _____

4. WHAT DID YOU ENJOY THE LEAST? _____
   _____

5. HOW WOULD YOU RATE THE AIRLINE SERVICE YOU RECEIVED? SPECIFY WHICH
   AIRLINE(S) BEST AND WHICH WORST AND WHY _____
   _____
   _____

6. HOW WOULD YOU RATE THE HOTELS, IN GENERAL?

   ❏ WHAT I EXPECTED　　❏ LESS THAN EXPECTED　　❏ BETTER THAN EXPECTED

   WAS THERE ANY PARTICULAR HOTEL WHICH WAS NOT GOOD AND WHICH YOU
   WOULD DEFINITELY NOT RECOMMEND OUR USING AGAIN FOR A FUTURE TOUR?

   ❏ NO　　❏ YES　　❏ SPECIFY _____

7. GENERALLY, HOW WOULD YOU RATE THE LOCAL SIGHTSEEING GUIDES?

   ❏ POOR　　❏ LESS THAN AVERAGE　　❏ AVERAGE　　❏ GOOD　　❏ SUPERIOR

   WAS THERE ANY PARTICULAR GUIDE OR CITY WHERE YOU FELT THE LOCAL GUIDE
   WAS OUTSTANDING AND WHERE YOU FEEL WE SHOULD REQUEST THIS SAME GUIDE
   AGAIN BY NAME ON FUTURE TOURS?

   _____
   _____

   WAS THERE ANY PARTICULAR GUIDE OR CITY WHERE YOU FELT THE LOCAL GUIDE
   WAS NOT AS GOOD AS YOU HAD HOPED AND WHERE YOU FEEL WE SHOULD NOT USE
   THIS GUIDE AGAIN?

   _____
   _____

Figure 14.4　Client post-tour questionnaire.

8.   WHAT IS YOUR OPINION OF YOUR TOUR MANAGER? STRONG POINTS? WEAKNESSES?

_____

_____

_____

_____

9.   HOW WOULD YOU RATE THE PRE-TRIP SERVICE AND ASSISTANCE YOU RECEIVED FROM OUR OFFICE—INFORMATION BULLETINS, ANSWERS TO YOUR QUESTIONS AND SO FORTH?

☐ POOR   ☐ LESS THAN AVERAGE   ☐ AVERAGE   ☐ GOOD   ☐ SUPERIOR

10.   IF THIS TRIP WERE TO BE REPEATED, IS THERE ANYTHING YOU WOULD LIKE TO SEE ELIMINATED FROM THE TRIP?

_____

ANYTHING ADDED? (EVEN IF IT INCREASES THE PRICE?) _____

_____

11.   WHERE HAD YOU TRAVELED BEFORE THIS TRIP? _____

_____

_____

12.   WHERE WOULD YOU NEXT LIKE TO TRAVEL? _____

_____

13.   DO YOU BELONG TO ANY CLUBS, CHURCHES, BUSINESSES OR ORGANIZATIONS WHICH DO GROUP TRAVEL—FOR PLEASURE, BUSINESS, STUDY, CONVENTIONS OR MEETINGS? IF YES, PLEASE NAME THEM: _____

_____

_____

14.   NAMES AND ADDRESSES OF FAMILY OR FRIENDS WHOM YOU FEEL MIGHT ENJOY KNOWING ABOUT OUR TRIPS

a)   Name _____
      Address _____
      Town _____ State _____ Zip Code _____

b)   Name _____
      Address _____
      Town _____ State _____ Zip Code _____

c)   Name _____
      Address _____
      Town _____ State _____ Zip Code _____

15.   COMMENTS (ADD SECOND SHEET IF NEEDED) _____

_____

_____

Figure 14.4 (Continued)

already have been advised about the unfortunate delay you encountered on the way home with XYZ airline, and we have asked for a full report from the airline management in this regard." This will deflect their anger somewhat so that it does not color the entire post-tour report.

One helpful marketing technique is to have a place on the questionnaire asking them where they would like to travel next, a place for referrals of friends whom they believe might enjoy a similar tour, and a question asking if they belong to any clubs or organizations that travel as a group.

FINANCIAL CLOSING

Now comes the important day of reckoning—the day when financial facts must be faced, when the **profit/loss status** of the project must be determined. Did the tour make money or not? It is as simple as that. Did it make as much as was anticipated? Was it priced adequately? Or in retrospect, were many expenses overlooked?

Before one can reach these decisions, it is necessary to close out any financial matters pending. The following are some of the areas at which to look.

❑   Has the tour manager's salary (if any) been paid?
❑   Have all promotional expenses been paid? The brochure? Flyers? Advertising? Promotional evenings?
❑   Are all suppliers' bills settled—hotel, airlines, cruise lines, motorcoach companies, receptive operators?
❑   Are there any sales fees or donations still to be paid to the organizer or sponsoring club?
❑   Are there any refunds due that the office has not yet received?
❑   Were there any over-ride commissions promised by the airlines, cruise lines, or other suppliers and has the company formally applied for these?
❑   Are all client payments completed?

If all of the above are settled and if all deposits and payments on this tour were accurately credited or debited to the accounting code number assigned to this tour at the outset, the company's accountant should be able to supply an accurate profit/loss status fairly quickly.

The results should be assessed honestly. It is easy to make excuses and say "If Mr. and Mrs. Smith hadn't canceled at the last minute, we'd have had the 20 participants we planned on and we would have made money" or "If we hadn't had to do that second promotional mailing, we would have made so much." The figures should be used as a learning experience for the future. Perhaps the next time, plans for a last-minute cancellation or an extra promotion can be costed into the tour from the outset.

PACKING AWAY FILES

Once all pending matters have been settled, the tour files can be packed and filed away. Taking an hour or two to put the tour files in order will make it possible for anyone on the staff to locate needed information later. This could be for booking the tour again in the future. It could be for looking up a client's financial record if he or she is being audited by the Internal Revenue Service and asks for help. It might be in referring to the tour manager's report with suggestions for the future.

Certainly all things financial should be filed together (i.e., the original costing and the post-tour profit/loss statement). If a similar tour is planned in the future, these costing sheets can be used as reference.

One sample set of all form letters and information bulletins that were sent out to the participants should be kept. (The master can be stored in your word processor for future use.) The samples may be used in modified form for a different tour to a different destination. One sample of all ads, invitations, and so forth pertinent to the project should be retained. And, before throwing away supplies of surplus brochures, a supply should be set aside for reference or for use as an interim sales piece until next year's brochure is printed, if there are plans to repeat the tour.

Brochures can also be used effectively as sales pieces when recruiting new groups for a similar trip. They also serve to showcase what your company is capable of producing and may impress a potential new client organization, whether the organization is considering the same destination or a totally different one.

ADDING NAMES TO THE MAILING LIST

Assuming that the company maintains a mailing list of all clients who have traveled with them, the names and addresses of these tour participants should be added to that list at this time. If you do not maintain such a list, now is the time to start one. Such a list makes it possible to do a couple of important things.

❑ To send out periodic mailings to past tour participants, thus keeping a rapport going with each client. These mailings could be future tour or cruise announcements, perhaps a company newsletter, or an invitation to a promotional evening.

❑ To refer to the client's travel history with accuracy should he or she book with the agency again. For example, if a previous tour member books again, the welcome acknowledgment letter could be modified to read: "Welcome aboard your third tour with LSI Travel. It's nice to have you along again, and we hope this trip will prove as enjoyable as the Europe one did back in '92." This makes the client feel remembered and important.

If these records are kept stored in your computer (or even alphabetically in a card index file), personnel can be trained to check each time a booking comes in to see if the client is a repeat customer or not. The file (see Figure 14.5) can include such information as name and address, tour and year, destination, and name of the tour manager. One can even add little comments for use in the future, such as "difficult tour member—do not solicit again" or "good prospect for the Orient."

In fact, if this information is readily accessible, a company can develop some interesting marketing and sales ideas, such as forming a travel club and giving each tour participant a membership card after the first trip with the company. Another idea is to give past tour participants a discount on future tours or a discount against their own tour if they bring along a friend who has not traveled with the agency before.

Of course, depending on the size and volume of group tours in the office, some system is needed for getting these names onto a mailing list. Companies with large lists may employ a direct-mail house or may maintain their own computer list in-house. At the completion of each tour, the names and addresses of the tour participants are added to the list. Then you can run off mailing labels when they are needed, sorting them by zip code rather than alphabetically. (This makes it possible to use the lower bulk mail rates, which are not allowable for small lists or for lists sorted alphabetically).

Small companies that have few group tours may prefer to keep a simple alphabetical card index and then also type up each tour list of passengers alphabetically on plain white paper (three rows, eleven names and addresses to the vertical row). This is suitable for running off on photocopy label sheets whenever a mailing is planned. The disadvantage of this method is that the names are not listed by zip code nor are they integrated alphabetically with other tours. Each tour list stands alone.

```
┌─────────────────────────────────────────────────────────────┐
│ Name: __Wing, Mr. Elliott/Mrs. Marilyn_____ │
│ Address: 2433 Brown Derby Road_____ │
│ City: __Rosemont____ State __CA____ Zip Code: __94526_____  │
│ Source of booking: _____Elaine Whittaker_____  │
│                     name of organizer, outside sales rep etc.│
│                                                               │
│ Name or Tour/Cruise and Destination  Year      Leader        │
│    Rosemont Country Club-Europe       19XX      Kimberly      │
│    Sun Line Orinoco Cruise            19XX      Carley        │
│                                                               │
│ _____    _____    _____    │
│                                                               │
│ See continuing card for more ...............................│
│ Comments: _Experienced travelers, but Mr. Wing has_____  │
│            heart condition._____   │
└─────────────────────────────────────────────────────────────┘
```

Figure 14.5 Sample of past participant client file card. This can be kept on a rolodex or in a computer database. (Courtesy Howard Tours Inc.)

LOOKING TO THE FUTURE

Now is the time (while pleasant tour memories are fresh in the clients' minds) to start the wheels in motion for the future. If this was a tour for a private club or organization, a meeting with the club organizer, chairperson, or president is advisable to assess the success and/or problems of this last tour. Of course, if this same person also acted as tour manager, this would already have been accomplished at the debriefing session. Whatever the case, in preparation for this meeting it is good to have two or three new destination ideas in mind with ballpark figures as to price and suggestions for time of year. Often, if the club is left to its own devices, to its own inner politics of election of new officers, and so forth, by the time it is ready to book the next tour or cruise, it is too late! The club officials need to be prodded with the assumption that, of course, they are going to do another tour and, of course, they are going to do it through the same company. The decisions regarding next year's tour must be reached now while the same club officers are involved in the decision-making process, not delayed until a new board of directors comes into power (perhaps with its own travel plans, own travel agent, and own vested interests).

One thought that might be planted is the idea of having a tour reunion to show films, relive the happy memories of the trip, and enjoy the camaraderie of newfound friends. This sort of reunion often can be a springboard for future trips by announcing next year's tour at the reunion and by giving past participants first chance to sign up for a new trip. You might even want to invite each tour participant to bring a friend, (athough this will change the spirit of the reunion and alter the group dynamics). It can also be effective if one of the tour participants acts as host and catalyst for the reunion, with the company representative and/or the tour manager attending as invited guests.

All in all, by the time the tour files are packed away and you move on to other things you should: (1) have a new nucleus of happy tour members; (2) have decided whether to repeat the same tour next year for a new clientele; (3) have decided whether to offer a new tour next year but to this same clientele; (4) have a financial picture of the tour; (5) have learned a lot—both from the successes and from the mistakes encountered on this tour.

❑ *SUMMARY*

The post-tour wrap-up phase of any tour is important, although many tour operators seem to lose interest in the tour once it has departed. Upon the tour's return, it is important to meet with the tour manager for a tour debriefing to elicit his/her comments and to obtain his/her financial report so that you may close out the tour books. You should send the tour participants a welcome-home letter along with a questionnaire to solicit their comments. All financial records should be reviewed and a profit/loss statement on the tour drawn up. All operational files should be packed away in an orderly fashion for future reference, and tour members' names and addresses should be added to the company's permanent mailing list of clients.

❑ *REVIEW QUESTIONS*

1.   **If something went terribly wrong on a tour, why is the tour manager usually eager to meet with you right away?**

2.   **Once a tour is over, why is it important to get in touch with the tour members on their return home?**

3.   **How can referrals to future potential passengers be obtained from returning tour members?**

4.   **Why is it important to take the time to put the tour files in order and pack them away in an orderly fashion after a tour?**

5. A group has just returned from a trip sponsored by their club. Why should you contact the club decision makers now regarding next year's tour rather than waiting until their new board of directors comes into office?

6. How would you use a left-over supply of brochures from this year's tour?

7. How would you plan a post-trip reunion party for a group? Specify what steps you might take to ensure the party's success.

8. How would you ensure that the tour manager submits his/her post-tour financial report in a timely fashion?

☐ *ACTIVITIES*

1. Write a "welcome home" letter to group participants returning from a fictitious tour.

2. If members of the Rosemont Garden Club had just returned from their trip to Europe, what new destination would you suggest to the club for next year's trip? Do a quick rough plan of a trip you might suggest to them along with a ballpark price estimate. Be prepared to show why this trip is particularly pertinent to those interested in gardening.

3. Consult a direct-mail house in your town and investigate what they would charge you to set up and maintain your past passenger mailing lists rather than your doing it yourself in-house. Discuss costs of initial data entry, periodic address changes, sorting and printing of labels for future mailings, etc.

▷ 15

INCOMING GROUP TOURS

LEARNING OBJECTIVES

After reading this chapter, you should be able to:

❑ Understand the reasons to consider opening an incoming tour operation
❑ Ascertain if your company is qualified to open an incoming tour operation
❑ Start designing some incoming tour products that can serve as catalysts to bring you incoming business
❑ Know where to promote your product
❑ Know special requirements of inbound tourism not pertinent to outbound tourism
❑ Know what to look for in locating motorcoaches, hotels, and flights for inbound groups
❑ Be prepared for some of the frustrations unique to inbound tourism

KEY CONCEPTS AND TERMS

Balance of Payments
Custom-Designed Itineraries
Deadhead Charges
Destination Management Company
Ground Operator
Hospitality Desk
ITB
Inbound Tourism
Incoming Tourism
Motorcoach Companies
Multilingual Services
Pow Wow
Producer
Sample Itineraries
Sightseeing Company
Special-Interest Tour

Step-On Guide
Supplier
TIAA
Tier Pricing
USTTA
Visit U.S.A.

Once a company has some experience in operating an outgoing tour program, it may be time to consider opening an incoming tour division as well. In this sense, **incoming** (or sometimes called **inbound**) means handling groups of foreign visitors or groups from other parts of the United States. The incoming tour business, whether from abroad or from other states within the United States, is *big* business. According to the National Tour Association, the escorted tour industry generates $13.2 billion annually in North America, 5.9 million jobs, $73.3 billion in payroll, and $142 billion in tax revenues. And it's growing.

The United States Travel and Tourism Administration (referred to as the **USTTA** and part of the United States Department of Commerce), indicated that U.S. international travel receipts—including foreign visitors' international air fare payments to U.S. carriers—has increased from a deficit in 1984 to a projected 19.5 billion dollars in 1993. (See Figure 15.2.) Canada, Mexico, and Japan lead the way in Foreign Visitor Arrivals. Based on international travel receipts (dollars, not number of passengers), the top four producers of inbound visitors are Canada, Mexico, Japan and United Kingdom, and in that order.

Where could you fit in? A company could, of course, elect to be simply a local receptive operator also sometimes called a **destination management company** providing *local* transfers, city tours, and so forth. But the money is to be made by becoming a full-service receptive tour operator—handling a complete **Visit U.S.A.** package. Under such an arrangement, one combines hotels, sightseeing, motorcoach transportation, meals, social events, tour manager, and technical visits all into a total package, adds a markup, and then offers it to a tour operator or travel agent overseas (or elsewhere in the United States) for sale to his or her specialty group.

Under this arrangement, the selling agent or tour operator overseas is often called the **producer**, since this is the company producing the group or clientele. Conversely, the company operator in the United States that puts together the components of the package and operates the tour is often called the **supplier** or the receptive operator or sometimes the **ground operator**. In other words, the roles are now reversed; the agent is no longer the agent.

A small company that can offer a good incoming specialty tour product and promote it properly over three or four years should find it possible to build an operation of 20 incoming tours or so per year, earning $4,000 to $5,000 minimum per each small-size group. Of course, many companies can build a much larger volume.

In many countries, travel agencies and tour operators regularly handle two-way travel. However, in the United States, most travel agencies and tour operators have

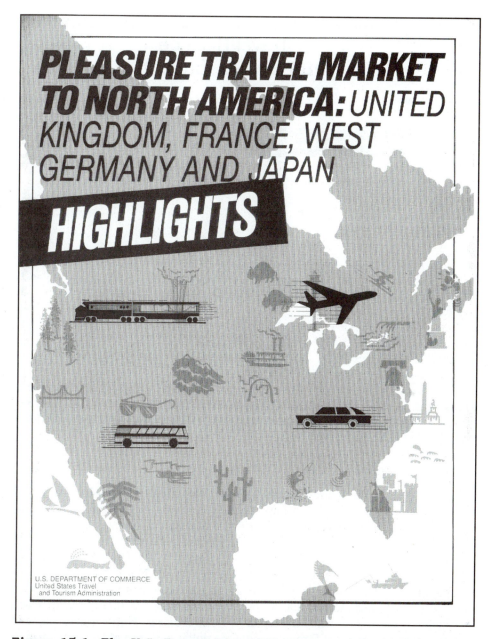

Figure 15.1 The U.S. Department of Commerce and U.S. Travel and Tourism Administration publishes pamphlets like this with statistics and information on foreign visitors to the U.S. This information is helpful to U.S. inbound tour operators and local U.S. receptive services operators. (Courtesy of U.S. Travel and Tourism Administration, Department of Commerce.)

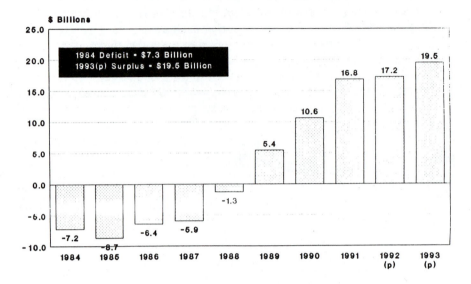

Composition of Receipts & Payments*
Travel Balance
1984 - 1993 (projected)

Figure 15.2 This chart shows that foreign tourism to the U.S. has increased steadily since 1984. (Source: U.S. Travel and Tourism Administration, Department of Commerce.)

concentrated on outgoing tourism and have left incoming traffic to incoming specialists. Companies with some group expertise have now begun to look at incoming tourism as a new market, a new product, a new source of revenue.

Incoming tourism is not a business for the inexperienced. Nor is it a stable business, since it usually fluctuates with the strength of the United States dollar. At times when the dollar is strong on foreign markets and North Americans find it a bargain to travel overseas, it is very difficult for foreigners to buy dollars with their weak currencies and a vacation in the United States is totally out of reach financially. Conversely, when the dollar is weak overseas, North Americans tend to travel close to home and foreigners find the dollar easier to obtain and a trip to North America a bargain. So, for the company with solid group operational know-how, incoming tourism should be looked at for a number of reasons.

REASONS TO CONSIDER OPENING AN INCOMING TOUR DEPARTMENT

❑ As a balance to outgoing business, filling weak seasons in the office.

❑ As an additional source of revenue, which is particularly important if outgoing business is down during an economic slump.

❑ As a means of generating **balance of payments**. Foreigners spending money for United States packages are infusing money into our economy, money that circulates and provides jobs in tourism in the United States—often jobs at the lowest end of the economic spectrum, where they are needed most. Visitors to one's city or state make purchases and support local restaurants, shops, and businesses.

❑ As a method of diversifying a company so that it does not have "all its eggs in one basket" should any one segment of business take a downturn.

❑ As a means of developing a new area of business that, except for start-up promotional monies and some cash flow for deposits, does not take a great deal of new investment capital. Also, it does not require a lot of new personnel *if* the company already has a good group department.

DESIGNING AN INCOMING TOUR PRODUCT

Probably the easiest way to start with incoming tours is to develop a specialty tour program that can be marketed both overseas and in other areas of the United States. You may want to start out small and not try to compete with large-volume operators who can easily underprice the small operator, nor should you try to sell to the extremely large producers who may sometimes expect to be carried financially for a lengthy period.

Therefore, it would be best to appeal to the moderate-size operator and to design a **special-interest tour** or tour service that someone else does not appear to be doing. A tour for European women visiting American families, homes, and schools? Tours of the Southwest stressing Indian culture, the desert, and turquoise jewelry? Horseback trips, rock climbing, or backpacking into our national parks? Decide what your company staff knows the best. Theatre? Opera? Fashion? Perhaps check with the state tourism board and the local convention and visitors' bureau to see what they believe is lacking and, conversely, to see what is already being done and what the competition would be.

The next step is to put together and price a few **sample itineraries**. Remember, these itineraries will probably not be sold "as is," but will serve as a showcase for overseas tour operators. In actuality, the final itinerary designed for a particu-

There is so much to see in California you'll need a guide.

We'll send you one...FREE!

It's the *Discover The Californias*® guide. Full of What-To-Do's, What-To-See's and Where-To-Go's in America's favorite vacation destination.

There are tips on how to enjoy *The Californias*® in a fresh new way. The State is divided into a dozen different regions, each with its own special surprises.

Order your guide today by writing the California Office of Tourism, P.O. Box 9278, Dept. C2007, Van Nuys, CA 91409 or

PHONE, TOLL FREE, 1-800-TO-CALIF, ext. C2007

The Californias.®

Figure 15.3   This ad, published by the California Office of Tourism was designed to bring tourists to the state. (Courtesy of California Department of Commerce.)

lar group may bear no resemblance to the original sample. But the sample will serve as the catalyst, as food for thought. The tour operator overseas, upon seeing these samples, may contact you requesting that a similar tour be custom-designed for his or her clientele.

Take into consideration that ultimately your final **custom-designed itinerary** should be tailored to the likes and needs of the incoming traveler. Europeans seem to love our national parks, our deserts and open spaces, whereas visitors from southern Chile and Argentina (areas with lots of open spaces and wonderful scenery) are not as impressed. Germans and Japanese are not so caught up in shopping for the latest electronic gadgets, whereas those from developing countries may see our country as one vast shopping temptation.

Remember that things we take for granted can prove intriguing to visitors; they may very well want to visit a mall or supermarket. I once had a group virtually buy up all the plastic tablecloths in Macy's. Another group I accompanied could not get over an all-you-can-eat, self-service buffet lunch; they filled their plates time after time after time until I was sure the restaurant management might ask us to leave!

TOP STATES VISITED BY OVERSEAS TRAVELERS 1991 (IN MILLIONS)

5. Nevada — 1.3

3. New York — 4.3

1. California — 5.2

2. Florida — 4.3

4. Hawaii — 3.1

Source: U.S. Travel and Tourism Administration, June 1992

Camera Ready Art

Figure 15.4   Foreign tourists to the U.S. prefer to visit some states more than others. (Source: U.S. Travel and Tourism Administration, Department of Commerce.)

Once the sample itineraries are drawn up, you should produce an attractive brochure that can be used as a sales piece *for the trade*, not for the consumer. Rather than listing tour prices right in the brochure, it is best to print a separate tariff insert sheet. In this way, the tariff can be updated and reprinted annually, or as needed when prices change, without having to reprint the basic brochure. It is a good idea to price each tour on two different levels: one based on standard hotels and one on more deluxe properties.

Remember, if marketing overseas, that many foreigners are not knowledgeable about distances within the United States or the length of time it takes to get from one city to the next. Quite often, if left to their own devices, overseas operators will ask to travel too far in one day at a pace that would exhaust their passengers if one complied. A brief day-by-day sample itinerary (or several) in the brochure, illustrated with a good route map, can be an immense help in their planning a realistic schedule for their group.

The brochure should answer other important questions. Who is your company, how long has it been in business, what are its credentials, and who are its credit and banking references? What are payment policies? It is helpful to state that a minimum deposit is expected in order to begin reservations proceedings for a tour. A request for, say, $500 per tour group does not seem unreasonable. Final payment schedule should be explicit. A suggestion would be to indicate that payment in full, in United States dollars, is due 45 days before the tour begins. This enables you to prepay hotels and other suppliers at 30 days prior, the usual requirement. If this is not stipulated, final payment may not arrive in time to provide the cash flow needed. I have seen incoming group tours arrive with payment in foreign currency cash in a flight bag!

Once the brochure and accompanying tariff are published, where do you begin to look for clientele? Remember, the buyer is the overseas or domestic tour company or travel agent selling groups, *not the individual traveler*. Promotional monies or efforts would be wasted on the general public. After all, you want incoming groups that another agent or tour operator forms and that arrive as a pre-formed group entity. You do not want individual clients. These prospective client groups are going to need a local travel agent or tour operator in their country or city to process their bookings, handle their air reservations to the United States, assist in securing their U.S. visas, publish a brochure in their language for promotion in their country, and so forth, just as if the situation were reversed and a group were being formed here to send to their country or city.

PROMOTION

Promotional efforts for incoming groups may be directed to several areas:

❑   Tour operators and group-oriented travel agents overseas and in the United States that your company particularly wishes to cultivate. Start with those that

Visit California and the U.S.A.

THE U.S. – A PHENOMENON IN AGRICULTURE

The United States represents one of the true world phenomena in agriculture. In contrast to most European and Asian countries, it is "under-populated" in terms of food production per inhabitant. The country is fortunate in having vast acreages of fertile soil, moderate climate and abundant water. Add to this a combination of technology, research and education — all provided through a vast network of universities, government agencies and agricultural support industries. The result is a most productive food machine.

By concentrating the nation's resources on food production, some remarkable gains in crop yields, livestock production and ability to feed the country's 220 million citizens have resulted . . . particularly in the last 25 years or so. In 1950, the nation harvested 345 million acres (140 million hectars), of which 295 million were used for domestic consumption and 50 million for export. Recently, in 1976, 330 million acres were harvested (134 million hectares), of which only 230 million were used for domestic purposes and 100 million for export. Twenty-five years ago, the average North American consumed two acres of food production; now one acre maintains a citizen at a higher nutritional level than a quarter century ago. We cordially invite you to visit the U.S.A. and learn about its Number One industry — Agriculture.

CALIFORNIA IS THE NUMBER ONE FARM STATE – COME SEE IT!

*Because of California's mild climate and intensive irrigation, this one state **alone** produces 25% of the nation's table food (the food humans eat — not what's fed to livestock or used in other ways), and 50% of the country's vegetables, fruits and nuts. However, biggest dollar producer for California agriculture is milk-dairy products, followed by cattle/calves. And 90% of the wine produced in America comes from California, rivaling the best of Europe. Agricultural land values here are among the highest — up to $40,000 per acre ($15,320. per hectar) for orchard or vineyard land. The state's farm strength lies in its diversity production of some 250 commodities, and marketing boards and farmer-owned cooperatives play a large role. Exports are also a vital part of the state's farm economy, exporting some 48 commodities valued at 2.8 billion dollars.*

Figure 15.5 This map is from a brochure published by an incoming tour operator that specializes in agricultural tours. It is aimed at foreign travel agents who are interested in bringing agricultural tour groups to the U.S. (Courtesy of Harvest Travel International.)

you may be using to receive your groups overseas; they are already friends. Then expand. One can obtain a list, for example, from *Travel Weekly's World Travel Directory.*

❏ Our U.S. embassies overseas, particularly the department pertinent to your specialty tour operation. For example, if specializing in theatre/ballet/opera tours, one might contact the Cultural Attaché at each United States embassy, alerting them to this specialty product so that they can refer any local inquiries they may receive to your company in the United States.

❏ Airlines. Remember, local airlines sales managers do not receive revenue from business into their territory, only on tickets sold from their territory. Therefore, the local airline sales office personnel have nothing to gain by helping you promote an incoming tour division. But if you acknowledge this fact and simply ask for help getting in touch with the airlines' various sales managers overseas, they may give that help. Then you can write a letter of introduction to these overseas airline managers directly, including your incoming tour product brochure and asking them to call it to the attention of tour operators and travel agents in their country when the airline staff makes sales calls. Sometimes overseas airline salespeople are looking for exciting new products they can bring to the attention of their travel agents and tour operators. Perhaps, if a travel product is distinctive enough, it will catch their eye.

❏ USTTA. You may contact the regional offices overseas, alerting them to the product and asking them for referrals; contact the USTTA head office in Washington (see page 378) for a list of these regional offices overseas.

❏ **Travel Industry Association of America (TIAA).** Although this organization will not actively go out and promote or refer your tour products, it is helpful to be a member of the club. This is the organization that sponsors the annual Pow Wow trade show. It also publishes a newsletter and a directory of members and can be helpful in terms of networking or providing background information. Membership fees for travel agents and tour operators are based on the gross sales volume of the company.

❏ Trade shows, such as Pow Wow. Trade shows are probably one of the most effective promotional methods, since it is possible to meet several hundred potential client companies within a three- to four-day period. **Pow Wow is** sponsored by TIAA as a once-a-year marketplace, bringing together North American suppliers and overseas buyers. The meeting is held in a different United States city each year and you are prescheduled, by computer, for an appointment with a different overseas tour operator or travel agent every twenty minutes.

In addition to Pow Wow, which covers travel suppliers from the entire United States, you might attend the Big One, the International Tourism Bourse (**ITB**), held every February in Berlin. It is pointless to waste valuable promotional monies on trade shows that are open to the public, giving away free brochures, free trips, free time, and energy. It is better to select only those shows that are for the travel trade itself, being selective even there.

❀ RIESLING-FREUNDESKREIS TRIER ❀

STUDIENREISE FÜR WEINBAU UND KELLERWIRTSCHAFT IN DIE USA
VOM 01.-13.09.1992

Endgültiges Programm:

1. Tag, 01.09., Dienstag   Frankfurt/M. - Sacramento

05.45 h Treffen der Teilnehmer am Friedrich-Wilhelm-Gymnasium,
        Weberbach 75, 5500 Trier (bitte denken Sie daran, daß
        hier keinerlei Parkmöglichkeiten bestehen!).
06.00 h Abfahrt per Bus (Sie fahren mit dem Busunternehmen
        "Kylltal Reisen") nach Frankfurt/M.
09.15 h Ankunft am Flughafen Frankfurt/M. Erledigung der
        Einreiseformalitäten.
11.00 h Abflug mit UA 941 nach Chicago. Mittagessen an Bord.
14.00 h Ankunft in Chicago.
15.21 h Weiterflug mit UA 499 nach Sacramento.
17.49 h Ankunft in Sacramento (Ortszeit: - 9 Stunden zu uns,
        d.h. bei uns ist es mittlerweile 02.50 h). Treffen mit
        unserer Reiseleiterin, Frau Margret Tanner, die Sie
        nun in Ihr Hotel begleiten wird und Ihnen von nun an
        den Rest der Reise beratend und hilfreich zur Seite
        steht: Frau Tanner kennt sich in Sachen Wein sehr gut
        aus, da sie einen eigenen Weinberg nördlich von San
        Francisco besitzt.
        Übernachtung im Hotel HOLIDAY INN CAPITOL PLAZA.

2. Tag, 02.09., Mittwoch   Sacramento - Lodi Gegend

08.00 h Frühstück im Hotel.
09.00 h Abfahrt vom Hotel zum einem ganztägigen Fachbesuchen
        mit Weinproben. Die besuchten Weingüter sind haupt-
        sächlich Familienbesitze, die über Generationen wei-
        tervererbt wurden. Die Vielfalt von Lodi Weinen bein-
        haltet zum Beispiel Cabernet Sauvignon, Chardonnay,
        Sauvignon Blanc, Chenin Blanc, Zinfandel, French Co-
        lombard und Flame Tokay.
        Mittagessen unterwegs ist eingeschlossen.
        Rückfahrt zum Hotel am späten Nachmittag. Der Abend
        steht Ihnen zur freien Verfügung; wir empfehlen Ihnen
        ein Abendessen im nahegelegenen Restaurant "OLD
        SACRAMENTO" in einer Gegend mit vielen Restaurants,
        Boutiquen und viel Nachtleben...
        Übernachtung im HOLIDAY INN CAPITOL PLAZA.

Figure 15.6 This is the first page of an itinerary for a 13-day in bound tour to the U.S. It was planned by a German travel agency for a group of German wine enthusiasts. The tour includes visits to California wineries and lectures in viticulture at the University of California. The tour uses Harvest Travel International as the receptive operator. (Courtesy of Reiseburo Globus.)

To attend these trade shows, a company preregisters and rents a booth for the duration of the show. In addition to the booth registration cost, there is an enrollment fee for each staff member who attends and works in the booth. One must also budget for personal staff expenses, such as airfare to the city of venue, hotel, and some meals (sometimes many meals and festivities already are included in the enrollment fee). Attendance at these social events is an excellent way to meet potential clients informally.

When attending one's first trade show, it is possible to go equipped with no more than brochures, tariff sheets, a sign to identify your company, and a good supply of business cards. Later, you may have a professional booth backdrop made, which should fold down so that it can be shipped from show to show. Such a backdrop, complete with lighting, can run as high as $5,000, but it is a promotional investment that can be amortized as a capital investment over several years.

Also, as you attend more shows, you may wish to carry other handouts besides brochures: perhaps a one-page synthesis of the company's operations translated into several different languages, perhaps a tabletop slide presentation or a video. At the first show or two, it is a good idea to take time to visit the other booths to get ideas.

OPERATIONAL SETUP

If the promotion is a success, your company may suddenly receive requests for quotations and itineraries. The office should be prepared to move quickly when this happens. The same general requirements would apply for an incoming tour department as for an outgoing tour department, that is:

- ❑ A separate room or a work area away from office traffic.
- ❑ Adequate insurance.
- ❑ Personnel adept with group operations.
- ❑ Photocopy machine.
- ❑ Fax.
- ❑ Separate phone line(s).
- ❑ An accounting system to separate out expenses and income for each different tour.
- ❑ Computer with word processing software for storage of city tour descriptions and standardized paragraphs to enable you to put together tour offers quickly.

In addition, incoming business has some special requirements all its own. These are:

- ❑ *Ability to respond immediately* to requests for quotes and suggested itineraries. Someone able to do this should be in the office at all times. All of the incoming tourism staff should never be away at the same time. The client who has to wait a week for an offer will go elsewhere. Often such producers are under pressure to get back to their own clients quickly with a suggested itinerary and rough price estimate, or lose the business themselves to their local competition.

❑ *Accessibility to multilingual tour managers and translators.* Although it is not mandatory that an agency's in-house staff be multilingual, it is helpful. But it *is* mandatory that an agency be able to provide **multilingual services** by contracting with good, professional, free-lance tour managers who can conduct a tour with fluency in the foreign language concerned and with native-speaking translators who can put the itineraries and other written materials into various languages. This usually means being located in a large urban area or a university town.

❑ *Ability to work with minute details.* In outgoing tourism, you usually work with an overseas receptive operator who is responsible for the day-to-day details like making luncheon reservations, checking mileage, and reminding the bus company to pick up the group on time. When the situation is reversed and your company becomes the receptive operator, it carries the same responsibility. Someone on the staff must have a fine eye for detail to be sure that nothing slips by.

❑ *Staff availability 24 hours a day.* Tour managers must be able to reach someone from your company when out in the field with a tour in case of problems encountered enroute. There is no such thing as being unavailable on weekends or evenings.

❑ *Necessity to understand foreign traditions,* viewpoints, dietary likes and dislikes, and so forth.

COSTING INCOMING TOURS

The principles of costing, be they for incoming or outgoing tours, are basically the same (see Chapter 7). Individual variable expenses and fixed group expenses must be separated out just as they are for outgoing tours. But there are also a few differences:

❑ *No air commission.* Remember, all earnings must come from markup on ground expenses. The passengers' flights most likely will be booked and ticketed by their local tour operator or travel agent (the producer) who will then, obviously, get the air commission.

❑ *No promotional expense.* There is no need to cost-in for promotional efforts. The producer takes the risk for promoting the trip and foots the bill for printing the brochure (perhaps in a foreign language), advertising the tour, and so forth.

❑ *Tier pricing.* The producer will expect **tier pricing** from you—a quotation of graduated prices, based on the volume produced. For example:

$800   per person, basis 40 paying passengers and one
complimentary (expressed $800 pp 40+1)

$875   per person, basis 30 paying passengers and one
complimentary (expressed $875 pp 30+1)

$950   per person, basis 20 paying passengers and one
complimentary (expressed $950 pp 20+1)

It is the producer, not the receptive operator, who is taking the risk, so it is the producer who gets the price break for producing volume. Regardless of how many tour members they produce, they still will charge their tour members the same price; they usually will not lower the price to their customers as their tour fills. But as their tour fills, they realize an escalating profit—the incentive for their risk venture.

Even if the overseas producer requests that your company quote, for example, 40+1, it is wise to also quote prices on 30, 20, and so forth. This forces the producer to face the fact that they may not actually produce 40 passengers and, therefore, should be conservative and price their tour on 30 or 20. If tier pricing is not given at the start, later, when they have only sold 20 or 25, they may try to pressure the receptive operator to honor the price quote that was given them based on 40 and may, in fact, become angry when they are then quoted a higher per person price based on only 20 in the group at that late date.

Overseas quotations should always be made in United States dollars, letting the overseas producers convert into their local currency and take the risk for exchange rate fluctuations. Also, a company should be sure to quote net and state that rates are net, noncommissionable, when making the offer. The overseas producers will add in their promotional expenses, airfare, and markup before establishing their selling price.

As many tour managers and complimentaries as needed must be priced in. If, for example, one complimentary is allowed by the hotels and it is used for the tour manager, you will need to cost-in another complimentary for the incoming group leader or maybe two, depending on the producer's request. Since the group size probably will not warrant hotels' granting that many complimentaries, the extra complimentaries will have to be prorated over the clients booked, so that each client actually absorbs part of each additional complimentary required.

Do not try to bid too low. Many larger operators can easily underbid a smaller concern; many of them do, hoping to make their profit by selling the tour members optional trips after the group arrives. Instead, you can offer a quality tour with many private functions on which a financial value cannot be placed, functions such as private receptions, home hospitality, meetings with key leaders, and access to private clubs or businesses. Be prepared, however, for the producer's trying to negotiate the price down; it is best to have a small extra margin in there that can be given away if necessary. The first offer should state that the prices are estimates only and that final and firm prices will follow after the agency has been given the go-ahead to book and after the final price confirmations have come in from the hotels, from the motorcoach company, and so forth.

Booking

Once the company has been given the go-ahead to book and has collected a nominal good-faith deposit from the producer, the next job is to secure all necessary reservations—the hotels, the motorcoach, and perhaps to start looking for a bilingual tour manager. The finishing touches (such as meal reservations, social events, and so forth) may be added later, when it is certain that the group is really materializing. However, these items should be costed in now, and adequately so, even if each and every menu is not actually booked at this stage.

Motorcoaches

One of the most important decisions to be made is the selection of the **motorcoach company** with which the company will deal. Good or bad motorcoach services can make or break a tour. Everything can go well on a trip, but a coach that breaks down, a public address system that does not work, an air-conditioning unit that fails, or a rude, disagreeable driver can ruin an entire day. Therefore, when it comes to motorcoaches, it pays to get the best, not necessarily the least expensive. Table 15.1 provides a checklist of factors to consider in leasing motorcoaches.

TABLE 15.1   Checklist for Leasing Motorcoaches

_____ Adequate licenses and insurance confirmed? Permission for airport pick up and drop verified?

_____ Adequate equipment—air-conditiong, lavatory, public address system confirmed?

_____ Mileage charges based on exact destination and usage details?

_____ Number of coach seats verified? Seats set aside for tour manager, incoming tour leader, and city guides or hosts?

_____ Equipment points (for service of equipment) verified?

_____ Deadhead charges (for driving coach back to home base empty) clarified?

_____ Driver's hotel, meals and other per diem costs included in the coach company's price quote?

_____ Bridge tolls, turnpike charges or parking fees included in the coach company's price quote?

_____ Formal reservation order made?

Now let's look at each of these considerations in more detail.

- ☐ Be sure that the motorcoach company selected has all the necessary licenses, both intrastate and interstate, if the group will be traveling over state lines. Also be sure that it carries adequate insurance and that it has permission to pick up and drop at any airports that the group will be using. Often less expensive coach companies are lacking in one of these areas.
- ☐ Specify the equipment desired—air-conditioning, lavatory, public address system.
- ☐ Give the coach company exact details on where the group is going, the number of hours the coach will be needed each day, and so forth, so that they can calculate time/mileage charges. The tour manager must be told later how the coach is priced so that he or she does not run up extra time and mileage charges while on tour and authorize sending the bill to your company after the fact.
- ☐ Verify the number of seats available for sale. One seat should be set aside for the tour manager, one for the incoming group leader, and perhaps additional ones as needed for local step-on city guides or hosts if these will be used. The producer should be told from the outset the maximum number of seats that he or she may sell to avoid an oversell situation. A company may not want to sell the back-row seats, or those over the rear wheels. If a coach with a lavatory is ordered, the two seats across from the lavatory may be better left vacant. In the United States, most coaches are forty-three seaters. A problem may be encountered when the group size is small, say fifteen to twenty. Not many small coaches are available, particularly for interstate use, and when using a van or minibus, there are problems with luggage storage space and with driving long distances, particularly over mountains.

  Also be sure the producer understands that if one coach is oversold and a second one must be operated, it may be more expensive. A group of eighty (two forty-three-seat coaches with forty passengers each) is economical; a group of fifty (two forty-three-seat coaches with twenty-five passengers and eighteen empty seats each) is not.
- ☐ Verify the coach company's equipment points (places where they service their equipment or have other coaches available). Obviously, a company with many equipment points around the state or the country and the ability to get a replacement coach immediately in case the original one breaks down is of prime importance.
- ☐ Verify if the coach company is charging **deadhead charges**; that is, charges for driving the coach back to home base empty. If so, the itinerary might be redesigned, or you might wish to look for a company that is large enough not to charge deadhead mileage or dropoff charges.
- ☐ Verify that the coach driver's living expenses, (e.g., hotel, meals, and so forth) are included in the price quote. If not, you will need to budget in for these costs at the time you cost and price your tour.
- ☐ Verify if there are any additional out-of-pocket charges your tour manager will have to pay enroute such as bridge tolls, turnpike charges, or parking.

❑ Verify availability of the coach and put in a formal reservation order. Do not wait, because many motorcoach companies book up their equipment, particularly during peak periods. If not reserved in advance, you might have to locate a coach later on through another company, perhaps at a higher rate, wiping out a substantial part of the profit just to keep faith with the overseas customer.

Hotels

A company planning to handle incoming tours will have to become familiar with hotels in the immediate area and across the country. At first, this seems like a formidable undertaking, since there are so many. Perhaps the best way to start is to make a hotel inspection in one's own city, trying to locate two or three properties in a moderate price category and another two or three in a more deluxe category. Remember, you cannot always count on first choice being available, so it is best to have several and to build a rapport with the sales managers of these properties.

In selecting properties, the same criteria would apply as in selecting properties for outgoing tours (see Chapter 6), such as bus-loading zone, dining room, meeting rooms, ambience, and efficient group handling. In addition to these criteria, some other criteria may prove particularly important in dealing with foreign groups:

❑ Will the group feel comfortable in the atmosphere of the hotel?
❑ Do front-desk personnel speak foreign languages? In short, is the hotel geared to the foreign market?
❑ Is there a concierge to help foreigners who do not speak English or know the city?
❑ Is there a money exchange facility at the hotel (or nearby)?
❑ Are dining room menus available in other languages?

If the itinerary is a full one, with most free time taken care of, the above factors may not be so important. But if tour participants have free time on their hands and must make independent arrangements for dinner reservations, shopping, and optional sightseeing activities, it can be extremely important. If there are no such services in the hotel, the company may end up having to run a **hospitality desk** or having the tour manager on call around the clock to assist members who do not speak English.

Sightseeing

While the group is trekking along through the countryside, enroute sightseeing and commentary probably can be handled by the tour manager, assuming that this individual has been well selected and has done some homework before departure by reading up on areas to be visited.

However, no matter how educated and well-read this tour manager may be, you cannot expect such a person to know the history, facts, and figures of each and every city on the itinerary. Also, in some cities in the United States (just as in some cities overseas), only licensed guides are permitted to give city tours. Therefore, a more formal type of sightseeing may be arranged in some of the major cities—either by prehiring a local guide (called a **step-on guide**) to give the sightseeing tour aboard the group's coach, or by letting the coach rest for a day here and there and hiring a local sightseeing company to tour the group, which is complete with its own coach and driver/guide. For example, Greyhound is a coach company only; its drivers are not guides. Gray Line, on the other hand, is basically a **sightseeing company**. Its drivers are also guides and will give a tour as they drive. However, many are not bilingual, in which case they give the tour in English and the bilingual tour manager translates—a lengthy and not totally satisfactory solution. It is preferable to contract for the tour to be given directly in the language of the visiting group and to work with a sightseeing company that can provide this service. In pricing the tour, check to determine if entrance fees to museums, public buildings, and other places listed on the itinerary are included. And what about the guide's tip? It will be necessary to cost these miscellaneous items to assure a quality tour.

Air

Arrival and departure flights will be handled by the producer, not by the receptive operator. However, domestic flights within the itinerary as part of the tour are not so clear. If coming from overseas, it may be best for the passengers to purchase these domestic flights overseas in conjunction with their international ticket. In other cases, it may be more financially advantageous to the passenger for the receptive operator to do it and include the United States domestic flight segments in the land tour package. When booking these flights within the United States and checking on airfares, always be aware that there may often exist Visit U.S.A. fares—special advantageous promotional airfares designed for overseas visitors coming to the United States. These special fares are not available for sale in the United States to U.S. citizens and are not in your airline computer; you may have to call the airlines' rate desks to obtain this information.

Perhaps the best solution at the outset is to take the initiative and book the group flights within the itinerary that seem best for scheduling purposes. You can then advise the producer of the flight schedule and price of the domestic air portion and offer to release the group flight space to the producer for ticketing at time of tour finalization if the producer so desires and if more advantageous financially to the travelers.

Transfers

The company will have to book transfer service to and from airports in conjunction with the tour, assuming that the group is arriving and departing as a unit. If involved with a group in which participants are arriving individually, it probably is best to have the tour start officially at the hotel on the first night with a hospitality desk check-in. In costing transfers, compare the prices of sightseeing companies versus motorcoach companies. It is not unusual to find that sightseeing companies, which charge a flat transfer fee, may be less expensive in some cases than a motorcoach charter, which often requires a five-hour minimum.

THE WAIT

Once your company has quoted a price to the producer and has been given booking go-ahead, you will reserve all space, get final confirmations and price quotes, and then get back to the producer to advise of hotel confirmations and final prices (which should not differ too much from the original quote once the agency staff becomes adept at pricing).

During the next six months, the file probably will be dormant while the producer is busily promoting and selling the tour. This can be one of the most frustrating periods for the receptive operator, as the success of the project rests totally in the hands of this producer; there is nothing you can do to help. When dealing with outgoing tour business, during this period you would be promoting and selling and would have a feel as to how the tour is progressing and would know what the outlook is for success. But when the situation is reversed, you are excluded during this important period. Nevertheless, during this waiting period, you should require periodic progress reports and should send a fax requesting them if the producer does not take the initiative and send them on.

At 60 days before the group's arrival, it is time to begin to cut back some of the space if it appears that it will not all be used. It is important to play fair with the hotels and other suppliers to build credibility with them. The producer should again be reminded that at 45 days before arrival, final payment is expected and at 30 days, final rooming lists. This gives you time to turn around and send rooming lists, send any necessary advance payments, and send final instructions to the hotels, motorcoach companies, and other various suppliers involved.

FINALIZING THE TOUR

At 30 days before arrival, it is time to finalize with the various hotels, motorcoach companies, sightseeing companies, the tour manager, local guides, and others servicing this tour. At this point the company cancels any unsold space, formally commits to the tour manager, and goes into high gear in the finalization process just as on an outgoing tour. It is at this time that rooming lists and payments to hotels should be sent out, finishing touches put on social events, menus for group meal functions selected, and technical visits finalized. At this time you should mentally walk through the tour day by day, hour by hour, to be sure that nothing has escaped attention.

The staff will also be busily preparing information packets to be distributed to the group as they arrive. These packets will contain their day-by-day itinerary (translated into the native language of the arriving group), perhaps a map showing the route that they will be following, dining suggestions for meals on their own, and other information that may be helpful. Perhaps it will even be necessary to provide name tags or baggage tags if the producer is not doing so; double-check to verify.

As arrival time draws near, the tour manager should be brought in for briefing. All documents and background information must be turned over to him or her for reading and clarification, and travelers checks and other funds must be prepared.

Once the group arrives, the tour should be operated on a day-by-day basis in the field by the tour manager. If you have selected a good manager, most problems can be solved as the tour moves along without frequent call-ins to the office. However, no matter how qualified the tour manager, there will be times when quick assistance is required from the office (e.g., if a tour member is ill, if someone's flight schedule must be changed, if the group's return flights must be reconfirmed, and so forth).

While the group is in town, it might be helpful to the future business relationship to make a special effort to spend an evening with the group personally or to invite the incoming leader to dinner. It may even be prudent to accompany the group personally for a day or two or to invite the entire group for an evening of home hospitality. This is strictly a management decision to be made on the basis of the importance of the account. When accompanying such a group for a short period of time, it is important *not* to erode the leadership position of the tour manager; he or she must remain at the helm throughout.

FRUSTRATIONS AND PROBLEMS

Although incoming tourism can be one of the most satisfying and profitable segments of the travel industry, it can also be extremely frustrating at times, with more than its share of problems and areas of misunderstanding. Let us look at a few of these:

❑ *Travel agents or tour operators overseas who do not operate as professionally as one would like*, such as those who do not send in booking reports, rooming lists, or payments when due, requiring constant follow-up and sometimes requiring harsh treatment to get the job done when it is supposed to be done.

❑ *Difficulties in obtaining visas* to come to the United States. Many times, foreigners wishing to visit us encounter lengthy delays when applying for tourist visas or are made to feel like immigrants rather than welcome guests when they approach our embassies overseas.

❑ *Misunderstanding on the part of the tour members and the incoming leader* as to what services are to be provided and how the itinerary is to be followed. Your initial commitment to the producer may have been perfectly clear, but perhaps it was not conveyed properly by that company to the incoming leader or to tour participants. For this reason, it is wise to include a detailed itinerary and list of included services in each tour member's arrival packet.

❑ *An underdeveloped incoming tourism industry* in the United States. Hotels without staff with foreign language ability. Hotels with no money exchange. The assumption in most public places that everyone speaks English. Encounters with some unsophisticated North Americans who may not know a foreign group's country, history, customs, or sensitivities and who may, perhaps inadvertently, cause hurt feelings or tensions.

❑ *Incoming tourists who do not wish to follow the program,* preferring to strike out on their own to shop, *cherchez la femme,* and so forth—some without the courtesy to advise the tour manager that they will not be attending certain functions.

❑ *Participants who are not always easy to get along with,* perhaps continually late, not thoughtful of their fellow tour participants or of those hosting them, perhaps critical of the United States and its way of life.

❑ *Dependence on the economic and political climate.* The fluctuations of foreign currency versus the United States dollar, inflation, and international disputes can have an undue influence on incoming tour business—something over which you have absolutely no control. A Panama invasion, Tiennamin Square crackdown, Persian Gulf crisis, or other incidents can totally undo plans for an expected group on which much time and money have been spent.

❑ *Last-minute group bookings* from overseas companies that sell a group first, then contact you for help in booking it at the last minute—a nightmare! Of course, they want Yosemite Park in midsummer, Hawaii at Christmas, Las Vegas over Thanksgiving weekend, or some other equally impossible request. Don't be afraid to turn down a group if you cannot do it justice.

❑ *Agents who want partial services only,* who want a receptive operator to provide the technical program, social events, or other services in which it specializes (and on which it makes no money) but who want to book their own hotels and tour services directly. Learn to say no!

But, all in all, the positive outweighs the negative. Developing an incoming tours segment of the business can be a satisfying and positive addition to the company's mix if approached in a professional way with knowledgeable staff, a promotional plan, nominal startup monies, adequate cash flow, and without pressure to produce a group or a profit immediately. You must not look at it as an immediate solution to a business downturn in other areas of the company, since the first group will probably not arrive for well over a year. You should look at incoming tourism as an exciting way to diversify a travel company's operation for the long haul.

SOME HELPFUL CONTACTS

International Tourism Exchange (ITB)
c/o U.S. Travel and Tourism Administration
Ross Markt No. 10 600
Frankfurt/Main Germany
(For information on ITB annual trade show in Berlin)

International Tour Management Institute
P.O. Box 3636
San Francisco, CA 94119
(For referral of tour managers or training courses)

National Tour Association
546 East Main Street
P.O. Box 3071
Lexington, KY 40596
(An organization of over 2,100 suppliers and 575 tour company members who package and sell escorted tours)

Travel Industry Association of America (TIAA)
1899 L Street, N.W.
Washington, DC 20036
(For information on Pow Wow)

Travel Weekly
500 Plaza Drive
Secaucus, NJ 07096
(To purchase their *World Travel Directory*)

United States Travel and Tourism Administration (USTTA)
United States Department of Commerce
14th and Constitution N.W.
Washington, DC 20230

❏ SUMMARY

Incoming tourism can be an exciting new endeavor for a company that already has an outgoing tour department in place and a staff with previous group experience. The simplest way to begin is with a special-interest tour product. You should prepare several sample itineraries and then publish a brochure, along with a tariff insert sheet that may be updated annually as prices change. Promotional efforts should be directed to group tour operators overseas and elsewhere in the United States. You should become involved in the various associations and trade shows associated with the incoming sector of the travel industry. It will be necessary to have on staff those who are adept at detail work to properly operate inbound tours. While there are many frustrations and problems surrounding inbound tourism, the positive outweighs the negative.

❑ *REVIEW QUESTIONS*

1. **What are some reasons for an existing travel company to consider opening an incoming tours division?**

2. **Why is a specialty tour product a good idea for a small operator new to the incoming tour business?**

3. **Why would your local airline sales offices not be a particularly good source of help in marketing your incoming tour product?**

4. **What can attendance at Pow Wow do for you if you recently opened an incoming tour department?**

5. What are some of the special requirements an incoming tour department would have in addition to those an outgoing department would have?

6. What are some of the points to double-check with a motorcoach company when requesting a quote?

7. What are some of the frustrations/problems you may encounter in the incoming tour business?

8. What are some special factors to be on the lookout for in selecting hotels for foreign visitor groups?

9. How does the pricing of incoming tours differ from that of outgoing tours?

10. In incoming tourism, who is your overseas buyer to whom your promotional material is directed?

❏ *ACTIVITIES*

1. You are about to enter the inbound tour sector of the travel industry and are researching what kind of special-interest tours are needed. Contact your nearest convention and visitors' bureau to ascertain what they think is lacking or what is oversaturated and thus constituting competition for you.

2. Make several hotel inspections in your town. Try to visit three hotels in a standard category and three in a deluxe category. Talk to the sales managers and obtain their best net group rates. (Check if they have Visit U.S.A. rates and ascertain which are least expensive.) In inspecting the hotels, be on the lookout for those things particularly important to foreign visitors such as ambience, foreign-language ability of staff, money exchange, and so forth.

3. If you were suddenly to receive an inquiry for a foreign-language tour in an uncommon language in your area (Swahili? Farsi? Hindi?), determine how you would go about locating a bilingual tour manager to escort this tour if it were to materialize.

4. Make a list of sites in your area that you think might be of particular interest to incoming visitors. Don't overlook the obvious sites you take for granted but which might prove unusual to them.

▷ 16

AND . . . FOR THE EXPERIENCED GROUP OPERATOR . . . CONVENTIONS, INCENTIVES, SPECIAL-INTEREST, TRADE MISSIONS, AND MORE

LEARNING OBJECTIVES

After reading this chapter, you should be aware of some specialty travel formats suggested only to the experienced group operator, namely:

- ❑ Incentive travel groups for corporations and their sales forces
- ❑ Special-interest tours ranging from skin diving to opera
- ❑ Trade missions, the ultimate business group travel
- ❑ Meetings and conventions—where you make money and where you don't
- ❑ Overseas study programs and the academic market

KEY CONCEPTS AND TERMS

Academia
Adventure Travel
Conventions
Conditions Statement
Incentive Trips
Inventory Control
Meetings
Seminars
Trade Missions

Once you have had experience in groups, you may be ready to handle some more difficult assignments, such as meetings, seminars, conventions, trade missions, and incentives. Also included in this category would be academic overseas study programs and special-interest tours such as opera tours, wine and gourmet trips, trekking, and the like.

Make no mistake, all of these are for the sophisticated group operator with a strong background in group operations, costings, and promotion. They are for the operator with excellent knowledge of suppliers within the industry, with heavy in-the-field tour-operating and tour-managing experience. They definitely are not the kinds of tours with which to experiment as learning experiences or with which to break into the field of group travel.

A brief look at the idiosyncracies of some of these more sophisticated trips will make them more easily recognizable and will help you know when to attempt them and when they are out of your league.

MEETINGS, SEMINARS, AND CONVENTIONS

An area drawing a great deal of interest and being attempted by a number of newer, smaller companies is the area of **meetings**, **seminars**, and **conventions**. For many retail travel agencies, this is an offshoot or logical development of their regular commercial business.

Unfortunately, many members of the travel industry simply assume that volume business automatically means volume profits, and many newcomers become terribly excited at the prospect of handling such big business. The truth is that unless the potential exists for packaging the trip (and thus costing-in a markup), the venture may not prove to be as profitable as hoped, regardless of the numbers of clients traveling.

If the meeting is at a destination within driving distance and if the organization basically wants nothing more than hotel or resort accommodations for a couple of nights, some meeting room space, and a meal function or two, it is somewhat difficult to package it and make any real money other than commissions. If, however, you can include air, sightseeing, and transfers in the basic package and may also package an optional post-meeting tour (or perhaps sell a group cruise), it may become a viable project.

Many companies prefer not to handle such meetings here at home but do become involved when the meeting is offshore. For example, a meeting in Honolulu can be packaged quite successfully with a basic program of round-trip air transportation, convention hotel, lei greeting, arrival transfer, hospitality desk, meeting room space, and a social evening or two such as a luau. If the meeting is no more than three to four days, usually many of the group will extend their trip to include one or two additional islands as short post-convention tours. A number of operators are successful also in packaging their own trips even farther afield to

Japan or Tahiti, for example, as extensions. Quite frequently the bulk of the profit is made from the post-convention trips, with only minimal earnings realized on the basic package.

Large conventions are best left to the specialty handlers in this field. Such large events have requirements all their own that the small to average size company may not be prepared to meet. These requirements include the following:

❑ Computer programming capability of **inventory control** that can automatically pull up rooming lists for each hotel, flight manifests for the many different flights from various gateways, membership lists for each optional post-convention tour, and so forth. Computerized tour invoicing and computerized tour documentation are also musts.
❑ Financial ability to make sizable deposits, publish promotional materials, or handle other up-front expenditures if necessary.
❑ Necessity to reorganize the office and staff around the project—perhaps hiring and supervising a great many temporary employees to meet the crunch. I have been involved in one convention of 16,000 participants where it actually was necessary to lease additional office space, put in extra banks of telephones, and print separate stationery and document supplies.
❑ Necessity to spend time, money, and entertainment on the sponsoring organization. This undoubtedly would involve inviting their decision makers on an inspection trip to the convention site to see the hotels, meet the local managers, and generally gain confidence in the selection of the convention site and your company.

TRADE MISSIONS

The **trade mission** is group travel in a business format. This is the group from a particular industry, company, or city that makes a trip abroad to ascertain the potential of the overseas market, to show off its product, or to meet with prospective overseas importers.

Samples of these would be a group of California vintners traveling to Asia and hosting wine tastings for restaurateurs and hoteliers in Hong Kong, Taiwan, and Manila as part of an effort to induce them to feature California wines instead of European wines on their menus. Or a cooperative of cotton growers visiting China after United States-China relations were first normalized to investigate the possibilities for selling United States cotton to Beijing. Or a city-to-city or sister city type of visit by a government delegation. It could be a city's port authority directors visiting with comparable port authority officials in their respective countries—the purpose being to induce more shippers to use its port facilities.

The trade mission takes many forms, but all are dominated by a common thread—*the basic purpose of the trip is to develop business,* whether it's short-range purchase of a product or service or long-range development of an elaborate

a)

b)

Figure 16.1 Hotels, airlines, and even cities compete within their industries for the lucrative meetings and conventions business. (Courtesy of a) Ryder & Schild Advertising Inc. and The Boca Raton Resort & Club, b) TWA Meeting Services, TWA.)

scheme for business cooperation. Some of the characteristics of this type of travel might be:

❑ Shorter lead time than the normal vacation tour, often responding to a sudden economic or political need.

❑ Usually a short, snappy trip with a purpose—bearing in mind that those participating often are business or political leaders who cannot justify being away for long periods.

❑ The financial tab for the trip is rarely being paid by the individual participant. Usually, it is picked up by his or her company or a government entity; or perhaps it may even be an invitational trip by a sponsoring organization here at home or by an overseas entity.

❑ Pressure from certain participants—participants who may think that because of their status in the community they can get it wholesale or can persuade certain airlines or other segments of the travel industry to donate their services.

❑ Spouses usually do not participate in the trip; if they do, they do so at their own expense.

Since this is essentially business travel—although business travel on its highest plane—it must be approached from the standpoint of business and not vacation travel. Handling a project of this nature requires strong control on your part, a willingness to spend a great deal of extra time involved in the project (often outside the office attending frequent directors' committee meetings), and a tremendous amount of tact and graciousness, since you often are dealing with community and business leaders who have a strong sense of their own importance. The attitude that usually works best with this type of project is one of extreme professionalism; that is, presenting yourself as a professional peer, businessperson, and adviser to the project—not as a travel clerk who simply takes instructions on providing and hotel reservations. If you want to become involved in this type of business, you're well advised to join the Chamber of Commerce, a service club like Rotary or Kiwanis, and generally be active and visible in the business community.

A typical package to present for such a trip (after a preliminary consultation to determine the needs) might include the following:

❑ *Round-trip airfare* (wherever possible, a group fare to ensure the participants staying together as a group and not each one doing his or her own thing, thus deteriorating into a group of 30 FITs).

❑ *Hotel accommodations throughout.* Note that many business groups require all single-room accommodations rather than share-twin arrangements.

❑ *Quick early breakfast* at the hotel each morning.

❑ A *tour manager* to handle all business details of the trip as it moves along, thus leaving the group director and members free to conduct their own business and not be bothered with behind-the-scenes tour problems.

WORLD FEDERATION OF ENGINEERING ORGANIZATIONS

Dear Colleagues:

The World Federation of Engineering Societies (WFEO) will hold its thirteenth General Assembly and Technical Congress at the International Conference Center in Arusha, Tanzania, September 23-27,1991. As Chairman of the AAES Board, I will lead the U.S. delegation to the General Assembly, during which William J. Carroll of the United States will assume the Presidency of the Federation for the 1991-93 term.

Montgomery Travel Service (MTS) of Silver Spring, Maryland, will offer its services to members of the U.S. delegation in arranging their transportation to Arusha. Flight information and reservations assistance is available from Ms. Claudia McLeod, Manager of MTS. Telephone: 800.862.3322; 301.587.2121.

Abercrombie and Kent (A&K) International, one of the largest safari operators with offices in Nairobi, Kenya and in Arusha, has designed two alternative one-week safaris for members of the U.S. delegation who wish to take a post-meeting tour of the world-famous game parks in northern Tanzania or nearby Kenya. The two safaris are described on the other side of this flyer. Further information is available from Ms. Becky Hoselton at A&K's office in Oak Brook, Illinois (telephone: 800.323.7308; 708.954.2944).

Additional information on the Congress and General Assembly, including agendas, will be supplied as soon as it is received from the Tanzanian Institution of Engineers or from the WFEO Secretariat.

In order that we may inform the WFEO Secretariat of the names of the members of the U.S. delegation, please advise Mr. Harry M. Tollerton, AAES Director of International Affairs at your earliest opportunity if you, or a representative of your society, will attend the WFEO General Assembly. If you have any questions, please feel free to call Mr. Tollerton at 202.296.2237.

Albert A. Grant
Chairman AAES, Board of Governors
American Association of Engineering Societies

1991 WFEO
General Assembly and International Congress

Meetings Program

September 20 • Finance & Admin. Committee
September 21 • Executive Committee Focus Session
September 22 • Meetings of Technical Committees
September 23 • Opening Ceremonies-General Assembly and International Congress on Alleviation of Natural Disasters
September 24 • International Congress
September 25 • Executive Committee
September 26 • General Assembly
September 27 • General Assembly
September 28 • Executive Committee

Registration Fee

13th WFEO General Assemble	Nil
Delegate to International Congress	US $300
Accompanying Person to the International Congress	US $100

Once paid, cancellation penalties apply.

AIRFARES

Individual Apex Fares	*Round Trip*
New York to Nairobi	$2082.00
Washington D.C. to Nairobi	$2214.00

Group Fares	
New York to Nairobi	$1834.00
Washington D.C. to Nairobi	$1966.00

Group fare requires 5 persons travelling together round trip–Europe to Nairobi

Figure 16.2 Some group tours like this one to the 13th World Federation of Engineering Organizations General Assembly and International Congress are formed to promote international technical exchange and professional relationships. (Courtesy of American Association of Engineering Societies (AAES).)

❑ *Round-trip transfers, baggage handling, and tipping* in and out of all overseas airports and hotels.

❑ *Printing of a roster* of participants with photos and biographical sketches of those on the trip. This can be designed as an insert for a wraparound cover that serves as a brochure and carries the itinerary, tour inclusions/exclusions, responsibility clause, and other requirements.

❑ *A kickoff meeting and meal function* overseas—the first chance for the group to be together, make introductions, review the operational plan for the rest of the trip, and ask questions.

❑ *Perhaps meeting room space*, product display rooms, or other public room space.

❑ *Perhaps motorcoach charters* for days of field inspections, moving the group around from one point to the next for rapid business meetings.

❑ *Perhaps a bilingual interpreter* to accompany the group to various business and related social events.

❑ *Perhaps air freight charges* if the group plans to ship samples and demonstration items, projectors, and films—more than will fit into the standard two suitcases per person limit.

❑ *Perhaps certain other meals or social meal functions*, often banquets or cocktail receptions hosting overseas guests. (If the group is visiting several cities on the itinerary, this function might be repeated in each city with a new set of overseas guests at each party.)

❑ *Occasional sightseeing*, primarily on weekends, as incidental features or to augment the basic business nature of the tour—never preempting the business format.

Note that just as on a pleasure vacation tour, the product should be presented as a *whole package*, with a flat all-inclusive per person rate (based on a certain stated minimum number in the group, on which the package has been priced). It is not presented in breakdown fashion (i.e., so much for air, so much for hotels, and so forth). You will be working with net rates and adding your markup/profit margin just as is done with pleasure tours.

It is important to have a clearly written statement of specifically what is included in the package and, conversely, what is not included so that there is no misunderstanding and to make it crystal clear that participation and prices quoted require all members to conform to the group program, stay at the group hotel, travel on the group flights, and so forth. It often is a lifesaver to cost-in a small contingency (e.g., $50) for an extra amount to cover those things that the organizers somehow forgot to mention, such as the extra guest(s) for dinner, the extra tips that you will have to pay to secure the real service these people have grown to expect, and the storage charge for displays sent on ahead.

It is also important to mention the number of daily hours for which motorcoach charters are contracted. Groups of this nature have a way of extending on-site inspection days well beyond the allotted coach time. This is particularly true if they are working with overseas laymen hosts who may map out their day's activities with no real understanding of just how much can be squeezed into a day when moving a group, which often results in long and arduous days running well into the night.

In addition to the statement of what is and is not included in the trip, it is imperative to have a clearly worded **conditions statement** covering such things as final payment date, last date to make any changes in individual travel plans; and financial penalties for cancellations, changes, or breaking away from the group.

Although vacation tour travelers have grown accustomed to the need to adhere to certain group restrictions, the independent business traveler is accustomed to changing travel plans frequently as business needs dictate. Those people in the travel industry who work with commercial accounts are well aware of business travelers who may change their travel arrangements, request refunds, and rebook almost daily. Many of these same business travelers, on joining a group project, are surprised to learn that they may be penalized if they make changes or cancel. I have worked on projects of this nature where participants have notified me virtually on the eve of departure that they are not going and are sending a substitute from their firm. They seem genuinely amazed when it is pointed out to them that their visa and their APEX air tickets are not transferrable!

Note that one of the additional roles you play is that of liaison with overseas contacts on behalf of the group. For example, you may find yourself dealing with the commercial attaché at the U.S. Embassy in a particular city overseas, as this individual may be the pipeline to the local business community with whom your group wishes to meet in that city. If you are including a social function on tour to which overseas business dignitaries and key people are invited, it may very well be that the invitations to the "right people" can be initiated by the Embassy. Many times the contacts with overseas business leaders will originate with the sponsoring business organization here at home on their letterhead to give it legitimacy, but the follow-through work will fall in your lap, since the business leaders here will not have the time in their busy schedules (or perhaps the know-how) to complete the matter and work out the many minute details involved to see it through to completion.

OVERSEAS STUDY PROGRAMS

Arranging study tours, overseas campuses, or other such educational travel projects is an exciting venture into a new arena. It's an arena into which most travel agents and tour planners have not stepped—**academia**.

Perhaps they are convinced that there is no money to be made in this arena, under the illusion that all students are nineteen years old and travel with a backpack or that all professors are shopping for the cheapest deal in airfares and Eurail passes and nothing more.

Fortunately for those who have entered this field, these perceptions are not necessarily true. Although overseas study tours or in-residence campus programs often are not high-priced products, many of them do attract a moderate-income participant. This is usually the participant who is looking for a trip or overseas living experience with educational overtones. Often it is the client who is well read and somewhat traveled, now looking for a new experience. Many want to stay in one city or country for a while and experience it in depth rather than join another three-week whirlwind rat race. Many are interested in one particular field, whether it's art, theatre, or learning a foreign language.

Some are teachers or educators themselves, who are anxious to increase their knowledge, to give themselves a new reservoir of material with which to return home and face the new academic year, or to earn teacher's salary increments often granted for continuing education. Still others may simply be those adults who wish to expand their travel and intellectual horizons but don't quite know how to go about it on an independent basis.

The possibilities in this field are endless. For example:

❑ *The small, privately escorted tour*, revolving around one key academic person, often a professor or noted expert, selling to his or her own following. (See Figure 16.3.)

❑ *A complete series of tours for a local college or university*, officially sponsored by the college. These tours are often to a variety of destinations and draw on instructors from a variety of academic disciplines who may escort the trips and teach their specialties enroute. Usually, the success of such a program requires a fairly sizable off-campus promotional campaign to attract sufficient numbers. Typically, such a program will fall under the jurisdiction of the college's summer session or continuing education division and will be announced in the appropriate catalog of courses, with the bulk of the participants coming from throughout the country, and not necessarily from a local market, much less from a local professor's following or from the students on one campus.

❑ *The overseas campus.* Just as in the previous example, this, too, may be under the auspices of one academic institution in the United States but will draw its clientele from across the country. But, rather than being a moving tour, it will feature an in-residence program in one place overseas—perhaps actually on campus, utilizing off-season dormitory space or a private home residence program.

Some programs may be for the summer months only. Others may be for a full semester or even the full academic year. Most carry academic credit through the sponsoring educational institution in the United States. Such programs usually involve weekly classes while overseas, with weekend field trips and then optional post-session tours. Most are geared to college-age or adult travelers, although there are some good high school (and even occasional elementary school) programs.

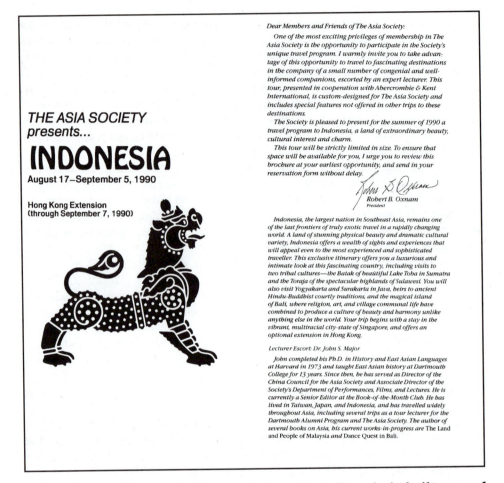

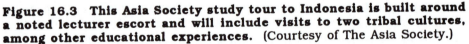

Figure 16.3   This Asia Society study tour to Indonesia is built around a noted lecturer escort and will include visits to two tribal cultures, among other educational experiences. (Courtesy of The Asia Society.)

Attempting to work in this market requires a strong understanding of the world of academia and feeling comfortable discussing undergraduate versus graduate units, salaries of full professors versus associate professors, and the whys and wherefores of out-of-state tuition fees, transferral of academic credits, or ADA (average daily attendance) funds. It is helpful to have an understanding of academic institutions' financial needs to provide programs that generate revenue for them. It is also helpful to understand how such a successful travel and study program can enhance the reputation of an academic institution and excite faculty wishing to be affiliated with it.

In this type of program, as in the trade mission, your role will be that of true business adviser to the project. Businesspeople, who make up the bulk of trade mission programs, are aware of the needs for a businesslike arrangement, for promotion, and for upfront financial expenditures. But academia often is blissfully unaware of many of the business and financial facts of life behind a successful travel-study program. They may assume that all they have to do is announce the project in their school catalog and it will sell itself. They may be genuinely amazed to learn that a promotional campaign is necessary, that the company has to supply upfront monies on their behalf for ads and brochures, and is in fact investing in a risk venture on their behalf. In fact, some may even be offended if you ask that they share in this financial risk.

Typically, handling such a project means individual client counseling (usually by phone and correspondence) with each of the participants. Although the school sponsors the project, at least from the academic point of view, its personnel do not have the time or knowledge to counsel or sell prospective passengers. Although you will want to refer specific academic questions to the school, all other client handling will fall to you, including individual billings, information bulletins, and liaison with the school to mail out preregistration materials, reading lists, and other academic materials. Therefore, strong and detailed backup personnel in the office will be needed, since you are not dealing with one entity, one client (the school), but rather with many (the individual participants).

INCENTIVE TRAVEL

The incentive trip is totally different from the previously discussed groups. Here there is one client only—the corporation buying your company's services. Although ultimately there may be several hundred travelers in the group, still the overhead corporation is the only client. It makes the decisions. It pays the bills.

An incentive trip is given by a corporation to its top producers as recognition for a job well done. This is the insurance company that sends its one hundred top salespeople on a seven-day cruise. This is the automobile manufacturer inviting the 50 top dealers and their spouses to Hawaii. It is called an **incentive trip** because the trip is the carrot dangled in front of the salesperson (and often the spouse) all year long as the *incentive* to do a better job. This better job may be to sell more cars, to increase overall production figures a certain percentage over the preceding year, or to reach a certain monetary sales volume. In other words, the terms of the contest may vary but the contest always exists.

For years, large corporations sponsored such incentive trips for their sales forces, and these trips usually were handled by the giant incentive houses such as The E.F. MacDonald Company, Maritz, S & H Motivation and Travel, and others. In fact, incentive travel was only a small percentage of the total incentive picture; by far the biggest portion was in merchandise—stereos, televisions, cars, and furniture.

But travel is becoming more and more the preferred "carrot" to dangle in front of the salesperson. Qualifying for a company's incentive trip brings recognition among one's peers, labeling the winner as successful. Travel is a benefit that endures for life; it is not like the car that is surpassed by a newer model next year or the household gadget that has broken down by the time next year's sales contest rolls around.

Travel is seen more and more as a motivating force; also, it is no longer associated with just the larger corporations. Many small corporations now consider travel as its annual sales motivation tool, and they are open to proposals for interesting and innovative trips. Moreover, many travel companies, once they have had a thorough grounding in other types of group travel, are venturing into these waters.

This kind of business is just right for the travel counselor with a high sense of theatre, innovative thinking and creativity. Here is an opportunity to design theme-night banquets complete with show, music, and Hollywood stars. Tony Bennett was the surprise star at a recent insurance company incentive in San Francisco, walking on stage to the strains of "I Left My Heart In San Francisco"—all to the gasps of the amazed insurance salesperson guests. Sophisticated treasure hunts, private limo airport pickups, samba shows, fabulous awards banquets, and schooner cruises all can form part of an unforgettable incentive tour package—a package which thanks the attendees for a job well done and which whets their appetite for the job to be done in the future. In fact, a feature of many incentive tours is advance notice of next year's fabulous incentive destination. Another feature of typical incentive tours may be the unveiling of a new product that the sponsoring company is bringing into its line for sales in the coming season.

The bottom line on all these incentive trips is to "wow" the winners and make the sponsoring corporation and its hierarchy look good in the eyes of the attendees—no matter what it takes out of you in the way of special requests (e.g., a midnight private transfer to the airport for a company director, special treatment for a company VIP by the hotel staff, a last-minute engraved recognition plaque for an individual overlooked). To handle incentives means being on call 24-hours a day while the trip is in progress. It means knowing resources to fill the most impossible demands.

If you are attempting to attract incentive travel business, it is good to remember that you will not only assume the role of business consultant, tour operator, and travel agent to the project, but also that of marketing expert par excellence. One job is to put together an exciting, attractive travel package within the client corporation's budget, and ultimately to operate it successfully in the field. But your prime job is to act as marketing and motivational leader throughout the entire campaign before the trip. If the client's salespeople are not inspired to get out there and sell more insurance or more cars (thus earning their corporation the necessary additional profits out of which to pay the tab for the trip), the trip does not stand on its own financially. The corporation has bought the idea only because it was convinced that the revenues from the additional sales or productivity within the corporation will more than cover the cost of the prize(s)—that is, the trip.

To keep salespeople selling insurance over a year's time, through thick and thin, ups and downs takes some doing. They need to be revved up, patted on the head, coerced, seduced, and convinced that they can make it—that success lies just around the corner, that this trip is something that they (and their spouses) really want in the worst way and cannot buy elsewhere.

It will mean preparing endless promotional mail pieces for the salespeople striving to earn the free trip, perhaps showing films or even doing a song-and-dance act. I have sent chopsticks (with instructions on how to use them) to groups striving for Hong Kong. Talk with anyone in the incentive field; they will tell stories of mailing out giant fortune cookies with custom-written messages inside, of sending singing telegrams, or of mailing hundreds of postcards postmarked from the overseas city of the incentive destination. A fertile imagination and many extra hours of involvement are musts for the success of an incentive project.

SPECIAL-INTEREST TOURS

Perhaps, in a sense, all the kinds of travel projects mentioned in this chapter may be seen as *special-interest* in that none of them is your straight "If It's Tuesday, This Must Be Belgium" tour.

Yet, to the trade, a **special interest tour** has come to mean a tour that truly revolves around a very special interest and is marketed to those with that interest. In this category falls wine and gourmet tours, agricultural tours, opera and theatre trips, and certainly **adventure travel**. The last has almost become a case of the tail wagging the dog, and most catalogs of special-interest tours today are dominated by treks in Nepal, white-river rafting in the western United States, and backpacking in Peru.

There is also now a sub-specialty of adventure travel called *soft adventure* (as opposed to hard adventure). These are trips that offer adventurous off-the-beaten-track itineraries but that do not necessarily involve "roughing it." Often, they stay in inns or hotels instead of camping. Hiking may be an optional daytime activity, returning to the base hotel at the end of the day, thus permitting the tour members who don't feel up to hiking a particular day to remain in town. Soft adventure trips may often include cruises to unusual areas such as the Amazon or Galápagos Islands, but on non-luxury vessels accompanied by naturalist guides. Soft adventure trips are often the natural maturation process of an adventure tour company that wishes to retain its clients as they, in turn, mature. This type of clientele often grows to expect more comfort but still wants a trip with educational or naturalist content.

Study Spanish in Avila, Spain

June 23-July 7, 1993

through Vista Community College
Berkeley, California

Vista opens doors.

Figure 16.4 This group program to study Spanish in Avila, Spain will appeal to a small "special-interest" group. (Courtesy of Vista Community College.)

There seem to be four strong characteristics of special-interest trips and the companies and people who operate them. First, the trip revolves totally around the interest, whatever it may be. The special interest is strong, almost all-consuming; and transportation, accommodations, and other tour services wrap themselves around this paramount interest. Rarely is it the other way around, wherein occasional special-interest activities are merely dropped into a regulation tour. In fact, that is often a sign of a phony special-interest tour.

Second, most special-interest tour companies are the outgrowth of the efforts of one or two key individuals, often idealists with a great love for a certain sport or activity—individuals who want others to share in the experience. Often they have learned the travel business merely as a means of bringing their particular interest or philosophy or passion to others, whether it's skin diving, a love for the opera, or a love for fine cuisine.

Perhaps the founder of a West Coast tour company specializing in opera tours had no intention of going into travel, but as a lecturer on Wagner, he found that forming groups of opera buffs and taking them to European opera festivals was a natural outgrowth of the teaching process. Similarly, the founder of one of the early diving specialty tour companies found a way to combine his great love for Tahiti and diving with a background as a retail travel agent. Another individual started organizing South Pacific tours that stayed in villages and lived with the local people. This was an idealistic and personal experience in which he once had participated and that he wanted to make available to a limited segment of the travel public who would appreciate the close human contact involved in such a travel program. These three people typify those who are behind many of the special-interest travel companies that have come to the fore.

Third, the key person in most of these companies is an expert in the special interest; this person is able to answer the client's most sophisticated questions about types of ski boots or diving equipment and able to train staff to do likewise, thus he or she does not depend on outside experts for the answers.

Fourth, many of these companies have elected to sell directly to the public as well as act as a wholesaler and sell through travel agencies, rather than to rely solely on retail travel agencies for their success. They find that a great many retail travel agencies do not handle individual client sales well on special-interest trips, since the agency sales staff may not have the necessary background in hiking, Wagner, French wine vintages, or whatever the tour specialty may be. (Many travel agents have stated that they resent selling a client on a tour with such a company, since they feel the company will steal their client and get him/her to book direct next time, thus pushing the retail agent out of the picture and thus representing a loss of income in the future). If there is someone on staff who is truly an expert in a particular field, you may want to attempt using that person's expertise and putting together a special-interest tour. If not, it is best to book through an operator who is familiar with that particular field.

One word of caution—since these special-interest tours revolve around the interest, it is of primary importance to be able to provide what one promises. Just because you are an opera buff and have gone to the Bayreuth festival every year, if you do not know the ropes for securing group seats to the festival and cannot truly come through with the tickets, it is best not to attempt it in the first place! Many knowledgeable, well-meaning operators have virtually been ruined by not being able to provide the Super Bowl tickets, the seats to La Scala, or the grandstand positions for the Carnival in Rio parade that their brochures offered. Therefore, before agreeing to take on such a tour, it's wise to ascertain how you will secure such tickets, what upfront non-refundable monies you may have to risk to obtain them, and what other surrounding requirements may be attached to the tickets (such as purchasing a minimum number of days' land tour in conjunction with the tickets from a certain operator, and so forth).

THE FUTURE?

It is obvious that the market is rife with possibilities and exciting kinds of travel projects. We have seen incentives and special-interest programs, nostalgia cruises promising Big Band dancing to music of the '40s, and overseas professional meetings with flair. Group projects have been developed to attend foreign cooking schools, to learn to sail in Caribbean waters, or to ride horseback and cook out in the backwoods.

What will be next no one really knows. But an imaginative and innovative person with a good solid group tour background may have the ideas that will be the next contribution to this constantly changing travel industry. The industry will welcome these ideas.

❑ SUMMARY

There are many exciting group travel possibilities. These include such specialty trips as meetings and conventions, trade missions, overseas study programs, incentives, and a broad range of what are termed special-interest tours. Each has its own particular requirements and method of handling. It is suggested that these be looked at as future possibilities for the group operator who already has experience in operating and marketing group travel programs.

❑ REVIEW QUESTIONS

1. **What is the difference between hard adventure and soft adventure travel?**

2. **Why is sightseeing not stressed on a trade mission?**

3. **Who pays the bill for an incentive trip?**

4. **What personal capabilities are helpful to a person going into the incentive travel business?**

5. **What is the basic purpose of a trade mission?**

6. **Where would you start looking for business for a potential trade mission?**

7. **Why do salespeople find a trip more attractive as an incentive for a job well done over the year than tangible products?**

8. **Name one problem you may encounter in dealing with business travelers participating in a group travel program.**

9. **Why do many people in the travel industry overlook the possibilities of dealing in the academic market?**

10. **Name four major requirements for handling large conventions.**

❑ *ACTIVITIES*

1. You have been asked to put together a trekking tour to the Andes. Contact several specialty tour companies that operate this type of tour and compare the programs they offer.

2. Talk to someone in the business community. Interview this person to find out what they would require in the way of services if you were going to handle a meeting or convention for them. Then estimate what your company's profit might be on such a project if you were really to operate it for them.

3. Select a destination for an incentive tour. Then write a sales "pep" piece (a postcard or letter or some other type of item that can be sent through the mail). The tone of the piece should be to enthuse the salespeople who are striving to earn their free trip.

GLOSSARY

A academic market–That segment of the marketplace whose travel dates and travel plans revolve around the academic calendar, such as teachers, students, school administrators, and the like. Prime prospects for study abroad programs, summer session trips, tours and cruises with intellectual enrichment or college credit.

ACs–Author's corrections. In preparing tour brochures and similar printed promotional materials, refers to corrections initiated by the author, thus incurring additional expense.

accordion fold–A method of folding paper so that it opens like the pleats in an accordion. May be used for a tour brochure or a direct mail letter if the printer has the necessary equipment.

account executive–Person responsible for the management of a client's account. Often used today in place of "sales representative."

acquisition cost–The cost of acquiring something. For example, the cost of acquiring an inquiry regarding a tour might be the advertising cost divided by the number of inquiries the ad generated, resulting in the advertising cost per inquiry.

add-on–A supplementary charge, for example the extra airfare charged from the home city to the published tour gateway city.

adjoining rooms–Rooms or cabins sharing a common wall, not necessarily connected by a common door. See also **connecting rooms**.

adventure travel–Trips designed for the active traveler often including hiking, trekking, white-water rafting, camping, rock climbing, or other similar activity. Typified by out-of-doors rather than city tourism. See **hard adventure, soft adventure.**

affinity group–Membership organization, such as a school, business, trade association, religious group, club, or other organized membership entity, which may sponsor group travel programs.

after-the-fact monies–Promotional monies received by a tour operator from a supplier only if a tour project has materialized.

air/sea–Travel programs or itineraries using some combination of both air and sea transportation. In cruises refers to flying the passengers to/from the ship, which is positioned elsewhere. Sometimes also called fly/cruise.

à la carte–Each food item on a menu is prepared, priced, and ordered separately. As opposed to limited choice, a fixed menu, or table d'hote. Usually an indication of a higher priced, deluxe tour.

allotment–In tourism, a certain number of rooms, cruise cabins, airplane seats, etc., which the tour operator may retain for free sale until a specified date, at which time the operator must submit a manifest of names and release unsold space. Does not imply responsibility to sell the entire allotment. See also **block; bulk buying.**

amenity package–A cluster of special features, for example, complimentary shore excursions, bar or boutique credit, or wine at dinner offered to clients on a given tour or cruise, usually as a bonus or extra feature. Usually used to induce clients to book through a particular travel agency or organization.

American plan (AP)–Hotel accommodations including three meals per day in the price of the room. Usually means breakfast in accordance with the custom of the country concerned, plus full lunch and dinner, which may be set menu or may be limited to a specific monetary value. The hotel may require meals to be taken in certain dining rooms or only at certain times. See also **full pension.**

AP–See American plan

APEX (Advance Purchase Excursion) airfare–Special promotional roundtrip airfare. It must be paid for and issued within a stated time before departure, and often cannot be cancelled, changed, or reissued without penalty. Other restrictions often apply.

ARC (Airlines Reporting Corporation)–Membership organization made up of United States domestic airlines. An administrative body, appointing sales agents (travel agencies and others), making available the area settlement bank for airline ticket sales reporting/payments, and many other functions previously administered by the Air Traffic Conference (ATC), which was eliminated January 1, 1985. See **ATC.**

arunk (arrival unknown)–Often used in a passenger's airline itinerary to refer to a surface segment being traveled by rail, ship, or motorcoach for example or noncontiguous sector for which no flight is provided.

ASTA (American Society of Travel Agents)–Trade association of United States travel agents and tour operators, which includes international and allied memberships for trade-associated industries.

ATC (Air Traffic Conference)–Formerly a division of the Air Transport Association responsible for setting standards and establishing agreements regulating activities of domestic airlines among themselves, with international carriers, and with the travel industry in general. Eliminated January 1, 1985. See **ARC.**

B **back-to-back**–A series of tours or charter flights wherein one group leaves as the next one arrives. The group operator uses the carrier in both directions, thus avoiding dead-head expenses.

ballpark figure–A rough, advance financial estimate, not to be interpreted as final or as a commitment.

bid–(1)(Noun) An offer to perform a certain service at a certain price. For example, a printer offering to print a tour brochure at a specified price or a tour operator offering to operate a certain tour at a specified price. Usually based on detailed specifications. (2) (Verb) To bid on a certain job, tour, project as to offer to undertake it at a specific price under certain specifications.

blackout–A period during which a certain fare, rate, or offer is not valid, as for example during the Christmas holidays or some other peak period.

bleed–A term signifying that the printed image or color extends beyond the final edge of the paper. More expensive than a "nonbleed" because paper must be over-sized and then trimmed down.

block–A number of rooms or seats reserved far in advance, usually by wholesalers or group tour operators, who intend to sell them as components of tour packages. See also allotment.

blow-up–A larger version of an illustration, particularly a photo.

blueline–A proof for a brochure, flyer, or similar material presented to the client after the job has been photographed, but prior to printing. Appears in various shades of blue only, not in the actual colors of ink in which the job will be printed. Used for one-color and two-color printing jobs, not for full-color (four-color) jobs.

body copy–Basic printed information in a tour brochure or ad, as opposed to the head-lines, photos, or art.

boldface–A heavier, darker type, often used for headlines or paragraph sub-heads in a tour brochure or ad.

breakage–Expenses budgeted for in a tour but not used or expended, thus resulting in additional profit to the tour operator. For example, meals budgeted but not consumed, currency fluctuations in favor of the tour operator, or the tour selling much larger numbers of passengers than anticipated.

brochure–Printed promotional literature offered by a tourism business. Usually implies a printed, folded piece as opposed to a one-page flyer or poster.

bulk buying–Buying in quantity. Often implies assuming risk for selling an entire block of seats, rooms, etc.

bulk fare–Net fare contract for a specified number of seats. The tour operator contracting for these seats assumes the risk of selling them, as in a charter.

bulk mail–Third class mail, requiring a special bulk mail permit number, zipcode sorting, and a certain minimum number of pieces.

C   **CAB (Civil Aeronautics Board)**–At one time, the United States government regulatory body designated under the Federal Aviation Act to consider aviation matters affecting the public convenience and necessity, including supervision of routes, passenger and cargo fares, conditions of service, and schedules. Phased out January 1, 1985.

cabin assignment–Actual assignment of a client's specific cabin location on a cruise. Gives deck and actual room number. Normally assigned by the cruise line close-in to departure date as opposed to previous guarantee of space by category and price only.

cabin category–Cruise line's division of the various cabins on its ship into pricing categories, so that all cabins within a given category carry the same tariff. May vary by deck or aft/fore location, with tub or merely with shower.

calendaring–The act of carefully posting important dates on your calendar so that no task related to the operation of a group travel program is overlooked.

camera-ready–A brochure, flyer, or similar material completed to the point of being ready to photograph.

capacity-controlled–Space on a particular flight apportioned among different fare bases with a limited number of seats for sale in each fare category.

caption–Copy accompanying and explaining photos or illustrations.

cash flow–Monies available to meet the tour operator's daily operating expenses, as opposed to equity, accounts receivable, or other credits not immediately accessible.

charter–To hire by contract the entire capacity of an aircraft, motorcoach, cruise ship, or train.

classified advertising–Small print ads, listed by category, and usually without illustrations, as in the "classified" ad section of a newspaper or magazine. See also **display advertising.**

CLIA (Cruise Lines International Association)–An association of cruise lines seeking to promote cruises by offering promotional materials, training guides, and educational programs for travel agents. Also administers the functions previously administered by the Pacific Cruise Conference (PCC) and the International Passenger Ship Association (IPSA), such as appointments of new travel agencies.

client load–The number of clients one travel counselor can reasonably and effectively handle at a given time.

clip art–Pre-prepared art that can be used in preparing ads, flyers, or tour brochures. May be purchased from an art service or sometimes obtained from a supplier, such as a cruise line or airline.

clipping service–A subscription service that keeps track of and clips samples of the client company's ads and editorial mentions in newspapers, magazines, flyers, and other publications. Often a function of a public relations firm.

closeout–Finalization of a tour, cruise, or other similar group travel project, after which time no further clients are accepted, any unsold air or hotel space is released, and final passenger lists and payments are sent to all suppliers.

coach–(1) in railroads, a car for ordinary daytime short-haul travel; (2) in airplanes, the economy class section as opposed to first class or business class; (3) a motorcoach or deluxe bus.

cold list–A mailing list untried by a particular advertiser, as in a direct-mail list of names and addresses that one might purchase to solicit group tour or cruise clients.

color key–A printer's proof presented to the client prior to printing, showing all colors in place. Used for full-color (four-color) process.

complimentary ("Comp")–Free. A product or service (e.g., a night's lodging, a drink, or a dinner) given without charge, in recognition of past patronage, a promise of future patronage, or to rectify some mistake. In group business, usually the free trip accrued with the airlines, hotels, and other suppliers as a result of producing a given number of passengers in the group, may be passed on to the tour organizer. See **TC**.

concierge–Employee in many major hotels, especially in Europe, often multilingual, who is in charge of personalized guest services such as dinner reservations, theatre tickets, and letter mailing.

connecting rooms–Rooms or cabins that share a common wall and connecting door. See also **adjoining rooms.**

consortium–An affiliation of many privately owned companies so as to secure bulk-buying power, over-ride commissions and other leverage with suppliers. Many small and mid-size travel agencies now doing this to maximize their profits and to compete effectively with larger travel agencies or chains.

consumer disclosure notice–See responsibility clause.

consumer protection plan–A default protection plan to protect travelers who may lose their monies should their tour services, purchased through member companies in the plan, default. For example, in the United States the plans of the United States Tour Operators' Association, the American Society of Travel Agents, and the National Tour Association.

continental plan–Hotel room that includes both the use of the room and a light breakfast consisting of a beverage, toast or rolls, and sometimes juice.

convention–(1) business or professional meeting, usually of large numbers of people. The term congress is a common term outside the United States; (2) an international agreement on a specific matter, especially the outcome of a meeting.

co-op advertising–A cooperative arrangement in which a supplier and a tour operator or travel agency share the cost of placing an ad.

copy–The written material for a brochure, flyer, ad or similar promotional material. Includes body copy and headlines.

copy fitting–Determining what copy will fit in a certain amount of space on a piece to be printed. When writing a tour brochure, writing the copy to fit the particular space and layout restrictions of a shell or original brochure.

costing–Process of itemizing and calculating all costs the tour operator will pay on a particular tour. Usually the function of the operations manager. See also **pricing**.

crop–The process of selecting the most interesting portion of a photo or illustration for impact and eliminating the rest.

CRS (Computer Reservation Service)–Refers to the airline reservations system a travel agency or tour operator has elected to use in-house. For example, Sabre (American Airlines), Apollo (United Airlines), etc.

CRT (Cathay ray tube)–Refers to airline computer terminal screen used by most retail travel agents.

cruise–Voyage for pleasure rather than for transport, often departing from and returning to the same port.

customized–Custom-designed, drawn up to satisfy the specific wishes of a client or client organization. For example, designing a customized itinerary made-to-order for a traveler or group rather than selling an existing, standard itinerary. Particularly common when dealing with special-interest groups and designing itineraries around the particular interest of the client organization. Usually more expensive than buying standard existing packages.

D   DBA (Doing Business As)–Used wherein the business name differs from the corporate name. For example, LSI Travel Agency, Inc. DBA Specialty Tours Abroad.

deadhead–Aircraft or other transportation vehicle operating empty, without a payload of passengers or cargo. Usually done to reposition the vehicle.

deck plan–Visual layout of each of the decks of a cruise ship indicating location of various public rooms as well as various cabin numbers and their layout.

demi-pension–Half board. Hotel rate including bed, breakfast, and a choice of one other meal—lunch or dinner. Breakfast is in accordance with the custom of the country concerned (not necessarily full American breakfast). Lunch or dinner is usually on a set menu or *table d'hote* basis, not *à la carte*. The hotel may require that meals be taken in certain dining rooms or only at certain times.

deregulation–The act of deregulating the travel industry, specifically the Airline Deregulation Act of 1978, amending the Federal Aviation Act of 1958. Provided for the end of the Civil Aeronautics Board's (CAB) regulating authority over domestic airlines on January 1, 1985, for removing travel agency exclusivity, thus paving the way for carriers to appoint and pay commissions to nontravel agents, and for removal of antitrust immunity for travel agents.

desktop publishing–A method of preparing camera-ready material to be published, such as ads, flyers, and brochures, utilizing an in-house system of computer keyboarding, page layout and graphics, thus avoiding using a graphic artist and typesetter.

diluted revenue–A term usually used by a supplier to signify sale of a company's product at less than its normal profit. For example, an airfare offered to a tour operator at a very low net fare (or with an unusually high commission on the gross), thus resulting in less profit to the supplier.

direct mail–A form of advertising that reaches the individual through the postal services, usually third class.

display advertising–A form of advertising distinguished from classified advertising by the use of illustrations, white space, headlines, and other attention-getting devices.

double–Sleeping room provided with a double bed. Sometimes erroneously used to mean any room accommodating two persons, as in a twin-bedded room. See also **twin.**

double double–Hotel or motel room with two double beds. Found mostly in the United States.

double occupancy–The rate per person if sharing a twin-bedded or double bed room. The usual published tour price.

downline–All segments (legs) of an air itinerary after the originating flight.

draw–(1) a famous name or individual who will attract or draw clientele to the travel program with which he or she is associated; (2) an advance of funds to a commissioned sales person against later actual sales and commissions.

dummy–The layout for a brochure or booklet. Also sometimes called a mockup.

duotone–A photograph reproduced in two colors, usually black and one other color. An effective way to give additional depth or warmth to a photo in a tour brochure.

Dylux–A trademark name for the more generic term blueline.

E **ecotourism**–The marriage of tourism and ecology awareness, providing trips to ecologically sensitive areas such as the Amazon rain forest, the cloud forests of Costa Rica, the Pantanal region of Brazil, etc.

errors and omissions insurance–Coverage should travel company's staff make an error causing a client great hardship or expense. Travel industry's equivalent of malpractice insurance. Referred to as E and O.

ETA–Estimated time of arrival.

ETD–Estimated time of departure.

European plan (EP)–Hotel accommodations with no meals included in the price of the room.

ex–Out of, departing from. As in ex SFO or from San Francisco.

F **fam trip**–Familiarization trip/tour. Trip or tour offered to travel writers and travel agency personnel by airlines, cruise lines, and other suppliers as a way of informing the customer and influencing segments of the industry.

fare quote–A price on a specific route or air itinerary, as quoted by the airline concerned. In today's deregulated market, may mean a negotiated airfare lower than market price and guaranteed by written fare quote number.

fax–Facsimile transmission of a visual message (type or art) via the telephone wires. Very widely used in the travel industry, particularly to expedite international correspondence.

final documents–Final materials sent to a client after payment in full, enabling him or her to make the trip. May include air tickets, cruise tickets, rail tickets, tour vouchers, baggage tags, name badge, departure instruction bulletin, list of participants in the tour, and mailing lists to leave with friends and family.

finish–The texture or feel of paper to be used for tour brochures or other printed promotional pieces.

FIT (Foreign Independent Tour)–An international preplanned, pre-booked, and prepaid trip with the itinerary and components planned to the traveler's specifications. Custom-designed itinerary, as opposed to buying an existing travel package.

fixed expenses–Expenses related to the tour as a whole, which do not vary with the number of passengers in the group. For example: promotional costs, tour manager's expenses, charters, and so forth. See also **variable expenses**.

float–Amount of money represented by checks outstanding, in process of collection. Monies advanced in lump sum to a supplier toward future bills.

flop–To turn a photo over and print it so that it is the mirror image of the original. Particularly pertinent to using photos in tour brochures or ads so that the photo faces inward, directing the reader's eye to the brochure or ad rather than facing outward to the edge.

flush–To set printed copy even with other copy that is lined up vertically. Flush left means that the left edge of the copy is aligned, but the right edge (ragged right) may not be. A solid even box of copy would be flush left and right. Flush right means that the right edge of the copy is aligned.

fly/cruise–See air/sea

flyer–Printed advertising distributed to potential customers by hand or by mail. Usually fairly simple in format, as opposed to a brochure, which is more complex and detailed.

force majeure–From the French, literally a stronger force. In the context of a tour operator's responsibility clause, referring to something beyond one's control, as in an act of God.

four-color process–A printing process that produces full color photos, art, and graphics. Allows the designer to make full use of all colors of the rainbow in the design and to use color transparencies instead of black-and-white photos. Most expensive brochure method; usually beyond the budget of the average small tour operator.

free sale–Available for sale without having to call and request space. Automatic availability. See **sell and report**.

full pension–Full board. Hotel rate including bed, breakfast, and two principal meals. Breakfast is in accordance with the custom of the country concerned (not necessarily full American breakfast). Lunch and dinner are usually on a set menu or *table d'hote* basis, not *à la carte*. The hotel may require that meals be taken in certain dining rooms or only at certain times.

G **galley proof**–Initial printer's proof, often in long column or "galley" form as opposed to a "page proof," with type laid out as it will appear on the finished page with headlines and illustrations indicated.

GIT (Group Inclusive Tour) Airfare–A special promotional airfare available to tour operators to utilize as a group tour basing fare in conjunction with a *prepaid* land package. Similar to the ITX fare, but for groups only. A restricted fare with limitations on such things as number of days, stopovers permitted, and minimum numbers of passengers required to qualify as a group. Requires that all group members travel on the same flights throughout the international portion of the journey.

glossy finish–A shiny finish, coated paper stock, as opposed to a matte finish.

graphic artist–An individual skilled in coordinating a promotional piece and its components: original art, clip art, typesetting, design, pasteup, photo selection and cropping, etc. Particularly accustomed to working with printers in the practical workaday world of commercial art. Acts as a contractor for the client, pulling all parts together to produce the final promotional piece—a brochure, flyer, ad, etc.

gross rate–Rate prior to deducting the commission. See also **net, net net**.

ground operator–See **receptive services operator**.

group desk–Desk or department within an airline that handles group reservations. Not to be confused with the airline's tour desk.

guarantee–Holding a reservation by giving a client's credit card number as a "guarantee" that the client will appear, for example, with a hotel property. The understanding is that if the client does not appear, the supplier in question will charge the client's credit card for the service whether utilized or not.

guide–Person licensed (wherein necessary) and employed to take tourists on local sightseeing excursions. Not to be confused with the tour manager, escort, leader, or director. See **step-on guide**.

H **halftone**–Printer's term for a photo or illustration. Refers to a method of rephotographing the photo or illustration through a screen so it may be reproduced.

hard adventure–Adventure travel of an active nature, designed for hardy travelers in good physical condition. In addition to physical activity throughout the itinerary, may also include "roughing it" style sleeping arrangements.

hospitality desk–A desk or series of tables, usually in the lobby area of a hotel or convention center, for a specific tour or convention. Staffed with individuals who provide such varied services as making dining suggestions, selling optional local tours, answering questions, etc.

Hotel and Travel Index–Quarterly publication listing over 30,000 hotels, resorts, motels, guest ranches, and lodges worldwide. Includes their addresses, telephone contact, and published rates. Published by Ziff-Davis Publishing Co., 1 Park Avenue, New York, NY 10016.

I **IATAN (International Air Transport Association Network)**–Worldwide association of international airlines.

inbound tourism–Receptive tourism, whether from other countries or other cities in our own country. Sometimes also called incoming tourism. Usually makes its profit on markup of net land arrangements, not on sale of air tickets.

incentive tour–Group travel program rewarding a client company's successful sales people with a bonus in the form of an expense-paid trip. Distinctive from other kinds of tours in that the entire bill is paid by the client company, not by the individual traveler. Such tours are usually short, to a single or limited destination, and may feature convention or learning activities such as classes, seminars, unveiling of a new product, awards, and so forth.

incidentals–Items understood to be excluded from most tours, cruises, or pre-packaged travel programs. Examples: cocktails, laundry, phone calls.

incoming tourism–See **inbound tourism**.

independent contractor–Person contractually retained by another to perform certain specific tasks. The other person has no control over the independent contractor other than as provided in the contract. In the context of group travel, a tour manager or tour brochure designer/writer might be retained in this capacity. Not to be interpreted legally as an employee but rather as self–employed.

in/out dates–Refers to arrival/departures dates in a hotel/motel. To avoid error, used in lieu of the term from date x to date x.

interline–Used in conjunction with another word to describe anything involving two or more airlines, such as interline itinerary, interline reservation, interline stopovers. See also **online**.

inventory control–System enabling the tour operator to keep track of the inventory of hotel rooms, flight reservations, and other suppliers' products he/she is holding for resale.

ITB (International Tourisme Bourse)–World's largest international tourism trade show, held annually in Berlin.

IT number (itinerary number)–Code number assigned to an international tour or package by the sponsoring/originating air carrier. Serves as an identity number to be printed on air tickets issued in conjunction with the tour or package in question, often serving to ensure additional commission to the travel agent issuing the air ticket and to ensure additional override commission to the wholesale tour operator whose tour package it is. Being phased out by many airlines since deregulation.

ITX (Independent Tour Excursion) airfare–Special promotional airfare available only in conjunction with a prepaid land package. Similar to the GIT fare, but available to passengers traveling independently.

L **layout**–Final arrangements of material to be reproduced by printing. A detailed plan, on paper, as a guide to a typesetter or printer, as for example a tour brochure or layout. Sometimes called a mock-up.

lead time–Advance time, length of time between initiating a tour and its departure date.

leg–Sector, segment of an itinerary.

legal clause–See responsibility clause or consumer disclosure notice.

line art–Artist's drawings, illustrations, graphics, etc. In printer's terms, refers to art which will be reproduced by the camera without screening.

lowercase–Small letters, as opposed to capital letters or uppercase. Signified by the initials l.c. when marking copy or reading printer's proofs.

M **MAAS**–Meet and assist. Often used to mean meet, greet, and facilitate at the airport but without a transfer into town. For example, meet a group arriving by one flight and assist them to connect to another departing flight.

manifest–Final official listing of all passengers and/or cargo aboard a transportation vehicle or vessel.

M–Thousand, as in 5M means five thousand.

MAP–See modified American plan.

margin–(1) Spare amount, measure, degree allowed for contingencies or special situations; (2) As in profit margin, the difference between the price one charges and what one pays out, earnings.

market segment–A limited portion of the total consumer market.

markup–A percentage of the net then added to the net cost to form the gross (sell price). Thus, the difference between the cost and the selling price of a given product (i.e., profit). Often confused with profit margin, which is calculated as a percentage of the gross. Example: $100 net price + 25% mark*up* on the net, or $25, = $125 sell price. (The $25 markup = only 20% of the $125 gross but 25% of the net).

matte finish–Rough or unglossy finish on a paper stock.

media release–Current term for news release or press release. Implies releasing news story to all type of media—the print media (magazines, newspapers), as well as the electronic media (TV, radio). See **news release.**

meet and greet–Pre-purchased service for meeting and greeting a client upon arrival in a city, usually at the airport, pier, or rail station, and assisting the client with entrance formalities, collecting baggage, and obtaining transportation to his or her hotel or other destination. Often includes an arrival gift such as a lei. Often associated with arrival transfer service. Sometimes referred to as meet and assist (MAAS).

meeting planner–An individual particularly skilled in all of the details of putting together a successful meeting for an organization or business. May work separately or within the framework of a travel agency.

mockup–See **layout.**

modified American plan (MAP)–Hotel accommodations including breakfast and either lunch or dinner in the price of the room. Usually means breakfast in accordance with the custom of the country concerned, plus one principal meal, either lunch or dinner, which may be set menu or limited to a specified monetary value. Originated in beach resorts in the Western Hemisphere, where the clientele did not wish to come in from the beach to dress for lunch, preferring to take only breakfast and dinner at the hotel. It may be required by the hotel that meals be taken in certain dining rooms or only at certain times to qualify for the plan. See also **American plan, demi-pension.**

montage–Combination of several pictures or parts of pictures into a single unit. May also be a blend of pictures plus art.

motorcoach–Deluxe bus designed to carry passengers in comfort; often includes a bathroom, air conditioning, microphone, and wrap-around windows for maximum viewing.

N **name draw**–A noted personality whose name when affiliated with a travel project, may draw people to join the trip.

negotiate–To confer with another so as to arrive at the settlement of some matter. In a group travel context, usually refers to discussions between tour operator and suppliers to obtain most favorable rates and conditions.

net–Rate after deducting the commission, but prior to adding applicable tax and service charge. See also **gross, net net.**

net net rate–Gross less commission plus applicable tax and service charge. Actual out-of-pocket amount to be paid for a given service or product. See also **gross, net.**

net rate–Confidential, wholesale rate that must be marked up for profit prior to resale to the customer. See also **gross, net net.**

networking–The act of using an interconnected or inter-related chain, group, or system. A method by which members of the travel profession become known among their peers for mutual self-help in referrals, locating new positions, locating worthy employees, making themselves visible and their talents known. Female version of the "Good Old Boys" club.

news release–Typed story about a forthcoming tour or travel program, submitted to various media sources such as newspapers, magazines, radio and television stations with the hope of receiving free publicity. Also called press release, or media release.

niche–Specialty, market segment. Often used as in "niche advertising" or "niche marketing", meaning a travel product not marketed to the general public but rather to a very specific, smaller segment of the potential market.

no-name–Practice of holding a space on a given flight, tour, or hotel room without giving the supplier a client's name. Usually means asking the supplier to hold the additional space "on faith" for a short period of time to allow you to sell it and submit the passenger's name, since once the space is released, it may be difficult to obtain it again.

NTA–National Tour Association.

O **OAG (Official Airline Guide)**–Monthly publication of flight schedules. Two versions available in the United States: Worldwide Edition and the North American Edition. Annual subscriptions available from Official Airline Guides, Inc., 2000 Clearwater Drive, Oak Brook, IL 60521.

occupancy rate–In hotel/motel industry, the percentage of total number of available beds or rooms actually occupied. Derived by dividing the total number of rooms occupied during a given time period (night, week, year) by the total number of rooms available for occupancy during the same period, to arrive at the occupancy percentage.

OHRG (Official Hotel and Resort Guide)–Three-volume worldwide directory of hotels, resorts, and motor hotels, edited especially for travel agents and related industries. Listings in geo-alpha order provide a description of the property, location, facilities, basic tariffs, commissions paid, rating information, and reservation information. Published by Ziff-Davis Publishing Co. Ordered from OHRG, P.O. Box 5800, Cherry Hill, NJ 08034.

online (intraline)–Used in conjunction with another word to describe anything over one airline only, such as online connection, online stopover, or online itinerary. See also **interline.**

opaque–Not allowing light to pass through. The opposite of transparent. Important to consider in selecting paper stock for a tour brochure or flyer.

operations–Performing the practical work of operating a tour or travel program. Usually involves the in-house control and handling of all phases of the tour, both with suppliers and with clients.

operations manager–Individual in charge of performing the practical and detailed work of tour operations. See **operations.**

option date–Date by which an extended offer will be withdrawn. For example, a tour space held on option for a client until a specified date may be released if the client has not paid a deposit by that date. Conversely, hotel space held on option for a tour operator may be released if the operator has not paid a deposit to the hotel by the stated option date.

organizer–An individual who recruits a group for travel purposes. Often called a "Pied Piper" or sometimes a "Name Draw."

originating airline–Airline carrying a passenger on the first portion of an itinerary. In group international travel, usually refers to the first international airline, also sometimes called the sponsoring or controlling airline of the particular tour group. The airline that obtains and controls all the downline continuing airspace. In group context, implies the sponsoring airline of the tour.

over-ride–Extra commission paid by suppliers such as airlines, cruise lines, and so forth to group tour operators as an incentive for group and volume business.

overtonnage–Phenomenon in the cruise industry in which there are too many ships in a given area or market. For example, overtonnage in the Caribbean in winter, or in Alaska in summer. Implies a competitive atmosphere.

OW–One-way travel, as opposed to roundtrip.

P   pacing–Fullness or emptiness, fastness or slowness of a tour itinerary. The scheduling of activities within an itinerary to make for a realistic operation and to give certain balance of travel time, sightseeing, social events, and free time and rest.

package–(1)(Noun) Pre-arranged combination of elements such as air, hotel, sightseeing, and social events packaged together and sold as an all-inclusive package price, not sold by component parts; (2) (Verb) to package, meaning to combine elements as above into an all-inclusive package product, sold as such at a package price.

page proof–A printer's proof with type laid out as it will appear on the finished page with headlines in place and areas indicated for illustrations and photos. See "galley proof."

PATA (Pacific Asia Travel Association)–Membership organization of government and private business that seeks to promote and monitor travel to and within the Pacific/Asia area. In addition to the overhead PATA, which accepts only organizations and government members, there also exist local chapters of PATA to which individuals may belong.

pax–Passengers.

per diem tour cost–Cost of the whole tour divided by the number of days to arrive at an average per day cost. Often the land/sea price (published price less air), divided by actual number of hotel nights to arrive at an average per night land cost. A method used within the travel industry to compare the cost of seemingly similar travel products.

Pied Piper–An individual with a following. Used in the travel industry to refer to a person who may recruit a group. See also **draw; organizer.**

plate–Originally a very thin layer of metal on a surface of base metal, nowadays usually plastic, as in a credit card. Distributed by airlines to travel agents appointed to represent them and then used by agents when issuing airline tickets on behalf of the participating airline concerned. In group tours it is customary to use the plate of the originating or controlling air carrier for the particular tour in question, even though a great many other airlines may be involved in the interline itinerary.

PMS colors (Pantone Matching System)–A standardized system of matching colors of ink; used by printers to assure exact color.

Pow Wow–United States' largest tourism trade show. Held annually at rotating venues. Primarily of interest to inbound tour operators and other United States suppliers interested in making their travel products known to overseas buyers. For the trade only; not open to the consumer.

preferred supplier or vendor–A supplier that a tour operator or travel agency may prefer to use due to preferential prearranged rates, overrides, or other volume considerations.

pre/post convention tour–Extension of a convention tour whereby, for an additional charge, extra days or destinations may be added to the beginning or end of a basic convention itinerary.

press release–See **media release; news release.**

pricing–Decision-making process of ascertaining what price to charge for a particular tour once total costs are known. Involves determining the markup, or profit margin, studying the competition, and evaluating the tour value for the price to be charged. Usually a management function. See also **costing.**

profit margin–The difference between what one pays out in expenses versus what one takes in as receipts (i.e., the profit). Usually expressed as a percentage of the sell price. See **margin, markup.**

promotional assistance–In travel industry terms, usually financial assistance from a supplier to the travel agency/tour operator. Can be in many different forms: cooperative advertising, free brochure shells, sharing direct-mail costs, and so forth.

promotional fare–Fare, lower in cost than normal fares, that may carry restrictions, be valid only on certain days, times, or flights, and require a minimum stay abroad or at the destination. Designed to attract passengers who may not otherwise travel, so usually aimed at the non-business traveler.

promotional evening–Social event to promote enrollments in a group tour, cruise, or other similar travel program.

proof–Sample of an ad, tour brochure, or other printed material supplied to the client prior to publishing so that the client may check for errors.

property–Hotel, motel, resort, or other place of lodging.

prorate–To divide, distribute, or assess proportionally.

protect–(1)(Verb) To obtain confirmed air, hotel or other such reservation protection when one's first choice is unable to confirm; (2) (Noun) Protect (with accent on the "pro"), meaning protection at a second choice when one's first choice is waitlisted.

Q   quote–(1)(Noun) A firm price; (2)(Verb) To offer a firm price.

R   rack rate–Regular published rate of a hotel or other tourism service. Highest rate.

rate desk–Department of an airline that fares various itinerary routes and issues written fare quotations to tour operators/travel agencies.

receptive services operator (RSO)–Person, firm, or corporation providing vehicles, guides, or local services to a tour operator or travel agent. Sometimes called a local operator, receiving agent, ground operator, reception agency, sub-contractor, land operator, inbound operator or destination management company. May be a division of a full-service retail travel agency, or only a receptive operator without air appointments or full-service travel agency ----capabilities.

receptive tourism–See **inbound tourism.**

reconfirm–In travel, usually refers to an airline's requirements that the passenger call the continuing airline of each flight segment and reconfirm enroute his/her intention to travel as planned.

release–(1)(Noun) Signed form giving the tour operator permission to use a person's name, picture, or statement in a tour promotion; (2) (Verb) to release space, as in returning unsold air reservations, cruise cabins, or hotel rooms to the supplier who originally allotted them.

responsibility clause–Detailed statement of conditions applicable to the sale of a tour package; one of the printed sections of a tour brochure. Often called the legal clause or consumer disclosure notice.

retroactive–Made effective as of a prior date.

reverse–A white on black print, as for example white type on a black background. Sometimes called a reverse-out by those in the graphics/printing trades.

review dates–Dates on which the supplier will ask to review the inventory of space a tour operator is holding and perhaps take back part or all of the space if it is not being sold quickly enough.

risk monies–Funds that one would not recoup should a tour not materialize. For example: nonrefundable deposits to suppliers, promotional expenditures, printing expenses.

room assignments–Placement of individual members of a tour group in specific rooms in a given hotel, resort, or other property. Usually, but not always, done by hotel personnel.

rooming list–List of names of passengers on a tour or other group travel program, submitted to a hotel, motel, or similar. Names are not alphabetized as on a flight manifest, but rather are listed room by room indicating who is rooming with whom. Twin-bedded rooms, singles, and triples are usually listed in separate categories.

RT–Roundtrip.

run-of-the-house rate (ROH)–Flat rate for which a hotel or other place of lodging agrees to offer any of its available rooms to a group. Final assignment of rooms is at the discretion of the hotel.

run-of-ship (ROS)–An arrangement wherein a cruise line agrees to offer its cabins at a flat rate rather than in a variety of price categories.

S **sales representative**–The employee of an airline, hotel, tour operator, cruise line, or other supplier who calls on travel agents, group operators, or potential group accounts. See also **account executive.**

sector–One part of a trip, travel between any two points on a multi-destination itinerary; also called a segment or leg.

segment–One part of a trip, travel between any two points on a multi-destination itinerary; also called a leg or sector.

sell and report–To be able to confirm automatically a reservation and then report it to the supplier, rather than having to request space prior to confirming. Not usually possible for groups. See **free sale.**

seminar–Educational or informational meeting. Used in the travel industry to signify a one-time learning situation wherein one learns about new travel products. Often sponsored by suppliers or industry associations for travel agents/tour operators.

senior market–Mature potential travelers—some retired, some still employed, or partially employed. A desirable market for the tour operator, as many of these individuals enjoy group travel and, as seniors, are free to travel midweek and off-season.

service charge–Amount of money automatically added to the bill in many hotels, restaurants, and night clubs in lieu of the "voluntary" gratuity or tip. Usually determined by a percentage of the bill rather than a set monetary amount. More frequent in Europe than in the United States.

shell–A partially pre-printed brochure, usually obtained from a supplier, already containing graphics, illustrations, photos, a map, and perhaps some generic copy. User adds his/her own copy in white spaces intentionally left blank. Usually done in four-color process, thus making expensive full-color photos available to the small operator at a reasonable price.

shore excursions–Planned land or air tours available for purchase by cruise passengers at scheduled ports of call.

short sector–Flight or segment of a trip of short distance. A portion of a longer, continuing flight or journey. Often a sector on which it may be difficult to obtain space since blocking the short duration inhibits the carrier's opportunity to sell the longer, full journey.

single supplement–Additional amount of money to be paid by a client for single occupancy of a hotel room, especially when participating in a tour that specifies double occupancy accommodations. Calculated by the tour operator by subtracting the share-room cost per person from the single cost—the differential being the single supplement. Sometimes called the single room supplement.

soft adventure–Hard adventure grows up. Adventure travel modified for the adventurous traveler who is in his/her middle/older years and prefers more comfort, or for the beginning adventure traveler with an adventurous spirit but no desire to "rough it." See **adventure travel, hard adventure.**

soft sailing–Cruise sailing or departure date on which bookings are low or on which it is anticipated they may be low due to projections based on these dates in the past. A sailing on which it should be possible, therefore, to secure best possible rates and concessions from the cruise line.

spec–Term describing the "specifying" of type face and sizes for a specific printing project. Usually done by the graphic artist or designer planning the brochure or ad rather than leaving it to the discretion of the typesetter.

spec sheet–A typed sheet laying out the specifications of a job on which a price quote is requested; for example, to a printer for a brochure printing cost quotation.

special interest tour–Prearranged, packaged itinerary designed to appeal to or respond to requests by a group of persons with unique interests. Such tours may focus on horticulture, law, gourmet dining, backpacking, music, religious events, sports, or any other specific field.

spread–Selection, as in a spread of cabins on a cruise, meaning a selection of cabins in each of the major categories on the ship.

stack–(Verb) Term used in typesetting and graphics, meaning to put one on top of the other and run vertically rather than horizontally. As in several photos running vertically in a column or a headline broken into three short lines of type, one on top of the other.

step-on guide–A local guide hired to step on a motorcoach tour for a short period; for example: to give a half-day or full-day tour.

stock–Name, weight, and finish of the paper or cardboard to be used for a given printing job.

study program–Encompasses a study tour, a cruise with an academic program aboard, an overseas campus, a summer session, etc. Involves travel combined with study in some fashion.

supplier–Airline, railroad, cruise line, motorcoach company, or other entity offering travel-related services and products as component parts making up a package tour.

T **table d'hote**–Fixed price meal. A complete meal as described on the menu for a set price, as distinguished from *à la carte* listings in which each item may be ordered separately and is priced separately. Usually a feature of full pension or demi-pension meal plans.

tariff–(1) Fare or rate from a supplier; (2) class or type of fare or rate; (3) published list of fares or rates from a supplier; (4) official publication compiling fares or rates and conditions of service.

tc–Complimentary trip for the tour conductor.

TIAA (Travel Industry Association of America)–An organization made up of the private sector, related primarily to the domestic, inbound segment of the travel industry. Sponsors the Pow Wow annual trade show.

tier pricing–Quoting a variety of tour prices based on volume. For example: one price per person if the tour group materializes at 25 paying passengers, a slightly lower price at 30, and so forth. The organization or agency may elect to pass these savings on to the participants or, as is most frequent, may prefer to keep the savings as additional revenue.

tix–Tickets.

tour–Any prearranged, prepaid journey to one or more destinations and returning to the point of departure. Usually includes transportation, accommodations, meals, sightseeing, and other components, and is sold as a unit without price break-outs by component.

tour basing fare–A special airfare on which tour operators may build a tour. Not available to the traveler unless purchasing a prepaid land tour in conjunction. See **GIT, ITX** as examples.

tour conductor–See **tour manager**.

tour consultant–Individual affiliated with a travel agency selling and advising clients regarding a tour. Sometimes a travel consultant or sales person with particular expertise in group tour sales.

tour courier–See **tour manager**.

tour designer–Used in this text to define the individual actually designing a tour itinerary and qualified to do so professionally, though the term is not frequently used in the travel industry. May be a retail travel agency employee, a tour operator (wholesale or retail) or a consultant/ independent contractor.

tour desk–(1) Desk, table, or counter space often located in the lobby area of a hotel and staffed by a hotel employee or representative of a local travel agency or tour operator for the purposes of answering questions, selling local sightseeing tours and excursions, and providing information on things to do. In the case of conventions, or large group tours may be combined with the hospitality desk; (2) desk or department at an airline staffed by an airline employee who sells the airline's own official tours and packages directly to passengers or to passengers through retail travel agents. Not to be confused with the airline group desk, which books group air reservations.

tour director–See **tour manager.**

tour escort–See **tour manager.**

tour leader–See **tour manager.**

tour manager–Person employed as the escort for a group of tourists, usually for the duration of the entire tour, perhaps supplemented by local guides. The term tour director, leader, escort, conductor, and in Europe, courier, have the same meaning and are used interchangeably.

tour operator–Company that arranges tour packages by assembling the components such as hotels, air, sightseeing, and so forth and then markets them either thorough travel agents at a commission to the agents (a wholesale tour operator) or directly to the public, or to a tour organizer (a retail tour operator). Tours may be for groups or may be independent packages.

tour organizer–Person who recruits participants to join a given group travel project. Also called Pied Piper or draw. An individual with a following. Often compensated with a free trip and/or named titular tour leader.

tracking–Following. Keeping track of, as in tracking which ad in which publication produces a certain number of inquiries, and how many bookings result from those inquiries.

trade mission–Group tour with a business rather than vacation purpose. Usually planned for business or government representatives traveling overseas to secure new business in foreign markets for their product, city, or other entity.

transfer–Service provided for arriving or departing travelers to transport them to/from an airport or an air, sea, or rail terminal to their hotel or vice versa. May also be between one terminal and another. A standard element of an inclusive tour. For groups usually includes more than just transportation: meet and greet service, baggage handling, guide, etc.

twin–Hotel or motel room having two single beds for use by two persons. Not to be confused with a double, which is one bed for two persons. See **double.**

U **unable**–Unable to confirm, not available.

upfront–In advance, as in upfront expenses referring to monies expended prior to launching a tour or receiving passengers' monies. Monies at risk.

uppercase–Capital letters, as against lower case. Signified by the initials u.c. when proofreading.

USTOA (United States Tour Operators' Association)–An organization of many of the leading tour operators doing business in the United States. Membership is voluntary. Operator of the USTOA Consumer Protection Plan.

USTTA (United States Travel and Tourism Authority)–A government entity under the United States Department of Commerce. Maintains a few key offices overseas to promote travel to the United States.

V   **variable expenses**–Expenses related to the individual passenger and for which the tour operator will not be charged unless the passenger is present to use them. For example: hotel accommodations, meals, tips. See **fixed expenses.**

VAT (Value Added Tax)–Government-imposed tax, based on the value added at each stage of the production and distribution of a product or service.

velox–A particularly sharp photographic print suitable for reprinting. An effective means of sending the same tour or cruise advertisement to many different publications. Sometimes also called a stat.

W   **waitlist**–List of clients awaiting confirmation on a flight, cruise, tour, and so forth that is currently sold out. Space is confirmed to waitlisted clients as cancellations of confirmed clients occur.

white space–The part of an ad or brochure layout that has no copy or illustration, purposely left blank, often indicative of an elegant or more expensive product.

wholesale tour operator–Company that arranges tour packages by assembling the components such as hotels, air, sightseeing, and so forth, and then markets the total travel package at a total package price through travel agents at a commission to the agents or at net rates, rather than marketing directly to the public or a tour organizer. See **tour operator.**

Y   **yield**–(Noun) The actual financial value of a sale or transaction. For example, the "yield" on a group of 50 passengers traveling on a highly discounted airfare (called a diluted fare) may be lower than the yield on a group of 25 passengers traveling on a non-discounted fare. In negotiations, suppliers will be willing to grant more advantages on potentially high yield groups than on groups utilizing low yield, diluted rates.

APPENDIX: TOUR COSTING EXERCISES

You learned in Chapter 7 that a tour can be exciting and well-planned yet still be a failure if it doesn't make a profit. When your tours don't make a profit, you don't stay in business. You can make every tour profitable by costing it properly. This appendix presents costing exercises for three tours: #1, Overnight Retirement Group Trip to San Francisco; #2, a 16-Day Tour of South America; and #3, an 18-Day Rotary Club Tour to the Orient. Each exercise represents a different degree of difficulty— #1 is the easiest and #3 is the most difficult. Compute the totals and put your answer in the space provided in each costing problem, then answer the following three questions for each tour: 1. What is the selling price of the tour? 2. What is the profit if the minimum number of people go on the tour? 3. What is the profit if the maximum number of people go? See how well you did by checking your answers with the correct ones at the end of the appendix.

COSTING EXERCISE 1

Overnight Retirement Group Trip to San Francisco

Your profit margin is 15%. The minimum number of tour members is 30; the maximum number is 40.

Scenario

Your mother lives in a retirement complex in Stockton and you are associated with a travel agency there. You're aware that her friends in the complex want interesting daytime activities, but have a limited disposable income. You propose that they go on an overnight trip to San Francisco to see the opening of a new art show at the DeYoung Museum and take in some theatre and shopping. Since it is your mother's organization, you promise to escort it personally and cost it as modestly as possible. You promise the president of the complex Activities Club a free trip. You tell them you need 30 paying passengers to operate the trip.

The Itinerary You Design

Day 1: At 9:00 a.m. the group meets in the parking lot of the complex and boards chartered bus to San Francisco. In San Francisco, group checks into St. Francis Hotel around 11:00 a.m. and has independent lunch and a chance to rest. At 1:00 p.m. the bus will pick them up and take them to the museum show opening and champagne reception. At 4:30 p.m. they will return to the hotel. At 7:00 p.m. they meet in the lobby/bar area for cocktail(s) and then group dinner at hotel and stay overnight.

Day 2: The group has breakfast at the hotel and the morning free for shopping and independent interests. The group will have lunch on their own, but must check-out of the hotel by noon. After a 2:00 p.m. matinee at Geary Theatre, the group will walk back to the hotel and meet the bus by 5:15 p.m. They will return to Stockton around 7:15 p.m., depending on traffic.

Here Are the Costs You Find Out
(What it Will Actually Cost You Out-of-Pocket)

Flyers & posters to distribute in-house to residents' mail slots & a couple bulletin board announcements. Informal do-it-yourself type thing ... *$20.*

Bus charter, 43-seater, $600/day × 2 days (includes driver & his expenses, bridge tolls, overnight bus parking in SFO, mileage & times you've told the company) ... *$1200.*

Hotel $170 per night gross, less 10% commission plus 7% tax. They give one free bed with 40 passengers. Note this is per room rate, not per person.

Museum show tickets including glass champagne ... *$25.00* per person, no free.

Cocktails at St. Francis - budget 2 per person at $5 each + tip = *$12.00* per person.

Dinner budget set menu, including tax, tip & coffee (no wine) ... *$28* per person.

Breakfast at hotel $7.50 + tip + tax = *$12.50.* No free.

Bell Captain tip for storing hand luggage while group at theatre ... *$20* per group.

Theatre tickets, orchestra seats, at group rate *$30* (instead of usual $32). No free.

Tip to bus driver at end of trip, *$1* per person per day.

VARIABLES	Per Person
Hotel @ $170 – $17 (10% comm.) = 153 net + 7% tax on $170 or	
$11.90 = $164.90 net net rate for two, divided by 2 persons	$82.45
Museum entrance fee and champagne reception	25.00
Cocktails, if each person drinks 2 drinks	12.00
Dinner	28.00
Breakfast	12.50
Theatre tickets	30.00
Bus driver tip at $1/day × 2 days	2.00
TOTAL NET PER PERSON VARIABLES	$_____

FIXED EXPENSES	Per Project
Coach charter, 2 days at $600 per day	$1,200.00
Tip to bell captain for entire group	20.00
Promotion—flyers/posters	20.00
TOTAL FIXED EXPENSES SO FAR	$_____

NOW WHAT ABOUT THE FREES

One free for Club President you promised. Variables only	$191.45
(Don't put in fixed as these would be paid anyway whether	
Club President rides along or not)	
One additional free for yourself as escort (as no frees at 30)	191.45
Total Cost for the two "Frees"	$_____
TOTAL FIXED EXPENSES PER PROJECT	$_____

PUT IT TOGETHER

Variables per person	$_____
Fixed expenses of 1622.90 divided by 30 pax = per person share of fixed	$_____
Total Net Cost per person based on 30	$_____

TO FIGURE PROFIT MARGIN

Net $245.55 divided by .85 (to make a 15% profit margin) = sell price	$_____
Less Net	–245.55
Net Margin of Profit Per Person	$_____

PROFIT PICTURE AT 30

Profit margin of $43.45 per person × 30 paying passengers = profit at 30	$_____

PROFIT PICTURE AT 40

Profit margin of $43.45 per person × 40 paying passengers = profit	$1,738.00
Plus one free escort at hotel only (savings)	82.45
Plus fixed expenses of $54.10 per person × 10 bookings	
(#31–40) = savings	541.00
TOTAL PROFIT AT 40	$_____

Note: You added only 10 passengers, but nearly doubled your earnings. You earn more on the last bookings than on the first. Therefore, when you reach your minimum number (30), don't stop promoting.

COSTING EXERCISE 2
16-Day Tour of South America

Your profit margin is 25%. The minimum number of tour members is 15; the maximum is 40.

Scenario

You have been asked to put together a 2-week tour to South America for a country club. The club has 2,000 members and its president, who has been to South America before, will act as combined tour organizer and as tour director. He wants a free trip for himself only (no wife), but no salary or expenses. The club has a monthly newsletter in which they will publicize the trip at no cost to you, the agent. However, they do not wish to undertake the expense of direct-mail to each club member, so you agree to do the direct mail and take that financial risk.

You have decided to book all land arrangements through a wholesaler who specializes in South America rather than trying to book direct. You have been asked by the club to book for 40 passengers and they are optimistic that they'll get 40 easily. You are not so optimistic and you decide to price it on a minimum of 15+1 (15 paying adults, 1 comp) and you guarantee the club that you will operate the trip if they sell 15.

Costs

Air: You have been quoted a gross airfare of $1251 ($1099 basic airfare + $152 Cuzco sidetrip = $1251). There is no automatic complimentary air ticket with this fare, but you negotiate with your airline rep and get them to grant you a government order air ticket at 25. You're getting 11% commission on the total air lift plus 5% over-ride on the net online airline revenue if you have a minimum 15 passengers, retroactive to booking #1.

Land: A South America specialty wholesaler quotes you $1,000 net for land services on the basis of 15+1, or $900 on the basis of 30+1. (This covers full land package: hotel room & tax throughout, share-twin basis; transfers, baggage handling at airport & hotels, welcome party, half-day city tour each place + additional sightseeing, a tango performance evening in BA and a samba show in Rio.) In addition to these charges, you wish to cost in a bang-up South American night at the club to promote sign-ups (with films, pisco sours, hors d'ouvre, etc). The country club gives you an estimate of $1000 flat rate for this function. Your brochure costs for 2,000 copies will be $900. Direct-mail charges (including envelopes, cover letter, bulk-rate postage, and labor) are $800. You plan on a 20% profit margin on the land costs.

Calculations
(Note we do the land first, adding air at the end)

Per Person Variable Expenses
Land price quote, basis 15+1 $1,000.00

Per Project Fixed Expenses
   Promotional Costs
   Brochures   900.00
   Direct Mail   800.00
   Promotional Party at the Club   1,000.00
   Total Promotional Expense This Project $ _____

   Tour Leader/Organizer
   Land Package, complimentary $0000.00
   Air–negotiated with airlines at 25, so at 15 cost in
     at $1251 gross less 11% commission = net air $1113.39
   Total Cost to Send Leader $1113.39
Total Fixed Expenses $ _____

Totals Per Person
Land variables, net   1,000.00
Fixed expenses $3,813.39 divided by 15 pax   254.23
Subtotal   1254.23
Net $1254.23 divided by .75 (to make a 25%
  profit margin) = sell price, land only   1,672.30
Plus Gross Airfare   1,251.00
Total Published Price, Air & Land $ _____

Profit Picture
Profit Picture at 15 Passengers
(a) Sell price land $1672 less $1000.00 net land variables =
    $672 net profit margin per person × 15 persons $10,080.00
(b) 11% commission on airfare of $1251 = $137.61 × 15   2,064.15
(c) 5% override on the net online airline revenue ($1251 less $152
    Cuzco sidetrip not airlines = $1099 base airlines online gross less 11%
    commission or $120.89 = $978.11 net online @ 5% = $48.91 pp
    add'l commission × 15 pax   733.65
Total Profit on Project at Minimum Enrollment of 15 $ _____

Profit Picture at 30 Passengers
(a) $672 net profit margin on land × 30 persons $20,160.00
(b) 11% commisison on airfare of $1251 = $137.61 × 15   4,128.30
(c) 5% override on net online airline revenue, per above,
    at $48.91 pp × 30 pax   1,467.30
(d) Savings at 30 because land quote drops from $1,000 net
    to $900 net pp, or $100 pp savings × 30 pax   3,000.00
(e) Savings of fixed expenses of 254.23 pp × 15 (passengers #16–30,
    as these expenses already defrayed by 1st 15 pax who joined tour)   3,813.45
(f) Comp air ticket for organizer at 25 (net cost)   1,113.39
Total Profit on Project at Enrollment of 30 $ _____

Comments

1) Note that because of the savings, once you reach your basic 15 pax, your profit at 30 is not double what it is at 15, but rather is more than triple. Therefore, rule-of-thumb, you double your tour membership and you triple your earnings. In other words, in a sense, the last 15 passengers who join are twice as valuable as the first 15, so don't stop selling once your tour is "successful" at 15. This is when you double your sales efforts to bring in the second batch of 15!

2) Note that of the total $33,682.44 profit, only $5,595.60 is from commission; the remaining $28,085.84 is profit from sources other than commission! So stop thinking like a retailer; stop thinking commissions. In groups, they're not that important!

COSTING EXERCISE 3

18-Day Rotary Club Tour to the Orient

The profit margin on land costs is 25%. The minimum number of tour members is 20; the maximum is 40.

Scenario

You are handling an 18-day Orient Tour for the local Rotary club, which will act as host club for the surrounding Rotary Regional District with a mailing list of 5,000. You have offered the president of the local club a free trip for himself at 20 paying passengers and a free trip for his wife at 40. The club president is not an experienced tour manager, so you will send a professional, paying the necessary salary and expenses to hire such an individual, since you cannot afford to be away from your office that long in order to direct the tour personally.

You have booked land arrangements directly through receptive services operators in each country: Japan, Hong Kong, and Thailand. You hope for 40 passengers, but will price it on 20 "just in case." The club wants a $50-per-person fee paid into their Rotary International scholarship fund. In order to hold hotel space in Tokyo during the convention, your receptive operator in Japan advises you that you have to put up $100 per room deposit one year ahead of time. You and the Rotary Club agree to split the cost of the mailing to 5,000 Rotarians. You agree to pay for the brochure; they agree to run three follow-up reminder announcements in their chapter newsletter at no charge to you. You hold a promotional wine and cheese evening with films and pay for it. The trans-Pacific air carrier offers to pay a 10% override commission on that airline's net revenue portion of the trans-Pacific air fare.

Costs

You are using a $1,000 gross airfare, which grants one complimentary for each 15 paying passengers. The net online revenue portion of this on your major trans-Pacific air carrier is $682; the balance is interline revenue on other airlines. You receive land quotes as follows: Japan $892 for 20+1, $869 for 40+2; Hong Kong $279 for 20+1, $259 for 40+2; Thailand $317 for 20+1, $298 for 40+2. In addition to these ground operators' charges, you cost in $10 per person for in-house handling and document preparation, a $7 airport departure tax, a $15-per-person fund to cover niceties such as occasional wine, birthday cakes, and so forth. The professional tour manager you hire requests $75 per day salary for the period while away on tour, as well as for the days in your office for pre-tour briefing and post-tour debriefing. In addition, you grant the tour manager a maximum budget of $10 per day for run-around money: taxis, telephone, laundry, plane headsets, and other items. The tour brochure costs $850 and the mailing costs $900. You plan on a 25% profit margin on your land costs. The promotional evening will run $300.

Calculations

Per Person Variables	
Japan land expenses, net, based on 20 + 1	$892.00
Hong Kong land expenses, net, based on 20 + 1	279.00
Thailand land expenses, net, based on 20 + 1	317.00
In-house handling and documents (name badges, bag tags, itineraries, and so forth)	10.00
Airport departure tax	7.00
Niceties fund	15.00
Total Individual Net Variables Based on 20 + 1	$ _____
Per Project Fixed Expenses	
Promotional costs	
Brochure	$850.00
Direct mail $900, your share half	450.00
Promotional evening	300.00
Total promotional outlay	$ _____
Tour Manager	
Salary, $75 per day × 20 days (18 on tour, two in office)	$1,500.00
Run-around monies $10 per day × 18 days out on tour	180.00
Tour manager's meals—estimate 18 days × $40 per day	720.00
Tour manager's airfare, free at 15 + 1	0.00
Tour manager's land tour arrangaments, free at 20 + 1	0.00
Total estimate for tour manager	$ _____

Free trip for Rotary president
(must cost in "free" trip because used "free" one for tour manager above)

Airfare of $1,000 less 11% commission = net to your company	$890.00
Land costs (see variables)	1,520.00
Total to carry president	$_____
Total fixed expenses per entire tour project ($1600 + $2400 + $2410)	$_____

Totals Per Person

Land Variables, Net	$ 1,520.00
Fixed expenses of $6,410 divided by 20 paying	
passengers, = each person's share	320.50
Subtotal	$ 1,840.50
Net $1840.50 ÷ .75 (to make a 25% profit margin) = sell price, land only	2,453.33
Plus $50 donation for Rotary Scholarship Fund	50.00*
Plus interest on monies that you have to deposit to hold	
Tokyo hotel (20 rooms held at $100 per night per room = $2000 divided	
by 20 persons minimum in the group = $100 borrowed per person if	
borrowing one year at 14% interest rate)	14.00*
Total sell price, land only	2,517.33
Plus Gross Airfare	1,000.00
Total published price, air and land (For sales purposes, perhaps	
round off to $3500 or $3495.)	$_____

Profit Picture

Profit Picture at 20 Passengers

Profit (markup) of $612.83 per person ($2453.33–1840.50) on	
land × 20 passengers	$12,256.60
11% commission on airfare of $1,000 = $110 per person air	
commission × 20 paying passengers	$2,200.00
10% override commission paid on the net online air revenue	
figure of $682 = $68.20 per person × paying passengers	$1,364.00
Total Profit on Project on Minimum Enrollment of 20	$_____

*Note: The $50 scholarship fund donation and the $14 interest are added on *after* calculating the land markup, as it does not seem ethical to mark up these two items.

Profit Picture at 40 Passengers

Profit (markup) of $612.83 per person on land × 40 paying passengers	$24,513.20
11% commission on airfare of $1,000 = $110 per person air	
commission × 40 paying passengers	4,400.00
10% override commission paid on the net online air revenue	
figure of $682 = $68.20 per person × 40 paying passengers	2,728.00
Savings of $1,600 promotional expenses divided by 20 = $80 per person	
already paid for by the first 20 people, so you do not have to pay this	
$80 per person out for tour members 21 through 40	1,600.00
Savings on $2,400 professional tour manager	2,400.00
Additional savings from overseas ground operators, since you reached	
40 passengers, but priced tour on their 20 + 1 figure:	

Japan now costs $869 instead of $892 = savings of	$23.00	
Hong Kong costs $259 instead of $279 = savings of	20.00	
Thailand costs $298 instead of $317 = savings of	19.00	
Total savings per person	$62.00	
Mutliplied by 40 persons in the group = total group savings		2,480.00

Total profit on project on enrollment of 40	$_____

Comments

Since you are utilizing the first complimentary land and air accrued for your paid tour manager, you must cost in the price of the Rotary club leader's trip as a full expense. When you reach 40 passengers, you receive your second accrued complimentary land from the suppliers (your air in this case actually already accrued at 30), so this second complimentary can be used for the president's wife at no additional cost to you or the tour members. Note that the second 20 passengers have paid for the cost of the Rotary president's wife's trip. Therefore, there is incentive for him to continue to promote after his trip is successful at 20 members, *if* he wants to obtain the free trip for his wife.

ANSWERS

Exercise 1

Total Net Per Person Variables	$191.45
Total Fixed Expenses So Far	$1,240.00
Total Cost For Two "Frees"	$382.90
Total Fixed Expenses Per Project	$1,622.90
Variables Per Person	$191.45
Per Person Share of Fixed	$54.10
Total Net Cost Per Person based on 30	$245.55
Selling Price Per Person	$289.00
Net Margin of Profit Per Person	$43.45
Profit with 30 People	$1,303.50
Profit with 40 People	$2,361.45

Exercise 2

Total Promotional Expenses	$2,700.00
Total Fixed Expenses	$3,813.39
Total Published Air and Land Price	$2,922.30
Total Profit with 15 People	$12,877.80
Total Profit with 30 People	$33,682.44

Exercise 3

Total Individual Net Variables Based on 20 + 1	$1,520.00
Total Promotional Outlay	$1,600.00
Total Estimate for Tour Manager	$2,400.00
Total to Carry President	$2,410.00
Toal Fixed Expenses Per Entire Project	$6,410.00
Total Selling Price	$3,517.33
Total Profit with 20 People	$15,820.60
Total Profit with 40 People	$38,121.00

INDEX